The Russian Century

A Hundred Years of Russian Lives

Edited by
George Pahomov
Nickolas Lupinin

Nickolas Lupinin
George Pahomov

UNIVERSITY PRESS OF AMERICA,® INC.
Lanham · Boulder · New York · Toronto · Plymouth, UK

Copyright © 2008 by
University Press of America,® Inc.
4501 Forbes Boulevard
Suite 200
Lanham, Maryland 20706
UPA Acquisitions Department (301) 459-3366

Estover Road
Plymouth PL6 7PY
United Kingdom

All rights reserved
Printed in the United States of America
British Library Cataloging in Publication Information Available

Library of Congress Control Number: 2008926468
ISBN-13: 978-0-7618-4067-1 (paperback : alk. paper)
ISBN-10: 0-7618-4067-2 (paperback : alk. paper)
eISBN-13: 978-0-7618-4175-3
eISBN-10: 0-7618-4175-X

∞™ The paper used in this publication meets the minimum
requirements of American National Standard for Information
Sciences—Permanence of Paper for Printed Library Materials,
ANSI Z39.48—1984

Contents

Acknowledgements	v
Introduction	vii
Glossary of Russian Terms	xi

PART I   THE VANISHED PRESENCE: RUSSIA BEFORE 1914 1

1	Viktor Chernov, Idylls on the Volga	3
2	Sergei N. Durylin, Domestic Love	18
3	Sofiia Kovalevskaia, A Thief in the House	28
4	Oleg Pantiukhov, A Student's Summer	41
5	Aleksandra Tyrkova-Williams, A Woman's Autonomy	54
6	Nikolai Volkov-Muromtsev, Memoirs	64
7	Vladimir Zenzinov, Coming of Age	74
8	Vasilii Nikiforov-Volgin, Presanctified Gifts	88
9	Mark Vishniak, In Two Worlds	95
10	Konstantin Paustovskii, Commencement Revelry	103

PART II   INSTABILITY AND DISLOCATION: 1914–1929 111

11	Georgii Altaev, How I Became a Cub Scout	113
12	Nikolai Filatov, A Soldier's Letters	120

13	Konstantin Paustovskii, Save Your Strength	130
14	Roman Gul, We're in Power Now	139
15	Sergei Mamontov, Civil War: A White Army Journal	144
16	Vera Volkonskaia, Orphaned by Revolution	155
17	Mikhail Gol'dshtein, My First Recital	168
18	Viktor Kravchenko, Youth in the Red	173
19	Vasilii Ianov, The Heart of a Peasant	181

PART III UNRELENTING ORDER AND TERROR: 1930–1953 189

20	B. Brovtsyn, Dearly Beloved	191
21	Tat'iana Fesenko, Internal Dissenter	199
22	Nila Magidoff, Only to Travel! Only to Live!	210
23	Tat'iana Fesenko, War-Scorched Kiev	225
24	Elena I. Kochina, Blockade Diary	236
25	N. Ianevich, Literary Politics	251
26	K. Vadot, The Terrorist	259

PART IV APOGEE AND FRACTURE: 1954–1991 265

27	Mariia Shapiro, A Soviet Capitalist	267
28	Valerii Leviatov, My Path to God	273
29	Valentin Kataev, A Paschal Memory	282
30	Kirill Kostsinskii [K.V. Uspenskii], A Dissident's Trial	285
31	Iurii Krotkov, The KGB in Action	290
32	Vladimir Azbel, Siberian Adversity	306
33	Leonid Shebarshin, Three Days in August	315

Acknowledgments

My gratitude is due, first of all, to Professor Nickolas Lupinin of Franklin Pierce University, gentle critic and steadfast friend, co-author, without whom this volume would never have appeared and also to Marina Adamovitch, editor of *The New Review (Novyi zhurnal)*, for her helpful advice and permission to translate and reprint a number of memoirs from that journal. Gratitude must also be expressed to a number of publishers and publications, some of them long-vanished, whose names appear in the brief introduction to each particular entry. I also wish to thank several colleagues and friends for their exemplary translations of various pieces: Professor Mark Swift, of the University of Auckland, for translating Filatov, "A Soldier's Letters," Leviatov, "My Path to God," and Fesenko, "War-Scorched Kiev;" Professor Karen Black of Millersville University for Paustovskii, "Commencement Revelry;" Sharon Bain, my colleague at Bryn Mawr College, for Shapiro, "A Soviet Capitalist;" Cindy Burr-Ramsey for Durylin, "Domestic Love," and Krotkov, "KGB in Action;" Julie Stetson for Vadot, "The Terrorist;" and Brian Boeck for Gul, "We're in Power Now." Finally, to my students at Bryn Mawr College who, in taking my course on Russian culture and civilization, provided incentive and manifested the curiosity and enthusiasm which is their valued hallmark.

Bryn Mawr   George Pahomov

Introduction

Russia has had a great influence on the twentieth century world. Russian music, dance, theatre, art, and literature have shaped contemporary life in significant ways. It is very unlikely that one reaches adulthood without reading Dr. Zhivago, seeing the films of Eisenstein or the plays of Chekhov. And any overview of 20th century art and music will prominently include Malevich, Kandinsky, Stravinsky and Prokofiev. But this influence also has a dark side. The Russian version of communism was a virulent ideology during a major part of the twentieth century, its global impact so profound that it has rightly become the source of countless studies and extensive documentation. While this focus on Russian communism is invaluable and completely justified, it too often overshadows the many other aspects of Russian life. There is still an unknown Russia, a Russia comprised of private lives as opposed to public history. This Russia includes the stories of real people who lived during the turbulent one-hundred years between 1890-1991, people from diverse backgrounds, a broad geographic spectrum, and various educational and socio-economic levels. This volume, which brings together letters, diaries, personal sketches, and memoirs—most of which are appearing in English for the first time—was put together to tell that fascinating story.

Beginning at the end of the nineteenth century, with the rapid growth of cities and industry and Russia's entrance into modernity, and proceeding chronologically to the collapse of the USSR in August 1991, the stories presented here do not simply trace linear change punctuated by great convulsive events. Those are the peaks of history. These accounts have been written by people who lived in the shadows of those peaks but who strived to make meaning of their lives. The selections speak in an intimate and personal voice of immediate experience rather than of the distant, general flow of history.

Personal matters—privations, suffering, joys, achievements—are recounted with candor and insight.

This book is not an examination of Russian reality in terms of Western ideas, concepts, or norms but an evocation of twentieth century life through the personal voice. The English-speaking reader will elicit for her or himself the values in Russian culture, both latent and manifest, which shape the attitudes and guide the behavior of Russians.

All too often the Russian experience has been presented as either horrific or heroic, absorbed in persecution and "victimology." The field is replete with Gulag accounts. This volume goes beyond that approach and deals with the personal and intimate—love, sexuality, courtship, marriage, family life, work, faith, and education. In choosing these selections, we were not guided by "historical objectivity" but rather by subjectivity, by an emphasis on the subject or the unique self. This approach intentionally counters and supplements the vast majority of existing works devoted to Russian history and culture. We offer the reader no great individuals, no overarching story lines, no plots conceived by an omniscient author. The private selves who wrote their own life stories did so in a language of common experience and common values without awareness of a greater meaning beyond the intimate particulars of their lives. In this sense the naive and unaffected recorder of history is its authentic witness.

It is a given in anthropology that a culture's collective self-view tends to be idealized and that such an idealization becomes a lens through which history and experience are viewed and understood. It is also true that a member of a given culture presents himself to outsiders in terms of that idealization. Many observers, both non-Russian and Russian, see only the idealization, the defining myths, and respond to them according to their own pre-existing needs and desires. Such needs and desires may be positively or negatively charged, but in either case they promote linear, monocausal interpretations of what has been observed, at the expense of the complex, contradictory, and even paradoxical realities of life. In 1943 in Amsterdam, confined to a secluded space, Anne Frank lived simultaneously in fear of the Nazis and in love with Pieter van Daan. To assume that she lived only in terror, that terror was the singular emotion of her life, would be to deny her full breadth of being and her full human dignity. Anne's case cautions us to be wary of simple explanations of human behavior and sensibility.

In its rich complexity human character is a source of numerous eventualities. So is a culture. When we try to understand a culture different than ours it is a mistake to assume that what is observed in a particular context or at a particular moment represents the totality of that culture. In fact, at any given moment most of a culture's characteristics and make-up lie latent, waiting to manifest themselves at a particular juncture or in a particular context.

In this volume we have let the writers decide what is to be revealed. They speak of events which endure in their memory. Often it is of universal human experience, the consciousness of self in the face of inevitable death. It is at such times that anguish, transformed by intelligence into recollection, loses its power to injure their hearts. Whether in its religious sense or removed from it, "bearing witness" stimulates a desire in every writer to open her or himself to other eyes, to testify and thus transform the sting of memory into some greater tempering idea which frees the rest of their lives from the burden of secrecy. In the process, their liberation becomes our gift.

All too often Russians, as well as other observers, assume Russia to be a homogeneous and corporate cultural entity. Such a view was doubtlessly influenced by the monolithic political structure of the Soviet Union as it drove to homogenize its subjects. Communist ideology tended to see human beings as a commodity and an instrument. Coercion and violence were used against those with contrary views. The result, to some degree, was an actual but also a presumed uniformity.

In cultures which tend toward uniformity and homogeneity the collective self-view and the self-image of the individual largely coincide. Such coincidence becomes especially apparent as one recalls descriptions of small and isolated cultures such as those of insular tribes and contemporary "cults" in which the individual is submerged within a corporate sensibility. In contrast, American experience is very heterogeneous and broad in spectrum. In a monolithic realm a people's culture is not only the sole source of self-identity but also the primary means of knowing the external world. This is not the case for Russia. It does not have a monoculture. If anything, its culture is far more heterogeneous than the cultures of its neighboring nations. Language, especially its lexicon, is an objective indicator of the openness and permeability of a culture. Russian, by borrowing from languages as diverse as Iranian, the Turkic group, the Scandinavian group, Greek, Bulgarian, Tatar and Mongolian, Polish, Ukrainian, Yiddish, German, French, and English, demonstrates its rich and productive variety.

In some minds such variety raises the question of whether a coherent, cognizable, and explicable Russian culture exists at all. This book does not attempt to answer that question nor define the culture but rather suggests the shape of its dynamic. In a classic formulation A.L. Kroeber affirms that every culture "derives most of its component elements from its own past" but also "tends to absorb new elements . . . and reshape them in accord with its own patterns."[1] In a thriving culture both processes are at work simultaneously. It has always been a debate among Russians what the proportions of the old and the new elements should be. This was the argument between the so-called "Slavophiles" and the

"Westernizers" in the nineteenth century and is currently the debate between the isolationists and the integrationists. The debate seems largely political but is driven by inchoate, deeply rooted attitudes and values.

The would-be fusion of the old and new elements always creates tension. And it is a tension which permeates the life of most Russians. Even though there is a saying in the language which proclaims that "The destiny of one person is the destiny of a whole generation," the epic and the private do not run an identical course. The line between collective and personal destiny may be difficult to locate, but it does exist.

This volume looks at private life, its satisfactions and discontents, its joys and sorrows. Yet, while looking at such life we do not presume that the mundane and the routine determine all. Russian life in the hundred years before 1991 did include much violent change and great hardship. We want to dispel the notion, however, that Russian life was one disaster after another, an endemic and unrelieved tragedy. Life, after all, is not lived in disaster. It may be lived through a disaster, but even then life assumes a routine, though perhaps an altered one.

We have spoken of Russians and Russian culture without any attempt at academic definition of the terms. We intentionally leave that to the reader. However, several points should be made. The English language, unfortunately, has only one word to designate people who are ethnically Russian and those who live in Russia, or more properly, the Russian Federation. This insufficiency makes for misapprehension and an awkward ambiguity. *Rossiia* (Russia) is the name of the state; the adjectival form is *rossiiskii* (of the Russian state). A citizen of *Rossiia* is called a *rossiianin*. A person who is ethnically Russian is called *russkii*, likely derived from *Rus*, the medieval Slavic principality and its people. As an entity Rossiia is analogous to Great Britain. Not everyone living in Great Britain is ethnically English and not everyone living in Rossiia is ethnically Russian. Yet in both nations a language is shared: English in Great Britain, Russian in Rossiia. The pieces chosen for this anthology were written by men and women who saw themselves as largely belonging to Russian culture and for whom the Russian language was the primary means of expression. These are the people of the Russian Century.

George Pahomov

NOTE

1. A.L. Kroeber, *An Anthropologist Looks at History,* University of California Press, 1963, p. v.

Glossary of Russian Terms

artel—a cooperative association of workers, craftsmen, or traders within a particular profession

borshch—a kind of vegetable soup usually made with a beef stock and with beets, cabbage, potatoes, tomatoes, carrots, and occasionally other vegetables

brichka—a carriage, heavier than a *drozhki,* with a collapsible leather or canvas top

dacha—a summer home, frequently having a glass enclosed veranda

desiatina—a square measure equivalent to 2.7 acres or 1.09 hectares

drozhki—a light, open carriage usually drawn by one horse

gimnazium—a classical high school, featuring the classical and foreign languages and a liberal arts curriculum as opposed to *real'noe uchilishche*, a vocational high school; pronounced with a "hard" g as in gimlet

Gulag—the system of prison camps throughout the Soviet Union; the administrative body of those camps

izba—a rural, peasant house in central and northern Russia constructed of logs either round or square in cross-section

kolkhoz—collective farm; largely the product of forced collectivization in Soviet times

kolkhoznik—collective farm worker

kulebiaka—fish baked en croute; an open-face Beef Wellington filled with filet of sturgeon instead of beef tenderloin

kvas—a kind of beer made by fermenting rye bread or rye flour, yeast, malt and, sometimes, sugar; served chilled

muzhik—an adult male peasant; also a term of derision

name(s)day—a holiday celebrating the patron saint bearing the same name as the celebrant, e.g., 23 April is St. George's day

Okhrana—the secret police in tsarist times

papirosa (plural: *papirosy*)—a cigarette with a long cardboard mouthpiece, widely smoked before the advent of the modern cigarette during WWI

pirog (plural: *pirogi*)—a generic term for pies, usually deep-dish and rectangular, with fillings ranging from berries and fruit to mushroom and egg, sautéed cabbage, and ground beef. *Pirozhok* (plural: *pirozhhki*) is the palm-size version of a *pirog*, similar to a hot pocket or the English pastie

primus—a heating apparatus with a single flame similar to a Bunsen burner but with fuel pressurized by manual pumping; from Primus, the name of the Swedish manufacturer of the device; used for cooking when nothing else functioned

samizdat—underground publishing of materials forbidden by the Soviet government; a compounding of the Russian words "self" and "publishing"

sarafan—a full length, freely cut, sleeveless dress worn almost exclusively by peasant women

sazhen—a linear measure equivalent to seven feet, or 2.133 meters

shchi—a soup made of pickled cabbage (sauerkraut) usually on a beef stock

stanitsa—a large southern Russian/Cossack village; also an administrative unit

tachanka—a two-axle wagon drawn by two horses, similar to a buckboard

taiga—the unbroken forest belt of Siberia

tsarevich—crown prince

verst—a linear measure equal to .663 miles, or 1.06 km. (The proper form is *versta*, we use the anglicized variant.)

zemstvo—rural self-governing body established in the reign of Alexander II

A note on transliteration. The Library of Congress system is used in all bibliographical notation and throughout the text, except that in the text the designation for soft sign (') has been dropped from the ends of words. Russian names which are widely known in English have been left in their popular spelling.

Part One

The Vanished Presence: Russia before 1914

On March 13, 1881, after numerous attempts, the terrorist group "Will of the People" finally succeeded in assassinating Alexander II, the "Tsar Liberator." The hoped for collapse of the Russian government did not occur. And initially it was not fully clear what the outcome would be other than the belief among the realists that terrorism would not vanish from the Russian political landscape.

During the reign of Alexander III (1881–1894), there was a legitimate reason to believe that the nation would stabilize. Industry went into high gear, railroad construction soared, and the nation's economy drew constant focus. These positive measures were countermanded by numerous policies aimed to lessen the impact of the Great Reforms, to further Russianize the nation, tighten the hold on minorities, and emphasize the role of the gentry. However, as Nicholas Riasanovsky correctly points out, this was precisely the class that was in decline. Political terror, as a result of severe government decrees issued in 1881, also declined.

Nicholas II (1894–1917), the last Russian tsar, has been much written about. The formalistic perceptions of him as a gracious and kind person in private, but a reactionary and limited ruler are safe to accept. Frequently vacillating, and not wishing to occupy the throne, Nicholas witnessed the demise of the Romanov dynasty and the Russian State. He was not a ruler capable of steering the nation through the turbulent years that lay ahead, particularly in that the belief in the efficacy of his autocracy continued to dominate his thought.

The Russian nation itself had frequently other agendas. Political parties and movements rose, demanding participation in government. A liberal coalition actually formed a "Union of Liberation." Protests and strikes increased almost yearly. And the Revolution of 1905 evolving out of these movements is not a misnomer. Shaken by these events, particularly that of Bloody Sunday (January 22, 1905), the loss to Japan in the Russo-Japanese War of 1904–05, and the unparalleled nationwide strikes of October 1905, the Tsar buckled and issued the famous October Manifesto. This gave the Russian people civil rights and a Duma, which in effect made Russia a constitutional monarchy. But the credibility of the Tsar and his government was very weak. Nicholas's desire to keep the Duma subordinate certainly did not help.

From this point on until the outbreak of World War I in the summer of 1914, the level of politicization in Russia was intense. Various parties and interest groups struggled for influence. The press was ablaze with every conceivable form of opinion. Social issues were intensely debated, and, after the assassination of Russia's most capable minister, Stolypin, in 1911, the situation intensified as the government began its slide again into disarray.

Revolutionary extremism throughout the whole reign did not abate. As Anna Geifman has pointed out, over 17,000 people were either killed or wounded in assassination attempts.[1] This extraordinary phenomenon, particularly when combined with other forces of politically motivated violence, had a devastating effect on the stability of the nation, already wracked by inordinate levels of dissent, problems, and an incapable government.

Curiously, in this period of great ferment, Russia was witness to a stunning cultural explosion, the fabled Silver Age. There are identifiable and innovative movements in literature, both poetry and prose, such as Symbolism and Acmeism. Music continues to excel in such major figures such as Scriabin, Rachmaninoff and Stravinsky, as well as the recrudescence of church choral music. Russian ballet was a sensation in Europe with Nijinsky in productions by Diaghilev. And Russian art, whether that of painting or theater set design, was truly avant-garde. Vrubel, Kandinsky, Malevich, Chagall, and Goncharova, to name just a few, barely need introduction. As to the perception of "naming," were we to merely list the names of writers and poets of the Silver age, the task would be dauntingly lengthy. Akhmatova, Pasternak, Mandelstam, Bely, Sologub, Gumilev, Tsvetaeva, Blok, Mayakovsky.

Juxtaposing the cultural explosion to the feverish political turmoil is tantalizing. Was it clear in the social circumstances that a serious fissure in the body politic existed? Was the cultural flowering one that was hurtling through a limited time frame? Were there instances where the idyllic estate life still existed? Educated Russians were keenly aware of the great debates in society. The fledgling civil freedoms were savored deeply. Where Russia should move as a nation was a time concern, though perhaps one that was less keenly felt thousands of miles from the major cities. Despite all of this acuteness and involvement, no one could be expected to see that entry into World War I was through the gates of doom.

Nickolas Lupinin

NOTE

1. Anna Geifman, *Thou Shalt Kill: Revolutionary Terrorism in Russia*, 1894–1917 (Princeton, N.J.: Princeton University Press, 1993).

Chapter One

Viktor Chernov, Idylls on the Volga

Viktor Chernov is best known for an intense political activism. While yet a teenager in the 1880's, he committed himself to the revolutionary cause and was a hunted man by the 1890's. A man of great independence, he nevertheless became a member of the SR's (Social Revolutionaries), a party he was later to head. Strong pro-peasant and terroristic policies were hallmarks of the SR's and Chernov was notoriously indefatigable in the pursuit of both. The Bolshevik victory in 1917 did not prove to be the answer and he ultimately had to flee Russia. The selection below describes a boy coming of age and hardly hints at the future terrorist. One could say that Chernov lived many lives, from the Volga region of his birth to his death in New York in 1952. This excerpt is from Chernov's *Pered burei* [Before the Storm]. New York: Izd. Imeni Chekhova, 1953.

    I was born amidst the boundless steppes beyond the Volga in the town of Novouzensk, Samara Province, but spent my childhood, boyhood and callow youth in the town of Kamyshin on the broad expanse of the Volga River. Kamyshin lay on the right bank of the Volga where the now-shallow Kamyshinka flows into it. But in the memory of the old-timers the shallow river was once a broad watery expanse covered by thickets of bulrushes. Back in those times, small flotillas of daring river pirates would hide there seeking refuge and freedom in the Volga wilderness from the burdens and laws of the Tsarist regime. They were constantly at war with the world which they had rejected. They would wait in ambush for lone commercial vessels or for whole fleets and shoot out like an arrow into the fast mid-stream while startling the waters with their local, non-Russian, shout: "Saryn' na kichu" (come out on the stern), which was a demand for immediate surrender to the mercy of the attackers.

Some of the old-timers would mix fact with folklore and even point out the favorite hide-outs of legendary pirates Vas'ka Chaloi, Erem Kosolap, and Kuz'ma Shaloput. But to the west of Kamyshin there indisputably was a huge fortress mound in the shape of a radically truncated pyramid with a flat and rather broad top. It stood out in its protruding loneliness amidst the flatness of the surrounding steppe. Local tradition tied it to the name of Sten'ka Razin [an 18th-century rebel], but it had to be much older. For a long time, visiting archeologists wanted to excavate it, but it never went further than talk.

Important sounding and authoritative words poured from such talk—Khazars, Cuman, and Uzzes. It seemed that these ancient names created a greater impression on the eavesdropping children than they had on their busy elders. The whistling sound of the name Uzzes had a magical impression on us. We imagined them as riders fused with their steeds, men who were almost centaurs. We loved playing at being Uzzes, clambering on to unharnessed horses with the help of hostlers as they led them to the Volga to drink and bathe. We enjoyed whooping wildly as we imagined our docile quadrupeds to be wild ponies of the steppe.

Listening in on the conversations of elders was one of my greatest pleasures. I would have given a great deal to be present at the lessons of my older sisters. But I was gently shooed away because no one believed that I could diligently sit though the lessons without interrupting. Then I resorted to a trick. Long before the lessons would begin, I would penetrate the revered room whose secrets were kept from me, hide under the long and broad table and sit there for hours, not ever coughing, sneezing, or budging. It turned out that I had a rare memory, something akin to perfect pitch in music. Soon, I, unable to read, would memorize almost everything that was taught to my older siblings, especially poetry, so that I was able to correct and prompt my sisters whenever they stumbled. Once, filled to overflowing with all this content, I could not control my excitement and openly entered the competition with my sisters when they were forced to show off their learning at a family gathering. My success was the greatest, but the general consternation was even greater: where did an illiterate child get all this, to the point of memorizing long poems by Pushkin? I could not provide a satisfactory answer. Then they began noticing that I would disappear during lessons and, guessing correctly, extracted me from underneath the table with great triumph and laughter. At that point, I was permitted to attend lessons, but silently and with decorum. After that my zeal cooled considerably. The forbidden fruit had been sweeter.

I grew up largely as an unsupervised, enterprising Huckleberry Finn. A boat, a pair of oars, and several fishing poles were my charter to freedom. I would stop by the kitchen for an old pot, a hunk of bread, two or three onions, as many potatoes as possible, and, most important but easily forgotten, a small packet of salt. I would catch all the fish I wanted, giving myself over to the task with a rare fanaticism and, at times, imagining that I had no equal in it. My chowder would cook up rich and thick; the fire would crackle merrily under the pot, and the potatoes baked in its embers were the sweetest of all victuals.

But if the fish were really biting, I would forget all about eating, and bring home all my plain ingredients. My vanity consisted in catching large fish in places where everyone was satisfied with small fry. I had become thoroughly knowledgeable in the ways of all the local fish and knew from the motion of the bobber whether I was dealing with a greedy perch, a slow tench, a lazy and imposing bream, or a powerful and persistent carp. In order to get to my beloved spots in time for the best fishing, I would leave long before the rising of the sun. Once there, hidden in the cattails and bulrushes, I would witness nature—untouched by humans and trusting—perform its mystery of awakening. Light as a ballerina, barely touching the lily pads, a snipe would race by. Once, having been clever enough to catch it, I discovered its secret: it was almost bodiless, almost pure down and feathers. Then a cautious duck would swim out followed by its scurrying young brood. On shore, they would be ravenously watched by a slim and graceful polecat. Sometimes, it would frolic in the sun. I have yet to see anything as delightful as its grace and lightness, its joyous rushes, leaps and rolls. But one had to lay in wait patiently for such a scene and I knew few people who managed to do so. Twisting in all directions, a water snake would swim by; a curious turtle would raise its head above the water. Close to the shore, a female hedgehog would prowl for mice and snakes, followed by her litter of young, whose needles were soft and not yet steel-gray, but brownish-green. Angling teaches a person two things—the discipline of endless patience and a profound sense of living nature.

From the beginning, the city to me was stifling, crowded and unpleasant, and the family home was largely alien for reasons I will explain later. I consciously fled both. What joy it was to steal away from the walls of the dull inhospitable house; to climb into a large boat at twilight, reach mid-stream and give oneself over to the will of the mighty current, imagining that we were being carried above buried palaces and tombs of Khazar lords, full of mysteries and uncountable riches which had been concealed by a shift in the river's channel. And on a night when the moon was full, what could be better than to be enchanted by the moon's sorcery as it lay down across the waters, a shimmering silver road barely trembling and wavering at its edges. And what an unimagined sense of vigor would flow into my heart as the big four-cornered sail billowed tautly in the wind and the boat would race against the current driving trees, fields, houses, and belfries backward.

But the Volga was not always indulgent or obedient. Calm and magical on a quiet night, it would become inclement and threatening when struck by a *moriana*. That is what we called a severe and persistent windstorm from the sea, "the broad Caspian." It blew from the south, but it was no southern breeze. It would make the enraged Volga rear up and whip its waves into whitecaps. Its raging was no joke. It would rip apart rafts of logs coming down from the Kama River and scatter the heavy timber like matchsticks. The steam ferries which ran between the high and low banks of the river, would not dare to venture out into the storm and would hunker down wherever they could when caught by the weather in the hope that the *moriana* would cease by nightfall and they could take up their whistling and huffing the next morning. Even the passenger steamers, wary of being smashed against piers, would seek a sheltered spot in the river and wait out the storm on all anchors.

Once two playmates and I almost drowned when caught by a *moriana* on the "other side" where our fishing passion had taken us. It seemed that my buddies in all our exploits were always younger than myself. I recruited them, was their leader, and they depended on me as their senior. At that time I was a bit shy of ten; one of them was nine and the other eight. A *moriana* sometimes struck unexpectedly, with a scant warning to the experienced eye that was a dark gray strip along the water to the south. I noticed it in time and we rowed ashore, having decided to get home on the steam ferry. But the ferry was not running at all that day. We were out of luck. The *moriana* stormed with all its might. Suppressing our disappointment, we decided to wait it out. And then, as if in spite, out of the undergrowth there came toward our beached boat four professional Volga fishermen. They were huge men and not cowed by the storm, having seen its like before. They were preparing to cross the river under canvas sail, the strength of which they trusted completely.

One of the men, noticing our envious glances, suddenly said, "Hey, lads, come with us. We'll tow you." He may have been half-joking, but we immediately seized the opportunity with joy. The oldest of the fishermen, clearly displeased, grumbled something to his mates. They seemed to pause, but the offer had been made and accepted. Their pride and self-confidence along with the Russian trust in the blind luck of "what if?" kept them from backing out. Once agreed, it was a done deal. A rope from our prow was tied to their stern and the sail was unfurled. Then everything followed with lightning speed. The sail billowed forward, and we took off. The shore quickly receded. We were in a happy delirium when suddenly a thunderclap resounded right over our heads. The trusted sail had split right in half, punished by the wind and the extra load. Suddenly the men's faces darkened. They quickly glanced at each other, and one of them clearing his throat said: "Well, lads, we'll have to take to the oars to get out of this one, but you had better go back, that shore is nearer." The rope was thrown back to us and we were left at the mercy of the raging waves.

I knew that we should not row back in a direct line because then we would be parallel to the waves and any one of them could overturn us. We had to go at an angle and slice the waves with our prow while slowly approaching the shore. I managed to explain this to my eight-year-old helmsman, but the rudder was mounted high on the boat and was useful only in calm weather. Now, every time the stern was lifted by a wave, the rudder spun uselessly in the air. Then we had to steer with the oars, and rowed with interruptions and half-effort. After all, we only had the strength of kids. The boat danced on the waves, but whether we were making progress or were being blown away by the wind, no one could tell. Shivering goose-bumps ran up and down my body. Nothing was helping, the only way out was to the bottom. I kept this thought to myself, pretending that everything was fine, but I think that the boys were not convinced by my show of courage.

Suddenly one of them, the one manning the second pair of oars, let them slip from his hands. He began to cross himself repeatedly and tell us in a breaking voice that all was lost, and that all we could do was get on our knees and pray to God. At that moment, my "helmsman" began to cry like a child and call for his mother. Aware that I was the oldest and responsible for them, I responded with some furious curse words and for some time desperately rowed for the three of us until they finally came to their senses and began to take part. I did not know how much time had gone by, but it seemed an eternity. To add to our troubles, water kept rushing in over the gunwales and had to be bailed out, but there was no one to do it. Vainly I looked around the horizon—there was no one in sight, no one was coming to help us. It was like being in a death agony.

Later we found out that my father, alarmed by my absence in such a storm, saw our misadventure with the strangers' sailboat through his binoculars and hurriedly notified the lifeguard station. There we were spotted through a telescope and a longboat with hardy oarsmen was sent to save us. But then they noticed that we, totally unaware of it, were struggling toward a sandy spit, though at a snail's pace. The promise of deliverance was becoming a reality. That's how it came out. But finally when it came to jumping into the shallow water and pulling the boat ashore, I discovered that my arms hung loosely at my sides like ropes and, God help me, were totally useless. This was a reaction to what I had just lived through. Apparently for the last couple of dozen minutes I was functioning not on muscle strength, but purely on nerves which made the physically impossible possible. Later we had many other waterborne adventures. We were older, stronger, and more experienced, and when a *moriana* was not overly violent we would go out and test our skills in struggle with it. I owe much to the river, magnificent in its quiet flow and terrible in its violence. Those who were raised by the river gradually developed an acuity of vision, a sureness of gesture, the strength of muscles, cool-headedness, self-confidence, and the habit of not fearing danger but looking it straight in the eye. In the generation of children that grew up on it, the river, in its image and likeness, instilled an elemental sense of stubborn and unsubmissive will. Some of this was bequeathed to me, for which I am eternally grateful. What would have become of me without the river?

But it was not only the river that drew us. It also opened before us the vistas of constantly new adventures on shore.

It was good, having jumped out of a boat, to stretch one's legs on the meadowy left bank, to wander without a predetermined goal, to go wherever your gaze and imagination took you. There would be thickets of willows where one would rouse all sorts of game; the sudden splash of a fish in a marshy lake grown thick with water lilies; further on, hayfields through which one had to proceed cautiously because they were the domain of proud and irate Ukrainian settlers, whom we called Cossacks, and who did not want their grass trampled. Sometimes there would spread before us a fantastic world: a solid sea of grass stretching as far as the eye could see. It was the tall and silvery feather grass, now slightly rippling and sparkling but suddenly roiled by the wind with gusts moving on it in broad and deep waves as if on a real sea.

And how many unexpected encounters did the steppe hide. Sometimes a herd of swine would rise up, wild and protected by no one except battle-scarred, tusked boars who would turn even our most feisty dogs to immediate and shameful flight. There would also be enormous, heavy steppe birds, bustards, resembling wild turkeys. To become airborne they had to run for a good stretch along the steppe and acquire the inertia of movement much as today's airplanes. But the steppe's most magical power was in its sheer vastness, the space that caught your breath, and pulled you to itself as sometimes you are pulled, even against your will, by an abyss or a whirlpool. At the same time, these wide-open spaces gave birth to an indescribable and unforgettable sense of free action and a yearning for yet-to-be experienced and boundless opportunities.

Who can describe a spring or summer day in the steppe, heavily soaked with the aroma of wildflowers and grasses, made soft and tender by the hot caresses of the sun. The spring air and the sweet aromas would make us weak and drunk with pleasure. We would stagger and collapse under the shade of bushes in order to replace this dreamy life with the dreams of sleep. The steppe, indeed, is a fervid fairy-tale of nature. Taste once its scented breath and your soul will forever hear its call which will not be silenced or erased by the many years you may spend away from it.

I and the companions of my childhood years were not destiny's favorites. Rather, we were its stepchildren. My life in my father's house was no better and generally not much worse than the lives of my peers.

My father was born into a family of serfs and as a boy helped his elders in all the common peasant labors. Even in deep old age he loved to show off his skill at mowing. And he did mow like a master. But his father, my grandfather (whom I, the youngest, had never seen), upon gaining his freedom made a firm decision to free his son from the onerous fate of a peasant. So my father was sent away to a district four-year vocational school. Having successfully finished the course of study, he received grandfather's blessing to enter the tsar's service, in an extremely responsible position yet, that of a junior assistant to the clerk of the district treasury. Beginning with that, he slowly, gradually and patiently rose up the ladder of the service hierarchy to clerk, head clerk, aide to the manager, bookkeeper, manager, and finally at the age of forty, district treasurer, the highest pinnacle of his service anthill.

In parallel to his responsibilities he ascended the Table of Ranks. He dreamt of receiving the Order of St. Vladimir, which would have made him a squire of the gentry. And he did achieve it along with the rank of Collegiate Counselor, which upon retirement was reduced to State Counselor and thus kept him from being addressed as "your excellency."

By all the signs, he married successfully and happily. The only meaningful memories of our mother were preserved only by the eldest of us, Vladimir, who was ten when she died. I was the youngest and last. Some of mother's favorite books were preserved after her death. They revealed her to be unusually cultivated for our backwater. These books belonged to the vanguard literature of her time, the sixties and early 1870's. There were also copies *The Russian Word*, *The Cause*, *The Spark* and an occasional issue of Herzen's *The Bell* [politically progressive or radical publications].

Once I found an item which our stepmother accidentally left on the table, but I was too young to appreciate it. It was, as I later understood, a traditional old album of the kind common in Pushkin's time. I was struck by its unusual calligraphy which could have only been produced by a soft goose quill of earlier days, with its exquisite alternation of fine lines and bold strokes, with its dandyish and ornate signatures, some of which were works of art in their own right.

My eldest brother and sister later revealed that they had found evidence of mother's familiarity with literature in the album. But the album was not in our hands for long. Our stepmother noticed its disappearance and grew very angry when she found us poring over it. She took it away from us and we never saw it again.

My father's level of education was not very high. However, in a provincial backwater he stood out above the average. In his forties, as I remember him best, he was the "soul of society" in the full meaning of that phrase. He was expansive in nature, hospitable and good-natured. He loved to receive and entertain guests, and many people seeing a "light in his window" would drop by, seeking comfort and relief from their cares. He was accomplished and agile with a billiard cue, a hunting rifle, and the fishing rod. He was considered a professor of whist and "preference" [a card game generically similar to whist and bridge].

In societal issues, he had not advanced very far. But he was absolutely firm on one issue: land ultimately was to be turned over to the peasants, for they were the true children of the earth with true filial love. The gentry was on the land for vain and self-indulgent reasons. They defiled the land, making it a means of oppressing the peasant. They stuck out between the peasant and the land as superfluous and useless, and getting rid of them would constitute a venerable act. It was clear that this attitude was deeply seated in his consciousness, ingested with the milk of his mother, showing the imprint of his rural origin. He never covered up the deficiencies of his education nor his lack of good manners and all that which was considered good breeding. He loved to repeat—whether from a sense of self-abasement or from plebeian pride—that he was "a peasant, a peasant born, and would die a peasant."

Though my parents' natures were different, their family life flowed smoothly, except that my mother's health was jeopardized by frequent pregnancies. Along with us who had lived, she had given birth to several (either three or four) children who had been carried off by various childhood diseases. Her general health was poor, and she died leaving father five children, the oldest of whom was nine and the youngest, myself, about one. Because of my young age, I could not comprehend the magnitude of our loss. But my older siblings were crushed by our orphaned and neglected state. [In Russian culture the loss of even one parent makes a child an orphan; the loss of both makes one a total, "all-around" orphan, a *kruglyi sirota*.]

Father totally lost his presence of mind from grief and was almost driven to drink. His lapses at work nearly cost him his job. Close to despair, he finally barely surmounted it. He had to leave the locale where everything reminded him of his irreparable loss, but the children could not be left without a mother's care. The only thing to do was to remarry. They found him a bride suitable for a man of years and burdened by a brood of children. The bride, an aging virgin, was a thrifty, rather pushy cleric's daughter. According to my brother and sisters, she was attentive and kind to us early in the marriage until the appearance of her own child.

As more and more of her own children appeared (she had five or six by the time I left home), all girls, she became transformed into the classic stepmother of gloomy Russian songs and fairy-tales. She developed enmity toward everything associated with our mother. One by one, mother's albums began to disappear, including the one which contained her girlhood diary. Then she began to transfer mother's books to the attic, where they were doomed to become food for mice. Father had no time to read these books, and she herself did not have the habit or interest. Next came the turn of the photographs of the deceased, removed by herself in our presence. This was not a manifestation of jealousy. This was the desire to reign in the household autocratically, rather than be a substitute for the one who had reigned there previously. Everything that reminded her of "that one" filled her heart with a malevolent vexation. And we, "her" children, were also constant, living reminders of "that one." And we were to pay for it dearly.

Soon she was to deliver a very cruel blow; to turn out of our home our beloved, quiet nurturer and constant intercessor—our grandmother. She was meek and timid, but whenever she saw one of us being unduly punished, she would grab the victim and rush him off into the children's room. No one could get her to change her behavior. The worst thing was that we could not help but notice the systematic efforts to get grandmother to leave of her own accord. Petty harassment, poisoning every minute of her life, carping, malevolent tricks, constant fault finding, demeaning reproaches, calumnies, mockery—all were used to effect. Grandmother would weep silently with increasing frequency and so would we, huddled around her, understanding each other without speaking a word. We did not weep only because of grandmother's injuries, but also because we realized, contrary to our young years, that falsehood and evil were stronger than truth and goodness. We wept bitterly, lamenting and not comprehending how father could not see or understand anything. In his distance from us, he was our highest authority. Whenever he came down to us from his invisible but undoubted heights, he was good, kind, joyous and strong, and his smile would warm us like the smile of the sun illuminating the bleakness of our being.

Those of us who were older understood everything in the simplest of terms: a new, relatively young wife was able to twist her middle-aged husband around her finger.

She convinced father that it was in grandmother's best interest to leave the cramped house which swarmed with kids. And he, with his usual good will and clear conscience, took up the task. He recalled that he had some distant relatives, a quiet, childless couple of modest means. For a small honorarium it cordially took in life's old veteran. Everything seemed to have worked out for the best. But there was one thing that father overlooked. After grandmother had constantly been told that she was good for nothing, the exile from our home totally crushed her as ultimate evidence of her uselessness. "There now, no one needs me and I'm being sent away to die," she murmured at our farewells, her voice muffled by the lump in her throat. Nor did father notice what she had been for us and what a loss this was. We had been orphaned a second time.

I was the youngest and, without grandmother, the most defenseless. But it did not turn out that way. I was a boy and had certain resources which my sisters did not have. Father's passion for angling, its peace and quietude, grew with the years. I would easily keep up with him, a can of first-class earthworms on the ready, a landing net for the chance big fish, and a basket for what we caught. Later, gladdening the heart of my sire, I became a skilled angler myself.

Life in our household began to stabilize through an uneasy compromise. The matter was greatly aided by an unexpected inheritance: a two-story wooden house. And so there came into being "the bi-cameral system" as we jokingly referred to it later as adults. The upper chamber comprised father, stepmother, and her children. The lower chamber was us and the servants except for the cook. We rarely came together, almost only for dinner, which was a tense and tedious ritual. Supper for the lower chamber was a separate affair. It was modest and always the same—cold boiled buckwheat and an earthenware tureen of milk (we had our own milking cow). The upper chamber had its guests: the so-called "local intelligentsia." It was made up of the public notary, a lawyer, the excise tax man, two doctors, the police chief, the district attorney, and later, the head of the district council. They would hold their sessions at card tables and fill their intermissions with hors d'oeuvre and "liquid" refreshment. We stood "in opposition" to such goings on, especially to the head of the district council because he had married a recent graduate of the girl's high school with whom I imagined myself to be in love, though the very word was for me a pale and bookish abstraction.

The shift from education at home to a boarding school one was an epochal change in the life of the young generation of a middle-class provincial family. And it lay in my life as a new and special geological stratum. The shift threw me from rural and backwater Kamyshin to the regional capital of Saratov [a major city on the Volga]. At that time, Saratov already had a quite decent and presentable city-center built around an excellent boulevard which, due to the predominance of a particular kind of tree, was called The Lindens. When the linden trees were in bloom, the boulevard was suffused with a most tender aroma. The Lindens were intersected by a network of four or five major streets with an abundance of very decent stores. "The kind that Moscow would not be ashamed of," in the words of one of my landladies. The liveliest of these streets, resembling the German [foreigners] quarter in pre-Petrine Russia was of course called Nemetskaia [German] Street. During World War

I the city council, embarrassed by the name, changed it to honor General Skobelev [a hero of the 1877–78 Turkish wars]. After 1917 the spirit of the times changed its name to Revolution Street.

But as one moved toward the periphery, the city's glitter became increasingly lusterless. It was initially replaced by the usual provincial ordinariness of buildings and streets. Further on, the ordinariness changed to shabbiness, which came to a low point in the neighborhood of Gorki: primitive huts of the urban poor who made a living by some indeterminate means.

On this general background the recently built center resembled an errant piece of elegant brocade brightly sewn into the worn clothes of a poor person. Of course, the center was the object of special attention by the city council which represented the merchants and property owners while the outlying areas were totally neglected.

A part of this beautiful brocade piece was our boarding school. It seemed that the rest of the city had not yet fully become accustomed to its existence, especially to the glistening buttons of its uniform overcoats which, beneath the dim street lights, resembled those of military officers. The resemblance was further enhanced by the intricate cockades on our hats. As an upperclassman, I had numerous comical incidents because of this confusion. Occasionally in the evening on some out-of-the-way street we would encounter a bunch of soldiers. Their tipsy and loud talk would suddenly go quiet, their figures would straighten, and they would begin to march in step as they readied themselves for a stiff-bodied, snappy salute and to "devour the officers with their eyes." But suddenly, having seen things clearly, they would roar with laughter and chastise each other for spotting "an officer who was nothing more than boarding school crap." Sometimes threats would be sent in our direction and sometimes the dark gray overcoats would threaten to take their chagrin out on us with their fists.

In the lower grades street adventures were an everyday occurrence. The mere sight of our school uniforms and cockades with the school's initials on them provoked the street kids into bloody challenges. The school's initials, S.G. [Saratov *Gimnazium*], were stupidly and maliciously decoded [in Russian] as "blue beef." The reddish-blue hue of rancid beef is familiar to everyone. Therefore, the provocative question, "Hey, you, stinkin' blue beef, how much a pound?" had the effect that a gauntlet thrown at the feet of a medieval knight would have had. In order to preserve his honor the knight had to pick up the glove and unsheathe his sword. With us the ritual was to roll up one's sleeves and fight for the honor of the school until one of the combatants was knocked off his feet or himself fell to the ground: the convention was not to hit someone who was down. The younger schoolboys who usually were waylaid by gangs while walking home from school would form groups and fight their way homeward by going "wall against wall." Both sides had outstanding fighters, their Hectors, Ajaxes and Achilleses.

I also took part in this ancient internecine strife which had been legitimated by tradition. My old Kamyshin habits pulled me to the banks of the Volga where I would go on Sundays or other holidays. I had to slip out of the house unnoticed for this, while everyone was only beginning to rise. It was a great pleasure to get to the water, observe the fishermen, watch the loading and unloading of barges, to mingle with the sawmill workers, to listen to the engaging, boastful tales of the Galakhov boys—hoboes who had received their name from the merchant Galakhov and his flophouse. Among them one occasionally encountered self-made raconteurs who were true masters of the word. When one of them would talk, it was as if he were weaving multicolored silks. After grandmother's tales and songs, it was here that I found an endless spring of authentic language of the people: fresh, strong, and juicy as an Antonov apple, extraordinarily rich in imagery and laced with maxims, proverbs, and sayings.

But an even greater curiosity was roused in me by two types of people. The first were wayfarers, collectors of funds for church buildings, defrocked priests and deacons, pilgrims who traveled from one place to another and had been to almost all the famous monasteries which preserved the relics of the righteous and had miracle-working icons. Among such people there were also zealous sectarians seeking "the city of God and absolute faith." The second group consisted of hoboes who maintained their existence by whatever means they could, including petty thievery when times were hard. They turned to thievery, especially in late autumn, to ensure for themselves a winter's warmth and food in the local jail. Later, when Maxim Gorky's play *The Lower Depths* created a public sensation, I remained indifferent to it. All his male types were not new to me. The memory of my teen-age years was filled with them.

Having lost my mother at an early age, I grew up virtually abandoned by my stepmother. And though she came from a clerical family, I received no religious education in the spirit of the Orthodox church. I took a discarded child's primer on the Old Testament to be a collection of fairy tales about a serpent which spoke the human tongue, of prophetic dreams of pharaohs, of the sea which parted before a procession of fugitives, of the miraculous survival of youths in a lion's den and in a scorching oven, of a stone from a boy's sling which brought down the invincible giant Goliath.

Later, when promoted from the elementary grades in school to the middle ones, I had my personal period of mystic-religious enthusiasms and secret, solitary, prayerful ecstasies. But they developed on their own, having ripened in the secret corner of a growing child's consciousness prematurely intent on becoming a young man. All this had no connection with the Orthodox church but rather had points of contact with the Tolstoyism of the intelligentsia and the god-seeking of the common folk.

There was not even a hint of a university in Saratov. For higher education, one had to go either to distant Kazan or all the way to "the second capital," Moscow. There was one *gimnazium* [a classical high school] for men and one for women, a vocational high school, a finishing school for girls of the nobility, a pedagogical institute, a school for doctors' assistants [paramedics], and in the nearby countryside, an agricultural school. In all, a smallish number for a city that called itself the capital of the Volga region. However, along with the official institutions of learning where the provincial "fruits of enlightenment" were cultivated there was another place of learning. By some odd quirk it was located in a corner of the Commercial Club, a venue for gatherings of the landed nobility, grand banquets, and balls. Though it had no official standing, it served as a magnet for all the local students. It was a rather substantial library under the supervision of Valerian Aleksandrovich Balmashev, a political exile under government surveillance. His charm and kind attention enabled him to gradually transform the book-loving young people into students of an informal and liberating self-education.

I grew to self-awareness at the end of the 1880's. It was an uncommonly dreary time, without a single bright moment of political struggle. In a revolutionary sense, society was completely bloodless. It resembled a clear-cut forest in which once mighty oaks were reduced to stumps. There remained only legends of "socialists" and "nihilists" who once had gone out to rouse "the people" and who served as examples of how to resist all power and laws whether God's or man's by use of the dagger, bomb, and revolver. A romantic mist shrouded these enigmatic and daring people. Everyone spoke of them with Philistine condemnation and also with a kind of inadvertent esteem. And this impressed youthful imaginations.

For me, growing up motherless under the daily and hourly oppression of a classical "stepmother," escaping from her persecution into the kitchen, the servants' room, the banks of the Volga, into the company of street kids, it was completely natural to absorb love for the people, especially as it was expressed in the poetry of Nekrasov. I knew almost all his works by heart.

Since I was myself constantly "humiliated and injured," I was naturally drawn to all those who had been "humiliated and injured" as well. This was my world and in unison with it I set myself against "the reigning injustice." Nekrasov broadened this world for me. Thanks to him, this world grew from the servants' room and my restless street buddies to include the world of all common people, peasants, and laborers.

Chapter Two

Sergei N. Durylin, Domestic Love

Born to a merchant family, Sergei Durylin broke with that world to become a person of enormous erudition. Known for a gentle manner and kindness, traits always mentioned by his friends and colleagues, he was also remembered for his accomplishments in theater, literature, archeology, art criticism, and philology. His memoirs are finely drawn. The selection chosen illustrates a family life in style, habit, and sensibility which disappeared after the 1917 revolution. Taken from S.N. Durylin, *V svoem uglu* [In One's Own Corner]. Moscow: Moskovskii rabochii, 1991.

Seventeen years after the death of my mother, I opened for the first time a small pile of his [her first husband's] letters which she had carefully preserved.

There turned out to be very few of *his* letters. They were *her* letters to him. Her, the bride's, letters were full of deep feeling, strong in their clarity and simplicity: "I am all yours." "All is in you." "All is with you." "All is for you."

And she's always waiting for his letters, but he never has enough time. He's handsome, his mother's darling, the darling of his family. He loves her, but he doesn't have a thoughtful heart. His love is always "seeking its own" and it doesn't think, it doesn't even see its counterpart. It's a love with eyes open to itself and closed to the loved one. And the love of the loved one "suffers quietly" and won't raise a hand to open his eyes. Oh, it's bitter to love a person with closed eyes! And my mother drank up this bitterness to the dregs. And her love was so great that it strangled another feeling, growing in her towards a different person.

I was sorry that I had untied the scarlet ribbon that had at one time held together this pile of old letters. I felt sorrow, pain, distress. But when I think that everything was covered with love, when I remember that my mother never, to my knowledge, reproached the person who gave her so little happiness and so much suffering—when I once again imagine with how much love she would always remember his love, and how joyful she perceived her first love to be, and how thankful she was to him for this love, I thank my mother for this pile of letters from years long gone. She gave me, an old man, a great lesson of a great love, one which "suffers quietly" and forgives all. And I'm glad that I bear the first name of this unhappy, kind, and noble man, whose burden (and not his fault) was that he lived by "a single law declaring / The passions' arbitrary cues."[1]

After the death of Sergei Sergeevich, my mother remained at her mother's-in-law. Her life was difficult. Childless, she couldn't take root in the family, and without those roots she couldn't become a true member of it. Her mother-in-law respected her, but this imperious woman, fortune's favorite, harbored neither love nor warm feeling for anyone.

Olga Vasilievna needed my mother. She was bringing up orphans, a boy and a girl, the children of her deceased daughter. She did not entrust their upbringing to their father. My mother raised them. They were difficult children who nonetheless made out well for themselves.

My mother lived on Bolvanovka Street as the widow of the favorite son of Olga Vasilievna, but she never received so much as pocket money from her. And all the while her heart was being torn apart by troubles: her father, Vasily Alekseevich, couldn't support his family and soon died. My grandmother and my aunt were left without any means. My mother had to make up her mind to do something, so as not to leave her mother without bread. And make up her mind she did: she married my father.

This was a heroic deed in the true sense of the word. She did it for her mother.

My father was a widower, twenty years older than my mother. She didn't marry him out of love; she only knew that she was marrying an honest and good person. She took upon herself a huge family—by today's standards, ridiculously huge: my father had eleven children, of which only the eldest daughter was married. All the rest—six daughters and four sons—lived with their father. The older ones could have been my mother's younger brothers and sisters, and the youngest one was four years old. The heavy burden of raising and managing this enormous family, which took up two floors of a spacious house in Pleteshki, carried with it the no-less-difficult burden of managing a house that was almost the size of an estate. And my mother entered into all of this at the age of thirty, in the bloom of her youth, which was cut off at the root. Here too she carried her burden with honor.

Of my father's marriageable daughters only one had been given away in marriage, and unsuccessfully at that: the husband drank, leaving her without any means, and she came back to her father's house, so that all of my father's eleven children wound up in my mother's care after all. During my father's life my mother married off three daughters, all into happy marriages and even wealth. When the children from the first marriage left my father after he went broke, only one of the three remaining marriageable daughters managed to get married. The dowry for the oldest of them had already been prepared by my mother, and her stepdaughter took it with her.

My father's older sons did not receive an education. The eldest son, Nikolai Nikolaevich, was at business trade school just long enough to get his feet wet, and the second son didn't even get into the water at some boarding school. I remember my father saying that kids only needed to be taught "readin,' 'ritin,' and 'rithmetic,'" and then—off to business, to trade! My mother vehemently protested this and insisted that the two younger sons, whom she had raised, not only finish high school, but also university. One was an assistant to the famous Plevako [a leading jurist], and the other, an engineer.

Like the older sons, the older daughters attended boarding school only briefly—of the five only two, as I recall, finished school. The two last ones, whose upbringing fell to my mother, finished the public *gimnazium* for women with honors.

There were no children from my mother's first marriage. In her second they came one after another—five boys. The births were painful. And so the "toil and suffering" which fell to her were great. Her single reward was the fact that she was able to take care of her mother: my grandmother and my aunt lived quietly and peacefully in a little apartment, on the pennies given to them by my mother. And these pennies were really half-pennies, compared to the work which my mother bore in that alien, endless family. But even these pennies elicited reproaches from the stepsons and stepdaughters! My father, on the other hand, loved and respected his new mother-in-law.

Surveying my mother's life, I often thought that it would have been hard to come up with two more striking opposites than her first and second husbands.

Sergei Sergeevich was young and handsome, a wit, carelessly trying out all the experiences of easy living, one after another, never thinking about the final end. He loved my mother, and she loved him. There was lot of glamour in him, along with that specific quality which can be designated by the untranslatable French word *charme*. He loved merrymaking, the theatre, thoroughbred horses, wine, and women. He had friends and foes, companions and enemies. He burned his own candle (and those of others) at both ends. My mother had no children with him. And his love in her life was like a dream— at the beginning luminous and happy, like a lilac evening, then, at the end, sorrowful to the point of tears, to the bitterness of wormwood.

My father was the complete opposite of Sergei Sergeevich in everything. He was brought up in the school of hard knocks. The only son of an old merchant family which went bankrupt during his early childhood, he lived as a servant-boy in the home of the miserly and cruel silk merchant Kaptsov, a veritable Scrooge, where he received more than his share of beatings. Sergei Sergeevich would go to the Nizhnii Novgorod Fair riding the train first class, while my father would walk there on foot with the carts carrying Kaptsov's goods. Sergei Sergeevich was rich, while my father was barely making enough to feed a family of twenty people.

My father never had a drop of wine in his life. He was a homebody; his only treats were red whortleberry preserve and almond spice cake. He visited taverns only with customers, and would take only tea with a bit of sugar. He was not lacking in true, kindhearted folk humor. But the style of the life that he led and that he wanted his children to lead was strict and proper. He didn't like anything new. My entire childhood and boyhood were spent in candlelight, when houses everywhere already had kerosene lamps, and some even had electricity. Life for him was work and ritual, not chance and play. There was no merrymaking in him—at most, a smile. I don't remember him ever laughing. "Sinful" was a strict and harsh word coming from him. It hardly needs to be said that he was a proper, irreproachably proper, family man.

And my mother, who had married him, a fifty-year-old, without love, had five sons by him, and knew all the joys and sorrows of motherhood that the one she had loved before didn't give her.

First she gave birth to a son, named Nikolai in honor of his father. He was one of those children who can be best described in the words of Lermontov:

> Of purest ether, in His wisdom
> The Lord once wove their living strings;
> The world will never mingle with them,
> Nor will they mix with worldly things![2]

The common folk would call such children "not of this world." The ones who were "of this world" were those who fit the narrow, crude measure of "base earthly existence." Fedor Sologub liked to write of those "not of this world"—children with large, pensive eyes which early on showed an orphan's fear of the cold misery of existence. Kolia was not of this world. He was a starry-eyed boy. His big, brown, wide and sorrowfully open eyes were striking, evident even in a Moebius photograph. These were not ordinary eyes, but something more deep and penetrating. The child amazed everyone with his meekness, with his early understanding of people and things, with his glowing abundance of love for everyone. Important and high-ranking clergy of the Church of the Epiphany in Elokhovo called him a "blessed child." "He is not of this world," his nanny Pelageia Sergeevna marveled in sad adoration. His half-brothers and half-sisters loved him.

I don't know what his godfather—"Brother Kolia," as we called him—gave him on the occasion of the cutting of his first tooth. My mother selected him as the godfather in order to strengthen the connection between the new brother and his half-brother. My miserly grandmother Olga Vasilievna celebrated the first tooth with generosity; my mother kept grandmother's gifts of heavy golden ten-ruble pieces from the age of Catherine the Great (two or three of them) until times of dire need. My father fell in love with his namesake, his first-born son by his second wife. And my mother just adored him: he was the joy of joys that bloomed for her in a family of strangers. I was the second child after him—and both I and the next brother, Georgii, had it hard: we were expected to measure up to Kolia's radiance and lovingness, but we were only of this world. For better or worse, we adapted ourselves to this "shadow of our times," which fell on those of this world but did not darken Kolia's existence.

For my godfather my mother chose her second stepson, Alexander Nikolaevich, wishing to strengthen our blood-bond. For godmother she chose her own mother, and she named me in honor of her beloved.

Kolia died at the age of three from diphtheria. My mother gave birth to a third son, Georgii, a handsome, curly-haired boy who was much loved by his godmother, my father's third daughter, Elizaveta Nikolaevna. But my mother was not to be consoled. Kolia's death was a blow from which she never completely recovered. I think that had Kolia lived, he would have helped her find a path to the heart of her new family. Without him this path was never found.

How cruel life is—or perhaps how merciful: it was not meant for her to be at the funerals of either her beloved mother or her beloved son. She was terribly ill and was nearly at death's door herself when those two left this earth. Life in the new family was fourteen years of daily hard work for my mother. It was one long continuous workday.

She had to feed and clothe a house of thirty people, including children, relatives, and servants. Before that my mother had never been in charge of a household. However, when she harnessed herself to my father's household affairs, she handled everything so well, so ably fulfilled the offices of minister of internal affairs, minister of provisions, and minister of education in my father's domain that she never received anything but well-deserved praise from my father. I remember our family dinner table, fourteen feet long, packed with place settings. At the table would be my father, my mother, four brothers (we were fed separately), six or seven sisters, the governess Olga Ivanovna, two distant female relatives of my father's first wife, who lived at our house. These fifteen or sixteen people were family, but dinner never proceeded without guests: we invariably had one or another aunt (my father's sisters), or one of the Tarasovs (my sisters' cousins). And we mustn't forget to add one of my sisters' girlfriends or my brothers' buddies who would stay for dinner. But even that's not all. Either my father or one of my older brothers would bring someone else from town to dinner—some customer or just a friend—and having brought him, would simply ask my mother:

"Mother," (if my father was asking) or "Nastasia Vasilievna" (if my brothers were asking), "Ivan Ivanovich is having dinner with us. Do you have something to feed him?"

And my mother would always give one and the same response, "Yes," and would only afterwards lament that she never received advance warning. In order to "feed the visitor," who was sometimes the very picky Ivan Ivanovich, she had to add two fancy dishes and good appetizers and wine to the usual simple but filling family meal. And for all this she would only have half an hour, for my father himself would hurry her: "Mother, it's time to eat. We're hungry."

And this visitor, Ivan Ivanovich from Gluttonville, rich in black soil, hogs, and grain, would eat and praise to the skies the appetizers, the first course, the second course, the third course, the homemade plum brandy, the St. John's Wort liqueur, the marinated sturgeon, and the pickled and marinated apples, grapes, plums, cherries, and lingonberries.

At the same time she had to feed the small children and make sure that the broth and the cutlets were prepared to the exact specifications of the military doctor von Reson.

And she had to look after a third table (the *third* table in the *same* house at the *same* time!), to make sure that the sales clerks in the employees' room were full and satisfied.

Of course, she couldn't forget about the *fourth* table: she had to make sure that the "servants' cook" Arina would make rich, filling *shchi* [cabbage soup] and thick porridge [traditionally of buckwheat] for the servants: the kitchen staff, the caretaker, the maids, and the nanny.

Sometimes there was also a *fifth* table, in the same house at the same time: if an infant had a wet-nurse, then the doctor prescribed a special diet for her.

But the family was large: either one or another member would be sick, and then a *sixth* table would be added with a special menu. And this just on the workdays—from day to day.

But in addition to the workdays there were namedays [holidays celebrating the patron saint bearing the same name as the celebrant] and birthdays, and there were plenty of those in a family which had 13–14 children, not to speak of the rest! What a great number of pies to be baked! And all with particular favorite fillings—otherwise there would be hurt feelings and tears. And the nanny, and the wet-nurse, and the sales clerk Ivan Stepanych—all had to have pies for their namedays. And those were just the namedays within the household—what of all the others? My fathers' sisters—there you had three more namedays, whose demanding celebrants knew all of the virtues and shortcomings of the pies, made with rice, sturgeon, sauteed cabbage, mushrooms, liver, carrots, and so on and so forth.

Holidays presented a different kind of toil. And what an abundance of food was necessary for this huge family: *kulichi* [tall, cylindrical baked Easter cakes] and *paskha* [cheese cake], made from sweet cream cheese, butter, and sour cream [often with a combination of raisins, nuts and candied fruit]. Here exact calculation was necessary: the "sacramental" *paskha* and the "sacramental" *kulich*, which were taken to be blessed at [Saturday] morning services before Easter, had to be of such a size that there would be enough for each person in the family to have a serving during every day of Bright Week [the week after Easter Sunday]. This was not only a complex culinary problem, but a mathematical one as well. Besides the "sacramental" *paskha*, it was necessary to make *paskha* "for eating." *Paskha* was so delicious and tender, so aromatic and sweet (oh, the vanilla, almonds, sugar, candied fruit, and candied orange peel that went into it!) that it was eaten like pastry, like whipped cream, or double-rich ice cream. But the difference was that while there would usually be a small portion of dessert only at the end of dinner, *paskha* was eaten in varying amounts during morning and afternoon tea for seven days. But not only that; the "unblessed" *paskha* would be made and eaten during the entire six weeks after Easter right up to the Feast of the Ascension. It's difficult to fathom how much *paskha* mother and Petrovna [the cook] had to make! *Paskha* was made according to different recipes and with different ingredients: they were both cooked and uncooked, made of sour cream or sweet cream cheese, with chocolate and pistachios. This was a difficult art, demanding focused attention and skill.

But the distribution of the *paskha* was not limited to the household. My father would often ask about three or four days before the holiday, "Mother, you didn't forget that Katerina Ivanovna needs a *paskha* and a *kulich*?" "No, I didn't." "And what about the poorhouse?" "I remember." "And for Serafima Pavlovna?" "I remember."

But sometimes he didn't ask anything in advance, but would simply inquire on the first day of the holiday, "Was a *paskha* and a *kulich* sent to Serafima Pavlovna?" "Yes, it was." But in order to be able to answer thus, she had to keep in mind not only the family of thirty people, but all the Serafima Pavlovnas, all the Katerina Ivanovnas, all the poor relations, inhabitants of the poorhouse, and just other people and families whom my father helped secretly, and send them *paskhi*, *kulichi*, and Easter eggs on time.

The same thing would happen at Christmas. And the same thing would happen at other times. In the fall, father would say: "Mother, we should send some pickled apples to Ustin'ia Petrovna at the home." (Ustin'ia Petrovna was the mother of my sister's governess, a respected noblewoman who had seen Pushkin in person.) "The apples really came out well this year. We should do something nice for the old lady."

"The nanny visited her three days ago with the children, and took her some," my mother would answer. Mention of the nanny would remind him of the nanny's aunt Elena Demanovna [sic], a wonderful old lady.

"Oh, by the way, we should send some to Elena Demanovna. Their poorhouse is short on money. I bet they feed them salt-cured fish."

And she would have an answer ready: "On Sunday the nanny asked for a day off. She's going to the poorhouse for craftsmen. I already told Arina to fill a jar with a dozen of the larger apples."

To feed and care for everyone, providing them all with an Easter egg, a pickled apple, a Christmas goose, or a nameday pie, required unending labor, care, and constant attention. And truly, the care devoted to the airiness and wafting smells of these pies, a care which some might find ridiculous, indicated a caring for people, something that was not ridiculous at all but worthy of great praise. And the care with which all those pies were baked, and all those Antonov apples pickled with cardamon, was taken seriously by my mother and father, and taught to us.

All summer our house would be humming with activity—my mother's activity, of course—according to the old proverb: "Make hay while the sun shines."

Not a single apple that fell in our garden was wasted. Round apple slices were strung on twine in bountiful garlands (we loved this task) and hung under the beams of our spacious attic. Our braziers glowed unendingly with golden coals in the garden on the path near the house; basin after basin of preserves were being simmered. Sour cherries were marinated in vinegar in a special way.

Closer to autumn the "pickling" season began: plums, grapes, and then apples. Crates of Antonov apples were purchased at the Boloto Market. The smell of apples — wonderful, cheerful as a September morning, clear as crystal — would reign for several days throughout the house. Amber-golden hay was laid down in the dining room, where the apples were sorted, the hearty ones separated from the weaker, paler apples. The cellar would become inhabited by tubs of apples. After that came the turn of the lingonberries, my father's favorite. We stocked them in tubs as well. We pickled whole vats of cucumbers, and they were unusually tasty and wonderfully strong.

We would pickle, marinate, and dry mushrooms. This was an art in itself and presented its own difficulties. After the cucumbers came the cabbage. The chopping of the cabbage passed quickly and merrily. Everyone took part. Everyone crunched on cabbage cores. But my mother had the most important task: she had to calculate how much cabbage to chop, how much to slice up, and how much to leave unchopped. It was important to choose the most auspicious time for the cabbage: when it was cheap and in season, just begging to be pickled.

The cabbage cares of autumn would come to an end, and then we had to salt the corned beef for the coming year, stock the year's salted fish, and also think of marinating the sturgeon and cod for appetizers for our guests. The supply of wine was renewed with only the guests in mind; hence, the amount wasn't large, but still highly varied. I remember the difficult process of preparing the plum brandy, which would take my mother several days. I remember the flavoring of all sorts of vodkas in rounded bottles and broad-shouldered decanters. All of this was selfless and even unpleasant work for my mother: neither she nor my father would taste even a drop of all these riches, since they couldn't stand alcohol. The only commonly consumed drink in our house was *kvas*, wonderful *kvas* made from bread that every member of the household would drink in all amounts at all times. [A kind of beer made by fermenting rye bread or rye flour, yeast, malt, and sugar; served chilled.]

Much more pleasing for my mother and for us children was the work involved in preparing other foods: all sorts of fruit spreads from figs, black currants, apples, cherries, and plums — all these were favorite victuals of ours.

All of this prodigious labor was in preparation for the winter. But there was also the labor of winter itself, and for the family, and for the house of thirty people and its large number of guests, and for those being helped on the side. And all this demanded unending work from my mother.

NOTES

1. A quotation from *Eugene Onegin*, Alexander Pushkin's 1831 novel-in-verse (Chapter Eight, third stanza, lines 1–2). Translation by Walter Arndt, in *Pushkin Threefold: Narrative, Lyric, Polemic, and Ribald Verse* (New York: E.P. Dutton and Co., 1972), p. 160.

2. From Lermontov's narrative poem "The Demon," Part XVI. Translation by Anatoly Liberman in *Mikhail Lermontov: Major Poetical Works* (Minneapolis: U of Minnesota Press, 1983), p. 411.

Chapter Three

Sofiia Kovalevskaia, A Thief in the House

Sofiia Kovalevskaia (1850–1891) wrote an engaging memoir of her youth. Well received, the book was translated into eight languages. Autobiographical works by women were not an uncommon feature of the Russian literary landscape. Kovalevskaia's case was unique because she was an internationally renowned mathematician and a professor of mathematics at the University of Stockholm. The introduction to the English language edition of her memoir cites mathematical circles proclaiming her as "the most important woman mathematician prior to the twentieth century." Her talented life was cut short by pneumonia at the age of forty-one. Taken from Sofiia Kovalevskaia, *A Russian Childhood.* Trans. Beatrice Stillman. New York: Springer-Verlag, 1978.

When I was about six years old my father retired from Army service and settled in his family estate of Palibino, in the province of Vitebsk. At that time persistent rumors of an imminent "emancipation of the serfs" were already making the rounds, and these rumors impelled my father to occupy himself more seriously with farming, which up to that time had been given over to a steward.

Soon after our arrival in the country an episode occurred in our household which remained vividly in my memory. Moreover, its effect on everyone else in the house was so strong that it was often recalled afterward. And so my own impressions became intermingled with the subsequent stories about it, and I was no longer able to distinguish one from the other. Therefore, I shall describe this episode as I understand it now.

Various articles suddenly began vanishing from our nursery: now one thing, now another. Whenever Nanny forgot about some article over a period of time and then needed it later, it was nowhere to be found, although she was ready to swear that she herself, with her own two hands, had laid it away in the cupboard or the bureau. These disappearances were treated rather calmly at first but when they began to occur more and more often and to include articles of ever increasing value, when a silver spoon, a gold thimble and a mother-of-pearl penknife suddenly vanished in succession, an alarm was raised. It was clear that we had a thief in our house. Nanny, who considered herself responsible for keeping the children's belongings safe, was more upset than anyone, and she resolved to unmask the thief at all costs.

It was natural that suspicion should fall first of all on poor Feklusha, the girl who had been appointed to serve in the nursery. True, Feklusha had been with us for about three years, and Nanny had never noticed anything of the sort in all that time. In her opinion, however, this fact didn't prove a thing.

"Before this, the girl was little and didn't understand the value of things," Nanny reasoned. "But now she's older and smarter. And on top of that, her family lives in the village. So she must be snitching the master's property for them."

Reasoning in this fashion, Nanny reached such a deep inner conviction of Feklusha's guilt that she began behaving toward her with ever greater harshness and severity. And the hapless, intimidated Feklusha, feeling instinctively that she was under suspicion, began to acquire an ever more guilty air.

But no matter how stealthily Nanny watched over Feklusha, she was not able to put her finger on anything specific for a long time. And meanwhile the missing articles did not turn up, and new items kept disappearing. One day Aniuta's money-box, which always stood in Nanny's cupboard and contained about forty rubles (if not more), was gone. The news of this last disappearance reached even my father. He summoned Nanny and gave strict orders that the thief must be found without fail. At this point we all realized that the matter was no joke.

Nanny was desperate. But then one night she woke up and heard something: a peculiar munching sound was coming from Feklusha's corner. Already inclined to suspicion, she stealthily, noiselessly stretched out her hand to a box of matches and lit the candle all of a sudden. And what did she see? There was Feklusha squatting on her heels and holding a huge jam jar between her knees, stuffing jam into both her cheeks and even wiping up the jar with a crust of bread. I should add that our housekeeper had complained a few days before that jam was disappearing from her pantry cupboard. To jump out of bed and grab the criminal by her pigtail was, it goes without saying, the work of a single second for Nanny.

"Aha! Caught you, you no-good! Speak up—where did you get that jam?" she shouted in a voice like thunder, mercilessly pulling the girl about by the hair.

"Nanny dear! I didn't do anything wrong, and that's the truth!" Feklusha implored. "It was the seamstress, Maria Vasilievna, it was her gave me the jam last night. But she ordered me not to show it to you."

This explanation appeared to Nanny implausible in the highest degree.

"Well, my dear, anybody can see you don't even know how to tell a lie," she said with contempt.

"A likely story . . . when did Maria Vasilievna take it into her head to start treating you to jam?"

"Nanny dear, I'm not lying! It's the God's honest truth. You can ask her yourself. I was heating up her irons for her yesterday, and that's why she treated me to the jam. But she ordered me, 'Don't show it to Nanny, or else she'll scold me for pampering you.' "

"All right then, we'll get to the bottom of this thing tomorrow morning," Nanny decided. And in anticipation of morning she locked Feklusha up in a dark closet, from which her sobbing could be heard for a long while afterward. The next morning, the investigation began.

Maria Vasilievna was a seamstress who had been living in our house for many years. She was not a serf but a freewoman and enjoyed greater respect than the rest of the servants. She had her own room, in which she dined on food from the master's table. She held herself very proudly in general and kept apart from all the other servants. She was highly regarded in our house because she was such a complete mistress of her craft. People said of her that she had "golden hands." She was, I imagine, getting on toward forty by then. Her face was thin and sickly-looking, with huge dark eyes. She was homely, but I recall that the grownups always said of her the she looked *distingue,* that "you'd never take her for an ordinary seamstress." She dressed immaculately and kept her room in perfect order, even with certain pretensions to elegance. There were always pots of geraniums on her windowsill, her walls were hung with cheap pictures and, on the shelf in the corner, various porcelain articles were set out which I highly admired as a child—a swan with a gilt beak, a lady's slipper painted all over with pink flowers.

We children found Maria Vasilievna especially interesting because there was a story connected with her. In her youth she had been a beautiful, strapping young woman, a serf in the household of a certain landowner's widow who had a grown son, an Army officer. This son came home on leave and presented Maria Vasilievna with a few silver coins. By ill luck the mistress entered the serf-girls' room at that very moment, and she saw the money in Maria Vasilievna's hands.

"Where did you get it?" she asked, and Maria Vasilievna took such a fright that instead of answering, she swallowed the coins. She became ill at once. Her face turned black, and she fell choking on the floor. They barely managed to save her life. She was ill for a very long time, and her beauty and freshness vanished forever. Shortly after this episode the old mistress died, and the young master gave Maria Vasilievna her freedom.

We children were entranced by this story of the swallowed coins, and we often hung around Maria Vasilievna begging her to tell us how it had all happened. She used to visit the nursery rather often, even though she and Nanny were not on the best of terms. And we too loved to run to her room, especially at twilight, when she willy-nilly had to put her sewing aside. She would sit down by the window then and, leaning her head on her hand, would begin singing various sentimental, old-fashioned romances in a plaintive voice: "Among the Even Plains" or "Black Flower, Sad Flower."

Her singing was terribly dismal but I loved listening to it, even though it always made me feel sad afterwards. Sometimes it would be interrupted by terrible attacks of coughing, which had been tormenting her for many years and which threatened to tear her dry, flat chest apart.

When, on the morning after the incident with Feklusha, Nanny asked Maria Vasilievna, "Is it true that you gave the girl some jam?" the seamstress, as might have been expected, responded with an expression of astonishment.

"Whatever have you got into your head, Naniushka?" she answered in an offended tone. "Would I pamper the brat like that? Why, I don't even have any jam for myself!"

So now it was all clear. And yet Feklusha's insolence was so great that she went on insisting she was innocent in spite of the seamstress's categorical assertion.

"Maria Vasilievna! As God is watching—did you forget? You called me last night yourself, yes, you did, you praised me for heating up the irons, and you gave me the jam," she kept on repeating in a desperate voice breaking with sobs, and shaking all over as if in a fever.

"You must be sick and raving, Feklusha," Maria Vasilievna answered calmly, her pale, bloodless face betraying no trace of emotion. And now neither Nanny nor anyone else in the household had any further doubt of Feklusha's guilt. The culprit was taken away and locked into a closet far from all the other rooms.

"Sit there without food or water, you nasty thing, until you confess!" Nanny said, turning the key in the heavy lock.

This event, it goes without saying, raised a commotion all through the house. Every one of the servants thought up some pretext to come running to

Nanny to discuss the interesting new development. There was a regular club meeting going on in our nursery all day.

Feklusha had no father. Her mother lived in the village and came to our house to help our laundress with the washing. Naturally, she soon found out what had happened and came at a run to the nursery with noisy and profuse complaints and protestations that her daughter was innocent. But Nanny was quick to quiet her down. "Don't make such a big noise, lady! Just wait a little bit, and we'll get to the bottom of things, we'll find out where that daughter of yours stashed the stolen goods!" she said so harshly and with such a meaningful look that the poor laundress lost her courage and took herself off.

Popular opinion was decidedly against Feklusha. "If she snitched the jam that means she snitched the rest of the stuff too," everyone said. The general indignation against the girl ran particularly high because these mysterious and repeated disappearances had been hanging like a heavy burden over all the servants for many weeks. Each one feared in his heart that he might be suspected, God forbid. Therefore the unmasking of the thief was a relief to everyone.

But just the same, Feklusha would not confess.

Nanny went to visit her prisoner several times in the course of the day, but she kept stubbornly repeating her refrain, "I didn't steal anything. God will punish Maria Vasilievna for harming a fatherless child."

Toward evening my mother came into the nursery.

"Aren't you being a trifle too harsh with the miserable girl, Nanny?" she said with some concern. "How can you leave a child without food all day?"

But Nanny would not hear of clemency. "What are you thinking of, my lady? To take pity on such a one as that! Didn't she almost manage to bring honest people under suspicion, the low, nasty thing!" she asserted with such conviction that my mother was unable to go on insisting and left without lightening the young criminal's lot by one iota.

The next day came. And Feklusha still refused to confess. Her judges were already beginning to feel a certain uneasiness when suddenly Nanny went to see our mother at dinnertime, with an expression of triumph on her face.

"Our little bird has sung!" she said happily.

"In that case," Mama very naturally asked, "where are the stolen things?"

"She still won't tell us where she hid them, the nasty thing!" Nanny replied. "She prattles all kinds of rubbish. She says, 'I forgot.' But just let her sit under lock and key for another hour or two—and maybe it'll all come back to her!"

And indeed Feklusha made a full confession toward evening, describing in great detail how she had stolen all these articles with the object of selling them later. Since no convenient occasion had presented itself, however, she had kept them hidden for a long time under the thick matting in the corner of her little closet. But then, when she saw that the disappearances had been noticed and that the thief was being hunted in earnest, she got scared. First she thought she would simply put the things back where they belonged, but then she was afraid to try that. So she wrapped them all up in a bundle inside her apron and threw them into a deep pond on the other side of our estate.

Everybody wanted so desperately to find some solution to this painful affair that Feklusha's tale was not subjected to very close scrutiny. After some lamentation over the needless loss of the articles, all satisfied themselves with her explanation.

The culprit was released from detention and a short, just sentence was pronounced over her. It was decided to give her a good hiding and then send her back to the village to her mother. Despite her tears and her mother's protests, this sentence was carried out immediately. Afterwards another girl was sent to serve the nursery in Feklusha's place.

Several weeks passed. Little by little order was restored in the household, and everyone began to forget what had happened. But then one evening, when everything was quiet in the house and Nanny, having put us to bed, was getting ready to retire for the night herself, the door to the nursery opened softly. The laundress Aleksandra, Feklusha's mother, was standing there. She alone had stubbornly resisted admitting the obvious and continued to maintain without surcease that her daughter had been "harmed for nothing." There had already been several strong altercations with Nanny on this point, until Nanny finally gave up and forbade her to come into the nursery any more, deciding that it was useless to try to reason with a stupid peasant woman.

But this time Aleksandra had such a strange and meaningful expression on her face that Nanny took one look at her and immediately realized that she was not there to repeat her usual empty complaints, but that some truly new and important event had occurred. "Now you just look here, Naniushka—look what a thing I am going to show you," Aleksandra said mysteriously. And, looking cautiously around the room to make sure that no outsider was there, she drew out from under her apron and handed over to Nanny a mother-of-pearl penknife—our beloved knife, that very knife supposedly among the stolen loot Feklusha had thrown into the pond.

When she saw the knife, Nanny spread her hands helplessly. "Wherever did you find it?" she asked.

"That's just the point—*where* I found it," Aleksandra slowly drawled out her answer. She said nothing for a few seconds, evidently taking pleasure in Nanny's discomfiture. Finally she said ponderously, "That gardener of ours, Filip Matveevich, gave me his old pants to darn, and I found the knife inside the pocket."

This Filip Matveevich was a German who held one of the leading positions in the servants' aristocracy. He received a rather large salary, was a bachelor, and although to the unprejudiced eye might have seemed no more than a fat German, no longer young and rather repulsive with his typical reddish squared-off sidewhiskers, still our female servants regarded him as a handsome fellow. Hearing Aleksandra's strange testimony, Nanny couldn't take it in for the first minute or two.

"But how could Filip Matveevich get hold of the children's penknife?" she asked in confusion. "After all, he practically never goes into the nursery! And anyway, how could it be possible that a man like Filip Matveevich would take to stealing things from the children?"

Aleksandra gazed at Nanny in silence with a long, mocking stare. Then she bent down right to her ear, and whispered several sentences in which the name of Maria Vasilievna was repeated more than once. Little by little a ray of light began to penetrate into Nanny's mind.

"Tut, tut, tut . . . so that's how it is!" she said, waving her hands helplessly. "Akh, you humble one, you! Oh, you no-good woman, you!" she exclaimed, filled with indignation. "Just you wait, we'll make you come clean!"

It turned out (as I was later told) that Aleksandra had been nurturing suspicions of Maria Vasilievna for a long time and had observed that the seamstress was carrying on a secret love affair with the gardener.

"Well, then," she told Nanny, "judge for yourself. Would a fine lad like Filip Matveevich love an old woman like that just for nothing? She was probably buying him with presents."

And indeed she soon became convinced that Maria Vasilievna was giving the gardener both gifts and money. Where then was she getting these things? And so she set up a regular system of espionage over the unsuspecting Maria Vasilievna. The penknife was only the final link in a long chain of evidence.

The story was turning out to be more fascinating and diverting than would have been possible to predict. Within Nanny had suddenly awakened that passionate detective instinct which so often slumbers in old women's hearts and incites them to rush fervently into investigating all sorts of complicated affairs which do not concern them in the least. And in this particular instance, Nanny's zeal was spurred even more because she felt that she had deeply wronged Feklusha, and she burned with the desire to atone post-haste. Right then and there she and Aleksandra formed a defensive and offensive union against Maria Vasilievna.

Since both women were filled with moral certainty of the seamstress's guilt, they resolved upon an extreme measure: to get hold of her keys and (seizing an opportunity when she would be away) to open up her trunk.

The thought is sister to the act. Alas! Their assumptions, as it turned out, were entirely correct. The contents of the trunk fully confirmed their suspicions and proved beyond any possible doubt that the hapless Maria Vasilievna was the perpetrator of all the petty thefts which had caused so much commotion during the past weeks.

"What a low, nasty thing she is! She even palmed the jam off on poor Feklusha to take attention away from herself and throw all the blame on the girl! Oh, the shameless woman! A little child, and she has no pity for her!" said Nanny in disgust and horror, completely forgetting her own role in the episode and how her own cruelty had forced poor Feklusha to give false testimony against herself.

One can picture the indignation of all the servants and of the household in general when the appalling truth was revealed and made known to all.

At first, in the heat of his anger, our father threatened to send for the police and have Maria Vasilievna put in prison. But in view of the fact that she was already a middle-aged, sickly woman who had lived in our house for so many years, he soon softened and decided merely to dismiss her and send her back to Petersburg.

One might think that Maria Vasilievna herself should have been satisfied with this sentence. She was such an expert needlewoman that she need never have feared going hungry in Petersburg. And what kind of position could she have held in our household after such an episode? All the rest of the servants had previously envied and disliked her for her pride and arrogance. She was aware of this and knew also how cruelly she would have to atone for her former grandeur.

Strange as it may seem, however, she was not only unhappy with my father's decision but, on the contrary, started begging his mercy. Some kind of feline attachment to our house came to the fore, perhaps, to her old familiar place in the world.

"I don't have long to live—I feel that I shall die soon," she said. "How can I go and live among strangers before I die?"

But Nanny, reminiscing with me many years later, when I was quite grown up, had an entirely different explanation. "It was just more than she could stand to leave us, because Filip Matveevich was staying on, and she knew that once she went away she would never see him again. If she, who lived her whole life as an honest woman, could do such a shabby thing in her old age, then she evidently loved him so much she couldn't stand it!"

As far as Filip Matveevich was concerned, he managed to come out of the water quite dry. It may be that he was really telling the truth when he maintained that in accepting presents from Maria Vasilievna he had no knowledge of where they had come from. In any case, since it was difficult to find a good gardener and our garden and vegetable plot could not be left to the whim of fate, it was decided to keep him on, at least for a time.

I do not know whether Nanny was right about the reasons impelling Maria Vasilievna to cling so stubbornly to her place in our house. Be that as it may, she went to my father on the day designated for her departure and threw herself sobbing at his feet.

"Better to let me stay on without pay, punish me like a serf—but please don't drive me away!"

My father was touched by this deep attachment to our household. But, on the other hand, he feared that if he forgave Maria Vasilievna, the rest of the servants would be demoralized. He was in great perplexity as to what to do when suddenly a plan came into his head.

"Listen here," he told her. "Stealing is a great sin, but I could have forgiven you anyway if your guilt consisted only in your thievery. But an innocent girl suffered because of what you did. Just think of it! On account of you Feklusha was subjected to such shame—a public whipping! For her sake, I cannot forgive you. If you truly wish to stay on with us, I can give my consent only on one condition: that you beg Feklusha's pardon and kiss her hand in the presence of all the servants. If you're willing to go that far, all right then—stay here!"

No one believed that Maria Vasilievna would consent to such a condition. How could she, a proud one like her, apologize publicly to a serf and kiss her hand? But suddenly, to everyone's astonishment, Maria Vasilievna agreed to do it.

Within an hour after her decision all the household was assembled in the entrance hall of our house to view the curious spectacle: Maria Vasilievna kissing Feklusha's hand. My father had demanded precisely that: that the event should take place with solemnity and in public. There was a large crowd. Everyone wanted to watch. The master and mistress were there too, and we children also asked permission to come.

I will never forget the scene which followed. Feklusha, embarrassed by the honor which had so unexpectedly fallen to her lot and fearful, perhaps, that Maria Vasilievna might avenge herself later for this compulsory humiliation, went up to the master and begged him to relieve her and Maria Vasilievna of the hand-kissing.

"I've forgiven her without it," she said, ready to cry. But my father, who had tuned himself up to a high key and convinced himself that he was behaving in accordance with the precepts of strict justice, only shouted at her. "Get moving, you little fool, and don't stick your nose into other people's business! It's not for you that this is being done. If I had been guilty toward you—do you understand me? I myself, your master—then I, too, would have to kiss your hand. You can't understand that? Then hold your tongue and be quiet!"

The cowering Feklusha did not dare interpose any further objections. With her whole body shaking in terror, she went and stood in her place, awaiting her fate as if she had been the guilty one.

White as linen, Maria Vasilievna made her way through the crowd which parted before her. She walked mechanically, as if in her sleep. But her face was so rigid and angry that it was awful to look at her. Her lips were bloodless and convulsively pressed together. She came up very close to Feklusha. The words, "Forgive me!" tore from her lips in a kind of sickly scream. She grabbed Feklusha's hand and brought it to her lips so violently and with a look of such hatred that it seemed as though she wanted to bite it.

Suddenly a convulsion twisted her face and foam appeared at the corners of her mouth. With her whole body writhing, she fell on the ground and began screaming with piercing, inhuman shrieks.

It was discovered later that she had been subject to these nervous attacks—a form of epilepsy—even before that. But she had carefully concealed this fact from her masters, fearing that they would dismiss her if they found out. Those of the servants who knew about her disease kept their silence out of a feeling of solidarity.

I cannot convey the effect her seizure had on those present. It goes without saying that we children were hastily taken away. We were so terrified that we were close to hysterics ourselves. But even more vividly I remember the sudden shift which took place in the mood of all our household servants. Up to that time they had behaved toward Maria Vasilievna with anger and hatred. Her act seemed so vile and low that each one derived a certain pleasure from showing her his contempt, from spiting her in some way.

But now all that was changed suddenly. She had unexpectedly appeared in the role of suffering victim, and popular sympathy shifted over to her side. Among the servants there was even a repressed protest against my father for the excessive severity of his punishment.

"Of course she was wrong to do what she did," the housemaids would say in undertones when they gathered in our nursery to confer with Nanny, as was their habit after every important event. "Well all right then, so the general could have given her a good tongue lashing, the mistress could have punished her herself, the way it's done in other houses. That doesn't hurt so much, you can bear it. But now, all of a sudden, see what they thought up! To go and kiss the hand of such a little cricket, such a snotnose as Feklusha, right in front of everybody! Who could stand such an insult!"

Maria Vasilievna did not regain consciousness for a long time. Her seizures recurred again and again over an interval of several hours. She would blink, become conscious for a moment and then suddenly start thrashing around and screaming again. The doctor had to be called from town.

With each passing minute, sympathy for the patient increased and indignation against the masters grew. I remember my mother coming into the nursery in the middle of the day. Seeing Nanny brewing tea with a good deal of fuss and concern at that unusual hour, she asked quite innocently, "For whom are you doing this, Nanny?"

"For Maria Vasilievna, naturally! What do you think—is it your opinion that she, a sick woman, should be left without tea? We servants, we still have a Christian heart!" Nanny replied, in such a coarse and challenging tone of voice that my mother grew quite embarrassed and hurried away.

And yet a few hours earlier, that very same Nanny, if she had been given her way, would have been capable of beating Maria Vasilievna half to death. The seamstress recovered within a few days, to my parents' great joy. She took up her life in the house just as before. No one mentioned what had taken place. I believe that even among the servants there was no one who would have reproached her for the past.

But as for me, from that day on I felt a strange pity for her, mixed with an instinctive horror. I no longer ran to her room as I used to do. If I met her in the hall I couldn't keep from pressing myself against the wall, and I tried not to look at her. I kept imagining that she would fall on the floor right then and there and start thrashing and screaming.

Maria Vasilievna must have been aware of my alienation from her, and she tried to win back my old affection by various means. I remember that almost every day she would think up different little surprises for me: now she would bring me colored scraps of cloth, now she would sew a new dress for my doll. But none of this helped. The feeling of secret terror would not pass, and I ran away the moment I found myself alone with her. And soon after that, I came under the supervision of my new governess, who put a stop to all my friendly relations with the servants.

But I vividly recall the following scene. I was already seven or eight years old. One evening, the night before some holiday—the Annunciation [25 March], perhaps—I was running down the hall past Maria Vasilievna's room. Suddenly she looked out and called to me.

"Young lady, young lady! Come in and see me. Look what a lovely lark I baked for you out of dough!"

It was half dark in the long hall, and no one was there but Maria Vasilievna and myself. Looking at her white face with its great, dark eyes, I suddenly felt an eerie sensation. Instead of answering her, I dashed away headlong.

She called after me. "What is it, young lady? I can see that you don't like me at all any more. I disgust you!"

It wasn't so much her words as the tone of voice in which she said them that shook me. I didn't stop, but kept on running. But then, on returning to the classroom and calming down after my fright, I couldn't forget the sound of that voice—hollow, despondent.

I was not myself all evening. No matter how I tried to suppress the unpleasant gnawing sensation inside of me by playing, by prankishness, I couldn't make the feeling go away. The thought of Maria Vasilievna wouldn't leave my mind. And, as always happens with a person one hurts, she suddenly seemed terribly nice to me, and I began to feel drawn to her.

I couldn't bring myself to tell my governess what had happened. Children are always embarrassed to talk about their feelings. Moreover, since we were forbidden to fraternize with the servants, I knew that the governess would in all likelihood praise me for my behavior. And yet I felt with every instinct that there was nothing praiseworthy about it.

After evening tea, when it was time for me to go to bed, I decided to drop in to see Maria Vasilievna instead of going straight to my room. This was a kind of sacrifice on my part, for it meant running alone down a long, deserted, and by now quite dark hall which I always feared and avoided in the evening. But now a desperate bravery came to the fore. I ran without stopping to take a breath. Puffing and panting, I tore into her room like a hurricane.

Maria Vasilievna had already had her supper. Because of the holiday, she wasn't working but sitting at the table, covered with a clean white cloth, and reading some religious book. The lamp glimmered in front of the icons. After the frightening dark hall, the little room seemed uncommonly light and cozy, and Maria Vasilievna herself so kind and good!

"I came to ask you to forgive me dear, dear Maria Vasilievna!" I said in one breath. Before I could finish, she had already grabbed me and started covering me with kisses. She kissed me so violently and for such a long time that I felt the eerie sensation once more. I was already trying to figure out how to get out of her grasp without offending her again, when a cruel attack of coughing forced her to release me from her embrace at last.

This dreadful cough tormented her more and more. "I barked like a dog all night," she would say of herself, with a kind of sullen irony.

With each day that passed she grew paler and more withdrawn, but she stubbornly resisted all my mother's suggestions that she consult a doctor. She even showed an angry irritation when anyone mentioned her illness. In this way, she dragged out another two or three years. She was on her feet almost to the end. She went to bed only a few days before she died; and her final hours, they said, were horribly painful.

My father ordered a very opulent funeral (by village standards) to be arranged for her. Not only all the servants, but all our family attended it as well, even the master himself. Feklusha, too, walked behind the coffin and sobbed bitterly. The only one missing was Filip Matveevich. He did not wait for her to die. He had left us a few months earlier for another and better-paying job, somewhere in the vicinity of Dinaburg.

Chapter Four

Oleg Pantiukhov, A Student's Summer

Ivan Bunin, Nobel laureate in literature, once wrote: "Our children and grandchildren will be unable to comprehend that Russia in which we once . . . lived, which we appreciated, failed to understand; all that might, complexity, wealth, and happiness." True or not, our understanding of that Russia is made substantially richer and clearer by the memoirs of Oleg Pantiukhov: Schooling. The cadet corps. Exams. Trips abroad. The Caucasus. Correspondence with parents. A visit to the monasteries on Solovki. The centennial celebrations of Pushkin's birth. Through all these descriptions we gain insight into distant values and sensibilities. Taken from Oleg Pantiukhov, *O dniakh bylykh* [Of By-gone Days]. Maplewood, N.J.: Durand Press, 1969.

Our Pushkin Troop, named in honor of the poet, decided to go hiking in the mountains after summer camp was over. The so-called "camp" did not provide us with hardship and adventure. The desire to be active in nature in the way that Baden-Powell would later recommend, but in our own simpler, Russian way, had been in us long before the appearance of the Boy Scouts. Our Pushkin Troop had rules of honor and friendship which were strictly followed even though they were not written. There was also the hope of being helpful to our country and countrymen. Our group was morally different from our environment.

We studied a map of the Caucasus Mountains for a long time and finally chose the itinerary which I had suggested. Suram–Kutaisi–Abastuman–Borzhomi. Because Suram and Borzhomi were very close to each other, the route resembled a triangle with legs of 70 kilometers.

It was a wonderful plan. We would see the famous Suram tunnel, the manganese mines at Chiatur, ancient monasteries, and cross the wild, desolate pass at Zekar. It felt good to plan the hike and from that point even the camp took on more meaning. I recall that I had taken from home a bar of birdcherry scented soap. It was cheap, but its aroma seemed heavenly and inspiring when it mingled with the morning scent of pines which were all around us.

It did seem to me that the last summer in Tbilisi ought to be spent with my parents. But even my parents agreed that we had to bid a proper farewell to the magnificent Caucasus which had sheltered us for the past twelve years.

We had parceled out our provisions and equipment among the hikers. Finally the awaited day came, and we were all seated in the coach of the evening train. We somehow managed to sleep on the hard benches and in the morning got off at Suram where we found a faucet and washed out in the open. Then we bought *chureks* of bread and set off westward along the railroad right-of-way. The railroad dove into the darkness of the tunnel but we followed the old abandoned line over the mountains. We stopped to light a campfire and make tea. I was overwhelmed by a mass of new impressions. We continued along the railroad ties thinking of the people who rode past that very spot in comfort. How diverse they must have been: some pleased and happy, others bored and lonely, but none of them seeing the beauty of the mountains beyond the railroad cars. All kinds of thoughts come when you hike along the ties.

We spent the nights around a campfire underneath a clear sky. When it was my turn to cook, I poured buckwheat groats into a pot of water, added salt, diced some smoked Ukrainian fatback and cooked everything over the fire. Before eating we added chopped onion and pepper. I was proud of my glorious Ukrainian mulligan stew. The boys even sang a Ukrainian song in my honor. We would take turns standing watch at night passing a revolver to each other. That was our only weapon. For the sake of security, we invented a story to tell inquisitive natives that we were the vanguard of a large body of troops which followed behind.

In Kutaisi we rested at the home of one of the hikers whose name was Gorokh. We visited very ancient Georgian monasteries. In one of them we were shown the extraordinarily large ring of [the Georgian] King David. There were stone walls clinging to cliffs over abysses and, as elsewhere in the southern Caucasus, palaces of Queen Tamara. In Kutaisi we counted up our money and decided to ride to Kobulety to see the Black Sea. It was a perfectly understandable desire: none of us had ever seen the sea.

We sensed its close presence later in the evening twilight as we strode on deep gravel smelling the sea, breathing it, hearing it, but not seeing it. And we could not see it for a long time until we came right up to it and even then could not discern it nor understand that the foam and the rush was the Black

Sea itself. In the darkness, the noise, the rumbling and surging, we could not tell where the sea began or ended, especially since we stood at a decent distance trying to keep our hiking boots dry.

Razgil'daev's relatives, with their constant banal chatter, also kept us from fathoming the sea. It was especially pointless since we could not hear what they were saying anyway. The gravel, churned by waves, made much noise. The moment it piled up in one place, some angry being would gather it all up and fling it back. And each time it was several wagon loads of well-washed multicolored stones.

We slowly got our bearings in this muddle and began to distinguish the pattern by which the azure-green, glassy water would gather into a wave, rise higher and higher and explode in watery fireworks. One could easily "get high" on this. Our new acquaintances, Razgil'daev's relatives, had to understand why we did not answer their questions and stood staring into the grayish-green mist.

In the morning before returning to Kutaisi we again came to the sea and saw that it had limits, although they were very foggy, indeterminate, and far beyond the horizon. We saw the waves glistening so brightly in the sun that our eyes hurt and that the foam resembled fanciful lace. Especially incised in memory was the translucent, glassy color of the waves and the unusual, "heavenly" purity of the whole watery mass.

Then we rode back scrutinizing the colorful garb of the natives and their fragile huts erected on stilts. Our toughest crossing was from Kutaisi to Abastuman—but what wild, primeval gulfs, what forests, what wilderness. When we spent a night near a roaring mountain stream the darkness was so thick you could not see your hand in front of your face. Our campfire cast light only as far as the nearest trees. Anyone could have crept up to our bivouac without any difficulty. But of course there was no one: only the sounds of wild animals from the dense forest. This was the most nerve-wracking night of our expedition.

The whole crossing was tiring. We were short of bread. The hard, yellow, unsalted cornpone which we bought at occasional villages was inedible. Worn-out and famished we climbed the pass, entering a realm of clouds and fog where nothing was visible except for patches of white hiding in the trees. There wasn't a soul for tens of kilometers. As it began to grow dark and the unpleasant thought of spending the night amidst clouds entered our minds, we suddenly heard pure Russian speech. It seemed to us fairy-tale sorcery or a hallucination, but then we saw the foggy outlines of buildings, either native huts or Russian log cabins. It was an outpost of a Cossack regiment on duty in Abastuman where the crown prince was in residence. What dear, Russian faces, what rollicking, expansive songs, what good-natured jokes, what tasty borshch and what blessed sleep on hay among your own people. That was our best night.

After that it was easier, mostly downhill. We spent a night in the outskirts of Abastuman at some lumber mill. It was worse than uncomfortable. The boards cut into my side and I dreamt that I was the dying soldier impaled on the rocks in Lermontov's "A Vale in Dagestan," left behind by my buddies. In my sleep I tried to scream to call them back and woke up.

Abastuman was attractive but different from Borzhomi. There were no natural springs, but the air was permeated with the scent of pine resin, very sweet air, and there was also the presence of the crown prince. It was said that the crown prince, Grand Duke Georgii Aleksandrovich, lived very modestly, unlike his brother in Borzhomi. It was said that the crown prince was a very likable young man. [He was a younger brother of Emperor Nicholas II and was next in succession until the birth of Nicholas' son, Alexis.]

We were approaching the end of our expedition, walking past Akhalpikh through a bare, sun-scorched plateau. The sun was rising. An old Turk on horseback stopped, faced the sun and covered his face with his palms. It must be that Mohammed and his followers were exquisitely sensitive to the beauty of sunrise. Our thoughts at the rising of the sun do not go past the mundane, but here, in a small village, a mullah atop a minaret fervidly sang praise and gratitude to the Creator.

Whenever we encountered Turks, we would say, "Salaam a leikum" to them. And they would hospitably answer, "A leikum salaam." Here, in this part of the Caucasus, we found a small corner of Turkey, or so it seemed to us. Miniature houses, almost without windows, dusty gardens and stillness. Quiet, placid people and not mean, but friendly, dogs. It was apparent that the Turks were a good people and it was a pity that we warred against them and that we sang derogatory soldiers' songs about them.

And then we reached Borzhomi. What an empty place it seemed without anyone we knew. Of course, there was something familiar in the effervescent fizz of Borzhomi mineral water, in the green glades, in the clean, sandy garden walks. But my companions, after having looked at themselves in the mirror at the railway station, decided that the luxury and indolent bliss of this spa was not for us, woodsmen, and that we would scare the local belles to death if we appeared before them as we were. We returned by train to Tbilisi and to our previous life in the military school. We were upperclassmen now, the special class of 1899, the centennial of Pushkin's birth.

In 1898 my family had moved to the now familiar Voznesenskii Street. There I got my own minuscule room which my mother christened a "studio." It had its own door to the staircase and was totally separate. It was so small that if one managed to shove a bed into it there would have been no room for anything else. So there was no bed, only a small desk and chair. Sometimes there was an easel and always a bookcase with the works of Aleksei K. Tolstoy, Lermontov, Pushkin, and Chekhov. These were my favorites. If you exited the room onto the landing you saw a medium-size mirror in a carved wooden frame. In the mirror there would be a reflection of a rounded, yet angular, face whose owner was quite unhappy with it, presuming that an attractive, handsome face was a guarantee of success in life just as a princely title was. But when you had neither one nor the other you were in for hard times. But, I would push out my chest, hold my head high and repeat to myself that I would be all right, I would be triumphant.

The Pushkin festivities swept through the academy. Throughout the city, in theaters and everywhere there were celebrations of the Pushkin centennial. Speeches were made and poems read at the Pushkin monument:

> The poet has perished, the prisoner of honor
> Has fallen, calumniated by idle talk.

I could never hear these words of Lermontov, his "cry of the soul," without exultation.

It was then that we decided to spend our Pushkin fund, about ten rubles, on a trip into the Caucasus Mountains which Pushkin had loved so well. And so we went to ancient Mtskheta where the parents of Gedevanov, our "enraged goose," lived. We expected to come upon a "prince's court" and "princely" hospitality, but when we saw a native house hardly different from the others, surrounded by several grazing sheep, with frightened faces of women in the semi-dark entrance, we realized our error. It was odd that Gedevanov himself was the initiator of this trip.

We quickly decided to celebrate the centennial in the lap of nature. After all Pushkin loved the grandeur of the Caucasus and he also loved its wine. He wrote about both in his "Journey to Erzerum." We had brought a goatskin bota of wine with us. And so with a song, we celebrated the hundredth anniversary of the birth of Pushkin [June 6].

Graduation day was fast approaching. It was final exam time. We had already been to the studio of Mishchenko who traditionally photographed all the graduating classes. The postcard size photographs were pasted on illustration board that had been decorated with watercolor views of Tbilisi and our school and photographed once again. The original large illustration board with a group photograph of the whole class was traditionally hung in the common hall of the First Company, the place where the names of the honor cadets appeared in gold letters cut into marble tablets. These young men were the "luminaries" of whom our chaplain, Father Mantstvetov, loved to talk. Should there ever be a war and our graduates be made Cavaliers of the Order of St. George, their names would also be displayed on marble tablets. And so, as a friend and I joked, the possibility of myself being immortalized here was not yet lost.

But it was not a joking matter when a rumor flashed by that our group, the Pushkin graduates, would not have its class portrait hung in the hall because of our insolent behavior during the year. In truth, we did do some outrageous, scandalous things. Never through malevolence, but rather because of an excess of youthful energy and the urge to pull off the unprecedented and extraordinary. For instance, we took to "busting" the new and totally innocent class master. In the dining hall, each time that he would bring a spoon of soup to his mouth, the whole company would thunder "uugggh."

Even worse, whenever some timid house master would do his rounds at bedtime or at night he would find the doors locked and barricaded. And when, with the help of the staff, he would break into our sleeping quarters, he would be met with unbelievable shouting and pillows flung in his direction. The director would come at night to chew us out. Grand Duke Constantine, the head of all military educational institutions, visited and spoke to us of the inadmissibility of such stunts. We ourselves understood that they were "inadmissible" and repugnant. But such judgments were risky. Maybe it seemed to some of us there was valor in such behavior. I can't say. Personally I never would have begun such doings but when some of the big guys such as Begiev or Chelokaev would start, other daredevils would join in, and all hell would break loose. There was something infectious and elemental in this "restlessness among the people" that may have been generically related to what later occurred throughout Russia.

At this time, the end of May 1899, my head was in a spin not only from exams but from various plans for the future. The class master kept asking me which military academy I had chosen. But I had other plans. Something on the order of forestry school along with "Popka" Bekilov. Besides I recalled with pride that father had deposited 100 rubles in my name in a bank. The question was what to do with them.

Before entering an academy, it would have been nice to see the world and especially those places in Europe which we studied so thoroughly in school. For instance, to go into the mountains of Schwarzwald or the Swiss Saxon Alps. There was also the town of Freiberg with its mining institute. It would be interesting to enroll there and see if I could become a mining engineer. In any case, even if I were to lose a year, I would learn German and one or two other subjects. And finally I could always enter the Pavlov Military Academy with the help of my friend Musin-Pushkin.

I laid all these plans out to my parents both orally and on paper. To my delight, father hardly objected to the European trip. He was opposed to the Freiberg plan. And so I graduated from military school. The passport for traveling abroad and the hundred rubles were in my pocket. Everyone seemed to be moving that year. My older brother was getting married and moving to the Crimea with his bride. He was encouraging mother and my other brothers to go there with him. My aunt was going there as well. Only my father in Tbilisi and Vania in Artvin were to stay in place.

My civilian outfit was of a kind fairly widespread in Russia. It consisted of a Russian shirt [with buttons on the left side of the chest], a broad belt, and a light, sand-colored overcoat bought in Gulaspov's store [in Tbilisi]. It was strange to see our Voznesenskii Street neighbor and buddy, Sandro, as manager there. He also sold me a stylish cap with a hard celluloid peak.

I am alone in the railroad car of a train heading westward to Batumi. I am traveling at night in order to save time and hotel expenses. It is uncomfortable on the hard bench and there are too many thoughts in my head to sleep anyway. I tour the city, write postcards and leave on a ship of the Russian Navigation and Travel Association. It is a third class ticket, but I can move into second class for an extra five rubles if the seas get rough. I do so in Poti, having spent a night lying on hawsers and inhaling oil fumes. In the second-class cabin I sleep on clean sheets like a lord. In the morning I marvel at the forested mountains on my right and the blue expanse on my left, and decide to stop at New Mount Athos on the way back, money permitting. Next we hit rough water and there was great relief when the ship entered the bay of Novorossiisk.

As proper for a tourist, I immediately set off to view the city. But there was no city. It was all piers after piers, wharves, a railway shop, dirt and endless dust. I pressed on in search of the vanished city and finally reached the public gardens. They were colorless and dusty, but I never did find the city, only insignificant rural buildings, insignificant shops, and the smell of anthracite. In memory that smell is Novorossiisk to me.

Next day at dawn we reached Kerch. What a lively place. Just outside the town is Mitridat Mountain [mentioned by Pushkin]. There is no sand or pebbles on the beach—only pea-size seashells. It was good to bathe in the clear, glassy water. The people here were different from those in Tbilisi. They behaved as if they had nothing to do but bathe in the clear water, dry in the sun and drink black coffee in the Turkish taverns.

Feodosiia was even more attractive. This was the real Crimea and the people on shipboard were in a mood of high anticipation: tomorrow at dawn we would be in Yalta. The Yalta where Chekhov himself lives. The city was still asleep; the sun barely breaking through the clouds in the east. It had just rained. The sand squeaked under foot and the air was such that words fail me.

I asked the captain's assistant how much time we had. He did not give me a clear answer. Two or three hours, he said, depending on the time it takes to unload and load. I'm off down the embankment hoping by some miracle to see Chekhov or at least his house. It would be unconscionable to disturb him at such an early hour. I ask a policeman for Chekhov's house but, alas, this name, so precious to us, is unfamiliar to the corpulent policeman. He knows neither house, nor Chekhov. I asked several passersby and one of them ventured a guess that the house was three or four kilometers away in Autka. I was in a quandary. Would I find the house? Would the ship leave without me? And then I shamefully surrendered: had tea in a restaurant built on pilings overlooking the sea. The tea was very good, and the sweet rolls even better. I tried to console myself with the fancy that perhaps Chekhov frequented this place, sat in this very chair and looked at the sea just as I was doing.

Sevastopol. What a celebrated name. The bay, the surrounding mountains, and even the earthen mounds and the old fortress. Where and how did they fight here? The question brings the recognition that my knowledge of the defense of Sevastopol is pitiful. I'll have to read Tolstoy's *Sevastopol Stories*. I hasten on to Kiev. The frequent changing of trains is quite tiring. At Tatiana Pavlovna's, a family friend, I rested up for two days while she spoiled me with all kinds of tasty dishes. The rooms smelled of mothballs, but even this smell seemed cozy and cool to me.

And Lida. I couldn't admire her enough. She was already in the upper classes of the *gimnazium*. She read a lot, daydreamed, and surely went out with her girlfriends. She was mother's favorite and I wrote home about her, Tatiana Pavlovna, and their farmstead.

I continued west to the border where I met a veterinary student who was a distant relative of one of my Tbilisi cadet friends. He convinced me to buy a ticket not to Freiberg, but to Zurich where he himself was going to university. In my father's absence it seemed best to follow his wishes and forget about the mining institute in the Schwarzwald and save my parents the money which would have gone for my tuition. As it turned out later, father had changed his mind and sent me a cordial and supportive letter to Freiberg in which he praised my persistence and promised to send tuition money. I never did get that letter, and found out about it only upon returning to Tbilisi.

In Vienna the veterinary student and I stayed in a splendid hotel not far from the Cathedral of St. Stephen. In the evening we went to the famous Prater where everything was very decorous except for the roller coaster which was the source of great screeching, especially when the cars would plunge into water. It also struck me that the fashionable women along the vaunted Ringstrasse were not as stylishly dressed as we at home imagined. "Viennese chic" was not evident. There was a strange combination of colors—bright yellow and violet. But expensive shops, especially flower shops, drew one's attention. The museums were overwhelming. Palaces, royal carriages, thousands of military men in strange, semi-civilian uniforms. Newspapers sold briskly on the streets. A nervousness was felt in the air, but perhaps it was Viennese everyday life.

We arrived in Zurich groggy, having spent the night in a packed car full of Tyroleans smoking their long ceramic pipes. A beautiful lake and beautiful mountains in the distance. But first we had to find a room for the week. We wandered around the city for a long time. Once, at the entrance of a house, we saw a sign advertising rooms, but we decided to investigate around the block and return. But we never found the house; it seemed to have been swallowed up by the earth. We kept wandering and for some reason attracted the attention of a dignified man in civilian clothing who asked us to go with him. We did so with mounting curiosity. It turned out that he was a policeman who brought us to a precinct where we were politely questioned and asked to show our passport and money. Then we were given the "For Rent" page of a newspaper and told how to get to a particular street. The incident struck us as curious—something to tell the folks back home. Later we encountered signs with "Entry to Russians Forbidden" written on them. This was offensive, but it became understandably cautionary when we learned that Zurich was the headquarters of Russian revolutionaries and terrorists. We once even visited a Russian students' eating house to peek at typical Russian "nihilists" of the sort found in novels. But the prices in the eating house were high and we retreated. I was saving my money for something more productive. I wanted to hike into the mountains and paint. So I bought a box of oil paints which cost almost all of ten rubles. I traversed the nearby mountains, saw the life of this toy-like country, beautiful as a wrapped chocolate, and painted the landscape.

Once on the climb up Etliberg I was passed by a German with a knapsack on his back and a walking stick in hand. He looked at the surroundings with such exultation and hummed the "Toreador" march with such exuberance that I was ashamed of my sluggish indecisiveness.

A week later I left my student friend and was on the way home with the regret that I had no major accomplishments but with an abundance of foreign impressions which were totally unlike our Russian ones. Zurich with its shadowy streets and broad embankments, with its unusual black automobiles working as cabs, its crowded Swiss Guards festivals, was left behind. Once again it was Innsbruck squeezed into a cleft amidst huge cliffs. Once again it was Salzburg, where during a two-hour layover I sketched a view of the city from the river. Passersby stared at me and I was pleased. Let them even send for a policeman. The city was famous for its sausage and I bought some thinly sliced Salami. I ate some and kept the rest for the folks at home to taste.

Thoughts of home occupied me more and more and at times it seemed strange to be traveling abroad when I could have spent time with my mother before my departure for St. Petersburg. It was clear to me that I was going to St. Pete. But it was not clear where to—maybe the Academy of Fine Arts.

Once again I was in Vienna, where I got a table in an expensive cafe on the Ring. I ordered tea and picked up a newspaper. There was big news from Russia: Crown Prince Georgii Aleksandrovich, who was being treated for tuberculosis in Abastuman, had died. The newspaper tried to assess this from the point of view of Austrian interests. And I was sorry that Zil'berg, our German teacher, did not give us more work with newspapers.

From Vienna there was the uninspiring trip to the border. I opened my knapsack, the only luggage I had, to pull out the trip-tattered book of Chekhov's stories. I read them like the Gospel, as revelation, as a true reflection of our Russian life, beautiful, free and untrammeled, so unlike the stale and alien foreign countries.

Across the border at the Russian station you could get an excellent borshch for ten kopeks. Everything here was inexpensive and easily understood. Only in Odessa, on the famous harbor steps, did I have an unpleasant experience. I was in a good mood and decided to support the commercial enterprise of some character and let him shine my boots. But the scoundrel, in response to my good intentions, sneered at the five kopeks I offered him and asked such a high sum that I was flabbergasted. The shoe polish alone cost him a ruble, he said. In order to lighten my mood I recited some Pushkin lines denigrating Odessa. Then once again I was on a ship. The Crimea seen from the sea. A brief stop at Alushka, transfer to a longboat and then I was on shore.

Autumn 1899. A group of us recent cadets was traveling northward via the recently opened railway through Baku, Petrovsk and Rostov-on-the-Don. Tbilisi and the best part of my life was left behind in the sweet-smelling clouds of Tbilisi dust. The beauty of the Georgian Military Highway. Vladikavkaz. The railway. Finally, Russian cities. We take in Russia with great curiosity. What is she like? How will she reveal herself? And we had a jealous, protective sense toward "our" Caucasus which was not "Russia" at all.

St. Petersburg—a totally different place. It seemed cold, dark, and dank. The city had a powerful effect on me. It was a typical, gray St. Petersburg short day. Icy mist covered the ruler-straight streets, so unusual to our Tbilisi eyes. In the city-center the noiseless streets were paved with wood blocks. They gave off a fine smell of pitch which was used to bind them to the base pavement. This was a totally different environment and totally different people. The center was filled with civil service types and the military. Simple folk were found on the periphery wearing old-fashioned full-length overcoats, cloaks, and caftans. I especially recall the street vendors selling juicy and tasty plums. The vendors wore white aprons and carried their trays on their heads. Near Haymarket Square and Apraksin Market there were many merchants' wives in colorful old-style broad capes and shawls typical of their social class. I managed to discern all this much later. My first task was to find my way to the Pavlov Military Academy.

The academy turned out to be located in the boonies of St. Pete and was totally different from the Alexander Academy in Moscow. It was a gloomy, gray barracks and not even ancient. Inside, it did not have the expected high-ceilinged halls and its corridors and rooms were low as well. It smelled of wax which was used to robustly polish the parquet floors which were the sole decoration of the place.

My first impression of the cadet corps was negative as well. What had I gotten into? Would I ever come to like this place? My thoughts flew homeward to my friends, Voznesenskii Street, and my parents who were left all alone.

The severe military training of the academy after my independent trip to Switzerland and after my unfettered life in our Tbilisi was hard. I was very homesick. There was the friendship with the contingent from our old school. There were some twenty of us here, if you counted all the classes. Meleshko, Boreisha, and Sasko were Tbilisi alums who were in His Majesty's Company because of their height. The Tbilisi contingent, just as all the other cadet schools, had their own table in the tea hall. We would gather there as at a club during the intermission between day and evening classes to talk of our affairs and recall Tbilisi. Prices in the tea hall were low, but if there was no money for rolls we simply drank tea with sugar.

At tea we gave each other friendly advice and shared information about the city: which horse cars or trolleys to take when you had a pass. We talked of our instructors and company commanders, but the most valuable were our shared memories of Tbilisi which kept up our spirits. Whenever someone received delicacies from home he, of course, shared them with the rest. A Siberian fellow named Makeev attached himself to our group. We immediately took him in and gave him the nickname of "walrus," which is what we *kintos* called all Siberians. [*Kinto*, meaning comic street entertainer/musician, was widely used in the Caucasus as a term either of endearment or mockery.] Homesickness for our distant lands brought us together. We would walk around the academy quadrangle and talk of the past and the future. The present, the barracks present, would go by very quickly. And, in fact, it did not just go by, it flew.

One brutally cold day of minus fourteen degrees or so, [five degrees Fahrenheit] the whole academy went to the funeral of General Rikachev, a one-time commandant of the academy. We marched along crowded streets with passersby carefully examining us. What did they think of us, future officers? Were they in sympathy or in opposition along with the majority of the "intelligentsia?" There was music, then a rifle salute. This was all new to us and we felt ourselves to be adults. Our fingers nearly froze and our shoulders and arms were extremely tired. But as always, fatigue provided satisfaction.

There was a momentous event at the Feast of the Epiphany. His Majesty's Company took part in a religious procession at the Winter Palace, and we saw, for the first time, the Sovereign Emperor and the Autocrat of all the Russias.

There were ceremonial halls—magnificent paintings on the walls, chandeliers, vases. And amidst this luxury we stood erect in two ranks looking with surprise and delight at generals, the Emperor's suite, the rare, exalted medals, liveried servants, courtiers, grandees, officers of the cavalry guards, hussars in their red dolmans, and Pavlov grenadiers in their tall shakos. We who had just left provincial Tbilisi, or Omsk, or Orenburg were astounded. What brilliance, what opulence.

Then the solemn religious procession began, moving through all the halls to the Jordan doors and out to the Neva River, the Jordan.[1]

And here is his Majesty the Emperor whom I longed to see. He is the epitome of modesty and simplicity, despite the glittering surroundings and haughtiness of the courtiers. His sky-blue eyes are plain, tender and familiar as if they were the eyes of thousands and thousands of Russian people. There is something very Russian, something dear in them and, strange as it may seem, something attractively shy. And his rank is only that of a colonel, something immediately apparent amidst hundreds of high-ranking generals. The thought flashes through my mind that he ought to be a general rather than a colonel. But it is also pleasing that he modestly declines higher ranks. But will this be understood, perchance, by the giants in the Preobrazhenskii Regiment who stretch like a wall down the corridors. But what thoughts don't enter the mind of a provincial youth at his first time at court. The chief thing is to prolong time and to gaze at him intensely. His Majesty walks by slowly and looks kindly and attentively into the eyes of each. And his gaze stopped at me for a moment and filled me with pride, as if I had become known to the tsar.

The empress walked next to him, slowly nodding to everyone with a benevolent and intelligent expression. . . .

Overall, the impression was magical and overwhelming, and later in the tea hall, answering everyone's questions, I spoke with enthusiasm of the court, parade, and of His Majesty. . . .

The next time we saw the emperor was when he came to inspect the academy. There was only one adjutant with him, but he kept to himself, and we all felt as if His Majesty was our personal guest. Nor did the academy administration surround the emperor except for general Shatilov, who, out of breath with joy, pranced behind the emperor trying to explain everything with his hissing, flu-ridden voice.

The emperor was obviously pleased with everything and perhaps most of all with the fact that he was out of his usual environment and in touch with Russia's youth which had just come from all corners of his extensive empire. Who knows, but perhaps we from Siberia, the Urals, the Caucasus, Pskov province brought with us the air of all the Russian borderlands and His Majesty unexpectedly became immersed in our youthful high spirits and sensed that very connectedness with the people which he so needed.

This was the time of the greatest flowering of our Russian state. There were Russian troops at far-off Kushka and even farther in immense Manchuria. His Majesty was the most powerful monarch in the world. Yet, here he was with us and we could see him up close and examine all the features of his Preobrazhenskii Regiment tunic and the historic adjutant's epaulets with the interwoven silver monograms of Alexander II and Alexander III, his grandfather and father. A gilded adjutant's braid ran down his sleeve from an epaulet. He approached us with tenderness, occasionally posing brief questions. At the doors, where everyone rushed to see him off, His Majesty put on his gray overcoat, wiggling a shoulder as if the coat was tight in the armpit, and said that he was glad to have seen our academy in such exemplary order and that he wished us success in our studies and training.

We were given silent consent to go out onto Spasskii Street and run alongside the emperor's conveyance. We shouted Hurrah! Then the driver went faster and the sleigh disappeared in the mists of St. Petersburg.

Classes were canceled for the rest of the day and that made us doubly happy.

NOTE

1. In the Eastern Orthodox Church Epiphany celebrates the baptism of Christ by John the Baptist in the river Jordan. The ceremony, which includes a blessing of the waters (hence the exit to the Neva River), occurs on the twelfth day of Christmas.

Chapter Five

Aleksandra Tyrkova-Williams, A Woman's Autonomy

Tyrkova-Williams's memoirs provide an indication of the mindset of idealistic (and frequently revolutionary) Russian youth. The author was much influenced by her mother who, she says, was a person of the 1860's—one who obtained her liberal views from Christian ethics and from broad reading. Her grandfather's copy of Lamartine's work on the Girondists was also very influential. She read it several times when she was thirteen. The poetry of Nekrasov found even more resonance in the young Aleksandra. The events of the day, disputations, political literature, and the arrest and exile of her brother to Siberia made certain that her path would become an oppositional one. Ultimately her own high sense of morality and justice made her turn away from what the Revolution spawned. Taken from Aleksandra Tyrkova-Williams, *Na putiakh k svobode* [On the Paths toward Freedom]. New York: Izd. Imeni Chekhova, 1952.

I am not writing a history. I do not have any books, or documents at hand, not even the notes which I occasionally jotted down. This is merely a remembrance, a story of what I saw and heard, of the setting in which I grew and lived. I write only of that which has remained in my memory. I began writing at the end of 1940 in Pau, a small town in the south of France with a beautiful view of the Pyrenees. Currently, I am writing in Grenoble with no less a gorgeous view of the Alps. Where will I end? Will I be able to complete this? Who knows? At the age of 73, one looks at tomorrow carefully, especially now, in 1943. But I will try to preserve in human memory that which I witnessed, sometimes as a participant, and relay the development and spirit of the events over which future historians will puzzle. Unless history, publishing, libraries, and archives, the building blocks of culture, are swept away by storms.

I have chosen to write my memoirs because I think it essential to retain a remembrance of our era which concluded a specific period of Russian life, perhaps not even just the Russian. I will try to speak less of myself, though I do so. I was a part, even though small one, of that oppositional ferment which was called the liberation movement. Now after all that Europe is going through, and all that Russia is suffering, I have different perceptions regarding that which occurred and the events in which I participated in one way or another. Our weaknesses, errors, and delusions have become clearer. But I do not disavow my past and those ideals which I served as well as I could— human rights, freedom, humaneness, and respect for the individual. I bitterly regret that our generation was unable to translate them into life, could not effect in Russia the free and democratic order for which we strove. Catherine II once said that she set the well being of each and everyone as her goal. There is much wisdom in these words. The term "each and everyone" denoted Russia to her. We transferred the center of gravity onto the person, each individual, forgetting the dictum of another great sovereign, Peter I: If Russia were only to live . . . We forgot this, not that we wanted Russia's destruction, but because of a childish, unthinking confidence in its stability.

The basis of our concern was a striving for universal well being, not for our personal bliss or enrichment, as was frequently the case with European politicians. Therefore, in the Russian opposition, there was much that was immature, naïve, unreasoned and, what turned out to be most dangerous, much simple-mindedness about the nature of statecraft.

The more that I recall the past, the more surprised I am to observe that the European calamity and collapse of today is a continuum of what we Russians thought and acted on a half century ago. If at the end of the last century, and at the beginning of this one, the more active, determined, and ardent segment of Russian public opinion had not been blind to Russian reality and not possessed by the passion of protest, there would not have been two European wars or Asian unrest. I would be peacefully writing my memoirs at home in Russia, and not in an alien land. But things turned out otherwise.

That which we considered to be our Russian cause, our Russian struggle for a new life, was transformed into the preface which awaited Europe and which was reflected in the life of people on all the five continents. That of which I write became a part of their history. Marxism, which now has such an enormous influence on the world's politics, became a real force thanks to the Russian Revolution, even though in the beginning it was only one of its components. It began on 14 December 1825. From that time on, revolutionary sparks either smoldered or flared in agitated minds until, in the XX century, they raced across all of Russia, and then the whole world, like fire in the steppe.

The underground revolutionary fervor was reflected in the lives of all thinking people, including those who fanned the flames and those who attempted to douse them. The flashes of this flame were reflected in everything that I had read, seen, thought, heard, and felt since my youth. In order to understand the Russian reality of the past one hundred years, one must be cognizant of this incessant, inflamed, irrepressible and rebellious agitation. It grew and strengthened until 1917, when it burst out in a crushing revolution, a fearful historical collapse, which initially destroyed the life of the cultured classes, and later shattered the life patterns of the peasants.

As for myself, the escalation of revolutionary rhythm coincided with a radical change in my personal life. It came to be that I had to support my children and myself. I was unprepared for this and did not envision the difficulties which life often presented to novices. I had no profession. Luckily, I seized onto journalism and made writing my craft. I serve it to this day. Later, this drew me closer to the active opposition. But, at the beginning, I felt myself very alone on the new road, the more so that I did not yet perceive social missions to pursue. In actuality, the clarification of these was just coming to the attention of public opinion. There were no beacons by which I could steer the course. This was practically the most difficult thing for me.

The only thing I recognized clearly was my responsibility for the children. I took them when I separated from my husband. One way or another, this had to be addressed. During the summers, I took the children to my mother in the country, and spent more time there than in the city. On the Vergezh River I was again immersed in my mother's warm and radiant life which merged with the beauty of our native country spaces. When school began again in the fall, my children and I returned to St. Petersburg. We lived in a small, cheap apartment in the Peski district. Living was cheap and similar to what I, as a *gimnazium* student, had seen in the life of my close friend Nadia Krupskaia [later to become Lenin's wife]. At that time I had wondered how she and her mother managed in such cramped quarters. Now I was forced to understand. Even for this kind of life there frequently was not enough money. There was almost no work to be had. I tore my children away from a secure life, but what was I giving them in compensation?

Having no money weighed heavily on me. I did not know how to push my way through life, to move ahead. I was acquainted with some writers. It was pleasant to be with them, and conversation was cheery. But none of them ever had the thought of helping me find work. Perhaps the fact that I was a landowner's daughter gave the illusion of material well being. The dresses which I had once bought in Paris, and which I somehow sewed up and wore down, also gave me the appearance of being wealthier than I was. My provocative and independent manner could also be deceptive—my ability to carry myself above my station.

The owner of *Mir Bozhii*, A.A. Davydova, with whose daughter I was great friends, once offered me a translation of a French book on the encyclopedists. This was then published as a supplement to *Mir Bozhii*. This gave me a breathing spell. Translating was not that easy for me. But newspaper work was immediately appealing. At that time, there were very few newspapers being published in Petersburg and I had no entry to them. I began by working for the provincial press, in the Iaroslavl newspaper called *Severnyi Krai*. There I sent my *Petersburg Letters*. It was easy to write them, even too easy and carefree. After a rather lengthy period of writing and social work, I took a look at my first satirical articles. I came upon the article on the *Peredvizhniki* [realist painters, second half of 19th century] and was terrified. So much superficial bravado and so little knowledge and understanding! True, at that time, in the writing on art, the creative process was not analyzed. The content and the thematics held sway. This was the narrow path that I treaded as well.

My relationship with *Severnyi Krai* became instantly fraternal and collegial, at first via correspondence. But the newspaper was poor. They could not afford to pay me more than three kopeks per line, and late at that. I would write for them once a week, some 300–400 lines. In the best case scenario, I would earn forty rubles a month. My apartment rent was thirty-five rubles. I also received several hundred rubles a year from a small brick factory that had been built on land rented from my father. The summer months on the Vergezh did not cost me anything. Nevertheless, it was sometimes so difficult to maintain myself and my children that I was periodically at a loss.

My affairs started to improve when I commenced writing for a second provincial newspaper, *Pridneprovskii Krai*, published in Ekaterinoslav. But my prosperity did not last long. A situation occurred which was characteristic of the position of the press and the mood of journalists. *Pridneprovskii Krai* was larger and incomparably wealthier than the Iaroslavl newspaper. I knew no one in the editorial office. But they liked my articles, embraced me right away, and asked me to write more. I wrote them of everything that came to mind—theater, books, news of life abroad and foreign literature. My first stories were published in *Pridneprovskii Krai*. I did not, of course, touch on political themes. The censor's office did not allow them. But no matter what we wrote about, the authorities sensed an obstinate oppositional spirit in our words and in those things which we passed over in silence. And they were right. But we were not at fault either for feeling constricted, for outgrowing the enclosures into which the government stubbornly forced Russian thought. The government did not wish to, did not know how to, provide an outlet for the accumulated social emotions and political needs. It did not understand that an energy was building and that it was dangerous to hold it back.

Censorship hurt us in the wallet as well. Both editors, in Iaroslavl and in Ekaterinoslav, accepted all my articles and were ready to publish them. Not infrequently, the censors disallowed them. No one paid me for these pieces. It was not easy to figure out what would pass and what would not.

In Ekaterinoslav a battle was also being waged between the lieutenant governor and the editor, Lemke. The latter was a retired military officer, feisty, and with a substantial desire to play a role in leftist circles. Later, he wrote several books on censorship and on the revolution. But at that time, he was a neophyte journalist. I do not know whether he was already a member of the Social Democrat Party, though later he became a member of the Communist Party. As editor of *Pridneprovskii Krai*, Lemke warred ardently against the local censors as did, by the way, many provincial editors. The sequence was as follows. The galleys of the typeset issue were sent to the censor. He would check off the unacceptable segments. When the sheet, marked up in red censor's ink, was returned to the editorial office, it had to be patched up hurriedly at night. The offending sections had to be somehow patched up by filling the devastated galleys with material previously passed by the censorship.

Lemke tried establishing a new procedure. He started to distribute the newspaper in the form in which it was received from the censor. The pages were replete with white spaces. The bureaucrats were angry, but there was no law forbidding blank spaces within articles and between articles. Finally, Lemke overdid it. I do not know if he put together an issue that was particularly severe or whether the censor was angry that evening. The galley proofs returned almost wholly smeared with red. No clean space was left, just the headlines and broken lines of unintelligible text. Lemke printed the bald newspaper and sent his subscribers the blank pages with scattered separate phrases.

The authorities went crazy. *Pridneprovskii Krai* was shut down. However, the newspaper's proprietor, the millionaire contractor Kopylov, was on good terms with the local administration and knew how to handle his affairs. He obtained permission to publish the newspaper anew but without Lemke. The latter, in response to his firing, immediately sent his colleagues a letter in which he announced that he had left the editor's post on a "matter of principle." He asked whether we were agreeable to signing a collective statement that we were also leaving and would not work for *Pridneprovskii Krai* without him.

For myself and for the majority of the contributors, this was a most unpleasant event. *Pridneprovskii Krai* buttressed my lean budget. They paid me five kopeks per line and paid punctually, something that could not be said about *Severnyi Krai*. But, nothing could be done. Such was the habit of Russian writers and journalists. We were employed by, and left editorial offices like small herds. I sighed, but wrote Lemke that he could use my signature.

A few days had passed when my servant led a stocky gentleman into my living room. He had a round beard, quick eyes, and a thick gold chain which gleamed on his colorful vest.

"Allow me to introduce myself—Kopylov."

With a dandyish actor's gesture, playing the part of a grandee on the provincial stage, he raised my hand to his lips and audibly kissed it.

"I am very pleased to meet you. Kindly be seated."

The contractor's sharp eyes surveyed my cramped room, estimated the cost of my chairs and couch, upholstered in cheap cretonne, noticed the sole bookshelf, a plain painted table, the floor without a rug, the pictureless walls, and then confidently they turned to me.

"And I, little lady, am happy to make your acquaintance. I wanted to do this for a long time. God has given you a bold pen. Even fit for a man . . . ha . . . ha . . . ha . . . The readers approve very much."

"Thanks for telling me. From afar it is difficult for me to determine whether they approve or not. We writers like to be praised by our readers. Thank you."

"No, thanks be to you. The news venders are asked: 'Is Vergezhskii in the issue? If not, I won't give you the five kopeks. Ha . . . ha . . . ha . . . All think that Vergezhskii is a man, but look at Vergezhskii."

He scrutinized me with unceremonious approval. He was amused at the "little lady" who worked for him, who received his money. Without giving me time to collect myself, he began to tell me about himself, attempting to make me understand that his sweep was wide.

"Come to visit us in Ekaterinoslav and see how people live there. You will meet your readers. You can stay at my place for a while. I will gather some guests to meet you. The whole district knows me; I not only own the newspaper but the theatre as well. I am a great lover of the theater. However, it consumes heaps of money. Much more than the newspaper."

"Tell me stories. I've heard that the newspaper gives you a good income."

He grinned, self-satisfied.

"You heard? Well, I can't complain, but the money could be better used. I didn't start the newspaper for purposes of income."

"Not for income? For what then?"

"For pleasure. A publisher of a large newspaper is someone, after all. But the theater, even though it is an expensive toy, is even more entertaining. I am a happy person and actors are cheerful people. Not to speak of the actresses. Ha . . . ha . . . ha . . ."

I demonstratively stayed silent. He understood. Such contractors who come from humble backgrounds to become millionaires were perceptive people and pretty good psychologists. Kopylov once again surveyed the cheap furnishings of my living room, wriggled in the chair, and looking past me out the window, offhandedly asked:

"Might you have a ready article? I'll send it in."

"No. You know . . . We . . ."

He didn't let me finish:

"I've heard, little lady, I've heard. These are trifles. I have a solid newspaper, and I know how to get on with the authorities. Write the way you wrote. We did not and will not offend you. We can raise the honorarium and set a fixed sum. Would you like to receive a little advance? Why bother with the mail when my office is in my pocket."

He pulled his office out from his jacket and opened the thick billfold. Habitually believing in the omnipotence of money, he might have truly thought that the sight of hundred-ruble notes would make me amenable. I did not get angry and just laughed.

"No, thank you. What advance? Your editor left and with him so did his co-workers. I left as well. That's it."

"In truth, little lady, why should you leave? I already have a new editor. He will continue things as before. And you, write as before also. We'll make a new agreement, a better one. Would you like to?"

My smile confused him. He saw how I lived and hoped that I was not so foolish as to refuse a good income. Patting the billfold with his hand, he gently attempted to convince me:

"Why refuse the money? Take an advance and we'll settle sometime in the future. I won't push you; you'll repay me whenever you want. Just write. Well, how much money shall I peel off?"

I stood up.

"None. We're all even. The office sent me everything. But I cannot write for you anymore. You find this difficult to understand. Every one of your worker's *artels* has its own rules. We writers are also an *artel*. If one is affected, all have to back him up. That's how it is with us."

He stood as well. In bewilderment, he rotated the billfold in his hands, still surprised that such a rich argument did not break a woman's stubbornness. He put it inside his jacket and, without the previous familiarity, somewhat tenuously offered his hand. I put mine in it. Why should I be angry with him? The more so, since I was told that he had given Lemke a full year's salary, something he did not have to do. His co-workers, however, did not benefit materially from this. I didn't know how I would pay next month's rent.

Kopylov stopped in the doorway. A sly smirk flitted across his smart peasant face.

"Oh little lady, little lady, how prickly you are . . . Unapproachable . . . And I was coming to St. Pete thinking Vergezhskii would go to Palkin's for dinner with me and then to the theater. Some theater! Some Vergezhskii!"

We exchanged glances. The sharp eyes of the wealthy peasant betrayed mockery at my inability to make a go of things. But there was a reflection of something else also. My polite but decisive refusal elicited a sporting approval in him.

"Yes, this Vergezhskii is something," I said also smiling.

"What can one say? Everyone has their own habits. There's nothing to be done. Good luck."

I never saw him again, did not write for his newspaper, and quickly became impoverished. I still did not know how to fight for survival and sometimes it was very difficult.

Then a catastrophe occurred. Lida died. She was thirty years old, full of life, energy, interests, and love. She occupied a position in which her talents, kindness, and social instincts could be broadly applied. She died from pernicious anemia. She passionately wanted to have children. She was pregnant several times and miscarried each time during the eighth month. Doctors warned her against pregnancy, that her life was at risk. But the maternal instinct turned out to be stronger than the sense of self-preservation. She tried to be a mother one more time. And again she failed to carry to term. The premature birth brought on acute anemia. She died slowly, cognizant that she was dying, but to the end maintained her cheer. Though bedridden, she continued to receive guests. She tried not to talk about her illness and forced her visitors to tell her about their lives, of what was occurring in literary circles, and of assorted day to day minutiae.

The death of Lida Tugan-Baranovskii saddened not only her relatives. For me it was an irreplaceable loss. In my new, still unsettled life, Lida's kind wisdom was a great support. Without her, life became colder and it was more difficult to find one's way. I frequently went to see Aleksandra Arkad'evna [Lida's mother]. I felt Lida's emanation while next to her. I came to be even closer to Mikhail Ivanovich [Lida's husband]. He was greatly saddened, became helpless and perplexed, muttered unintelligibly, stayed silent for hours, and could not work. I felt very sorry for him.

An unbeliever, during these dark days he circled around the eternal questions. In a childish way he grasped at the possibility of personal immortality, but without God. He did not join the church nor read the Gospels, but read Kant instead. He grasped at spiritualism. His sister, the pretty E. I. Nitte, who had inspired Kuprin to write the story "The Garnet Bracelet," organized a séance in her handsomely appointed and spacious apartment on Furshatskaia [street]. It was with Ian Guzik, a Lithuanian shepherd who had become famous as a powerful medium. Mikhail Ivanovich took me to one of these seances. Phenomena occurred which I will not attempt to explain, but I stand behind the accuracy of my descriptions.

We sat down around a long table in the living room. There were twelve of us, perhaps fifteen. Guzik's companion, his impresario, sat at one end of the table. He had collected money from us in advance, three rubles per person. It was he who told us how to conduct ourselves during the séance. Guzik himself stayed morosely quiet. He had a strange, hard gaze. The large room was weakly lit by a lamp under a dark shade which stood at the far end of the living room. But one could distinguish the outlines of people and objects. Tugan sat on one side of Guzik and V. K. Agafonov on the other. The latter was a young geologist who later became a well known scholar in France. Tugan and Agafonov held Guzik tightly by the hands. They put their legs against his and thus controlled all his movements. Only his head remained free. I sat next to Agafonov. All present held each other's hands and created a chain. But we continued to chat and joke until the impresario told us to be quiet. It became still. All that could be heard was the medium's breathing, becoming less frequent and deeper. After a few minutes, some object flew above our heads. Judging by the sound of the strings, this was the guitar which had been lying on a table at the opposite end of the living room. Certain sounds and rustling from the corners were heard. Right behind me, the sound of a spoon against glass resonated. This was the glass which had been placed on the floor, quite far from the table. Now, behind our backs, this glass made its way around the table. The spoon tinkled as if someone was tapping it against the glass. This was just like in the story of the mouse running around the dark room and ringing a bell in order to fool the evil stepmother.

One of the ladies screamed loudly:

"Oh, oh, I'm being hit with something shaggy across my face!"

"Something shaggy?" the impresario repeated. "That means the spirit of the Prussian soldier Wilhelm has arrived. Please sit still. This is a very crude spirit. If you resist, he can hit you very hard. If anyone feels that the chair is being yanked out from under you, one must get up right away or there can be unpleasant consequences."

As if in precise confirmation of his words, the chair under me began to be pulled. There was no one behind me. Agafonov was sitting on my left, another close acquaintance on my right. They would not tease me with such foolish stunts. Furthermore, their hands were in mine. I could not but have noticed their movement. Adhering to the instructions, I got up without breaking the chain while continuing to hold my neighbors' hands. After some moments the same mysterious being moved the chair back into place. Here something most strange and unpleasant occurred. I wanted to sit down but it turned out that someone was sitting in the chair and was not letting me sit down. But the chair was empty. In a few moments this strange presence seemed to melt away. The chair freed up. But no sooner did I sit down when something shaggy swept across my face, as if I was brushed with an animal's tail.

That is all that I saw from Guzik. I treated this with a cool curiosity. But poor Mikhail Ivanovich could not part with the insane hope of corporeally seeing, hearing, and sensing his deceased wife and imagined that Guzik would somehow link him with Lida. He insistently pleaded with the impresario and reiterated sadly and incoherently:

"You say this is Wilhelm? Can't you ask him to leave? Send someone else . . . The one we want . . ."

"We can't today. The séance is ended. The medium is already awakening."

Truly, one could hear how the rhythm of his breathing was changing, that Guzik was moving. During the séance he was completely motionless. The light was turned on. The medium was sitting and pale. The look of his strange eyes had become even more grim. All of this was unusual and extremely interesting for me. But why link the tinkling of the spoon and the shaggy strokes with the souls of the departed? I could not understand how Mikhail Ivanovich found solace in these disconnected phenomena. But I pitied him all the more! Involvement in spiritualism ended shortly. Tugan and I were arrested for participating in a street demonstration. He was sent out of St. Petersburg, though not for long.

Chapter Six

Nikolai Volkov-Muromtsev, Memoirs

Nikolai Volkov-Muromtsev was born in 1902 to a family of the nobility and gentry. The family lived on its estate, a productive grain and dairy farm near Viaz'ma, a city of 30,000 east of Smolensk. Young Nikolai was tutored in French and English and had in-laws who were members of the English upper classes. The choice of the three segments from his memoirs is not accidental. His ability to combine family and personal narrative with the tumultuous historical background is keenly apparent. He writes with pithiness and clarity. The evocation of life whether in the city or on the country estate carries the stamp of unforced authenticity. Rarely in memoir literature do we see a description of a city, Viaz'ma in this case, done so affectionately and informatively. Taken from Nikolai Volkov-Muromtsev, *Iunost' ot Viaz'my do Feodosii* [My Youth from Viaz'ma to Theodosia]. Paris: YMCA Press, 1983.

VIAZ'MA: THE TEXTURE OF A CITY

Viaz'ma had a population of 35,000. It was the center of the linen industry and had three leather and two match factories. The streets were cobblestoned and only the rich merchants paved in front of their homes with other materials, be it asphalt or wooden blocks. The Viaz'ma merchants were exceptional. Nowhere in Russia, I believe, was there such a congregation of old merchant families. In 1478 Ivan III conquered Novgorod, but the Novgorodians did not calm down. There were many other campaigns under Vasilii III and Ivan the Terrible. After one of these campaigns, the Muscovites decided that Novgorod would never be pacified while the old merchant class remained there. So they dispatched the merchants to Viaz'ma. It was enough to look at a list of Viaz'ma merchants to recall ancient Novgorod—Stroganov, Kalashnikov, Liutov, Sinel'nikov, Ershov, Kolesnikov, El'chaninov, etc. These families did not sit long in Viaz'ma with their hands folded. They became rich anew trading in linen and leather with the Hansa cities.

The major Viaz'ma merchants became linen czars. This was strange because the best flax grew in the light sandy soil of the Pskov, Novgorod, and Tver provinces. Smolensk had loamy soil, and the flax was coarser. But it was brought in from everywhere, and Viaz'ma became not only a Russian, but a European linen exchange.

The leather factories stretched out one after the other on a bend of the Viaz'ma River. They stank horribly but people were used to it and seemed not to notice. From the river one could see huge piles of sandal shavings that looked like red pyramids.

Beyond the Smolensk gate stood two match factories, the El'chaninov and the Sinel'nikov. They were very different. The El'chaninov plant was in the "latest style." It was rebuilt several years before the war and looked like a huge glass greenhouse. All the machinery was new with half being automated. Inside one heard the quiet hum of electric motors, central heating was everywhere, and the workers wore white coats as in a hospital. Around the factory was a new settlement for workers with small individual houses set in gardens.

Nearby, the Sinel'nikov match factory looked like a barracks. Assorted lumber and odd carts were sloppily strewn about. Everything was untidy. The workers lived in the city in no set location.

The El'chaninov matches were packaged in elegant raspberry colored boxes, 2 x 2 inches and less than half-an-inch thick. "El'chaninov Factory. 48 Matches" was stamped on them. The Sinel'nikov matches came in the simplest boxes. Incomprehensibly, Sinel'nikov workers were very proud of their factory, did not complain of their fate; management was always friendly. But El'chaninov's workers were always whining.

The linen and leather merchants were very rich. Their presence was very beneficial for the town. The merchants competed against each other as to who would excel in charity. Mikhail Ivanovich Liutov built one of the finest hospitals in Russia, Stroganov built schools, and Sinel'nikov equipped the fire department. When my mother undertook the creation of the Viaz'ma library, all the merchants wanted to build it so it would carry their name. Only after having purchased the land, and with great difficulty, was my mother able to convince the merchants to build the library jointly and to stock it. The merchants of Viaz'ma were not only rich but generous, a type of people common in Russia.

The Liutov hospital stood between the city and the railroad station. Liutov hired a superb architect for it and obtained the newest medical equipment from Switzerland. The wards and operating rooms had rounded corners so that dust would not collect there. He brought in Italian experts for the special floors. The walls were tiled. Needless to say, Liutov procured the best doctors and nurses.

In the market square there was a one-story building called the "Trading Row." This was an arcade with a covered passageway and shops in the interior. All kinds of merchants and storekeepers had businesses there. All of these merchants were either manufacturers or curriers, but they sat in their shops daily even though they had nothing to do with linen or leather. They sold necessities. The stores had boots, axes, scythes, harnesses, matting, hammers, nails, tar. There were barrels of herring, pickles, and all kinds of other things. The shops belonging to Stroganov and Kalashnikov were next to each other. One of the Stroganov brothers always sat on a barrel in front of his shop and played cards with Kalashnikov, also on a barrel instead of a table. You would arrive there and be greeted with a "What do you need?" "I need some nails." "Go find some nails for yourself, whichever you need. The smaller ones are in the boxes. Let me know later what you took." People walked around in the shops on their own. They took what they needed, tried on the boots without the owners even watching. In the Russia of those days, it was possible to conduct business in this fashion. Evidently, people were honest.

The eldest Stroganov brother, who was repeatedly elected mayor, was superbly educated and a natural scientist with a European reputation. He held honorary degrees from the universities of Edinburgh and London, and had doctorates from the universities of Heidelberg and Leipzig.

I think it was in 1912 that he went to London for a long time. His brother and Kalashnikov decided to visit him there. They did not have his address, all they knew was that he was in London. They arrived there and asked for the best hotel. They were told the Ritz. They booked rooms, sat down by a window facing the street, and began to play cards. Having stayed there for two weeks, they decided to return to Viaz'ma. "It's a hell of a city. We sat by a window for two weeks and did not see brother once."

The Viaz'ma merchants always wore dark blue homespun coats, similar wide trousers, boots, and peaked caps. They wore silk braided belts. And if the light, tight coat was unfastened, the whitest of white shirts could be seen underneath. The store smelled of tar, matting, herring, but everything was cleanly swept.

As in other cities, there were *artels* in Viaz'ma. I don't know when they started in Russia. These were voluntary associations of 30–40 people, though sometimes over 50. The smaller *artels* had about twelve men. There were construction *artels*, leather-working *artels*, and specialized ones. They built bridges, roads, did all forms of mechanical work, and excelled in shipbuilding. They had incredibly strict rules regarding honesty and professional knowledge of their craft. Everyone knew that if an *artel* took the job everything would be done as contracted. My father said that the *artel* was the most remarkable organization in Russia, and that an *artel* member was synonymous with honesty and irreproachability.

If someone needed machinery from Germany or cedar from Siberia, and *artel* was hired. "Here, I need 500 *sazhens* [one *sazhen* equals 7 ft.] of cedar, 12 feet by 9 inches, an inch thick—do you know where to get it?" "Yes." "Well, be sure to get the top grade." They came to an agreement and price. The merchant gave the *artel* man money without any signatures and the cedar planks were brought from Siberia at the best price possible.

No one ever worried that the *artel* people would cheat them. The majority of the *artel* men were from the peasantry, honest and smart. When I was already in England, the old Englishman Stanley Hogue used to tell me about the *artels*. He did business in Russia for 50 years and prior to that, his father did the same. They owned furniture factories in Moscow and Khar'kov, and they bought all their materials and wood through the *artels*. Not once in his fifty years in Russia did he ever actually sign a contract. He said that Russia was the only country where contracts were entered into orally rather than on paper. Transactions of twenty or thirty thousand rubles were agreed upon over a cup of tea. "No receipt was ever taken by them or me. I once gave an *artel* member 40,000 rubles, though I had never met him before. He delivered my order and provided an accounting down to the last penny. One could only do business this way in Russia." Only once did he hear that a merchant had been cheated by an *artel* member. The name of this person was made public and all the money that the merchant lost was returned by the *artel*. This person could never be accepted into any other *artel*.

One policeman stood at the market square in Viaz'ma. What he did there, nobody knew. A second one stood on Nikitskaia Square and one strolled the Sennaia Square on Thursdays, market day. I never saw any other policemen in Viaz'ma, but it was said that there were fourteen altogether. The son of one of them was in my class.

Viaz'ma was outside the pale of settlement, but there were many Jews. I do not know precisely what allowed Jews to live outside the pale at that time, but I think that if any Jew had a profession he could live anywhere. In Viaz'ma, for example, all three pharmacists, all six dentists, I do not know how many doctors, the oculists, public notaries, many storeowners, almost all the bankers, tailors, and shoemakers were Jews. I recall that on Troitskaia Street there were four houses next to each other which had brass plates reading, e.g., "Fel'dman—Dentist." Not one of them was a dentist or tailor in actuality. Evidently they sold goods of a sort. Everybody knew this and no one bothered them. There were about 2,000 Jews in Viaz'ma. Out of thirty boys in my class, eight were Jews and seven of them sat in the front row because they were good students.

There were many educational institutions in Viaz'ma: the First Alexander III men's *gimnazium*, the first women's *gimnazium* standing opposite, the second women's at the corner of Moskovskaia, the "realschule," the technical school, the first and second city schools, and several common schools. I have already noted that my mother always wanted to establish a university in Viaz'ma but the war came along.

And what about the city itself? Only in Russia could there be such contrasts. The roadways were absolutely bad. Only in the center of town were the sidewalks slabbed. On the remaining streets, the sidewalks were earthen, and raised a foot or two above the roadway. The Viaz'ma River was neglected. There were no embankments anywhere and the shoreline in the city was overgrown. It was sad. Only on the Bel'skaia side, under the precipice on which the cathedral stood, was there a boathouse. Otherwise there were no boats, not a landing, even in the city park. In spring, the Viaz'ma overflowed broadly into the flood plain meadows. How beautiful it was to look from the cathedral cliff upon this huge lake of two to three *versts* in length and more than a *verst* wide. The Bober River flowed into the Viaz'ma between the tanneries. The bridges crossing the river were old and wooden.

But at night, Viaz'ma lit up splendidly. Huge electric lamps, which illuminated the streets as if it were day, hung from cables. The town prided itself on its electric signs. Above the Nemirov Hotel on Moskovskaia a multicolored wheel spun at night. Some sort of electric feathers and flowers sparkled above the Nemirov movie theater. Above Krakovskii's pharmacy a large bottle poured red liquid into a glass which never filled up. A yellow and black shoe alternately flared above Izraztsov's shoe store. Truly, there were many fantastical billboards.

At night, the town shone like the capital. Prior to the war, the band of the heavy artillery division played in the shell at the city park on spring and summer evenings. The youth of Viaz'ma strolled beneath the electric bulbs which hung like pears from trees. High schoolers, apprentices, soldiers, vendors, and bureaucrats walked arm in arm with their ladies. To me, the park appeared to be too small for Viaz'ma. I always dreamed that upon growing up I would establish a park with tree-lined paths, gazebos, a landing, and boats for the strollers.

There were also some extremely handsome houses that were saved during the conflagration when the French were retreating from the battle of Viaz'ma. There were also new three- and four-story brick buildings. These were apartment houses with nice apartments with high ceilings and airy rooms.

Fires were rare in the city, perhaps because the houses stood far apart and had large gardens between them. The fire department with a high observation tower across from the city park always seemed to be closed. In actuality, a fireman was always on duty in the tower night and day. But I never saw the fire apparatus, nor the firemen racing anywhere.

All of the homesteads had stables, cowsheds, and barns. I do not know if Viaz'ma was famous for its cattle, or whether this was generally the case in provincial towns, but Viaz'ma cows were a lovely sight. Around five o'clock the herds returned from grazing. I often hung out the window looking at the cows. How gorgeous they were! As far as I remember, there were four herds in Viaz'ma of 150 cows, perhaps more: the Bel'skoe, Smolenskoe, Kaluzhskoe, and Moskovskoe. The herdsmen gathered the cows in the morning and brought them back in the evening for milking. All had their barns filled with hay and oil-cake for winter. Besides draught horses, there were few others. Some people had a *brichka* or *drozhki*. Only the more wealthy had carriages with one central shaft and a pair of handsome horses. Corpulent merchant's wives, all dressed to kill, used these carriages to go on visits. Rich storeowners also kept one-horse carriages.

Peasant wagons, loaded with hay and assorted viands, drifted from all directions to Sennaia Square where the Thursday market was held. Sometimes large fairs were held on the Torgovaia Square.

The city club stood on the Sennaia. All the merchants, bank directors, bureaucrats, etc. were members. I was never there, of course, but my father would go whenever serious matters concerning the town were to be decided.

The central telephone station stood on the corner of Sennaia and Kaluzhskaia. Many, many people had telephones in the city and in the countryside. When you called, a young lady would answer: "Whom do you wish, Petr Petrovich or Mariia Nikolaevna?" "Well, Petr Petrovich." "He's not home. Wait, I will ask. Dasha, where did you say Petr Petrovich was going? Aah, to father Aleksei, or maybe the pharmacy. Wait, I will find him and connect you." They all knew who was where, and who was drinking tea with whom, who was at the club, and all the news in general. The telephone station stood in a convenient spot, everything could be seen from its windows. And, in general, everybody knew each other—who got engaged, whose milk cow went dry, or who sprained a foot. Nothing malicious came to anyone from this.

The railroad station was a bit over a *verst* from town. Many people came to Viaz'ma on business. It was an important station, the principal one between Moscow and Smolensk on the Moscow-Brest railroad. A branch of the Nikolaevskii railroad to Rzhev and Likhoslavl terminated in Viaz'ma as well, and the Syzran-Viaz'ma railroad began here. Passengers from Europe who were traveling across Siberia to China or Japan transferred in Viaz'ma to the Trans-Siberian express. In Cheliabinsk, the train met the St. Petersburg express and, combined, crossed Siberia. The travelers all unfailingly bought the famous Viaz'ma gingerbread.

Viaz'ma had many cabmen. There were five carriages on the Torgovaia and five or six on the Nikitskaia. The rest were at the station. The cabmen were good, some even excellent. All of them were first-rate psychologists. Whenever someone arrived and hired a cabbie, the latter would engage the visitor in conversation. They always wanted to know what business one had. The uninteresting ones were taken directly to the Nemirov Hotel. To the more intriguing, the cabman would say: "Instead of stopping at the hotel, master (or mistress), why don't you go to Kolesnikov (or to Stroganov, Sinel'nikov, etc...) they will be hospitable to you." And truly, the merchant ladies liked to entertain visitors. They liked to joke and gossip with someone from the capital or even from just another city. The cabmen never made a mistake; they always brought only good people. Old Mr. Hogue told me: "I traveled all over Russia and never stayed in a hotel except in St. Petersburg, Moscow, Kiev, and Odessa. And it never cost me anything, either. The coachmen always suggested someone they knew. Having been driven to a house, I would be treated like a long-lost brother. A very hospitable people."

In the summertime, only officers and their ladies used the coachmen to ride around. But in winter, the coachmen harnessed two or three horses to a sleigh, and the youth would race around until dark. High schoolers, clerks, young merchants—all rode around beneath fur rugs.

We had a steady coachman named Stepan. He knew all of us well. His horses were superb and his carriage had rubber tires. When we needed a coachman, we would call Nemirov: "Is Stepan free?" "He'll be right over." His sleigh was also a fine one, with a spirited troika.

The coachmen were all monarchists and patriots. They knew everybody in town, and lectured our youth. They were listened to, since they were smart men.

THE SUMMER OF 1914

The author's family lived in Viaz'ma, a city mid-way between Moscow and Smolensk, but they summered on their ancestral estate to the north. This is the setting of the following passage.

This was the last summer that I spent in Glubokoe with the whole family. As always, we went there in May. The weather that year was magnificent. As usual, a crowd of people had gathered at Glubokoe. Grandmother had finally received permission from the department of the interior to start an archeological dig on Kamennoe Lake. The archeologist was to come from Pskov in June.

The heat which came in April melted the snows so quickly that the streams and rivers ran unexpectedly high. The lakes rose more than usual. The plywood plant had a millpond for soaking birch and aspen logs, but the lake rose over the breakwater and washed away many logs. We noticed the drifting logs the first time we went boating. Strangely enough, they floated vertically so only their ends showed. These foot-wide circles floated just above the surface. We hooked one with a gaff and pulled it back to the mill. My older brother Peter decided that it would be fun and a good turn to fish out all the logs. The next day we took iron hooks attached to ropes and went log-catching. After a day we be came so proficient that we would tow in ten or more logs at a time. In this manner we fished out more than 200 logs so that they became scarce in the lake.

One day grandmother suggested a picnic on Babinensk Lake. This lake, fairly narrow but two *versts* long, was on the road to Opochek. It lay amidst steep hills covered by a pine forest and for some reason was always light blue. On our side, the forest had been cut a number of years ago. The dense second-growth of pine and birch rose some fifteen to twenty feet and had not been thinned out.

There was a legend about Babinensk Lake and mountain. Supposedly a brigand named Lapin once had a hideout there. The place even had his name, "Lapin's Mountain." No one knew when he had lived there, but the peasants claimed that on moonlit nights Lapin would descend the mountain on horseback to water his gray stallion at the lake.

We went and arranged all the picnic paraphernalia by the lakeside. I got the urge to climb Lapin's Mountain. It was very steep. The paths on it were only those of animals turning unexpectedly either left or right, crossed by other paths just like them. People said that there were roe deer and elk and wild oxen there, but I never saw any. There were bears and wolves and an occasional lynx. The animals did not alarm me. The apparition of Lapin scared me more, but they said he never appeared in the daytime. I scaled to the top. The view from there was gorgeous. Below was the bright-blue lake and distant inundated meadows to the right. On the other side of the mountain lay the half-moon Garusovo Lake, as if of red copper. A bright green serpentine valley opened to the south with a river snaking through it. Bluish pine forests stood in tiers on both its sides. It struck me that Lapin chose this mountain for a good reason.

I sat and looked for a while and then decided to descend. The way down was more difficult than the climb. I started to zigzag down the paths. Suddenly I came out into a flat meadow. Although I missed it at first, I suddenly noticed a moss-grown log ruin that might have been a peasant cabin. There were only four or five courses of logs standing. "Strange," I thought, "it probably was a forester's hut." I walked around it and was dumbfounded. Behind it was a low, overgrown stone cross. My God, it was Lapin's grave.

I took off downhill, stumbled, rolled, stumbled, and rolled again. Finally I made it to the forest by the lake and, all out of breath, found the others. "What's wrong with you?" someone asked.

"Nothing, just running hard," I answered. For some reason I did not want to tell anyone about my discovery. Later I told only Nikolai Ermolaevich [a family friend] and he believed me: "Yes, I have heard of a cross and a log cabin, but I never could find it."

Nikolai Ermolaevich's wife was visiting him at the time. She also was from a family of lumbermen of Viatka Province but was then in medical school in Moscow. She was a slim, beautiful woman of twenty-five with auburn, almost red hair, and was very fun-loving. We kids simply adored her. After our snack of rusks [a browned, sweetened biscuit] we all ran along the shore to a sandy beach where we plopped down to rest. It was incredibly hot. "How about going for a swim," she said. We all undressed and dashed into the cold water. None of us were embarrassed by the fact that we were all nude. At Khmelita everyone swam in the nude, men and women together. I did notice however, without any furtive thoughts, what a beautiful figure she had. We swam for a while, then stretched out on the sand where we quickly dried out in the heat. We then dressed and went back for tea.

"Where were you?" asked one of the governesses.

"Swimming," answered Nikolai Ermolaevich's wife.

"Swimming! Nude!" shrieked all the governesses.

"Of course."

The group was gripped by horror. They all began to fuss and fume. A scandal was obviously brewing. I could not understand their agitation. At first I thought that we should not have gone swimming after a snack, but then realized that all these outlanders and city folk had never swum nude and were shocked. I was not an innocent kid and knew the difference between the bodies of men and women, but none of us ever thought of nude swimming as shocking or improper. Then I recalled the horror of the governesses when they once heard that I was present at calving-time. "Do you think that a stork brings calves?" I said to myself and decided that they were all ignoramuses.

The news of the murder of Franz-Ferdinand and his duchess came while we were still at Glubokoe. I remember what a doleful effect it had on everyone, as any murder would. Murders were so rare in those "uncivilized" times that every killing was the subject of conversation for weeks. Father said that they were "clearly killed by anarchists or some other lowlife, but that the Austrians, as usual, will exaggerate this and blame the Serbian government. And the Serbs, like jerks, will get all hyper and there'll be a crisis. It's up to the diplomats to quiet this thing down. Don't know why we guaranteed the independence of our 'little brothers' who may draw us into a war through their local intrigues."

Nevertheless, no one thought at the time that this would lead to war. Almost everyone assumed that it was an incident of only local significance.

Chapter Seven

Vladimir Zenzinov, Coming of Age

Vladimir Zenzinov (1880–1953) is an example of a quintessential revolutionary. Born in Moscow, he graduated from *gimnazium* in 1899 and went to Europe. There he spent four and a half years at the universities of Berlin, Halle, and Heidelberg studying philosophy, economics, history, and law. His contacts with revolutionary émigrés in Switzerland solidified the oppositionist views formed in his *gimnazium* years. Upon returning to Russia as a member of the SR's (Social Revolutionaries), he embarked on a life of active protest. He was arrested and exiled numerous times. He escaped numerous times as well. Like other revolutionaries of a moral suasion, he could not support the Bolsheviks and had to leave Russia in 1918. From then until his death he lived in Paris, Prague, Berlin and New York working and writing for numerous democratic and socialist publications. Taken from Vladimir Zenzinov, *Perezhitoe* [My Life's Experiences]. New York: Izd. Imeni Chekhova, 1953.

On Saturday evenings we always had many young people at our house. Insofar as I recall, they were exclusively from Siberia, and principally university students of medicine, law, and philology. There were usually ten to fifteen of them, mostly the same ones. They respected my father very much; as to my mother, they not only respected her but they loved her. They treated her with tender attention, like their own mother. And she attended to them with a motherly gentleness. She followed their destinies and knew the personal and family lives of every student. Apparently, for many of them, our home substituted for the family from which they were torn away. Muscovites and Siberians are famed for their hospitality and our home seemed to doubly justify this reputation. Things were always joyful, lively and pleasant. Needless to say, the principal activity was drinking tea.

Everyone gathered around the large table on which a boiling samovar stood. Without fail, mother herself poured the tea and washed the glasses. The table was filled with everything that Muscovite and Siberian hospitality could think of: jam, cheese "Danish," nougat, black Chinese fruit jelly, sweet cakes, candies, fruit. Spirited conversations took place on anything that interested those present—news and letters from home, current events, university life, concerts, theater. Strange as it may now seem, I do not recall political discussions or debates. There were animated debates, but I don't remember any which left a bad aftertaste. The atmosphere was almost familial, one of great sincerity. Many actually knew each other through their families in Siberia and had grown up there. After tea we went to the living room where the conversations continued or games were organized. There were happy games of forfeits, "opinions and comparisons," "cities," our "neighbors," complex charades, the "ring," and "madam sent one hundred rubles, buy what you want, don't say what it is and don't refer to black or white." Someone would begin playing the piano and we would dance. There were young women as well. Some had also come from Siberia to pursue higher education for women while others were my sister's friends who were studying at the first women's *gimnazium* near Strastnoi Convent. My sister was five years older than I.

Of course, in such an atmosphere there could not but be romances and infatuations. But at that time, this was of no interest to me. I even despised such things. I would repeat a phrase I had heard somewhere that "in courting there is something dog-like." But how could this not occur in the midst of joyful, lively, and boisterous youth? Only later did I find out about the "hopeless loves" which, as it turns out, were being played out before my eyes. Two students were in love with my sister (she was very attractive). One was the brilliant and handsome Mikhnovskii from Irkutsk, the other—our fat bumpkin Kolia Ocheredin, who resembled a Siberian bear. My sister rejected them both and married a doctor whom she met on the Black Sea.

Presumably, there were other romances. I recall that my sister had striking friends. One was a blonde (Davydova) with large eyes and a long braid. Another was a fiery Jewish brunette with a bright blush (Gortikova). Incidentally, I met her later while in emigration in Paris and together we recalled the distant days. She was then a mother of two adult sons and nothing remained of her former beauty. She had become a short, hunched old woman. My sister's best friend Bibochka Bari (Anna Aleksandrovna) was enormously popular. She was the oldest daughter in the very large family of Aleksandr Veniaminovich Bari, an Americanized engineer. He owned the Moscow factory where the famous Shukhov boilers were manufactured. Bibochka was a cheerful, plump blonde who radiated health and joy. My older brother Kesha was hopelessly in love with her. But only we, his brothers, knew of this and teased him unmercifully. Later she married Samoilov, a professor of physiology.

Late in the evening, after the dancing, there was always supper—*pirogi* [deep-dish pies] with meat, *pirogi* with fish, *pirogi* with [sautéed] cabbage, pickled mushrooms, hors-d'oeuvres and, of course, tea again—many cups and glasses of tea.

We, younger children, were never sent to our rooms. We had equal rights, participated in all the games, and stayed with the guests until the end. At supper I even had my own specialty: I masterfully cut the Swiss cheese into pieces as thin as paper. Because of this expertise, the students foretold a career as surgeon for me. My mother smiled, pleased: she wanted me to be a doctor.

Besides these weekly Saturday get-togethers, two or three times a year we had real balls. Sometimes there were even masquerade balls (on Christmas or Shrovetide). In those cases a ballroom pianist was hired and the pies and *kulebiakas* were ordered in a pastry shop. Usually there were fifty or so guests at these balls—sometimes more, and always there were young people. We danced to exhaustion through the night until morning. We always had a large apartment, and the dances were organized in several adjoining rooms. The adroit dancers waltzed from one room into another. After the quadrille, we would organize a "gran-pon" where all the dancers, holding hands, would race down the hallways, through the bedrooms and the nursery, bumping into chairs, and maneuvering between tables. I remember that once all the [pre-Lenten Carnival] mummers were dressed up in cooks' costumes with white chef's caps—this was quite striking and gay. There was much noise and laughter. The cook, the dishwasher, and even the caretaker looked on admiringly from the dark vestibule and the corridor at the merry guests.

I was the youngest in our family. Besides my sister Anna, I had two older brothers. Now I am the last of the clan. My oldest brother Innokentii (Kesha) died from tuberculosis in Paris in 1935, having contracted this disease in the difficult conditions of émigré life. My other brother, Mikhail, who was two years older, was executed by the Bolsheviks in 1920 simply for the fact that he had once been an officer (a second lieutenant in the reserves), doing his military service under the old regime. He was never involved in politics. For twenty years, I've heard nothing of my sister who remained in Russia. All my cautious attempts to find out anything about her were in vain.

It would be unfair for me, in telling of my family, not to mention our nanny because she occupied a place in it and even played a significant role. She was, of course, a member of the family as well. This occurred very frequently in Russian families. Entering a strange family, frequently at a very young age and looking after a first child, then a second, and then after all of them, the nanny became an organic member of that family. She became attached to its life with all her soul, frequently forgetting or rejecting her own. And if she had heart and character, she would not only leave a lifetime mark in the soul of each child but would become a valued, sometimes invaluable member of the family to which she had tied her own life and fate.

This was our Nanny precisely—and I capitalize this word because in our family this designation of a profession became a proper name. Her real name was Avdot'ia (Evdokiia) Zakharovna Gorelova. At first, we just called her Dunia, but out of respect for her, mother made us call her Niania [Nanny]. That is what we then called her for the rest of our lives. That is how she is imprinted on my soul. Nanny was twelve or thirteen when the serfs were emancipated. She remembered serfdom well and told us stories about it. It should be said, however, that she told us no horror tales—she lived under serfdom without being aware of it. (She was from Smolensk Province.)

While still a very young woman, probably in 1874, she came to Moscow from her village to earn some money. She had just given birth to her son whom she left behind in the village. (I did not know who her husband was or whether he was still alive. I only knew her brother, Gavriil Zakharovich, a Moscow cabbie who always stood on the Bol'shaia Dmitrovka in front of the merchants club. He would visit her for tea. This was a large, fat man with a very red face. He would drink innumerable glasses of tea in her room—until "the seventh sweat." This was the primary treat his sister could give him.)

It was natural in her situation to seek work as a wet nurse in a respectable home. So she showed up at Smolensk Square in Moscow where servants were hired in those naive times. It was there that Uncle Kolia saw her. He was looking for a wet nurse for his brother's wife, i.e., for my mother who was expecting her first child. In her youth, Nanny was a true Russian beauty if we are to judge by a photograph taken in our home which we saved. She was in a magnificent costume of a Russian wet nurse with wide tunic sleeves, decked in lace and ribbons, an embroidered shirt and several strings of beads. My oldest sister Mania, who died in childhood, was in her arms. It was said that Uncle Kolia was a great judge of female beauty, so it was natural that he would choose Nanny [as nurse] for his sister-in-law. From that moment on, until her death in 1908, Nanny lived in our family, having no other and not having one of her own. She nursed my oldest sister, then moved to Ania [Anna] and each of us in order. Later she reared my sister's children. She took care of us, was inseparable from us, and sat at the bedside when one of us, children, was sick.

I remember her from my very first moment of recall. Remembering my childhood illnesses, I always visualize her at the head of the bed. I would twist under her rough, kind hand as she rubbed me down with butter melted in a spoon over a candle flame. It tickles, it makes me laugh, it's hot and I complain and fidget. She quivers and groans as if she is ticklish too, and this makes me feel better. "Oh, oh, things are so hard for Afoniushka (she always had humorous catch-phrases from the village which seemed to be free improvisations to us) . . . there, that's the way Volodiushka... now your little hands and feet are resting . . . soon you'll be healthy again and running around the yard." And one fell sweetly asleep to her stories. She knew many of them and we knew them by heart from her, but we still kept insisting that she tell them to us again. She would wake us in the morning clapping her hands: "Wake up kids, the buns are ready!"

Nanny was illiterate and all of us children, in turn, taught her reading and writing. But nothing came of this. She remembered the letters and could point out each of them in a book. She even could pronounce syllables but could not combine them into a word no matter how hard we tried. She remained illiterate until her death. But I am convinced that she had a huge influence on all of us, perhaps just a touch less than that of mother, though perhaps equal to hers. Most of all she loved Misha, the second brother in age and likely the least fortunate of all the children. Maybe that is why she loved him more then the others. As a child, he was ill more than the rest of us and endured all the various childhood diseases. Perhaps he also reminded her of her own son Vania who grew up in the village. He was also a sickly child. Having grown up and come to Moscow, he, like Misha, was not distinguished by exemplary behavior and was "good-for-nothing," as she called him. When Misha was in military service ("Mishutka, Mishutka, this is no joke!") and had to go to the barracks very early in the morning before daybreak, Nanny would wake him and give him tea. At night she would clean his dress uniform, the buttons, the buckle, and the boots. And she was absolutely right when she would later say in all seriousness: "When Mishen'ka and I served in the army . . ."

As I recall all that I have lived through and reconstruct the past in my mind, I can only come to the conclusion that our family was a happy one.

I am not sure of the reasons, but in our family I developed in a way different from my brothers and sister. Our family was of the middle class not only in terms of income, but also according to its habits and its overall moral atmosphere. Nobody was absorbed in social issues, and politics were of absolutely no interest to anyone. My sister graduated from the *gimnazium*, attended the women's institute where she studied history and literature, and then married a doctor. She moved to the Black Sea and began to raise her own family there. Both my brothers were enrolled in the Alexander Commercial Institute on Staraia Basmannaia [Street]. From my father's perspective, this was perfectly natural. What else would the sons of a merchant be other than businessmen? Additionally, my eldest brother also graduated from the Moscow Imperial Technical College and earned a diploma in mechanical engineering. But he became a merchant and entered my father's business. My other brother—the "good for nothing"—did not feel the need to further his studies upon graduating from the Alexander Commercial Institute. Both of them led fairly dissipated lives and caused periodic trouble for our parents. Their friends were of little interest, especially those of Mikhail (whom the Bolsheviks later executed). This was how the youth of that circle lived, without any special spiritual interests.

I am not sure of the circumstances which made me different. From my youngest years, my biggest joy was to find an interesting book and hide somewhere. I could read a book for many hours. I can still recall the sensation: you sit for hours in an easy chair in a quiet living room—everything else is forgotten. Nothing outside of the book exists. Suddenly I am called to dinner or for something else. I would immediately come to myself as if recovering from some hallucination and look around without recognizing the familiar surroundings. My brothers laughed at me. Once I found a note pinned above my bed which read: "Philosopher—king of donkeys." (My brothers teased me by calling me "donkey" since I had protruding ears in childhood.)

Father would get angry because I would always arrive for family tea with a book. I would put it next to my place setting and try to read so as not to waste time over tea. Indignantly he would say, "And your books are all unusual, big and thick." (At that time, as I recall, I was reading Buckle's *A History of Civilization in England* in Pavlenkov's large edition.) I gobbled up many books in childhood—and probably did not understand many of them properly. But of those which I understood, I clearly remember *Robinson Crusoe, Gulliver's Travels*, Stevenson's *Treasure Island*, Verne's *The Mysterious Island*, and *20,000 Leagues Under the Sea*, Tolstoy's *Childhood, Adolescence and Youth* and *The Cossacks,* Emar, Mayne Reid, Cooper, Walter Scott, [Pushkin's] *The Captain's Daughter*, Gogol and Turgenev.

Here in America, every time that I see a group of school children in a museum under the supervision of a teacher, and see how they address their instructors with friendliness and trust, I become envious. We in Russia, at least my generation, did not experience this. During our school years there was always an abyss between us and our teachers. Even worse than an abyss— enmity which often turned into hatred. We did not like or respect out teachers and they, in turn, were deeply indifferent to us. Why this occurred I do not know, but I think the fault lay less with us than with the teachers. We, schoolchildren, were like the children of other countries during all times, i.e., children with good and bad inclinations. Like soft wax, we could have been molded into anything desired. But the majority of our teachers were poor pedagogues and educators.

Here is one of my first impressions of *gimnazium*. This, likely, was one or two weeks after I entered the *gimnazium*. I was then nine years old. What will children at that age do when forty of them are gathered in one room and left to themselves? Obviously, the first thing is to be naughty! This is as natural as for a school of fish to splash and gambol in the water. And should play exceed the limits of the permissible, a smart teacher should stop the overly zealous kids and explain to them why their fooling around was excessive and intolerable. Punishment should be meted out only after they disobeyed the rules.

All of this is elementary. But in our class, the following occurred. One of our pranksters thought up an amusement: he made a tube of paper and then, as from an air gun, shot chewed up blotting paper from it. If such a "bullet" hit a wall or ceiling, it stuck firmly. This activity was very absorbing and soon the ceiling in our classroom was covered with stars and constellations of red paper. I also participated in this joyous activity. Of course, this exceeded the boundaries of innocent play, but it is unlikely that this breach could be called a serious crime. Our class mentor thought otherwise. He did not attempt to explain to us why this mischief was unacceptable—he was only interested in who the offenders were. We, however, remained tight-lipped. Nobody made an admission or betrayed each other. For a long time he demanded confession and the remanding of the guilty. We remained resolute and among us there were no cowards or traitors. Then he turned to cunning and announced that, this being the first time, he forgave the guilty in advance. He simply was requesting that an admission be made so that he would know who was capable of doing this—the guilty would not be punished. We went for the bait and trustingly made the admission. Among those confessing was me. How bewildered—no, horrified—we were, when, despite the mentor's solemn promise, we were cruelly punished. We were left after school for two hours in a locked room! I recall that most of all we took this as a moral blow. Our mentor had made a promise, which we believed, and had fooled us right there on the spot. From this moment on, we would have no faith in our teachers.

In the eight years that I spent in the *gimnazium*, our relationship with our teachers was pretty much one of open civil war. Almost none of them were able to interest us in their subject. We felt that Greek and Latin were invented merely to torture us. Even the instructor in Russian language and literature, though he was Vladimir Ivanovich Shenrok, a Gogol scholar, could not engage us. Geography was a dead science—the mere enumeration of geographic names. It was particularly unpleasant when the "mute" map hung before us. On it we had to name and identify the mountain ranges, oceans and rivers of the world's five parts. Physics seemed a useless fabrication to us, as did, cosmography. I had a visceral revulsion for mathematics and, in all honesty, to this day cannot understand why we had to learn spherical geometry, trigonometry, Newtonian binomials, and suffer over logarithms. Even history failed to interest us.

We studied all of this only because it was demanded of us and the teachers taught it because that was the educational program dictated by the Ministry of Education.

When, as an adult, I began to study classical antiquity anew, I bitterly lamented that even those little bits of Greek and Latin which I absorbed in my *gimnazium* years, were almost totally forgotten. How I would love now to re-read and hear the commentaries of Caesar, Ovid, Virgil and Horace, Plato, and especially Homer! I had read all of this once, but it was all a dead letter, "lessons" to which I had to respond, and which I could either learn or not. Why did no one interest us in this, or even try? Forget about inculcating a love for the subject. One may ask, who was at fault here? Of course, it was not us, the school children, but our teachers and our lifeless and deadening school system.

The most fearful and unpleasant memories were of our history teacher—Viacheslav Vladimirovich Smirnov. This was a small and very quiet person with a short, dark beard. All his movements were in slow motion, his voice quiet. But he was the terror of the whole *gimnazium*. We all feared and hated him fiercely. He was very demanding. We had to be ready for anything that he might ask that was covered over the whole year. He never corrected the student, never interrupted him, or asked him to repeat. He waited—sometimes with malicious glee—until the student became entangled or stopped altogether.

Frequently, the following took place. He would call on a student—he always made him come to the front: "Kananov!" Kananov, a tall and confident student, a dandy, wearing an inordinately wide leather belt, would willingly jump from his seat. He would push his way along the long desk, hop loudly to the floor and walk to the front of the room. There he would assume an almost defiant pose, jutting one leg forward and shoving a hand inside his belt. "Tell me," the "historian" would say quietly, "about the events in Russia during the period of the War of the Roses in England." The question was a tricky one—it required knowledge of Russian and English history. Kananov remained silent and so did Viacheslav Vladimirovich. (A deathly silence always reigned in his classes because he noticed everything, saw all, and punished severely.) A minute would pass, then two. The silence became tense, unbearable to the class. Kananov put his other foot forward. Just as quietly, as if he had finished listening to Kananov, the "historian" would say: "Now, tell us how Alcibiades governed." Kananov immediately would liven up and begin in a confident tone: "Alcibiades was rich and famous. Nature endowed him generously with many talents . . ." and then suddenly he stopped, as if stumbling. Again the torturous silence. Kananov was terrorized and failed to comprehend anything. "The War of the Roses . . . what happened in Russia at that time? . . . Alcibiades . . . he was also, supposedly, famous for cutting off the tail of his favorite dog?" "Enough" the teacher would say dispassionately. Next to Kananov's name in the grade book, at the very center of the list, he would, with a slight movement of the hand visible to the whole class mark a "one" or "the stake" (i.e., the lowest grade). Poor Kananov would return to his seat, this time without any boldness.

A strange thing: in my eight years at the *gimnazium* I don't ever remember even one student having a friendly, purely human relationship with a teacher. We had nothing to do with our teachers outside of class. They never went with us to museums, galleries, or the theater. We studied our lessons, they quizzed us on them—that was the limit of our relationship. To me, this now seems impossible, but that is precisely how it was. I know that later the reciprocity between students and teachers in primary schools and *gimnaziums* was different. I heard stories about other *gimnaziums* (not those run by the state, but the private ones) where friendships between teachers and students were developed. In my case, however, things were exactly as I described them, even more so. This was the situation prevalent in our generation.

Despite everything said above, I nevertheless harbor good feelings and a grateful remembrance of the years spent in the *gimnazium*. Those years gave me much. They laid the foundation of my future life. But it is not the *gimnazium* that I must thank for this.

Herzen, in *My Past and Thoughts*, once expressed surprise as to why so much attention is given to first love in biographies, but that the first childhood friendship is rarely mentioned. Herzen, in recalling Ogarev, wrote: "I do not know why there is a monopoly of the memories of first love over the recollection of a youthful friendship." I am prepared to reiterate this observation. In any case, in my life, my first friendship played an enormous role, perhaps even the determining one, for my whole life.

His last name was Gorozhankin, and his name was Sergei. His father was professor of botany at the University of Moscow and director of the Botanical Garden. We quickly became friends. My other friend—even closer to me and one who had a decisive influence on me during those years—was of a completely different character and type. He had a large, irregular mouth, and dark fiery eyes. Were it not for his eyes, he would be unnoticeable. But when he became carried away—which happened quite frequently—and spoke of that which was precious and of interest to him, while ruffling his short hair with his right hand, his eyes burned like coals. Usually he stayed away from everyone and only during a fight would he dive into the center of the pack oblivious of the blows which rained on him from all sides.

I didn't notice him for a long time. But, having accidentally talked to him at length once, I was convinced that he read a lot and that his favorite books and authors coincided with mine. This instantly drew us together. We started walking home together from school and had endless conversations on the way. His name was Evgenii Voronov. In contrast to Gorozhankin and me, he did poorly in school. So poorly, that he was kept back for a second year in several classes and managed to stay behind for a third year in the fourth grade. Thus, Gorozhankin and I quickly passed him in grade. Finally, he was even expelled for his lack of achievement. Meanwhile, this was a smart and capable boy—even talented, it may be said. In any case, he was smarter and more talented than many of our "top students" whose names adorned the gold board [of honor]. Whenever he was called to respond to a lesson, he would invariably become dull and unintelligible. That was how he was perceived by all the teachers. I do not know the explanation for this.

What were the things that interested and linked us? Even now, I cannot fathom how boys of twelve to fourteen years old could have had the interests that we did then. We devoured an incredible number of books and lived in a state of feverish enthusiasm—shifting from one captivation to another. We read Adam Smith and Mill (always with Chernyshevskii's commentary), Darwin, Buckle. We studied astronomy; our idol was Tolstoy; we were fascinated by Chekhov. In Voronov's room, which was always filled with a multitude of books, there was a table on which the latest books lay—he called them "my sins." These were the books which he had to read first. This was pretty much the case with me as well. In imitation of Chekhov's story "Whist," we invented our own special card game. Essentially, this was the simplest of games which children called the "game of drunks." Its special feature was that instead of having four suits, we had four categories—belles-lettres, the socio-political, science and art. Rather than having face cards we had writers, publicists or public figures, scientists and artists. Tolstoy, Uspenskii, Chekhov, Darwin, and Beethoven were aces and the others followed according to rank. This game engaged us because we changed our aces and kings in relationship to our current enthrallments and had heated arguments and debates on this issue.

We overthrew our idols frequently, but in the end always came to an agreement. The one irreplaceable ace was always Tolstoy. The leading role in these arguments was played by Voronov. He was the most inquisitive among us, and Gorozhankin and I usually deferred to his ardor and pressure. I remember that for a time we were fascinated by Malthus. But then we realized that, in essence, his law of demographics was a deeply reactionary invention—and we threw him down in shame. He was replaced by Henry George with *Progress and Poverty*. It seemed that he supplied the key to solving all of humanity's social ills. I recall that right during the period of my fascination with Henry George, who saw all mankind's ills in land ownership and land tenancy, my father bought land in the Caucasus, and I experienced horrible moral suffering because of it. But, Henry George, too, was later removed from the pedestal. Our circle of interests was very broad. We even reached Herbert Spencer though, as Voronov said, his *Psychology* was as unpleasant to read as was the cod liver oil which had to be taken daily. The social sciences, such as economics and sociology, were of particular interest to us. I think that there was much in these books that we did not understand. But we took these books by storm, the way in which a fortress was attacked.

Our moral development instinctively paralleled the development of Russian societal opinion. We worshiped the Decembrists, knew lines from Ryleev by heart, were captivated by the 40's, and, as a substitute for their idealism, we accepted the nihilism and realism of the 60's. This was followed by a reaching out to the people and the recognition that we must serve them, the discharge of societal obligations, and the rejection of privileges. Secretly, I even imposed strict limitations on myself—I slept under a light blanket, refused sweets and other extras.

For a long time our idol was Mikhailovskii who was then writing and battling in the journals with a nascent Marxism. We waited impatiently, as if for an event, for each issue of *Russkoe Bogatstvo*. We would go to the journal's office, located near the Nikitskie Vorota [Gates], in order to receive it directly from the office manager. Someone told us that this was likely the uncle of Gleb Uspenskii, who was then in an institution for the mentally ill. We were especially fascinated by Mikhailovskii's theory of progress, by his doctrine of "hero and crowd."

Something that gave a specific edge to our intellectual concerns was the constant striving to apply each new discovery to everyday life and to engrained habits. We found the roots of animism and beliefs peculiar to primitive people, as well as countless survivals of the past, in contemporary society. We mocked these fiercely and applied the "hero—crowd" theory to everyday life. We would, in so doing, cite Taylor's two-volume *History of Primitive Culture*, Malthus, Henry George, Darwin, Spencer, and Mikhailovskii. The leading role in all of these obsessions was played by Voronov. He was the most temperamental, impatient, and fervent, the same Voronov who was expelled from the *gimnazium* for being "dull" and an "underachiever." Together, the three of us wrote letters to Leo Tolstoy, Chekhov, Mikhailovskii—we posed questions to them, expressed our enthusiasm and support and sometimes even criticized them. And what is most astonishing, we received replies from them. It is unlikely that they suspected they were dealing with fourteen to fifteen year old youths!

From the very beginning, social problems were at the very heart of our aspirations: thoughts of how society could be better governed, a society in which injustice could be seen at every step. How was humanity to achieve universal happiness? We knew that human life was short, that banality could soon crush us in its grasp, the way it crushed all those who had reached the age of thirty. So we rushed to effect our ideas into an actual project. We began to publish a [political] journal.

As I noted, Voronov undoubtedly had some troubles with the police and this forced my mother to request that I stop corresponding with him. But then my time came. When I was in the eighth year [final year of the *gimnazium*] and eighteen years old, my father received a summons to the *Okhrana* [secret police]. He was invited there for a discussion along with me. This was not much of a surprise for either him or me. I did not hide my political convictions from my family and my parents knew that I was growing up a revolutionary. Totally uninterested in politics themselves, they were very tolerant in this matter. Sometimes we even conversed on the issues, though very rarely, and even argued. But both mother and father were respectful of my views.

As I and my father were walking to the *Okhrana* department (this was February 1899), he coughed a few times (which was a sign of worry) and said: "Of course, I don't know what they'll be talking to us about. You must have gotten into some mischief. So don't be offended if I yell at you a little bit for propriety's sake!" I promised that I wouldn't.

A captain of the gendarmes greeted us at the *Okhrana*. This was my first encounter with the "blue uniform" which I already despised. "Young man," the captain said to me triumphantly, "we are aware of all your contacts with the revolutionaries who are abroad. I consider it necessary to forewarn you that if you continue these contacts in the future, you risk serious consequences." Turning to my father he said, "And I would ask you to pay more attention to your son's upbringing and behavior." Evidently, this upset my father who, instead of scolding me as he had intended, suddenly said: "I don't know what you are talking about, but I must say that I am proud of my son." This was a complete surprise for me as well. "You and I don't know," the captain replied, "but he (tossing his head in my direction) knows very well!" This was said in such a manner that I involuntarily looked closely into the captain's eyes—in them I read anger and hatred.

As we were returning home, father said with irritation: "Of course, from their point of view it would be better if you were involved in debauchery and drunkenness! Scoundrels!"

I was very pleased. I cannot but observe now that at that time even the "blue uniforms" were humane compared to many of our contemporary heroes who cloak themselves in a humanitarian mantle. They certainty had material evidence of my "criminal" contacts with revolutionaries abroad (intercepted letters from and to me) but they did not wish to destroy a youth. Later this became even more clearly apparent.

It was the spring of 1899. I was taking final examinations. I did not break off my foreign contacts; I just became more careful while my political convictions continued developing along the same lines. I already had a small collection of forbidden books: Kennan's *Siberia and the Exile System,* Kautsky's *Erfurt Program,* Renan's *Life of Jesus,* Bebel's *Women and Socialism*—all in German. I gave them to my father for safekeeping and he kept them for me at one of his storage facilities (he definitely knew from me what he was hiding). I asked him to bring them home to me the next day. He promised to do so. This was the 19th of May, on the eve of my Russian language exam. I slept peacefully before a dangerous and difficult ordeal.

In our apartment, my room was the last one. It could only be reached by going through my brother Mikhail's room. For some reason, I had always locked my door. Suddenly in my sleep I clearly heard the sound of spurs and then a loud knocking on the door. I immediately guessed what the matter was and managed to take Voronov's last letter from the table, crinkle it up and shove it into my mouth. Then I opened the door. Standing on the threshold was the same captain who had talked to my father and me at the *Okhrana*. Behind him was a suspicious looking character who turned out to be a detective in the *Okhrana,* and our caretaker Egor, a close friend of mine who had been invited along as a "witness."

"We have an injunction for a search and seizure here," the captain told me politely. And he showed me a written order signed by the director of the *Okhrana.* "Please." Both drawers of my desk were opened and all my letters taken. My large bookcase drew careful attention but nothing incriminating was found. Renan's book *Life of Jesus,* which I had received from abroad, went unnoticed, and this made me gloat. The night visitors went through my things for no less than three hours. Finally, they placed the seized items into a large packet and sealed it with wax. They then wrote a report of the search and forced me and Egor, the caretaker, to sign it. He wrote an X instead of a signature.

When we were passing through the dining room we found our whole family there in their nightclothes. My mother was in her nightgown. The captain and the detective walked ceremoniously through the room and, in parting, the captain said to my father: "It doesn't appear that we have found anything incriminating in your son's possession, but I do direct your attention to the tendentiousness of his book selections." My father did not answer and merely escorted him out of the apartment with an unfriendly look. Afterwards, neither my parents, sister, or brothers said anything to me, but I read no disapproval in their faces. What would have happened if I had asked my father to bring me my revolutionary collection a day earlier and it had been discovered during the search?

I could sleep no more that night. I doubt that my parents slept either. I went to the *gimnazium* in the morning for I had a difficult exam to take. I went to the examination that spring morning with a special feeling, a consciousness of the significance of what had occurred that night, and with a heightened sense of respect for myself. I did not, of course, say anything to any of my friends but, I must admit, I looked at them with a certain sense of superiority.

The exam went well. I had to write on the topic of "Positive Characters in the Works of Pushkin" (this was the so-called "Pushkin Year"—the centennial of his birth). I passed the exam. And I also passed all of the other exams. I graduated from the *gimnazium* and attained the diploma. For this I was obliged, after all, to the "blue uniforms" who allowed me to graduate from the *gimnazium*.

Now the doors of the university were open to me. But during the winter just passed, a different decision was coming to fruition within me. In some newspapers, and then in Mikhailovskii's *Russkoe Bogatstvo*, I read that a new socialist university had opened in Brussels. There classes were taught not only by leading Belgian and French scholars, but also by leaders of the workers' and socialist movements. So this intention entered my soul, to bypass a Russian university and go to Europe, to the sources of science, socialism, and revolution! When I approached my parents with this project, I was surprised that there were no particular objections. The decisive argument turned out to be my supposition that I would not be able to study at a Russian university anyway, because of the recurrent student disturbances—they were occurring yearly. My parents could not but agree with the logic of my arguments. My educational career was decided: I was allowed to go to Brussels.

Chapter Eight

Vasilii Nikiforov-Volgin, Presanctified Gifts

Vasilii Nikiforov-Volgin was born in 1900. Originally from the Volga region, his family moved to Russia's Baltic coast in search of a better life. When he started writing, Nikiforov used the pseudonym "Volgin" in honor of his original homeland. The son of a poor cobbler, he obtained his principal education in the Orthodox Church. His vignettes, two books of which were published during his lifetime, often dealt with the Soviet persecution of religion. After the USSR annexed the Baltic nations, Nikiforov-Volgin was arrested in May 1941 and executed six months later. Taken from Vasilii Nikiforov-Volgin, *Zemlia imeninnitsa* [The Earth's Nameday]. Tallinn, n.d.

After a lengthy reading of the *Hours* and prayers on bent knee, the choir in the apse began to sing in a solemn, grieving tone:

> In thy kingdom remember us, O Lord,
> When thou comest into thy kingdom.

The liturgy with the majestic and mysterious name of "Presanctified" began in a manner that was unusual. The altar and the *amvon*[1] were in the bright light of the March sun. According to the calendar, spring was to set in tomorrow.

Joyfully, like a prayer I kept repeating the word, stretching it: spri-i-ing! I went up to the *amvon*, lowered my hands into the sun's rays, bent my head to the side and watched the "sunspots" dance on my hands. I tried to catch them, but they wouldn't give in. The sexton, who happened by, tapped me on the arm and said, "Quit playing." I was taken aback, and began crossing myself.

After the reading of the first Exclamation the royal doors were opened. Everyone got on their knees with their heads bowed to the very ground. Into the noiseless silence stepped a priest carrying a lit taper and the censer. With the holy flame he made the sign of the cross over the bowed congregation and proclaimed: "Wisdom, O believers! The light of Christ illumineth all." My friend Vit'ka [Vitalii] came up and whispered barely audibly: "Kol'ka [Nikolai] is going to sing now . . . listen, it will be terrific."

Kol'ka lives in our court-yard. He's only nine but he already sings in the choir. Everyone praises him, and we kids envy him but treat him with respect. Now three boys came on to the *amvon*, with Kol'ka among them. They're all in sky-blue robes with gold crosses and remind us of the three adolescent martyrs stepping into the fiery furnace to suffer in the name of the Lord. It became very, very quiet in the church and only the silver censer trembled in the hand of the priest. The three boys sang in pure voices, fragile as crystal: "Let my prayer arise in thy sight as incense . . . Receive the voice of my prayer . . . Let the lifting up of my hands be an evening sacrifice."

Kol'ka's voice soars higher and higher like a bird and may drop at any moment, like a spring icicle, to shatter into minuscule crystals. I listen and think: "I ought to join the choir myself. They'll put a dressy robe on me as well and have me sing . . . I'll walk out into the center of the church and the priest will cense in my direction and everyone will look and say to themselves: 'Way to go, Vasia! What a great kid!'" And father and mother will be glad that they have such a clever son.

They sing; the priest first censes the altar, then the table of oblation; the whole church in the smoke of the censer seems to be amidst the clouds.

Even Vit'ka, the foremost rowdy in our yard, has grown quiet. With mouth wide-open he is staring at the sky-blue boys, and his hair is lit by a ray of light.

"You have golden hair," I tell him. He didn't hear me right and said:

"Yes, my voice isn't bad, but it's a little husky, otherwise I'd be singing." [In Russian the words for "voice" and "hair" are similar, "golos" and "volos."] An old woman came up to us and said, "Quiet, you rowdies."

During the [procession called the] Great Entrance, instead of the usual "Cherubic Hymn" the choir sang: "Now the powers of heaven with us invisibly do minister. For lo! The King of Glory entereth now. Behold the mystical sacrifice, all accomplished, is ushered in."

Very, very quietly, in the most soundless silence, the priest carried the Sacred Gifts from the table of oblation to the altar table while everyone stood on bent knee with heads bowed, even the choir.

And when the Sacred Gifts had been brought over, the choir movingly sang: "Let us with faith and love draw near, that we may become partakers of life everlasting."

The royal doors were then closed and the sanctuary curtain was drawn only half way which struck Vit'ka and myself as especially odd.

Vit'ka whispered to me: "Go tell the sexton that the curtain isn't drawn right."

I obeyed Vit'ka and went up to the sexton who was removing candle-ends from candlesticks. "Uncle Maxim," I said, "the curtain's all wrong."

The sexton looked at me from beneath his shaggy brows and snapped angrily, "You're the one person they should have asked! It's supposed to be that way."

After the liturgy was over, Vit'ka cajoled me into going to the grove. "There's snowdrops there, millions of them," he said in a high voice.

The grove was outside of town, near the river. We went through the perfumed early spring air, through glistening puddles and sun-gilded mud and sang off key but at full blast the prayer which had just echoed in church: "Let my prayer arise . . ." and almost had a fight over whose voice was better.

But then in the grove, which hummed in a special spring-like manner, we discovered the quiet, pale blue baubles of snowdrops, and for some unknown reason embraced each other, and then the whole grove resounded with our shouting and laughter. What it was we shouted and why we shouted we didn't know.

After that we walked home with little bouquets of snowdrops dreaming how good it would be to join the church choir, to don a sky-blue robe and sing, "Let my prayer arise."

A RADIANT EASTER SERVICE

The song from the day's liturgy was ebbing: "All human flesh is silenced as it awaits with fear and trembling."

The evening land was growing quiet. At home the glass doors of the icon cases were being opened. I asked father: "What is that for?"

"It is a sign. It signifies that at Easter the gates of heaven are opened."

Father and I wanted to get some sleep before the midnight service but couldn't. We lay side by side on the bed as he told me how once as a boy he happened to celebrate Easter in Moscow.

"A Moscow Easter, my boy, is a mighty event. Who has seen it once shall remember it to his grave. The huge bell from Ivan the Great [the name of a belfry] gives its first thunderclap at midnight and it seems that heaven with all its stars falls to the earth. And the bell, my boy, was six thousand *poods* [216,000 lbs.], and it took twelve men to get it swinging. The first clap would be timed to the striking of the clock in the Spasskii Tower."

Father rose up in bed and talked of Moscow in a trembling voice: "Yes . . . the Spasskii Tower clock . . . It would strike twelve and immediately a rocket would soar toward the heavens . . . and then the firing of the old cannons on Tainitskii Tower would commence: a hundred and one rounds.

"The ringing from Ivan the Great would spread like a sea over Moscow and the other forty-forties[2] would do second part harmony, like so many rivers in spring flood. Such a powerful force would flow over the ancient city that you weren't walking but bobbing on the waves like a small chip of wood. A mighty night it was, resembling God's thunder. Oh, my son, words can't describe Moscow at Easter."

Father grew quiet and closed his eyes.

"Are you asleep?"

"No. I'm looking at Moscow."

"Where is it?"

"Right here before my eyes. As if alive."

"Tell me something else about Easter."

"I also had the chance to celebrate Easter in a monastery. In its simplicity and sacred beauty it was even better than Moscow. The monastery itself was extraordinary, surrounded by a virgin forest with only the paths of various beasts, and by the monastery gates, the splashing of a small river. The trees of the taiga forest peered into it. The church was built of stout logs redolent of pitch. A great multitude of the faithful from surrounding villages would gather there for the radiant celebration. A most rare tradition was practiced there. After the service, maidens carrying candles would stream toward the river singing, "Christ has risen from the dead . . ." They would bow to the river waters, then affix the candles to wooden roundlets of wood and float them down the river one after another. A portent was anticipated: if the candle remained alight, the maiden would marry; if it went out, she'd spend her years in bitter loneliness.

"Just imagine what a wonder that was: a hundred flames floating on the water in the middle of the night, the bells joyously ringing, and the forest sighing."

"Enough reminiscing, you two," mother broke in, "you'd better get some rest or you'll be standing in church like sleepyheads."

But I couldn't sleep. My soul was gripped by a presentiment of something inexpressibly grand resembling either Moscow or the hundred candles floating along a forest river. I got out of bed and began pacing the floor, disturbing my mother's work in the kitchen, constantly asking whether it was time for church.

"Will you quit buzzing around like an out-of-joint spinning wheel," she gently chastised me. "If you can't wait, then go, but behave yourself over there."

It was two hours till the service but the courtyard around the church was full of kids. There wasn't a single cloud, no wind, and the night was frightening in its unusualness and grandeur. Tall Easter cakes covered with white napkins floated down the dark street; only they were visible; people seemed not to exist. In the dusky church, near the *Plashchanitsa* [a cloth representation of Christ's funeral shroud] stood a line of people desirous of reading the Acts of the Apostles. I joined the group and was asked: "Do you know how to read?"

"I do."

"Well, start reading then."

I went up to the lectern and began pronouncing the syllables[3] but stumbled over "Theophilios." I just couldn't get it out. I lost my confidence, stopped reading, and lowered my head in embarrassment. Someone came up to me and said: "If you can't read, you have no business here."

"I wanted to try it."

"You're better off trying Easter cakes," and they moved me aside.

I couldn't find a place to my liking in the church, so I went outside and sat on the steps.

"Where is Easter now?" I began to speculate. "Is it soaring in the heavens, or treading in the forest outside of town, through the marshes, on the fine needles of pine, on snowdrops, along the paths of heather and juniper, and what does it look like?"

I recalled a story that on the night of Christ's luminous resurrection, a ladder descends from heaven and down it comes the Lord to us with the Holy Apostles, saints, passion-bearers, and martyrs. The Lord walks throughout the land, blessing the fields, forests, lakes, rivers, birds, mankind, beasts and all that was created through His holy will, and the saints sing, "Christ is risen from the dead . . ." The song of the saints scatters like seed along the ground, and from these seeds fine-scented lilies-of-the-valley sprout in the forests.

Midnight was approaching. The courtyard was thick with human voices. Someone came out of the church-keeper's hut with a lantern.

"He's coming! He's coming!" the kids screamed madly, clapping their hands.

"Who's coming?"

"'Leksandr, the bell ringer. He's going to wham it now."

And he did. A huge silver wheel seemed to roll along the earth after the first strike of the bell, and then another wheel, and then a third, and the paschal darkness spun in the silver ringing of all the city's churches. Jacob, the beggar, noticed me in the darkness. "It's a light-bearing ringing," he said. "It's the sound of enlightenment," he said, and crossed himself several times.

The Matins service of Great Saturday began. Priests in white raiment raised up the *Plashchanitsa* and carried it into the sanctuary where it would lie on the altar until the feast of the Ascension. The heavy golden sepulchre was moved to its usual place with a rumbling sound. In that rumbling there was something paschal, significant. It was as if the heavy stone was being rolled away from the Lord's tomb.

I noticed my father and mother. Going up to them I said, "I will never offend you." And pressing myself to them, exclaimed, "What happiness!"

And the paschal joy kept rising like the Volga in flood, which father had described many times. The tall banners began to tremble like spring trees in a sunny breeze. People were getting ready for the procession around the church. The silver cross that stood behind the altar was brought out as was the gold-encased Gospel, and a great round bread—the artos.[4] The uplifted icons began to smile, and everyone took up a red, lit paschal candle.

Silence was upon us. It was transparent and so light that, if one were to blow on it, it would tremble like gossamer. And in the midst of this silence the choir slowly began: "The angels in heaven, O Christ our Savior, sing thy resurrection." And to this exalting song the procession began to stream in a sea of lights. My feet were stepped on; wax dripped on my head, but I hardly felt it, thinking, "That's the way it's supposed to be." It's Easter. The Lord's Easter—little "sunspots" danced in my soul. Pressed tightly to each other, in the midnight darkness, on the streams of the resurrection song, showered by the pealing bells and warmed by flames of the candles, we circled the church lit white by hundreds of flames and stopped in anticipation before the tightly shut doors. The bells grew still. My heart suppressed its beating. My face was afire. The earth disappeared from underfoot—I seemed to be standing on a heavenly blue. And where was everybody? They had all been transformed into exultant paschal candles.

And now that enormous event, which I could not encompass at first, occurred. They sang, "Christ is risen from the dead."

They sang it thrice, and the great doors threw themselves open before us. We entered the resurrected temple, and before our eyes, in the glow of the chandeliers, great and small votive lights, in the sparkling of silver, of the gold and precious stones on the icons, in the bright paper flowers on the Easter cakes—blazed up the Lord's Easter. The priest, wrapped in incense smoke, his face radiant, exclaimed joyfully and volubly: "Christ is risen!" and the people answered him with the tremor of a heavy snow avalanche: "Indeed, he is risen."

Grishka appeared next to me. I took both his hands and said, "Tomorrow I will give you a red egg. The best there is. Christ is risen." Fed'ka was standing nearby. I promised him a red egg as well. Then I saw Davyd, the yardman. I went up to him and said, "I'll never call you 'street sweeping martyr' again. Christ is risen."

All this time the words of the Easter canticle flew through the church like lightning:

> For meet is it that the heavens should rejoice, and that the earth should be glad, and that the whole world, both visible and invisible, should keep the Feast. For Christ is risen, the everlasting joy.

My heart contracted with joy; near the *amvon* I saw a girl with blond braids whom I had noticed at the Good Friday service. I went up to her in a dreamlike state, my face burning, and lowering my eyes said: "Christ is risen."

She was taken aback, dropped her candle, then quiet as a flame leaned to me and we kissed three times . . . and then, totally embarrassed, we stood a long time with our heads lowered.

And all that time from the *amvon* thundered the paschal sermon of St. John Chrysostom:

> "If any man be devout and loveth God, let him enjoy this fair and radiant triumphal feast . . . Christ is risen, and life reigneth!"

NOTES

1. In Orthodox churches the apse (referred to as the altar) is located on an elevated level (*amvon*) which extends beyond the icon screen (*ikonostas*, "ikonostasis" in Greek) out into the main space of the church. It is from here that the priest reads the Gospels and delivers the sermon. The word is derived from the Greek "ambon," (raised edge).

2. Tradition had it that there were 1600 churches in Moscow; it was customary to refer to them in units of forty.

3. Scripture was written not in Russian but in Old Church Slavonic; the relationship of OCS to contemporary Russian is somewhat analogous to the relationship of Chaucer's language to contemporary English.

4. The bread of eternal life. It is broken up and distributed on Saturday at the end of Easter ("Bright") Week.

Chapter Nine

Mark Vishniak, In Two Worlds

Mark Vishniak, who was trained in government law, was one of numerous highly educated Russians who joined the opposition to the monarchy. The events of 1905 pushed him into the camp of the Social Revolutionaries, an affiliation he was to maintain. However, his opposition to the Bolsheviks and the Russian Revolution of 1917 ultimately forced him into exile. As part of the Russian diaspora in Paris, where he arrived in 1919, Vishniak became a publicist and writer, helping to found and edit one of the more prominent journals there, the *Sovremennye zapiski* (Contemporary Notes). He authored a number of books, including a study of Lenin. Taken from Mark Vishniak, *Dan' proshlomu* [Tribute to the Past]. New York: Izd. Imeni Chekhova, 1954.

I cannot determine precisely what made the problem of personal guilt and responsibility primary in my consciousness. I was interested in this question for a long while. All the philosophers, legal philosophers, and criminologists with whom I became acquainted touched on this issue. The social side and the sociological school in criminal law and external conditions, wherein responsibility was not an issue, interested me less. But imputation and responsibility, guilt and misfortune were internally linked with morality and law as well as a human's biology and psychopathology. My attention was drawn to what, in pre-Freudian times, was referred to as moral insanity, i.e., the inability to distinguish right from wrong and resist amoral action. This was irrespective of whether one was conscious or not of the amorality of the deeds. A practical conclusion derives from this: philosophical speculation and jurisprudence were not enough to solve this basic problem. It was also necessary to know the nature of man, be it healthy or ill. But in order to "master" psychopathology, it was essential to take a course in medicine.

My legal studies did not take up much time or effort and I came up with the idea of combining jurisprudence with the simultaneous study of medicine in order to save time. But such a circumstance had been anticipated by the administration. The university office to which I went for the required paperwork explained that to be concurrently registered in two academic divisions was impermissible. The only solution was to continue the study of law in Moscow, and medicine—abroad. A romantic affair that had already commenced with my cousin Mania, my future wife, helped me to arrive at that decision. She had also chosen medicine as her field of education. She had no chance of entry into a Russian medical school without a medal [of academic excellence] and decided to go to Heidelberg. In three months, with my help, she was prepared for a supplemental exam in Latin. This was accomplished in approximately the same rapid-fire fashion that was used during World War II in the United States to train officers of the army and navy in Russian, Chinese, Malaysian and other languages.

Despite qualms, my parents nevertheless agreed to send me abroad and finance my trip. I was given only one mandatory condition: the university in which I was to enroll could not be the same one in which my cousin was to study. "Draper-Spencer" instilled the belief that marriages between close relatives did not lead to any good. And mother had good reason to fear that the event, which she definitely did not wish for me, might occur. I accepted the condition without hesitation, aware that the other university could well be close to mine. Let my cousin go to Heidelberg; I would go to Freiburg, only a three-hour ride away.

In the autumn of 1903, while still a third-year student in law school in Moscow, I left for Freiburg, in Baden, to study medicine. We left together with my cousin and my friend Boris Lunts, the son of a Moscow doctor to whom my family went in the event of a serious illness. I parted with my friends in Heidelberg, not without sorrow and sadness, and continued on the same train to Freiburg. It was not difficult to find a room and get set up—the charming town lived off its university and students. I set off for the post office to register my address in case I should get letters for general delivery. The clerk immediately gave me a telegram that was already waiting. It was from Heidelberg: my cousin informed me that she was leaving for Freiburg. I was amazed, happy, and saddened. It was unclear as to what had happened. The forthcoming meeting was gladdening while the cognizance of a broken promise was troubling.

The matter was a simple one. Heidelberg's medical school felt itself to be overburdened with female students and rejected the new entrants. My cousin had no choice other than to come to Freiburg, at least for mutual consultation as to what to do. Ultimately, it was not difficult to convince myself that a promise made under a set of totally different conditions cannot be considered binding. I kept my word honorably, but external circumstances proved stronger than I. I did not yet know the multi-leveled excuse of "rebus six stantibus" [given the current circumstances]. But I was already familiar with "force majeure," and that it was imperative to distinguish between "form" and "content" or essence.

It was much harder to convince my parents, to make them understand and believe everything had happened in precisely this way, that it was not the result of a plan worked out in advance.

As soon as my cousin was settled—in a room with a marvelous view of the famous Freiburg castle—we both took to the pen to inform our parents of the events. My parents were used to trusting me. "Our children don't lie," my mother liked to emphasize, boasting, and encouraging us to maintain our high reputation. And this tactic justified itself: I never deceived anyone. In the worst case, I stayed silent or did not speak the whole truth. But in this case, I sensed that I could not possibly convince them that all that had occurred was exactly as I described it and not contrived in advance. I attempted to make the letter reflect all the powers of conviction and sincerity that I possessed. But, nevertheless, I realized that had something similar happened to others, I would not have believed them myself. Everything happened too perfectly—this is not how things usually work.

I did not know to what degree my parents believed me. The withdrawal of fire and water, i.e. of the means necessary for my room, board, and tuition did not follow. In fact, I did not fear this. Our family relationships were too close. But there was no other reaction from my parents. They remained silent on this matter and this was, of course, the wisest thing, for even the sharpest rebuke would not have altered the situation.

My cousin and I were enrolled in the medical school without any complications. As required, she commenced with the natural sciences while I immediately became engrossed in anatomy. Professor Haup, a specialist on frogs who knew everything anyone had ever said or written about frogs, and who himself had published an enormous work called *The Frog*, was an excellent pedagogue. He attempted to provide a maximum amount of knowledge in the minimum amount of time to his students. Therefore, he arrived in class before the students and wrote a complete summary of his lecture on the blackboard. I worked for Haup in the anatomy laboratory—preparing a leg for experimental purposes, the names of the muscles of which I still remember to this day. I also attended the lectures of the famed August Weissman, an imposing elder of the Old Testament type. He captivatingly expounded his theory of heredity for which Soviet Lysenkoists posthumously labeled him a "formalist" and "obscurantist" in biology.

Like the rest of Russia, Moscow led a tense political life. But to a substantial degree it mirrored the life of St. Petersburg. The government was in St. Petersburg: Witte, Trepov, Durnovo, the grand dukes and the tsar. The central committees of the political parties were there. Finally, a new professional-political organization arose there and functioned legally—the Soviet of Workers Deputies. There was a branch in Moscow, though the fine-tuning derived from the St. Petersburg soviet. When it was decided to call a strike there at the end of November, the Moscow soviet could only join in support. The question of a strike was also discussed by the Moscow soviet. Mensheviks and SR's [Social Revolutionary Party] called for caution. But St. Petersburg's decision predetermined that of Moscow and on December 6th the Moscow soviet unanimously decided to commence a general strike on the next day.

Fondaminskii and I were assigned to the congress of railroad delegates. He argued for the necessity of a general strike and asked them to join it, while I was stitching together the corresponding resolution. The railroaders resolved to support the strike. The strike did not produce the desired result, and with an equal mix of spontaneity and premeditation "turned" into a revolt. The state immediately resorted to extreme measures. The meeting, which had convened in the "Aquarium," was fired upon. And in the center of the city, artillery was let loose against Fidler's Realschule [a vocational high school] where the so-called "volunteers" had gathered—most of these were youths who had not yet reached legal age and who were either students or from the working class. Following revolutionary tradition and for self-defense, barricades were set up in the streets of Moscow. They were also intended to impede the movement of mounted patrols.

I was not involved in the decisions. These were made by higher party functionaries. The building of barricades, however, was one of the responsibilities of the mid-level party member. Thus, together with others, in some square in the Arbat district, I hauled chairs, boxes, and barrels with a sense of great uneasiness and helplessness. I piled other things on top of them and unsuccessfully tried to topple a light pole with its glass already broken. I did not at all feel that the destructive spirit was simultaneously a constructive one. Those more adept, and, perhaps, less prone to reasoning, built barricades better and faster in other locations.

The headquarters of the SR committee during the insurrection was in the apartment of Lidiia and Lev Armand whom I knew from Rikkert's seminar in Freiburg. All the directives and guidance emanated from this alley in the Arbat—insofar as guidance was possible in a semi-elemental uprising. This was the center for news and people: news regarding what was happening and people to provide information on the situation and to receive proclamations, directions, and counsel. The proclamations were mainly written by Andrei Aleksandrovich

Nikitskii, our "scribe" as we called him. It was here also that the combatants and the volunteers came for weapons: revolvers, cartridges, and bombs. We spent all the days and nights of the uprising here, collecting and then discussing information, attempting to bring reason and order to chaos. Sometimes we had to carry out individual assignments ourselves. Thus, Lev Armand and I were sent to get cartridges. We reached the specified point safely. I was loaded up with cartridges hung front and back under my coat and headed back. The way led through the Prechistenka. A sentry stopped me at the house occupied by General Kostanda who was in charge of the forces.

"Where are you going?"

I answered. The soldier ran his hands along the overcoat and spouted out: "Go ahead, yid face!"

I did not feel insulted. The sensation of an incredibly lucky outcome crowded out all other feelings and thoughts. Had the guard run his hands on the front and back rather than along the sides, I would not have made it alive. Moscow had been placed on military alert, and those held on suspicion, let alone those caught red-handed, were frequently executed on the spot. While unloading the cartridges, I said to my friends:

"I survived my ordeal—a miraculous deliverance from death."

There were other risky assignments. Actually appearing on a street was accompanied by risk. One evening five of us went out. We had just approached the corner, when we heard the rhythmic clicking of horses' hooves. The clatter was so close that it was too late to retreat and there was nowhere to run. The leader of our combat units, Aleksandr Gudkov, who was later to die as a Russian volunteer on the French front during World War I, pulled out his revolver and stood first along the edge of the wall. Behind him, also with revolvers in hand, were Oskar and Aleksandr Vysotskii. Fondaminskii and I shuffled from foot to foot: we had no weapons, and didn't know how to use them anyway. Many tense seconds passed. My heart beat faster in rhythm with the approaching thud of the horses. Suddenly, a shaft of light from a lantern fell on a peacefully passing carriage, not on a dragoon patrol as we had supposed.

On a different occasion I was sent with another person to deliver dynamite in tea tins decorated with birds of paradise and other birds. The dynamite had to be brought to Chulkov's house on Smolenskii Boulevard. On the way back I stopped to see Sventsitskii who lived in the same neighborhood. He was also storing either dynamite or arms. I found Andrei Bely [the famous poet and novelist] there. I did not know whether he was an SR, an SD [Social Democrat], or a member of the Christian Brotherhood for the Struggle. One did not ask these things. But I can be a definite witness to the fact that at this time he "listened to the music of the revolution" and was captivated by it.

During the uprising, the Moscow soviet began to issue the newspaper *Izvestiia*. In principle, the editorial work was to be done by a collegium consisting of representatives of the soviet and the SR and SD parties. The SR's appointed me as their representative on the editorial staff. Having collected all the information that came in during the day from supporters in all parts of the city, I set out late at night through the quiet and snowy lanes of the Povarskii and Arbat neighborhoods to the address given me. There I found only one person—Ermanskii. I did not know whether he was a Menshevik or Bolshevik but soon became convinced that he acted like a Bolshevik. He greeted me affably:

"Well, how did it go? What have you brought?"

I laid out my material—reports from on site: conditions, morale, and losses.

"Leave it! Later we'll see what to include."

In next day's *Izvestiia*, there was almost nothing from the material that I had brought. When I met Ermanskii again next evening, I suggested that we decide jointly what material to include. He firmly rejected this and, after some wrangling, he unambiguously let me know that I had a choice: either leave the material and trust him, or take it back with me. Either choice was painful. Both were equally unacceptable but, in fact, I assented to both. At first I took the material and left. Then having walked two blocks, confused and angry—both at Ermanskii and myself for my own weakness and capitulation—I returned and left my papers. I could do nothing with them, and they would have been out of date by the next day, anyway. Perhaps the unscrupulous and factious Ermanskii might still use even a part of them.

Later it became clear that Ermanskii was a "left" Menshevik. The Bolsheviks accepted him into their Communist Academy, but he was expelled in 1930 and liquidated during Ezhov's purges.

The draft board gave me a one-year deferment and I left for Moscow the same evening. In an upper berth of a third-class railway car I gave myself up to sorrowful considerations of the immediate future. To knock about from house to house of relatives and acquaintances—a night here, a day there—seemed a boring and useless waste of time. Without a specific task—whether work or assignment—it was easy to fall out of the habit of systematic work. The thought of a personal life would also simultaneously surface. In order to marry, the law required an ID in the form of a passport or a residence permit. I had a university residence permit which I did not register with the police, but which was good until 31 August 1908. Only two days remained until its expiration. With acute awareness, I realized that this was my last chance to legally marry.

I went to my uncle's apartment directly from the train station. It was not difficult to convince my cousin that we had to marry within 36 hours. To postpone marriage meant the creation of new passport difficulties in the future. We split our tasks: I went to inform my parents, she—hers.

My father said nothing—giving his assent through silence. Mother, "for the last time," cautioned against marriage between close relatives, citing the sickly condition of my future "life's companion" and the like. Her objections were basically a formality—a self-justification rather than condemnation of my decision. In this fashion things on my front were settled. On my bride's side, aunt and uncle raised technical objections: how could a wedding be organized in the time span from Saturday to Sunday when all the stores were closed? One needed a wedding dress, a place in which to get married had to be found, guests had to be invited, and arrangements had to be made with the rabbi. Even obtaining the required wedding rings was a problem.

All of these obstacles, real or imagined, were easily overcome by our decisiveness.

I immediately went to see another uncle, Miron, with whom I had stayed periodically during my wandering years. He became a widower early on and had two young daughters. Tilla Ivanovna Sproge, a German from the Baltic region, looked after them and the household, not without a lively sense of humor. On the spot, my uncle agreed to the use of his quarters for the ceremony. We "arranged" for a rabbi and a portable canopy that was required for the ritual. The ten Jewish men of legal religious age, older than thirteen, who were mandatory to effect the prayer properly, were supplied by close relatives. As far as inviting friends, we had to limit ourselves to the very closest: Aniuta Koroleva, Sher, and the Ratner brothers.

With her characteristic resoluteness, the bride refused to wear a wedding dress. Very quickly one that was similar was sewn. A skirt was made out of a white silk dress and a white blouse with a bridal veil was added. The latter was obtained via the back door from the neighboring wig maker. Vasia Sher gallantly sent the bride an enormous bouquet of white roses. Everything turned out "as it is supposed to be." The most difficult items to get were the wedding rings. My future father-in-law went looking for them after the Sabbath rest had ended. Despite his efforts, he was unable to get anything better than rings made out of 14 carat gold. Which, by the way, did not impede their functioning in faith and truth for 46 years.

All of this seemed to be useless, though innocent ritualism, which one had to bear insofar as we had chosen the juridical, and therefore, according to Russian law, religious consecration of matrimony. Our wedding took place on August 31st, the day that my university residency permit expired. The religious ritual and the social ceremony were adhered to with minor deviations occasioned by the urgency in preparing the celebration and the particular circumstances of the groom.

The bride wore a white dress—not satin to be sure, but silk nevertheless. I wore a dark blue jacket. The parents and relatives were dressed up. The rabbi appeared. He was not the conventional Ia. I. Maze, but was a so-called spiritual rabbi, Weisbrem. He was a handsome elder with gentle facial features and a long white beard with streaks of yellow in it. He did not "torture" those gathered with a didactic speech, but limited himself to the minimum necessary to conduct the ritual. Those assigned to the task led us the required number of times under the velvet canopy with the golden fringe. As was customary, vessels were broken and crunched underfoot. We sipped the wine. We put the rings on the ring fingers and moved toward the refreshment table. Despite it being Sunday, the energetic Tilla Ivanovna was able to obtain various treats.

The whole procedure did not take much time. Though everything went well, one still felt that something was missing, that closure was needed. It was 10:00 PM, the program was spent, and it was time to depart. The young people decided to continue the celebration elsewhere. But where? Somebody suggested going to the Iar. This required the kind of money that I did not have. Dr. Rosenthal came to the rescue.

"Tell Uncle Abram, he will gladly give you a hundred rubles," he suggested. "At Vera's wedding (my father-in-law's eldest daughter) the horses alone cost more."

I became the possessor of one hundred rubles and, driven by six reckless cabmen, we left for Moscow's favorite place of revelry, which had a gypsy choir, individual compartments, and other attractions. It was only eleven o'clock, child's time for Iar. People came there after theater or for finishing up parties. There was no one there besides us. Here and there loose women loitered about, looking at us with astonishment since we were so unlike the usual guests and clients. We ordered coffee and liqueurs, also unlike Iar regulars, and soon felt out of place. We did not fit in Iar, nor did Iar fit us. It was decided to end the celebration and go home. The newlyweds departed as well: my cousin returned to her father's house and I went to sleep at Sher's.

Chapter Ten

Konstantin Paustovskii, Commencement Revelry

Largely forgotten now, Konstantin Paustovskii (1892–1968) was a talented writer whose works began to appear in print in the 1920's. His writing frequently expressed a lyricism not often seen in literature of the Soviet period. Steeped in the inheritance of Chekhov and especially Turgenev, Paustovskii wrote in the high style of Russian literature well into the 20th century. This selection is taken from his autobiographical work, *Povest' o zhizni* [Story of a Life]. Moscow: 1962.

The final examinations began at the end of May and dragged on for a whole month. All the grades had already been dismissed for the summer vacation. We were the only ones who came to the empty, chilly *gimnazium*, which seemed to be resting from its winter commotion. The noise of our steps resounded through all the floors.

In the auditorium, where the exams were taking place, the windows were wide open. Dandelion seeds floated around the hall in the sunlight like white, twinkling lights.

It was customary to come to the exams in uniform. The stiff collar of the tunic with its silver braid chafed our necks. We would sit in the garden under the chestnut trees with unbuttoned tunics and wait our turn.

We were afraid of the exams. And we were sad about leaving the *gimnazium*. We had grown accustomed to it. The future appeared dim and difficult before us, mostly because we would lose each other irrevocably. Our loyal, cheerful school family would break up.

Before the exams we held a meeting in the garden. All the boys of our class were invited except for the Jewish boys. They were not supposed to know anything about it.

It was decided at the meeting that the best pupils from among the Russians and the Poles should get a 'B' in at least one subject on the exams, so as not to get gold medals. We had decided to give up all the gold medals to the Jews. Without these medals they would not be accepted into the university.

We swore to keep this decision a secret. To the honor of our class, we didn't spill the secret either then or later, when we already were university students. Now I am breaking that vow, because hardly any of my school comrades are still among the living. Most of them perished during the great wars which my generation experienced. Only a few have survived.

Then there was a second meeting. We agreed on who was to help several of the girls from the Mariinskii Girls' *Gimnazium* write their essays. I don't know why, but they were to take the written exam on the History of Russian Literature along with us.

The negotiations with the schoolgirls were conducted by Stanishevskii. He had brought a list of the girls who were in need of help. There were six names on the list. I was assigned to help a schoolgirl named Bogushevich. I didn't know her and had never seen her.

We wrote the essays in the auditorium. Each one sat at a separate little table, the boys on the left and the girls on the right. The proctors paced along the wide aisle between the girls and us. They watched to make sure that we didn't pass notes, blotters, or other suspicious objects to each other.

All six of the girls on Stanishevskii's list had taken seats near the aisle. I was trying to guess which one of them was Bogushevich. The surname 'Bogushevich' brought to mind an image of a plump Ukrainian girl. One of the girls was plump, with thick braids. I decided that this was Bogushevich.

The director entered. We stood up. The director unsealed a thick envelope with a crackle, pulled out a sheet with the theme of the essay sent from the district school board, took a piece of chalk, and carefully wrote on the board: 'True enlightenment unites moral development with intellectual development.' An anxious moan passed through the hall—it was a ghastly topic.

I had no time to lose. I immediately began to write an outline of the essay for Bogushevich on a narrow strip of paper.

During the senior-year exams we were allowed to smoke. To do this we would ask permission and, one by one, to go to the smoking room at the end of the corridor. There the decrepit watchman Kazimir was on duty—the same one who had once brought me here to the preparatory classes.

On the way to the smoker I rolled the outline up into a thin tube and stuck it into my cigarette holder. I smoked the cigarette and laid the cardboard holder on the windowsill, in the place we'd agreed on. Kazimir noticed nothing. He was sitting on a chair and chewing a sandwich.

My job was finished. After me, Littauer went off to the smoker. He flipped his cigarette butt containing an outline on the windowsill, got the crib-sheet out of mine, and, returning to his place by way of the aisle, tossed it on Bogushevich's desk. After Littauer, Stanishevskii, Regamé, and two other boys pulled the same trick. Their work required adroitness and an accurate eye.

I had already begun to write my own essay when Littauer returned to the hall. I followed him with my eyes. I wanted to watch how, and to whom, he would toss my crib-sheet. But he did it so quickly that I didn't notice a thing. Only by the fact that one of the girls began to write spasmodically did I understand that the deed was done and Bogushevich was saved.

But it wasn't the girl with the thick braids who began to write; it was a completely different one. I could see only her thin back, crisscrossed by the straps of her white, dress apron and the reddish curls on her neck.

Four hours were allowed for the essay. Most of us finished it sooner. Only the girls still sat suffering at their desks.

We went out into the garden. That day such a multitude of birds was singing that they might have assembled from all over Kiev.

A quarrel almost erupted in the garden between Littauer and Stanishevskii. Littauer said that Stanishevskii's organization of all this help for the girls had been stupid. Stanishevskii flared up. He was radiant with the success of his enterprise and was expecting praise, not criticism.

"So, what was the matter?" he asked Littauer in a challenging tone that boded no good.

"The matter was that there was no damn need for us to know the last names of the girls we were writing for. Six girls—six crib-sheets. Any girl could get any crib-sheet. Why do I need to know that I'm writing for Bogushevich or for Iavorskaia? As if it made any difference! It only made things more complicated when we were dropping them."

"My God!" Stanishevskii shook his head sorrowfully. "You utter cretin! You have no powers of imagination. So get this: I did it on purpose."

"What for?"

"It just seemed more INTERESTING to me!" Stanishevskii said weightily. "Maybe a passionate love between the saver and the saved will blaze up out of this! Did you think about that?"

"No."

"What a dolt," Stanishevskii snapped. "But now—to François'. For some ice cream." After every exam we would binge on our modest means and go to François' confectionery shop, where we would eat as many as five servings of ice cream each.

The most difficult exam for me was trigonometry. Anyhow, I passed it. The exam stretched on into the evening. Afterwards we waited for the school inspector to announce the grades, and overjoyed by the fact that no one had flunked we burst noisily out into the street.

Stanishevskii hurled a tattered textbook into the air with all his strength. The pages sifted down from the sky onto the pavement, dipping and fluttering from side to side. That pleased us. All of us on signal threw our textbooks skyward. A minute later the pavement was white with rustling paper. Behind us a policeman whistled.

We turned off into Fundukleev Street, then onto narrow Nesterov Street. Gradually everyone trailed off in various directions, and only five of us were left: Stanishevskii, Fitsovskii, Schmuckler, Khorozhevskii, and I.

We set off for Galitskii Market, where there were many small snack bars and beer parlors. We decided to get drunk, because we considered that the exams were already over. Latin was the only one remaining, but no one was afraid of it.

We joked and laughed. A devil, as the old expression goes, had possessed us; passers-by were turning to look at us. At Galitskii Market we dropped in at a beer parlor. The floor smelled of beer. Along the wall there were booths built of planks, wallpapered in pink. They were called "private chambers." We occupied such a 'chamber' and ordered vodka and beef Stroganoff.

The owner foresightedly jerked the faded curtain closed. But we were making such a noise that from time to time one of the customers would open the curtain a bit and glance into our "chamber." Everyone who looked in we treated to vodka. They drank it willingly and congratulated us on our "successful graduation."

It was already late evening when the owner came into our chamber and, glancing sideways at the curtain, said in a low voice,

"There's a shamus hanging around outside."

"What shamus?" said Stanishevskii.

"One from Criminal Investigation. You have to get out into the courtyard as slick as you can through the back door. From the courtyard there's a passage to Kudriavskii Boulevard."

We attached no particular importance to the owner's words, but all the same, we went out through the back door into the dark, stinking courtyard. Past the trash bins and the wooden sheds, bending low so as not to snag our heads on the clotheslines, we made our way out to Kudriavskii Boulevard. No one was coming after us.

We came out through a passageway onto the dimly lit sidewalk. There, waiting for us, stood a stooped man wearing a derby.

"Good evening!" he said in an ominous voice and raised his derby. "Have you had a nice party, young gentlemen?"

We didn't answer and set off up Kudriavskii Boulevard. The man in the derby started after us.

"Mothers' milk not dry on their lips yet," he said with malice, "and they're crawling around back alleys!"

Stanishevskii stopped. The man in the derby also stopped and stuck his hand into the pocket of his long jacket.

"What do you want?" asked Stanishevskii. "You can go straight to hell!"

"Grubbing around in taverns," the man in the derby began, "and you—pupils of the Imperial *Gimnazium*! The penalty for visiting taverns is a citation for political unreliability, a wolf's passport.[1] Did you know that?"

"Let's go," Stanishevskii said to us. "He's an idiot and this is boring."

We started off. The man in the derby moved after us.

"I'm not the idiot," he said. "You're the idiots. I went to *gimnazium* myself."

"Oh, we can see that," said Schmuckler.

"See what?" the man yelled hysterically. "I was thrown out of the *gimnazium* for drinking and got a wolf's passport. And am I going to pardon your drinking party? No! I'm going to get even. I'm not going to rest until they hand you a wolf's passport apiece. Too bad about your exams. You're going to get a big nothing, not a university education. Were you talking against the government in the tavern? You were! Were you mocking the tsar's family? You were! I can put you away, easier than spit. I don't advise you to fool with me. I'll have you in front of the secret police."

We turned off down empty streets towards Sviatoslavskii Ravine. We thought the detective would be afraid to follow us into the dead-end ravine. But he stubbornly followed along.

"Surely the five of us can deal with him?" Stanishevskii asked quietly.

We stopped. The detective pulled a revolver out of his pocket. He showed it to us and gave a muffled laugh.

We led him around the streets for a long time, avoiding the intersections where there were police. Fitsovskii suggested splitting off one at a time and disappearing. In that case the detective would always follow the larger group—first four, then three, then two, then finally one. Instead of five, he could catch only one. But none of us agreed with Fitsovskii. It wouldn't have been comradely.

We jeered at the detective. Each of us made up a biography for him and recounted it loudly. The biographies were monstrous and offensive. The detective was wheezing with rage. He was clearly getting tired, but came dawdling along behind us with the persistence of a madman.

The east was beginning to pale. It was time to act. We agreed on a plan and, circling through alleys, came to the building where Stanishevskii lived.

The building was shielded from the street by a stone wall about half again as high as a man. A ledge ran along its base. At a single command we jumped on the ledge and whipped ourselves up over the wall. The gymnastics classes had done us some good.

A heap of broken bricks lay in a fenced flowerbed behind the wall. A hail of bricks rained down on the detective, left behind on the other side of the wall. He shrieked, jumped back to the middle of the street, and fired. A bullet whined inanely through the air.

We hurled ourselves through the flower bed and through the passageway to the second courtyard, ran up to the fourth floor into Stanishevskii's apartment, and in a few minutes were all lying around on the couches and hassocks in our shirtsleeves and intensely listening to the action out on the street. Stanishevskii's father, a bristly gray-haired lawyer, was pacing the rooms in his dressing-gown. He was in just as militant a mood as we were, but he implored us to lie calmly, and not jump up and go to the windows.

At first we could hear someone furiously shaking the gates and cursing at the porter. Then in the courtyard we heard the voices of the shamus and other policemen. To our good luck, the courtyard of Stanishevskii's house had a second outlet. The porter was assuring them that the schoolboys must have beat it out the back way. After making some noise, the detective and the police went away.

We fell asleep, slept like the dead, and didn't wake up until noon. We sent spies out into the street—Stanishevskii's sisters. There was nothing suspicious, and we dispersed to our own homes.

As strange as it may seem now, we had been saved from great danger: inevitable expulsion and a citation of political unreliability just two days before graduating. It would have been the ruin of our lives.

Finally came the marvelous day in the auditorium when the director stood at the large table covered in green felt, handed out diplomas and congratulated each of us on our graduation.

The next day there was the traditional graduation ball. All the girls who had taken the Russian literature exam with us had been invited. The school was brightly lit. Colored lanterns hung in the garden. An orchestra was playing.

Before the ball, Suboch made a speech to us:

"In your fourth year I merely endured you. In the fifth I began to nurture you, although there wasn't much chance of making real human beings of you. In the sixth year I became friendly with you. In the seventh I came to love you, and in the eighth I even began to be proud of you. I'm an unlucky father. I have too many children, no less than forty. Besides that, every few years my children change. Some go away, others arrive. Conclusion: forty times more grief falls to my share than to the share of ordinary parents. And forty times more trouble. Therefore I may not always have been equally attentive to all. I'm sad to part with you. I have striven to make good people of you. You in your turn have given meaning to my life. I have become younger with you. I forgive you, now and forever, all your stupid tricks and even your fights with the police. I forgive you everything. There is, of course, no magnanimity in this. But I summon you to magnanimity. Heine once said that there are more fools on earth than people. Of course, he was exaggerating. But what does that mean, nevertheless? It means that every day we meet people whose existence brings neither them nor those around them any joy or benefit. Be afraid to be useless. No matter what you might become, remember this wise advice: Not a single day without writing a line! Work hard! What is talent? Merely effort multiplied by three or by four. Love hard work, and may you always regret to part with it. Have a good journey! Don't think ill of your instructors, who have grown gray in their battles with you!"

We rushed to him, and he kissed each of us farewell.

"And now," said Suboch, "a few words in Latin!" He waved his arms and began singing: "Gaudeamus igitur juvenes dum sumus!"

We all joined in our first university song.

Then the ball began. Stanishevskii was master of ceremonies. He directed the schoolboy-saviors to invite for the waltz the schoolgirls they had saved. He introduced me to a thin girl with joyful eyes—Olia Bogushevich. She was wearing a white dress. Her eyes lowered, she thanked me for my help and turned pale with embarrassment. I answered that it was nothing at all. We danced. Then I brought her ice cream from the buffet.

After the ball we saw the girls home. Olia Bogushevich lived in Lipki. I walked with her at night under the warm foliage of the trees. Her white dress seemed too exquisite even for this June night. We parted friends.

I went to Fitsovskii's, where our little circle was spending what was left of the night. We had pooled our resources for a supper with wine and invited Suboch, Selikhanovich and Ioganson. Ioganson sang Schubert songs. Suboch played a virtuoso accompaniment for him on the bottles.

We made a great deal of noise and parted after the sun had risen but when there were still long, cool shadows on the streets. We embraced each other hard in farewell and each went his way with a strange feeling of sadness and good cheer.

NOTE

1. Such a document excluded the bearer from admission to university or from holding most government service positions.

Part Two

Instability and Dislocation: 1914–1929

It is difficult to imagine a nation that underwent the degree of instability and dislocation that Russia did in these years (1914–1929). When it entered World War I in 1914 along with the other major European powers, it was not only difficult, but inconceivable, to imagine that the result would have a world-wide effect for the rest of the century. Put another way, it was impossible to see Stalin and Soviet totalitarianism on the horizon of 1914.

Though World War I was devastating for all the European powers, it was doubly so for Russia. The staggering losses incurred at the front quickly began to strain the support systems "at home." The nation had increasing problems in maintaining the commitment to the war since the domestic economy could not meet obligations as basic as those of food supply. Furthermore, the government of the last tsar, Nicholas II, was not only perceived to be inept, but proving to be so. It is not an accident that the Zemstvo Union, the Union of Towns, and the War Industry Committee were more effective in aiding the army and the war effort than was the government itself. The government's continuous effort to bypass the Duma whenever possible, even in the face of such a national crisis, was extremely telling.

The monarchy fell in March 1917. It was not merely a question of Nicholas's abdication. The February Revolution (February 23–26, old style) was a popular revolt. Large numbers of street demonstrations, protesting lack of bread among other things, were joined by the troops and police sent against them. With the collapse of all authority, a new government was formed on March 12, 1917. Unfortunately, its very weakness was suggested in its name, the Provisional Government. It was to last only to November 7, 1917. Beset by an inability to rule, confronted with the continuation of the war, and increasingly challenged by the parallel power structure of the Petrograd Soviet, as well as the rapid radicalization of politics, the Provisional Government could not last.

Lenin, who had returned from European exile in April 1917, masterfully helped to engineer the great Russian Revolution of November 1917. The Russian Revolution has drawn vast attention. In recent years, leading historians such as Richard Pipes, Orlando Figes, and Rex Wade have written major studies on the Revolution and its effects. Points of interpretation aside, the inescapable conclusion remained there for the world to see. Russia became the first communist nation with all that would entail.

This did not come easily. Russia underwent a devastating Civil War (1918–1920) aggravating the destruction and dislocation of World War I. Lenin, ably aided especially by Trotsky, quickly moved to consolidate power in this period, frequently referred to as "war communism." The nature of the Soviet system was clearly marked and imposed. The very first months of the new reign saw the formation of the Cheka, the implementation of the "Red Terror," the creation of ravaging "food battalions," and the removal of individual rights as well as those of freedom of the press. In 1919, the first decree creating concentration camps was issued. The capacity of the world to fully comprehend the extremes of the new dictatorial model is still open to debate.

Lenin, the pragmatist, was never to be underestimated. With the nation reeling from the effects of World War I, the Civil War, and government decrees (Trotsky had openly stated that Russia was in a state of collapse unprecedented in history), Lenin proclaimed the New Economic Policy (NEP) in the spring of 1921. This substantially lowered economic restrictions and allowed the nation to recover rapidly. Though seen as a retreat from communist ideology, NEP proved to be necessary in saving the country.

This period, 1921–1927, also set the stage for the creation of the Soviet State. It was the political and organizational incubation for Stalin who used the years craftily to create his personal power base. This was accomplished through his detailed work in building the party structure and the attendant levels of personal loyalty. Painstaking and laborious, this was an organizational effort which more flamboyant leaders did not have the comprehension or tenacity to undertake. When Lenin died in 1924, with technically no formal heir, Stalin's political base, coupled with an ability for intrigue, proved a major determinant in his successful drive for supreme authority.

Nickolas Lupinin

Chapter Eleven

Georgii Altaev, How I Became a Cub Scout

This short piece tells a boy's story of the early years of the Russian Scouts organization. The creation of Russian scouting belongs to Oleg Pantiukhov who formed the first group in Tsarskoe Selo in 1909. Other units were soon organized in the larger cities. From them, the movement spread to smaller towns and outlying regions. A primary motive of scouting was patriotism. This was reflected in the motto of the scouts: "Be prepared—for Russia." With the vast Russian diaspora following the Revolution, organizations of scouts established themselves in practically every country which Russians inhabited. Taken from Georgii Altaev, "Kak ia stal volchonkom" [How I Became a Cub Scout] in *Sbornik,* San Francisco: Nats. Org. Russkikh Skautov, 1969.

 The year 1917 brought many new things to us, the boys of Gomel. The revolution took place in February. Suddenly everything was permitted: freedom. "Free-ee-dam." But in March, after a short exchange of rifle fire, Gomel was taken by German troops. The garrison was small and the Germans hardly interfered in the routine of the town.
 The life of the civilian population went on as usual, but it was a totally different kind of life. Everything had gone off the tracks. Even we, children, felt this. Almost every one of our fathers and elder brothers was gone. Some were slain in the war, others were wasting away as prisoners, and those still in the army were cut off from us by the war security zone. Values and customs were quickly crumbling everywhere. Even we, first-year *gimnazium* students, were visited by an upperclassman, a huge lanky fellow with a budding mustache, who conducted elections for the *gimnazium* "committee" and then gave a long speech of which we understood nothing and only remembered the word

"freedom." The teachers became far less demanding and even the inspector, a terror to the underclassmen, went soft and the golden buttons on his uniform lost their luster. With the coming of spring we would simply walk out of the afternoon classes and avoid going to [mandatory] church services altogether. It was such fun to use this freedom and slip away to the river Sozh, skip stones on the water and clamber up hawsers into empty barges.

The street began to rule our lives, and with the street, gang leaders appeared, rough boys with a devil-may-care attitude. They were ready for trouble anywhere and at any time. They would break windows in houses, especially if no one lived there; injure dogs with a well-aimed stone; tie a can to a cat's tail and chase the terrified animal with shrieks and yelps. When adults appealed to our conscience we had one answer for them: "It's our freedom, too." Gradually all adults, except for immediate family, became our adversaries and even enemies.

I was eight years old. I came, as it was said back then, from a good family. My father, who worked in private business, was drafted into the army and wounded in the shoulder. At his request he was placed in a military hospital near Gomel for recuperation. My mother had to take care of me and my two brothers, aged two and four. I was bored with their company and constantly listened for the summoning whistle of our chief, Stepka K. [diminutive of Stepan/Stephen]. He was a twelve-year-old hoodlum who had subjugated the wills and aspirations of all the kids on our street. Stepka was covered in scrapes and bloody bruises. He had a freckled face, pug nose, and steely gray eyes. With him at our head we fearlessly attacked gangs from neighboring streets. Stepka's father and older brother were killed in the war and his mother was struck down by paralysis. Perhaps this was why in Stepka's speech, movements, and habits there was a constant challenge, a desire for revenge, to force his pain on others. He stopped going to school, paid scant attention to his mother, who lived on a minuscule pension, and spent all his days in the street where he was the true boss. I knew that it was wrong to be in Stepka's gang, but there was such compelling power in his stare and in his body, that none of us had any control over ourselves. I would tell mother that I was going to my school chum's to do homework, but then, once with Stepka, I'd always be on the lookout for her.

Stepka was always thinking up new capers, but they did not always work out and some of the boys felt burdened by his doings. One fine day toward evening at the end of May 1917 Petka T., who had lived on our street, ran up to us shouting with excitement that young men were being rounded up on the town square and that they were to be sent to the front. Petka's excitement was so evident and the news so staggering that we all sprinted for the town square which was on the high right bank of the Sozh. It was true. On the green quadrangle of the town square boys were lined up in a U-shaped formation. They were in strange outfits, greenish shirts and pants only down to the knees, black socks and boots. They wore broad-brimmed hats with the left brim turned up with some sort of colored badge on it. On their left shoulders they had two multi-colored ribbons and blue scarves around their necks like girls. The bigger boys held smooth rods in their right hands, as soldiers held rifles, with the butts at the toe of their right boot. Some of the rods had pennants with some sort of images on them. Several young men stood in the middle of this troop, also dressed strangely except that they had many badges on their pockets and sleeves. One of them, apparently the leader, was explaining something with everyone attentively listening.

All this was so unusual that we held our breath while watching these little soldiers who were soon to be sent to war with the smooth rods. I looked for Stepka. He, aware of the huge impression the scene was making on us and sensing competition, smiled derisively and kept snorting louder and louder: "They're supposed to be boys' but they wear ribbons and scarves like girls. And the big guys are in short pants like they were too poor to have long pants." He began gathering cones from some near-by firs and throwing them at the smaller soldier-boys. We began throwing as well, aiming at their bare knees. There was disarray in the ranks and some of the boys began to complain to their leader. "Aha!" we cried, "Not only are they sissies, but they're snitches."

The troop leaders standing in the middle began looking at us and talking to each other as if consulting. We quit throwing cones anticipating what would come next. And then one of the leaders turned the right flank of his little soldiers, waved off an offered rod, and started toward us. We began to back up. But this young man, so strangely dressed, approached us with such a friendly wave of the hand and smile, that we stopped. He came right up to us and said, "Here's what guys, we're scouts. Come join us, you'll be our cub scouts." We were totally stunned. Adults only cursed us, street kids. Even now, we were the ones throwing pine cones but they were not angry, they heartily wanted us to join them. We glanced at Stepka. Even he was taken aback, expecting anything but this. Suddenly he seemed small and no longer fearsome. The young man asked us to sit with him. We walked off to form a semicircle on the grass, and he told us that they were boy scouts, that their detachment consisted of many troops of eight boys and that each troop carried the name of an animal or bird. He also told us that they were preparing for a parade and that, come summer, they would live in tents in the forest by the banks of the Sozh, swim, catch fish and cook chowder over a fire, play many exciting games and sing their songs.

"Do you want to join us?" he asked suddenly.

"Yes," we answered in one voice.

"Well then, line up in size places, two rows behind this troop," said our new leader pointing to the youngest boy scouts.

We lined up, and were divided into troops. Seven street kids and a leader from the detachment. We were taught how to march. This was fun, but it made no sense why we had to start marching with the left foot. Some of us did not even know our left foot. Our leader showed us the left foot and told us to pinch our thigh hard. Squealing, we pinched our left legs and forever remembered which was which. In marching, at first it was difficult to keep proper dress. But in half an hour we got it and vigorously stomped along behind the real scouts. A large crowd watched our exercises with interest. Toward the end, as we marched past the head scoutmaster, two tipsy dandies in round straw hats and light colored suits could not control their enthusiasm. "Look, Kolia," said one of them, "here comes the barefoot brigade." His buddy raised his hat and shouted, "Way to go, bareheels!" We were surrounded by friendly laughter and joyfully laughed ourselves. It was good to be accepted so simply and heartily. Only Stepka did not march with us. He stood aside screwing up his mouth, hissing, showing us his fist and pocket knife. Then suddenly he was gone.

Our leader told us that we needed written permission from our parents to join the scouts. Then a gathering was called for the next day. On our way home we tried to walk in step guessing whether we'd get permission and how best to break the news. There was a surprise waiting for me. Dad was home on his first furlough. He was still in uniform but without epaulets and signs of rank. His right arm hung lifelessly in a black sling. He asked me where I had been, and why I was late. Getting up my courage, I told him about the scouts and asked for permission to join. He frowned and said, "What scouts? They are simply a joke. Enough militarism," he continued decisively. "We have to build a peaceful life now. Look here, I marched and marched and now I can't move my arm, yet I have to work."

I sensed that there was no point in pushing my request. But I made up my mind that I would somehow sneak off to tomorrow's gathering. For the whole next day the clock seemed to have stopped. Father looked through all my homework and tested me on the multiplication table. I made only two mistakes, 8 x 8 and 8 x 9, but didn't have the nerve to ask for his permission a second time. Father sent me out for cigarettes. On the way I met some of the other boys. It turned out that only half had received permission. Some would not turn their sons over to a "joke outfit." Others did not have the money for a uniform. "Wear the clothing of your older brothers," was their response.

When I was already in our yard, I heard Stepka's familiar summoning whistle. I hurried to give father his cigarettes, climbed atop our fence, and from its height told Stepka that I wanted to spend time with father who was home, join the boy scouts and not be a street kid anymore. Stepka was obviously dejected. "Half the guys have gone," he said bitterly, "only the useless ones are left."

"Listen, Step," I said, "why did you leave yesterday? Come, there is a meeting today. You'll be the top guy with us. We'll live in tents in the forest, we'll go swimming and cook chowder over a fire."

Stepka thought for a while then said with bitterness, "They won't take me. I'm useless; they're from well-off families, rich kids."

"No, Step, they're not all rich kids, now it's . . .," I struggled for a word, remembered the class committee elections and blurted out, "it's freedom now." Stepka raised his head slowly and looked at me. His gaze turned placid. "I'll think it over," he said softly, walking away.

After lunch father was dozing on the couch, snoring lightly, his right arm stretched along his side. I sat in the corner with the multiplication table, watching the racing clock. Toward three father stirred and moaned quietly. His arm hurt. I coughed, and he raised himself and asked what I was doing.

"Dad, I learned the table by heart. Eight times eight is sixty-four. Eight times nine is seventy-two."

"Good boy. What do you want for a reward?"

"Let me go into town to play with Dima."

"All right, go but don't be late, and I'll go walk in the garden."

With that I immediately took off for the town square, hoping to meet the scout leader before the gathering. And he was there on the green sitting on a bench . . . with Stepka. Stepka was telling him something, waving his arms animatedly and spitting a lot. The scout leader sat a bit sideways, watching Stepka with absorption. He'd smile and ask Stepka something. When Stepka left, I told him, fighting back tears, that father would not let me join the scouts. The leader asked me for my name and address and then exclaimed that he knew the house that was surrounded by a large garden.

"What does your father do after lunch?" he asked. I told him that father napped and then strolled in the garden.

"Well, terrific," he said, "tomorrow at two-thirty there'll be a meeting of a troop in your garden. Is that OK with you?"

"It's OK," I answered slowly, hoping for a happy outcome. Then he told me to run home.

The next day while father was still asleep a troop came to our place and stopped by the broad garden path leading down to the river. They cut branches from a large wind-felled fir tree, tied their rods together and put up a lean-to. I was so involved in helping them that I did not notice father's appearance. He gave me a severe look, but as he came closer the scout leader presented himself and reported: "Eight scouts under my command building a lean-to, sir. Request your permission to remain and continue building." During the report father snapped to attention. Receiving a report is a sacred matter among military men. He examined the lean-to, then, addressing the leader, asked,

"What is the predominant wind direction in these parts?"

"From the south."

"Then why is your entrance also facing south? You'll get gusts right into the lean-to. There is a slope here. You ought to dig that up-slope ditch a little deeper in case it rains." Then he asked the leader to go off for a talk with him. We began rebuilding the lean-to. Some twenty minutes later not only did I get permission to join the scouts, but the scouts were allowed to gather in small groups on our property. My little world which up to now consisted of several streets, the cathedral, town square, and *gimnazium* suddenly became greater, compellingly engaging, and full of new mysteries. Our meetings were moved to the enormous estate of Count Paskevich which seemed to have been created for our activities and games.

Three magical summer months flew by, and in that time we matured as if it had been three years. It was wonderful that our leaders did not shout at us or order us about. Rather, they suggested things, and their suggestions had the power to attract and grip us for a long time. I remember that almost every boy on our street became a cub scout. The older boys became boy scouts right away. During the very first days our leader had a talk with us in which he said that every scout is a friend of children, the elderly, the weak, as well as the friend of animals and that every day he does at least one good deed. After that meeting we all rushed home vying with each other to compensate both people and animals for all the foul things we had done to them during the spring of that momentous year.

Old women no longer had to carry buckets of water from the town wells. "What's come over all of you?" they would say, puzzled. "Before we'd look both ways before going out, but now you've all become so good all at once. Must be the Holy Spirit entered your hearts. Well, thank you little grandkids; come into the house, maybe there's some candy for you," they would say and wink conspiratorially. But we, proud and pleased, always declined "payment" for our good deeds. I should add that during those hot summer days cats would serenely stretch out on the broad beams of gates, and dogs, relaxed to their fullest, serenely slumbered in the dusty streets. Also, after a premature cracking of our piggy banks, the broken windowpanes in town were all replaced.

I also want to say that from August on, my pack leader was none other than Stepka. At my insistence mother sewed a scout's uniform for him as well. He immediately became a scout and in two months' time so distinguished himself that he was transferred to the cub scouts as pack leader. Our pack was the best. Stepa had so much energy that beside his usual responsibilities he occasionally took charge of the "combined detachment" of cub scouts who gathered on their own initiative to play on our property. No one called him Stepka anymore; it was Stepa or Stepusha. He was rid of that onerous "-ka" ending.

Once after watching us, father called Stepa over and told him that when he grew up he would be the sergeant-major of the best regimental training unit in the whole division. Stepa shook his head and protested that he would become the leader of the scouts and cub scouts in the whole province.

In October of that year the second revolution took place. In 1918 after the German troops departed, the screams about "freedom" reached a frenzy, but freedom itself somehow vanished. The *gimnazium* was closed and the scouts were banned. We, the ex-scouts, met secretly for a long time without uniforms or any signs of distinction. The only distinction we had was our handshake with the left hand and our wonderful loyalty to each other, even though we had not been scouts for very long.

Two years later our family left Gomel. I lost from sight but not from memory the wonderful friends of my childhood.

Chapter Twelve

Nikolai Filatov, A Soldier's Letters

The views of Nikolai Filatov on the war and revolution are of historical and cultural interest, as is the manner of expression of this self-educated peasant soldier. The run-on text of each letter has been divided into paragraphs and capitalization of proper titles added, but an attempt has been made to preserve in translation other idiosyncrasies of the author's language without drawing attention to them with the conventional notation *sic*. They include punctuation errors, tense and person inconsistencies, run-on sentences, a few fragments, non sequitur clauses and questionable lexical choices. One ellipsis in brackets in letter 2 [. . .] is from the original. Other comments in brackets and footnotes are the translator's. Taken from Nikolai Filatov, "Soldatskie pis'ma 1917 goda" [A Soldier's Letters of 1917] in *Vospominania*. Paris: YMCA Press, 1981.

1. FRONT LINE TRENCHES

March 5th, 1917

How do you do greatly-respected Olga Valerianovna, I send you my greetings and wish you good health. I write you, Olga Valerianovna the following. We are still in position. The night of 28 February–1 March, precisely at midnight, in our entrenchments along the entire front we shouted "hooray" on the occasion of the English forces taking a city. At first we were told it was Gaa [Hague?], now they say it is an entirely different city, but that can be put off for now. Now lies ahead a more serious turnover, which happened in Russia. The matter is as follows. On March 4th at 8:00 PM we received at our position a telephoned telegram with news of the Russian Emperor's abdication.

This incident causes us much talk and discussions. Some say this means the end of the Russian State, and some say that the sovereign was deposed by Germans, of whom there are still many in Russia who occupy senior posts. But no one knows correctly. Today the officers announced that the sovereign himself no longer wanted to reign for reasons of health, but no one believes that. In response to our questions about who will be tsar, the officers say that everyone supposes that the brother of the former sovereign, Grand Prince Mikhail Aleksandrovich will be chosen.

I request, Olga Valerianovna, that you write what you know regarding this overthrow and where the former sovereign will go. The troops feel sorry for Nikolai Aleksandrovich, the only consolation is that Mikhail Aleksandrovich will be chosen. We have no newspapers that describe the politics of state, and so rely on rumors and what the officers say.

For now, Olga Valerianovna, good bye, be healthy, I wish you all the very best. Give my regards and wishes for good health and all the best to your mama Olga Petrovna.

Respectfully your acquaintance N. Filatov.

I have not received your books, from boredom I read fairy tales, though I do not like reading them, but in the evenings my comrades, who find them interesting, ask me to read them.

2. ACTIVE ARMY. FRONT LINE TRENCHES

May 12th of this year [1917]

How do you do greatly-respected Olga Valerianovna, I send you my greetings and wishes for all the very best. I first of all inform you, Olga Valerianovna, the following. Yesterday I received your letter of the 29th of last month, and today I received your 9 books in two packages. You ask me to write what is happening at the front, that is, what the general mood and discipline are like. I will endeavor to write you everything that has happened since March 5th. On March 5th I wrote you that we, that is the troops, do not want the New Government, but we want the old one. For this you probably called me a fool. But I deserve that name only in part, in that I could not wait for the matter to be resolved.

We were read some orders. These orders stated that a soldier has the right to travel first class and some other privileges, then it was said that discipline now will be severe, that for every minor infraction any officer has the right to shoot soldiers like [. . .] in a field trial, without sending a report to the upper command, as was formerly done. Then the officers explained what sort of minor infractions can be cause for summary execution. There were many such orders that made our hair stand on end and our skin crawl. We were very strictly forbidden to gather and talk about the tsar, it was strictly forbidden to say that the tsar had been deposed, and not that he himself abdicated. We were allowed to say that Mikhail Aleksandrovich will be chosen tsar. The officers scurried about and fussed as if caught in a trap. Finally the commander of our regiment, Colonel Velikopolskii, wrote a telegram to the Provisional Government. In this telegram the commander wrote that in my regiment there is utter antagonism, that soldiers desert their posts, nobody obeys anything, and that he demands discipline (that means extraordinary).

I do not need to repeat to you, Olga Valerianovna, what sort of situation we found ourselves in (between two fires). To think that there was antagonism in our ranks and we abandoned our posts. The telegram went through the headquarters of our 84th division, but when it reached the corps headquarters, it was sent back and two days later the commander of our Second Caucasus Corps came to visit us in our entrenchments. The corps commander spent a lot of time in the trenches, asked about all our needs and satisfied them, as he was able. We all loved him very much and he knew us soldiers well too, that's why he stopped the telegram and did not let it go further. He knew full well that under the old government we never caused antagonism, and under the new government we certainly shouldn't either. He knew that was all fabrications by the officers. When he came he told us the whole truth. After his departure the gentleman officers themselves began to incite unrest. They gathered us and said:

"Now you are citizens, just the same as us officers, so why do you not ask for better living conditions, like we officers enjoy. Why don't you demand cots, blankets, mattresses and so on? You live like swine, sleep on bough beds quite unsuitable for a citizen, and receive only 75 kopeks per month."

When we began to explain that in time of war conditions dictate that it is not permissible to have cots, blankets and mattresses in the trenches, the officers said that you are a fool, an ass and blockhead. They said "In our mess we eat your soup and leave you only water, and we still get a fabulous sum for rations and dinner."

And they said many such words, which could have incited antagonism, but we have our preachers, who ardently persuaded us not to believe the officers, to be patient and keep hope. We realized all this ourselves and acted as our conscience dictated. For now I will finish writing, and will write again the 14th or the 15th of this month, that is in two days.

I did not write you for so long, because I had a premonition that you are no longer in Tbilisi, and I don't know the address in Moscow. I have not received your letter in which you wrote that you moved to Moscow. Our spirit at the front could not be better, not one of our soldiers has deserted. I receive letters in which they write that there is desertion from the reserve regiments, but not from the front lines. You need not fear for the front. In my following letters I will write you about the general state of the war, that is I will write my views on the war and its conclusion. For now good bye, give my greetings to your mama Olga Petrovna. I wish you the very, very best.

—Respectfully yours N. Filatov.

3. ACTIVE ARMY

18. VI. 1917
Greatly-respected Olga Valerianovna,

Yesterday I received your books, sent June 5th of this year, probably from Yaroslavl. For kindly remembering me I send you my thanks a million times over. On May 17th I was summoned by a telephoned telegram from the 772nd regiment to our regiment. On that same day our regiment moved from the reserve to replace another regiment in position at the front. I spent on the road, that is marched, for two days, since the distance was seventy-five *versts*. When I arrived at my detachment, all the crews and machine guns were in position, with the exception of drivers [of horses] and six crew members. I was allowed to rest and I rest until today, but it is not rest, but worse than the front lines during battle. The problem is as follows. Prior to the first of June there was no committee in our command. But I lie! The committee existed, but from the first days when there was work to do they scattered. In our command there are, that is they are divided into two hostile camps. The drivers can't bear the sight of the crews in the trenches, and the trench soldiers regard the drivers likewise. I should point out that the drivers are few and all from the first mobilization, also the command of the machine gun detachments is benevolently disposed towards them, and there are many more trench soldiers.

In the former regime our kind chief himself settled everything graciously and would put this man on sentry duty for 8 hours, that one for 12 hours, and sometimes he had the charity to order someone put on post for 20 hours. Now he refuses to do this, while enmity has intensified. Everyone has the right to say what he wants, and here it has become my lot to be the go-between between the two warring factions. I'm the advocate of one and the other, and so enjoy the favor of both hostile camps. I took up this job from the first of June. At first this work was slow to progress, and I gave it all my energy. On the 14th the sergeant-major said to me the following: "Filatov, the whole unit is starting to come together, the former hostilities are no longer heard. Everyone is counting on you." He had a lot of other things to say, too. On July 1st we will have more elections. I think I'll ask to be relieved of this duty and go off to the trenches for a rest, because it's difficult to feed the wolves and have to answer for the safety of the sheep. Here you need a head as tough as a horse, I figure. The entire distribution of uniforms is my responsibility. All this time I'm up to my neck with things to do. In addition to that, there is often the desire to be at meetings and gatherings. I'd like to take a look with my own eyes at the head of the Minister of War, Kerensky[1] and see how he governs Russia in this troubled time. You know, Olga Valerianovna, when I've heard all I can of the various stories of the terrible unrest in Russia, I think that Russia can't take it any longer, if it goes on like this, Russia will not be able to endure, and all will be lost.

All is well at our front. Everyone is prepared to die for freedom. Only we have some deficiencies. The matter is as follows. Some sorts of diseases of malnutrition and heart palpitations from walking uphill have recently appeared along the front. We are fed well and I don't understand where this malnutrition comes from. These illnesses are thinning our ranks little by little, and there are no reinforcements. Few troops are coming up from the rear. Throughout our entire division, one no longer observes any hostile feelings towards the gentlemen officers, everywhere you can see friendly relations between soldiers and the officers. Twice I managed to be at the regimental deputies' meeting. I saw and heard how the officers address the soldiers with all sorts of questions, and how they light up *papirosy* for want of pipe tobacco. From this I can confidently say that for the time being there are no severe conflicts between soldiers and officers in our division. A soldier or an officer who returns late from leave is punished only in the rear. Our citizens are behaving badly. That only delays everything more and more and puts off long-awaited PEACE.

For now, Olga Valerianovna, good bye, be healthy, give my greetings to your mama Olga Petrovna. I wish you the very very best.

—N. Filatov

4. ACTIVE ARMY

25th day of June

Greatly respected Olga Valerianovna, I send you my greetings and well wishes. I have read only little of your books, and I have to read aloud, because I am asked to do so. For the most part I read about land issues, because issues about land are the most crucial for us tillers of the soil. I don't need to teach and explain things to you, Olga Valerianovna, you know full well what we need, and because I have to read the same booklet 3 or 4 times and forever stop and explain things. I have to define every foreign word, which is a problem because I don't know many of them myself, without an encyclopedic dictionary, it's very difficult. I myself am superbly educated: up until age 18 I knew neither how to read nor write, and books on political issues are not the same as the tales of Pushkin or Krylov.

Nothing exceptional has occurred at the front, everything is the same. The most diverse bits of information reach us from Russia. People return from leave and say that soldiers don't want to go to the front, that mass-meetings are held everywhere and speeches given that conclude with the words "down with the war." The rumors reaching us from Russia are more alarming by the day. I'm losing hope for Russia's salvation, now I think that all is lost, we will be crushed and that the monarchy will reign again. Our soldiers say that Kerensky is bloodthirsty, a second Napoleon. True, I adore Napoleon, I think he was a genius among geniuses. In difficult moments I always remember your words: "I fear for Russia, but I hope she will endure."

Good bye for now, Olga Valerianovna, be healthy, I wish you all the very best, give my greetings to your mama Olga Petrovna and my wishes for her good health. All the best.

Respectfully yours
N. Filatov.

5. ACTIVE ARMY, ROMANIAN FRONT

6/VIII/1917

How do you do, much-respected Olga Valerianovna. I send you my greetings and wish you good health. From your letter I learned that you still have not lost hope, you believe that Russia will endure, but I no longer hope for the salvation of our homeland. Our only possible salvation is peace, and the further continuation of war will be our doom. The best and brightest people in the upper command ranks are leaving, they flee and abandon us to the tyranny of fate. Newspapers shamelessly describe the failure of the revolution [of February 1917], and even the disorder in the active army—this in my opinion exacerbates Russia's pain. No matter what sort of disturbances there may be in Russia, anything could be at work behind our back, and when riots broke out at Tarnopol [in western Ukraine] there was a new scent in the air and everyone became alarmed.

From the 16th of July we began a slow retreat, surrendering every hill with a battle. Our Second Corps had just one road to take. The Germans really wanted to cut off our retreat, they charged drunk into an attack, and we treated them properly to machine-gun fire. The 25th of July Germans, Austrians and Turks launched attacks 8 times, we killed whole heaps of them. We suffered no losses on our side, and we practically have no soldiers anyhow. We've had no reinforcements since September of last year, we capture and maintain our positions with machine guns, and at night the company soldiers take up posts ahead of the machine guns and go back to the reserve for the day. And in the trenches machine guns always stand ready, very many of them. Besides these, we have extra machine guns at hand, at the slightest alarm these extra guns are placed on the front line. Sometimes we have three machine guns aimed at a single target: be our guests, Gentlemen Germans, Austrians or Turks.

We have withdrawn towards the rear about 20 *versts*, but covered nearly 100 *versts* in the process. During our dislocation, that is retreat, we knew no hunger, everything was distributed in advance, we were issued tea and sugar before the retreat. Nothing was left behind for the enemy, not as it was before, with the old government. I received your two packages of books, during our retreat I handed the books and my field office to the transport unit. Misfortune struck and my field office was lost, so I have only a single pen, quill and inkpot, and paper and envelopes I borrowed from my comrades. I will have to cease correspondence for a couple months. We are now in position, with no action thus far. The mood is happy. I read everything I can get my hands on. We spent 3 days constructing ourselves a sturdy, comfortable, winter dugout. Yesterday at 2 in the afternoon a 3-inch shell danced off our dugout, causing no harm. Our dugout can protect us from six-inch shells.

When I read your letter I was surprised to learn that you have become a country preacher for the New Age. You probably have had to endure much deprivation. I think that you have had to experience many, many hardships, and on top of it all you have to remain composed. I read in the papers about how our country folk understand the New Age. It's amazing how stupid and ignorant we are! Just to explain something insignificant would probably take about 20 hours.

I ask you, Olga Valerianovna, to give my greetings and wishes for good health to your mama Olga Petrovna. All the best, good bye for now, be healthy, and I wish you, Olga Valerianovna, great success in educating our people.

—Respectfully yours N. Filatov

6. POSITION IN THE KIMPOLUNGSKII SECTOR

November 15th day, 1917

Much-respected Olga Valerianovna, I send you my greetings and wish you good health, I also send regards to your mama Olga Petrovna and wish her good health and all the best.

First of all, Olga Valerianovna, I will write you the following. At the same time that you had a battle in Moscow, the Germans here at the front were not napping and broke through the front in two places, at Baranovichi [in the Brest region of Belorussia] and in Romania, at Okna [Okna-Muresh on the Muresh River]. Then they began to prepare for an assault on Iassy [in Northeast Romania near the Moldavian border]. I heard the following story. A division, that is this division maintained contact with our division, under the instigation of provocateurs, split along Bolshevik and Menshevik lines, left their positions and began fighting amongst themselves, and the Germans took their trenches with no losses. Our situation became critical. To re-establish our position, we brought up artillery, machine guns and a handful of soldiers to the place where the Germans broke through, after three hours' artillery bombardment there wasn't a living soul left in the trenches. Our troops recaptured the trenches with no losses and set-up machine guns. The Germans, after a two-hour artillery bombardment, moved to counterattack in tight formation. We let them come into close range, then the 132nd machine gunners and the 94th battery opened fire all at once. It was a horrible sight. The Germans advanced on our trenches with a pitiful battle cry, we let them in close and then mowed them down at point-blank range. Towards evening the Germans became convinced that it was impossible to take our trenches and the battle ceased.

I absolutely cannot understand how the Germans manage to break through our lines. Never have I seen troops abandon their position, that is, voluntarily leave their entrenchments, though I hear such stories and read about it in the papers, I still don't believe it. I have witnessed how our soldiers in the trenches, out of ammunition, bore the storm of German artillery fire, but did not think of leaving. Now I believe that our military technology is superior to that of the enemy, we have more than 50 machine guns in our regiment, and more were sent to us, but were not accepted because there are no horses to haul them. We have all the ammunition you could want, in answer to every German round our soldiers send 7.

We began voting for the Constituent Assembly from the 11th of this month. Most votes are cast for no. 3, and a small portion for nos. 4 and 6.[2] The soldiers were not prepared to vote, there are many misunderstandings, no conflicts. Yesterday I went to the regiment headquarters, and had the good fortune to be in the trenches. An Austrian prisoner came and said that they are given nothing to eat. From our reconnaissance men I obtained Austrian newspapers, magazines and all sorts of other works. I read little, had no time. The Austrians curse Kerensky for continuing the war to appease the bourgeois classes.

I have not received your books, no news is foreseen at present, we await peace. For now, Olga Valerianovna, good bye, be healthy, I wish you all the very best.

—N. Filatov

7. ACTIVE ARMY

December the 6th day, 1917

Greatly-respected Olga Valerianovna, I send you my greetings, wishes for good health, and all the best. Also greetings to your mama Olga Petrovna, whom I wish good health and every blessing.

I foremost write you, Olga Valerianovna, that yesterday I received your letter of 14 November, for which I thank you. You rightly predicted, Olga Valerianovna, that there will be many changes. True, we've had a little peace. The new war has not overpowered the old one, it ran off someplace, probably after the old war. There is no firing at our position, fraternization has ceased. The first of December we heard artillery and rifle fire in the Austrian deployments. From what the Austrians tell us, they are rioting and want peace.

Our mood has changed recently. Since we learned that the Cossacks have abandoned the front and are creating disturbances in Russia, now everyone has nothing but curses and threats for the Cossacks. They'll be in a bad way when the war is over, people want to destroy them forever. Any of their movements and uprisings will be put down right away. The Cossacks formerly enjoyed the reputation of being invincible, but in this war they served in headquarters, a safe distance from the action, they are considered cowards, they fear the Germans, went off to war to fight against women, but encounter soldiers with the character of Hindenburg.

You, Olga Valerianovna, imagine the break-up of Russia. That will never ever be, because we will not stand for German aggression, and Russia will become a strong and fearsome state. Do not trouble yourself, Olga Valerianovna with concern for my existence, I never worry for myself, because my life is cheerless. Just imagine, for all the hardships, the cold, hunger and difficult marches that I have endured and experienced in this war, when the war is over I will have to go to work in the mines or in a factory and I will again be regarded as a criminal element. I really don't want to go there, but am driven by need; there is no chance for me to take up farming. There is little land available and no capital to re-establish operations. I regret that on 14 September 1915 that shell didn't blow my head off, but now I'd like to live a bit more and see how the war ends.

I am dreadfully bored, my only entertainment is reading books, and I don't spare my eyes, anything to forget my gloom. I thank you, Olga Valerianovna, for your kindness towards me, your books alone sustain me, if not for the books, I would die from boredom and melancholy. I am quite fed up with living in the mountains. We are fed poorly, and the animals are fed very poorly, so that they can barely pull even empty carts. I cannot imagine, what will be next. I request, Olga Valerianovna, if you have the time, that you write what is happening in Moscow. For now, Olga Valerianovna, good bye, be healthy, I wish you all the very very best.

—Respectfully yours N. Filatov.
Village Shvartstal

NOTES

1. Aleksandr Fedorovich Kerensky became the Minister of War and Navy in the Russian Provisional Government a month prior to Filatov's letter, in May 1917. That same year Kerensky became prime minister in July and commander-in-chief in September.

2. The November 1917 elections to the Constituent Assembly were the first and only free multiparty elections in Russia until the post-Soviet era. Each of Russia's five wartime fronts constituted an electoral district. The remote Romanian front, on which Filatov fought, was largely insulated from Bolshevik agitation for immediate withdrawal from the war and confiscation of land and voted predominantly for the Socialist Revolutionaries. Of 1,128,000 votes cast by Russian soldiers on the Romanian front, 679,000 went to the Socialist Revolutionaries, while the Ukrainian Social Democrats received 181,000 votes to 167,000 for the Bolsheviks. Party lists were identified by numbers, and Filatov's numbers correspond to these three parties. On the Western front, by contrast, where Bolshevik agitation was rife, these proportions were reversed: the Bolsheviks received 653,000 votes of 976,000 cast, to 181,000 for the Socialist Revolutionaries.

Chapter Thirteen

Konstantin Paustovskii, Save Your Strength

Please see note to the previous Paustovskii entry.

[. . .] But everyone was convinced that the war was not in vain, and that justice finally would be restored.

"Worst of all, there ain't no truth or justice!" said a village shoemaker, a puny fellow with a sunken chest. "Travel around Russia, ask all of them people and you'll see that each one's got his own idea of truth. A local idea. And if you put them all together then you'd get the one and only, an all-Russian truth, so to speak."

"Well, and what sort of local truth have you got?" I asked.

"Why, it's standing over there, our truth!" answered the shoemaker and pointed at the hillock over the river. There a decrepit manor house was visible in the midst of a gnarled apple orchard. It was not very large, but it preserved all the features of the "Empire" style that had flourished on Russian estates during the reign Alexander the First: a pediment with peeling columns, narrow and tall windows rounded off at the top, two low semi-circular wings, and a broken cast-iron railing of rare beauty.

"Please explain to me," I asked, "what does this old house have to do with your local truth?"

"Why don't you go and visit the owner of this house, then you'll understand. If we're going to talk about truth, draw your own conclusions: who should this house, and this garden, and this land—the grounds around the house alone are two *desiatinas*—who should this belong to? But the owner over there is odd. The landowner Shuiskii, an unbelievable wretch. I doubt he would even invite you in. You better think up some sort of business to see him."

"What kind of business?"

"Well, something like you wish to settle in there for the summer, to rent a dacha. And you've come to make arrangements."

I approached the house along a path barely visible in the snow. The windows were shuttered with old rotten boards. The front porch was swept with snow.

I walked around the house, saw a narrow door upholstered in torn felt, and knocked loudly. No one responded nor opened the door. I strained my ears. The house was silent as a crypt. "Who am I kidding," I thought. "Surely no one lives here."

All of a sudden, the door flew open. On the threshold stood a little old man in a threadbare, black quilted robe belted with a towel. On his head was a little silk cap. His whole face was wrapped in a dirty gauze bandage. Tufts of cotton, brown with iodine, stuck out from beneath the bandage. The little old man looked at me angrily with eyes that were absolutely blue, like a child's, and asked in a high-pitched voice:

"What may I do for you, my dear sir?"

I answered as the shoemaker had told me to.

"You're not of the Bunin clan, are you?" the little old man asked suspiciously.

"No, of course not!"

"Follow me, then."

He led me into what appeared to be the only inhabited room in the house. It was crammed full of tattered rags and junk. A little iron stove was burning in the middle of the room. Trains of smoke belched out of it with every gust of wind.

In the corner I saw a magnificent round stove inlaid with decorative tiles. Almost half the tiles were missing; in their place were small niches filled with medicinal vials buried in dust, little yellowed paper bags, and shriveled worm-eaten apples.

Above a trestle-bed covered with a worn sheepskin there hung a portrait in a heavy golden frame; it was a portrait of a woman in an airy blue dress, with powdered hair combed up and the same blue eyes as the little old man's.

It seemed as if all of a sudden I was back in the early nineteenth century, visiting Gogol's Pliushkin. Prior to that I had never imagined that there still remained houses and people of this sort in Russia.

"Are you a nobleman?" the little old man asked me.

Just to be safe, I answered that I was.

"What you do professionally is of no interest to me," said the little old man. "These days such new occupations have come into being that it would trip up even a policeman. Kindly imagine, there is now even something called a "taxator" [an agricultural and forestry assessor]. It is all nonsense! The Romanovs' nonsense! I will let you the house for the summer, but under one absolute condition: you will not keep any goats. A certain Bunin lived here three years ago. A suspicious gentleman! A real Judas! Got himself goats, and sure—they were plenty happy to gnaw away on my apple trees."

"The writer Bunin?" I asked.

"No, his brother, the excise official. The writer came to visit. A somewhat more decent character than his bureaucratic brother but also, let me tell you, I don't understand what's there to boast about. Such petty gentry folk!"

I decided to stand up for Bunin, but on the old man's terms.

"Come now," said I, "The Bunins are old nobility."

"Old?" the little old man mocked me. He looked at me as if I were a hopeless dimwit and shook his head. "Old! Well, I am a bit older! My name is listed in the Velvet Books.[1]—If you have properly studied the history of the Russian state, then you would know how ancient my family is."

Only then did I recall that the shoemaker had given me the name of this little old man—Shuiskii. Could it really be that in front of me was standing the last descendant of the Tsar Shuiskii? What the hell!

"I'll charge you," continued the little old man meanwhile, "fifty rubles for the whole summer. This is, of course, no trifling sum. But my expenses are not trifling either. My spouse and I separated last year. The old witch now lives in Efremov, and from time to time I have to cough up five or ten rubles for her. But it's useless. She spends the money on her lovers. She's just asking to be hanged from the nearest tree."

"But how old is she?" I asked.

"The hussy is past seventy," answered Shuiskii crossly. "As to your residence here, we will write a point-by-point contract. I won't have it any other way."

I agreed. I felt as if the most extraordinary performance was being acted out in front of me.

From a tattered folder, Shuiskii pulled out a piece of yellowed stationery with a double-headed eagle embossed on it, picked up a quill, sharpened it with a little broken knife and dipped it into a vial of iodine.

"Damn it!" he said. "And why is it always like this? All because that damned fool Vasilisa never puts anything back in its place."

From the ensuing conversation it became clear that an elderly woman, Vasilisa, who used to bake communion bread, came over to Shuiskii's from Bogovo twice a week to clean up a bit, chop firewood, and make porridge for the old man.

Shuiskii found a little jar that had once contained "Metamorphosis" face cream but now served as an ink-well, and began to write. As he wrote, he grumbled about the new times:

"Nowadays everyone speaks and writes as if in Chinese. All around you see this nonsense of the Romanovs! Taxators, ameliorators! They say this good-for-nothing Nicholas dines at the same table with some debauched *muzhik* [an allusion to Rasputin]. And he calls himself tsar! He's a whelp, and not a tsar!

"Why do you wrap your face in cotton!" I asked.

"I apply iodine to my face and then, naturally, cover it up with cotton."

"What for?"

"For my nerves," Shuiskii answered tersely. "Now then, read and sign it."

He gave me the piece of paper written in precise old-fashioned handwriting. Listed there were all the conditions of my residence in the dilapidated house, point by point. One item I remember particularly well:

"I, the aforementioned Paustovskii, am bound not to avail myself of the fruit from the orchard, in consideration of the fact that the above-mentioned orchard has been rented to Gavriushka Sitnikov, the petty landholder from Efremov."

I signed this strange and absolutely useless piece of paper and asked about the deposit. I understood that it was foolish to pay for a house where I was not going to live anyway. But one had to play the role to its end.

"For goodness sake, what deposit!" answered Shuiskii angrily. "If you are indeed a nobleman how dare you mention such things! When you come then we'll settle up. It is my honor to bid you farewell. Cannot see you off—I have a cold. Shut the door tightly behind you."

I walked back to Efremov and the further I got from Bogovo the more fantastic this whole encounter appeared to me.

In Efremov, Varvara Petrovna confirmed that the little old man was indeed the last prince Shuiskii. Truth be told, he had had a son, but some forty years ago Shuiskii sold him for 10,000 rubles to a childless Polish magnate. The latter needed an heir, so that after his death all of his enormous entailed estates would not be dispersed amongst his relatives but would remain in a single pair of hands. Some deft secretaries at the assembly of the nobility found a boy of noble blood, Shuiskii, and the magnate purchased and adopted him.

It was a quiet, snowy evening. Inside the hanging lamp something buzzed softly.

After dinner at Rachinskii's I stayed behind—I was engrossed in Sergeev-Tsenskii's "The Sorrow of the Fields."

At the dinner table Rachinskii was composing pieces of advice for women. After having written a few words, he would lean back in his chair, read them over and smirk—obviously, he liked everything that he was writing very much.

Varvara Petrovna was knitting. Having withdrawn to an armchair, the fortune-teller was thinking about something as she looked at her folded hands with their diamond rings.

Suddenly somebody knocked sharply on the window. It startled us. Judging by the sound, which was quick and anxious, I understood that something serious must have happened.

Rachinskii went to open the door. Varvara Petrovna crossed herself. Only the fortune-teller didn't stir.

Osipenko burst into the dining room—with his coat and hat still on; he didn't even take off his galoshes.

"Revolution in Petersburg!" he cried out, "The government's been overthrown!"

His voice suddenly broke; he collapsed into a chair and burst out sobbing.

For a moment it was dead quiet. You could only hear Osipenko crying, like a child, gulping air convulsively.

My heart began to thump madly. I was short of breath and felt tears streaming down my cheeks. Rachinskii grabbed Osipenko by the shoulder and cried out:

"When? How? Say something!"

"Here . . . Here . . ." Osipenko muttered and pulled out of his coat pocket a long and narrow telegraph tape. "I've just come from the telegraph office . . . Here it is . . . everything."

I took the tape from him and began reading aloud the appeal of the Provisional Government.

At long last! My hands were shaking. Although the whole country had expected these events for the last few months, still the blow was all too sudden.

Here in sleepy, manure-strewn Efremov, one felt especially cut off from the world. The Moscow newspapers arrived three days late, and even they were not very numerous. In the evenings, the dogs howled on the Slobodka, and the watchmen lazily beat their clappers. It seemed as if nothing had changed in this town since the sixteenth century, that there was no railroad, no telegraph, no war, no Moscow, and that nothing ever happened.

And now—the revolution! Everyone's thoughts flew about in confusion, but only one thing was clear: something great had happened, something that could not be stopped by anyone or anything. It had happened just now, on this seemingly very ordinary day—precisely that which people had been anticipating for more than a century.

"What should we do?" Osipenko was asking frantically. "We must do something immediately."

Then Rachinskii pronounced the words that instantly exculpated all his sins:

"We must print this appeal. And post it around town. And get in touch with Moscow. Come on!"

The three of us took off: Osipenko, Rachinskii, and myself. Only Varvara Petrovna and the fortune-teller remained at home. Varvara Petrovna stood in front of the icon-case, rapidly crossing herself again and again while whispering: "Dear God, it's come. Dear God, it's come." Just as before, the fortune-teller stayed motionless in her armchair.

Somebody ran towards us along the deserted street. Under the faint light of a street lamp I noticed that he had neither a hat nor coat and was barefoot. He carried a shoemaker's last in his hand. The man dashed up to us.

"My dear friends!" he cried and grabbed me by the hand. "Have you heard? The tsar is no more! Only Russia is left."

He kissed each of us heartily and rushed on, sobbing and muttering something under his breath.

"But why haven't we congratulated each other?" said Osipenko.

We too stopped for a moment and kissed each other heartily.

Rachinskii went to the telegraph office to follow all the news from Petrograd and Moscow, while Osipenko and I searched for a small, out-of-the-way printing shop, where they published notices, announcements, and decrees from the military commander.

The printing shop was closed. While we were trying to break off the lock, a fidgety man with a key appeared, opened the shop and turned on the lights. He turned out to be the only typesetter and printer in all of Efremov. We did not ask why or how he had turned up at the printing shop.

"Go over to the font case and start composing!" I said.

I began dictating the text of the appeal to the typesetter. He set type, pausing now and then to wipe with his sleeve the tears which were welling up in his eyes.

Soon another piece of news arrived: an order from Nekrasov, the transportation minister of the Provisional Government,—to everyone, everyone, everyone!—for the detention of the imperial train, wherever it might be found.

Events were bearing down on Russia like an avalanche.

As I read the first off-print of the appeal, the letters jumped and blurred before my eyes.

The printing shop was now full of people who had somehow found out that the announcement of the revolution was being printed here. They would take stacks of appeals, run out into the streets and glue them up on walls, fences, and lamp posts.

It was already 1:00 AM, a time when Efremov was usually fast asleep.

Suddenly, at this unearthly hour, a short and vibrant clang of the cathedral bell rang out. Then a second and a third. The ringing gradually increased. A taut pealing was already audible all over the little town, and soon the bells of all the surrounding churches joined in.

Lights came on in all the houses. The streets filled up with people. The doors of many houses stood flung open. Complete strangers embraced each other, weeping.

The solemn and joyous whistles of steam locomotives soared from the direction of the railroad station. Somewhere in the distance people began singing the Marseillaise.[2] First their singing was barely audible but increasingly it grew in volume:

> Let's renounce the old world,
> Let's stamp its dust off our feet.

Then the resounding notes of a brass band burst into the choir of voices:

> We'll go to our suffering brothers,
> To the starving people we'll go!

On a table smeared with printer's ink, Osipenko was writing the first decree of the Provisional Revolutionary Committee of the town of Efremov. No such committee had been organized. Nobody knew, or could know, who its members were because there were no members. Osipenko himself was improvising the decree.

"Until the government of liberated Russia appoints new authorities in the town of Efremov and in Efremov Township, the Provisional Revolutionary Committee of Efremov appeals to all citizens to maintain complete order and thus decrees:

The administration of the town and the township is to be entrusted to the local *zemstvo* administration and its chairman, citizen Kushelev.

Citizen Kushelev, until further special instructions, is appointed the commissar of the government.

All police and gendarmes are to turn in their weapons to the local *zemstvo* administration.

A people's militia is to be established on the streets.

All offices and trade enterprises are to continue working without interruption.

The garrison stationed in Efremov (a reserve company) is to swear allegiance to the new government, following the example of the garrisons in Petrograd, Moscow, and other cities of Russia."

At dawn Rachinskii appeared at the printer's, looking tired and pale, but determined. Pinned to his coat was an enormous red ribbon.

He entered and, in a theatrical gesture, with great clamor, flung a gendarme's saber and a holstered revolver onto a table. It turned out that the railway workers had disarmed the bearded gendarme at the station, and Rachinskii, who witnessed the incident, claimed the weapons as the first trophy of the revolutionary committee.

Then came a tall gray-haired man with a kind, bewildered face—the new commissar of the Provisional Government, Kushelev. He didn't even ask how it came about that he was appointed to this high office.

Instantly a new decree was issued, over his signature, congratulating the populace of the little town on Russia's liberation from her age-old yoke. A meeting of representatives from all levels of society was scheduled for 1:00 PM in order to discuss immediate concerns related to the latest events.

Never in my life have I seen as many happy tears as in those days. Kushelev wept as he signed the decree.

His daughter had come with him—a tall, shy young woman wearing a kerchief and a short sheepskin coat. As her father was signing the decree, she stroked his graying hair and spoke in a trembling voice:

"Papa, don't get so agitated."

In his youth Kushelev had spent ten years in exile in the far north. He had been sentenced for belonging to a revolutionary student group.

A boisterous, incoherent, happy time began.

A people's assembly met for days on end in the hall of the *zemstvo* administration. This *zemstvo* administration became known as the "convention." It was steamy in the "convention" from the breath of hundreds of people.

Red flags fluttered in the February wind.

People from the villages streamed into town for news and instructions. "If only they'd hurry it up with our land," said the peasants. All the streets around the *zemstvo* were blocked with wide sledges and strewn with hay. Everywhere people shouted about land, redemption payments, and peace.

Elderly men with red armbands and revolvers at their belts—the people's militia—stood at the intersections.

The astounding news would not cease. Nicholas abdicated the throne at the Pskov railway station. Passenger train service was interrupted throughout the country.

Prayer services were conducted in honor of the new government in Efremov's churches. Almost all convicts were released from prison. Classes were suspended, and schoolgirls ran around the town ecstatically distributing orders and announcements of the commissar.

On the fifth or sixth day, I met the shoemaker from Bogovo at the "convention." He told me that Shuiskii, having learned of the revolution, was preparing to leave for the city. Just before leaving he climbed a ladder to the top of his tiled stove and pulled out from beneath the uppermost tile a small bag of gold coins; then he missed a step, fell, and was dead by evening. The shoemaker had come to town to hand over Shuiskii's money to the commissar of the Provisional Government.

It was as if the town and people were no longer themselves. Russia had found its voice. Out of the blue, inspired orators appeared in tongue-tied Efremov. They were, for the most part, workers from the railway yard. Women cried their hearts out listening to them.

Gone was the typical dejected and sullen appearance of Efremov's residents. Their faces grew younger, and their eyes thoughtful and kind.

They were passive townspeople no longer. They were all citizens now, and this word brought with it obligations.

And, as if on purpose, the days stayed sunny; crystalline ice thawed, and a warm breeze rustled the flags and carried joyous clouds over the little town. The breath of early spring was in the air—in the thick blue shadows, and in the damp nights that hummed with people's voices.

I was in a frenzy. I was exhilarated. I could hardly grasp what would happen next. I couldn't wait to go to Moscow, but the trains were not running yet.

"Wait and see," Osipenko was saying to me, "this is only a prologue to the great events advancing on Russia. So try to keep a cool head and a warm heart. Save your strength."

I went to Moscow on the very first train, carrying a pass signed by Kushelev, the commissar of the Provisional Government.

Nobody saw me off. There was no time for farewells.

NOTES

1. *Barkhatnye knigi* were the ancient registers of the Russian nobility.
2. The stanzas cited do not correspond to the standard text of the Marseillaise.

Chapter Fourteen

Roman Gul, We're in Power Now

Roman Gul was born in Penza in 1896, a city he romanticized and loved. After World War I he served briefly in the White Army during the opening phase of the Russian Civil War of 1918–1920. Barely managing to survive the early Red Terror, he wound up an émigré. He spent many years in Berlin, Paris, and ultimately New York. He chronicled the cultural life of Russian émigrés in Berlin and Paris in a two-volume memoir from which this selection is taken. He was well known as a novelist with several works, most notably *Azef*, being translated into several languages. In New York, in 1959, he was chosen to be editor of *Novyi zhurnal* (New Review), the leading Russian language quarterly in the United States. Taken from Roman Gul, *Ia unes Rossiiu* [I Carried Russia with Me]. New York:Most, 1981.

In those December days of 1917 Russia was at the height of its time of "damnation." A previously unseen and unknown passion for universal destruction, universal extermination and a wild hatred for law, order, justice, peace, and tradition spewed forth from the bowels of the populace. Just as in [Dostoevsky's novel] *The Possessed*, "everything shifted from its foundations." As the formulations said, "Everything has to be turned over and placed bottom-side up." "It is necessary to unleash the lowest, the most vile passions, so that nothing will hold back the populace in its hatred and thirst for extermination and destruction." All these wild ravings of Bakunin were incarnated now in everyday Russian life. It was precisely the sort of all-out popular rebellion which Pushkin had called "senseless and merciless." During this loathsome rebellion, we . . . lived. "Pillage what's been pillaged!" went the slogan and in Penza they senselessly pillaged all the stores on Moscow Street. "Burn the landlords' estates!" "Kill the bourgeoisie!" And they burned and killed all who were "marked for annihilation." After all, there were no longer courts and judges, prisons nor police. Everything was torn from its foundations, just as Shigalev and Verkhovenskii desired.

In Penza on the square in front of the railroad station a captain passing through the city was killed by a mob just because he hadn't taken off his insignia. After stripping the dead man naked they whooped and laughed while dragging the large white body to and fro through the snow of Moscow Street. Then a drunken frenzied soldier bellowed "The power is ours now! The people's." They burned Grushetskii, the notary, alive in his estate, not allowing him to escape from the burning house. The landowner Skripkin was killed in his estate and his naked corpse was stuffed into a barrel of sauerkraut "just for amusement." All this was done with wild laughter. "The power is ours now! The people's."

In hatred and passion for extermination they killed not only people, but also animals: the non-plebian, non-proletarian kind. In the horse-breeding farm of an acquaintance they broke the backs of the trotting horses with iron bars because they belonged to the "master." During the plundering of our estate a "revolutionary little peasant" took our female trotter named Volga and, harnessing her to a plow, began to whip her maliciously. Let her croak, she was the master's.... "Trotters are of use to masters, but now there ain't no masters." In another estate they cut out the tongue of a stud horse, and in *Days of Damnation* Ivan Bunin described how on an estate near Elets peasant men and women ("the revolutionary people") tore out all the feathers of the peacocks and let the bloodied birds loose "naked." Why? Well, because "*now* there's no need for peacocks, *now* everything is for the laboring classes, not the masters." Bolshevik agitators screamed this *now* until they were hoarse. And this had a mystical effect. "*Now* everything is different," "*Now* power belongs to the people," "*Now* we are all free," "*Now* there are no prisons!" "*Now* there aren't any police or constables," "*Now* everything is ours, the people's." I saw with my own eyes how the people believed in this *now* out of foolishness and blindness.

I'll tell you about another wild, senseless murder. At the estate next to us in the village of Evlashev they murdered Maria Vladimirovna Lukina, an old woman landowner. Fearing for her, her friends tried to talk her into leaving the village and moving to town. But the stubborn old woman answered: "I was born in Evlashev and I'll die in Evlashev." She indeed died in Evlashev.

Her murder was conducted according to all the rules of "revolutionary democracy." The peasants of Evlashev debated the bloody deed in a village gathering. Anyone could speak. A deserter from the front, the Bolshevik hooligan Budkin, incited the people towards murder, but other peasants spoke up against murder. When the majority, enflamed by Budkin, voted to kill the old woman, those who did not agree asked for a decree stating that they were not involved. The gathering pronounced a "resolution" to kill the old woman and to grant those who did not agree a decree.

Straight from the gathering, armed with fence stakes, the crowd thronged to the Lukin estate to kill the old woman together with her daughter, whom the whole village had known since childhood and half-affectionately and half-jokingly called "little chick." One of the peasants warned M.V. Lukina that they were coming to kill her. But the old woman didn't even make it to the barn. The "revolutionary people" killed her in the yard with the stakes. But "little chick" experienced a miracle. All bloody, she came to her senses near the carriage house with her Irish setter licking her face. Accompanied by the setter, she managed to crawl to the nearby farmstead of the Sbitnevs and they took her to the hospital in Saransk.

I emphasize that the whole peasantry was not totally possessed by the madness of murder, pillaging, and arson. There was also a minority which did not agree, but it was overwhelmed by the Bolshevik fervor of the deserters, who gushed into the countryside from the front.

I remember how "little chick" Natalia Vladimirovna Lukina came to see us. Her head was bandaged, and she could move her neck only with great difficulty. Telling about the murder of her mother, she cried plaintively, while pathetically smiling at something. As strange and as unnatural as it may seem, she didn't bear any malice towards those who murdered her mother and the peasants who nearly beat her to death.

"They're beasts, simply beasts. . . . But when they found out that I wasn't dead, but in the hospital, women from Evlashev started to visit. They took pity on me, cried, brought eggs, cottage cheese . . ."

"Oh, they were probably afraid that they would have to answer for their deeds!"

"No, what are you saying? Whom would they have to answer to? There are no authorities. No, it's true. They pitied me . . ." Then "little chick" cried, drooping her bandaged head. In my opinion, in her spiritual condition there was something Christian, but at the same time there was a submission to an all-engulfing evil that I found unpleasant.

I would like to emphasize one fact of the Russian Revolution that has never been written about by anyone, i.e., how Russian people of wealth and means (whom the Marxists called the "propertied classes," "bourgeoisie," "exploiters," and "capitalists") accepted the loss of their property. Bolshevik writings talk about the "resistance of the bourgeoisie," the "conspiracy of the bourgeoisie" and how the "heroic Bolsheviks" finally triumphed over the pernicious bourgeoisie. It is all a shameless lie. The Russian "bourgeoisie" (if one wishes to call it by that name) lost its property in isolation (without trying to organize), without a whimper, without resistance. While it is true that during the February Revolution there was a so-called "Union of Landholders," it existed primarily on paper. All it did was send reports to the revolutionary Minister of Land Affairs about disorders, pillaging, and arson. The minister, busy with revolutionary affairs, probably never even answered any of these communications since he had other concerns. By October, this "union" had already dissolved.

In general, Russians easily part with material things. In my opinion, they do so much more easily than Westerners. I recall what the chairman of the Penza local government, a young well-educated landowner named Ermolov (a relative of the famous general Ermolov), said when at a huge gathering some Bolsheviks and Mensheviks began to interrupt his speech with demagoguery: "Well, what about your land?!" He answered scornfully: "My land? You know gentlemen, I won't stoop down to join the crush of the crowd rushing to pick up fallen apples. I once had land. Now I won't. That's it."

The same gloating shouts were heard at a meeting in Petrograd at which the chairman of the State Duma M.V. Rodzianko was speaking. "That's all fine and good," they shouted, "but what about your land?" He replied: "As the Constituent Assembly decides, that's how it will be." Like all sound-minded people, he clearly understood that in Russia all land belonging to landlords, the state, and the nobility would be transferred to the peasantry. There wasn't any attempt at "resistance" by property owners.

In Penza during those accursed days I ran into Olga L'vovna Azarevich (her first husband was prince Drutskii-Sokol'ninskii, and by birth she was a princess of the Golitsyn family). She had lost everything. Through ill fortune there wasn't even any money left in the bank. In fact she had much to lose: her estate Muratovka with 3000 *desiatinas* of land [8,100 acres], a distillery, a sheep-raising enterprise, many horses, cows, a well-furnished home. Everything was plundered and pillaged. She managed to donate some valuable paintings to the museum of the Penza art school so that they would not perish. In spite of everything she did not despair. "Oh well," she said, "God gives, God takes away." I don't think the Lord our God could ever be involved in parceling out latifundia, much less employing insane, wild, drunken soldiers to misappropriate them. Nonetheless, such a degree of not being bound by the bounties of this world is, in my opinion, wonderful. And this very Russian feeling I have observed among many property owners. Russians are not strongly bound to land. As Marina Tsvetaeva wrote: "I know, I know that earthly wonder is a wonderful carved cup, which is no more ours than the air or the stars."

In emigration, in the city of Nice, Olga L'vovna ran a tiny café for Russian emigrants. Day after day she worked, went to the market, and cooked. She died in Nice at a venerable old age. Nobody ever heard a complaint from Olga L'vovna, or lamentations about lost silver and gold, although she once possessed it in abundance. In her life, as in many others, there was something else, something more precious than silver or gold.

Chapter Fifteen

Sergei Mamontov, Civil War: A White Army Journal

The Russian Civil War (1918–1920) is the setting here. A soldier in the White Army, Mamontov provides a unique perspective on the war in his book of memoirs. He notes: "It is often difficult to distinguish one's feelings. Simultaneously there was fear and valor, loathing and compassion, timidity and a sense of duty, desperation and hope." He is relentlessly truthful and markedly dispassionate in his judgments. His two-page introduction to the memoirs is as cogent a summation of the Civil War as one can find anywhere. Taken from Sergei Mamontov, *Pokhody i koni* [Marches and Stallions]. Paris: YMCA Press, 1981.

TO THE UKRAINE

My brother and I became totally convinced of the inability of various political groups to get us south. I even doubt whether such groups existed, and if they did, whether they were not Bolshevik fronts. It was easy to fall into a trap and best to count on our own resources. Once in the hallway my brother simply said to me:

"Let's go."

"Let's go. But when?"

"Now. Why put it off?"

"Good. Let's go."

And that was all. Mother silently packed a small suitcase for the two of us. Father saw us off at the Briansk Railway Terminal, gave us money, and blessed us. We parted forever. He died of typhus in 1920.

A railroad man put us into a freight car. The train set off southward into the unknown. The next day we arrived in Zernovo, the last town under Bolshevik control. Beyond lay the Ukraine, occupied by the Germans. We were lucky; there were no border guards in Zernovo. I waited at the station while my brother went to the farmer's market. He found a peasant from the Ukraine who agreed to take us south for a hundred rubles. In the meantime he advised us to walk out of town and hide in a wheat field along a road where he would pick us up at night. That's what we did.

When the peasant drove by at night, he was followed by a whole group of people. His feisty wife sat on the cart. On foot there were food smugglers, a family of the "bourgeoisie," and three German prisoners-of-war. It was an irony of fate that we, Russian officers, trusted our recent enemies, the Germans, most. They were obviously fleeing from the Bolsheviks. And we spoke some German. We walked along behind the wagon for a long time. It was a moonlit night.

"This village has the first Bolshevik checkpoint."

We made a large semi-circle around the village and marched for an hour. There was another checkpoint. We went around it as well. "This village has the third and last checkpoint. It's the worst, because they send out patrols."

The whole night the peasant's wife was angry at him. She was to give up her place to the father of the family and a small child who could not walk anymore. Her husband had not bought her the promised new items of clothing. She began to carp at him in a high, angry voice. In the still of the night her voice carried far, and she could be heard by the Bolsheviks. "Shut up, you witch! You'll get us into trouble," said the father of the family.

"You're the devil yourself," screeched the peasant woman

"I'll cut your throat if you don't shut up." He pulled out a penknife.

"Oh, yeah. I'll show you. Help! Help! Murder!"

"What can I do with this crazy woman?" said the frightened peasant. "Run, quick. The Reds will come any minute. Down this road to the right, left at the gully, the second road on the right and then the border is not far."

The Germans and the two of us began to run. Down the road to the right, to the gully, but there the road turned right and not to the left. "Let's not get lost. Better wait."

We went off a hundred strides from the road and lay down in the grass. Soon our peasant drove by. We waited to be sure that he wasn't followed and started after him at some distance.

Then I made a mistake.

I stopped to relieve myself. The Germans and my brother went ahead. I was going after them at a run, when out of the wheat on both sides of the road soldiers appeared and put their bayonets against my chest.

"Stop!"

Chapter Fifteen

A thought flashed through my mind: "Should I run? But my brother . . ." I stayed. Had we been together, we would have escaped. The Germans ran off. My brother stayed because of me.

The soldiers took us to the place where our whole group was being held, except for the Germans. I stood apart from my brother. There was a Bolshevik commissar, about forty soldiers and five mounted men.

"Where are you going and what is your business?"

We all said that we were going to the Ukraine for flour since there was famine in Moscow. The commissar then announced that we all could go except "you and you," pointing to my brother and myself.

"Why are you holding us, comrade commissar, we're all part of the same crew."

"Is that right?" he asked the others. To our relief, they all answered "yes."

"Nevertheless, you stay."

The others joyfully left.

"So why are you holding us?"

"You want to know? I'll tell you. Your mugs are White."

Things were getting bad. He had guessed our identities. We, of course, denied everything.

"I'll take you to headquarters. They'll decide what to do with you."

We had no desire to go to headquarters where we would have been shot on the spot. We weren't searched and proceeded as a group, talking to one another. Seizing a moment my brother whispered: "The letters. Do as I do."

We had been given letters of introduction to all sorts of White generals. What stupid carelessness. Each one of those letters was a death sentence. We had divided the letters. I had some and my brother had some.

My brother began to scratch himself which in these times was not unusual. All the trains were louse-infested. He shoved his hand into an inside pocket and I heard the sound of crumpling paper. I began to chatter away in order to deflect attention. My brother crushed the letters in his fist, put them in his mouth and began to chew, while ripping off small pieces which could be thrown away unnoticed. A large piece couldn't be thrown away because of the brightness of the moon. It would have been noticed. He looked like a person pensively chewing a blade of grass. I kept chattering away. Finally my brother spoke—he had gotten rid of the letters.

It was my turn. I remembered that they were in my billfold. I had to open the billfold within my pocket and pull out the letters. It was high-quality paper and when I crushed the letters it seemed that the whole world could hear the crackle. At a moment when my brother had the attention of the guards I shoved the letters into my mouth. But I couldn't chew them; there wasn't enough saliva. Tears ran from my eyes, and I became nauseous. Through an act of will I forced myself to chew slowly. Everything came out well. Rid of the damming evidence, we offered to be searched by the commissar. But he declined.

We kept trudging toward headquarters. My brother looked at one of the soldiers. "I know you, but I can't remember where we met. Where are you from?"

"Vladimir Province."

"Which village?"

"Nikitovka."

"Nikitovka! I know it well. I was on leave there two years ago."

I became cautious. My brother was up to something, but he didn't know Vladimir Province or Nikitovka.

"You know Nikitovka?" The soldier was surprised.

"Do I? Of course, that's where I saw you, you must know old . . . what's her name . . . auntie Anna, the bent-over one with the hunchback?"

"Not Anna, you must mean Mariia?"

"Of course, Mariia. Stupid me, Anna is in a totally different place. So how is old, dear aunt Mariia, grouchy as ever. You know her?"

"How could I not know her, she's my aunt."

"You're kidding. That makes us kinfolk. Strange running into each other like this."

My brother inquired in detail of news from Nikitovka, about Petr's family, our new relative, and of aunt Mariia. Petr was happy to find a kinsman and talked with relish. Then my brother repeated the same back to him with some variations. We had acquired a friend and even a relative amidst our convoy. In a similar fashion it turned out that a soldier named Pavel had been in the same regiment as my brother. Or, rather, my brother had been in his regiment. They reminisced of battles (all battles resemble each other) and the deeply moved soldier gave my brother a cigarette. My brother didn't smoke, but he had that one with obvious pleasure. The other soldiers listened sympathetically. My brother had created a good-natured mood among our guards.

Then my brother suggested that our case be put to a vote (such voting was popular at that time) and without waiting for a decision took the matter into his own hands. "Well, Petr," he said to our relative, "what do you say, shall we go or not?"

Petr was confused, but finally he said, "I don't know . . . I'll go along with the others." The formula was found.

"One vote to let us go," said my brother. "And what about you, Pavel?"

Pavel repeated the previous response. Soon everyone had agreed except the commissar who was asked last.

"My decision is to take you to headquarters," he declared.

"What is this comrades?" exclaimed my brother. "Forty-two votes to let us go, only one against but he wants to do it his way, disregarding your will. This is an overstepping of authority. Where is equality and justice I ask you? He thinks that he is an officer with golden epaulets and he can do whatever he wants. No, comrades, those days are over. Nowadays everyone is equal under the law. The will of the people and the opinion of the majority should be respected. Comrades, will you put up with such an attitude towards yourselves? He's behaving like one of the bourgeoisie with contempt for the will of the people. Am I right, comrades?"

Such an unexpected turn had its success. The soldiers in the back became concerned. Voices could be heard: "Of course, he's right. And you commissar, are you better than us?" "You'll catch a beating if you keep this up." Apparently there was no love lost for the commissar. He was taken aback but soon regained his self-control.

"Comrades, these are clever counter-revolutionaries, they're deceiving you."

The crowd grew silent. Things were getting bad again. But the commissar wasn't sure of his men. He decided to get rid of us.

"All right," he said to us, "you go straight down that road. We'll catch up to you in a minute." We did not want to move because that is how people get shot in the back of the head.

"We don't know the way, give us two guides," and my brother pulled the hands of our new friends. We moved away a bit. The commissar gathered his men in a circle and began to talk quietly.

"Petr, friend," said my brother, "you ought to arrange something. I don't want to go to headquarters at all."

"You're dead right. They will shoot you there, no questions asked."

"You see. Go talk with the commissar in a friendly way. Ask him what he wants? I'm ready to give him a bottle of vodka."

"Hey, that'll do it. Wait here, I'll go talk." He came back very quickly. "The commissar agrees."

"Luck's with us. How much does a bottle cost?"

"A hundred rubles."

"A hundred. You can get one in Moscow for forty. But OK. A hundred it is." My brother counted out a hundred rubles in coin. It was foolhardy to appear to be rich. Nothing prevented our friends from robbing us.

"Here's a hundred rubles and three for a drink for you."

The arrangement was made, but it was shaky. Would the commissar keep the bargain? He probably made it against his wishes. Will he have us shot at the last moment? The difficult part now was to leave our new friends. We went back to the group. The commissar was again talking quietly and stopped as we approached. My brother shook his hand with feeling.

"We lost our heads before and said things we shouldn't have. We didn't mean to offend. Peace is always better than a quarrel."

My brother kept close to the commissar not giving him the chance to conspire with his henchmen and finish us off. We settled down in a circle and cigarettes were passed all around. My brother and I did not smoke, but we lit up and began relating the news from Moscow.

My brother glanced at the moon. My nerves were so taut that I understood him without words. A large cloud was about to cover the moon. It would be dark in a few minutes. We would have to use this darkness to escape. It would shield us from bullets and pursuit. As the cloud covered the moon, we stood up.

"It's been nice talking to you, but we have to catch up to our companions. Otherwise we'll lose our flour money" (we made this up to facilitate our escape).

"Don't hold us up on our way back, and most of all, don't confiscate our flour. Goodbye, Petr. A low bow from me to Aunt Mariia. Goodbye, Pavel. Nice to see you again. You and I lived through things which are hard to forget. Goodbye, friends. Here's hoping we'll see each other again in this life. Thank you for your kind, humane treatment."

We shook everyone's hand. The commissar tried to detain us. "Wait a bit," he said.

"No, no. We can't. We've stayed too long as it is. We'll never catch our crew."

It was dark now. We turned and walked away at a rapid rate. The commissar began to talk with his cronies. We were almost beyond their field of vision.

"Run, on your toes" (to muffle our footfalls), whispered my brother. We sprinted for all we were worth in order to put as much distance between them and us as possible.

"To the right, into the wheat, zig-zag and then hit the ground." We ran into the high wheat and zig-zagged not to leave a clear trail, hit the ground, covered our faces with our sleeves and froze. (A moonlit face is very visible.)

Right away horsemen galloped down the road. Searching for us. They galloped past us, returned, and swept into the wheat fields. We heard muffled voices and horses rustling through the wheat. Then it grew quiet. We did not move. They might have set and ambush. An endlessly long time went by. Can one measure such moments? I heard a faint rustling in the stalks, looked up carefully—it was a hare. "If it's a hare," I thought, "then chances are there are no men." I took off my cap, raised myself no higher than the wheat, looked about with one eye, listening intensely. Silence. Then I whistled softly as we did when hunting. My brother answered. We found each other.

"Only not the road. We'll cut through the wheat." After an hour we saw several huts. One of them had a feeble light. An old woman was baking bread. She gave us milk and indicated the border: a small river.

We caught two horses from a herd and crossed the river on them. We were in the Ukraine. Then we collapsed beneath some bushes and fell asleep. That night we had walked more than sixty *versts*. Our feet were chafed raw.

In the evening we came to Iampol, where we met our three Germans. They got us a pass from the German commandant.

A bottle of vodka for two lives, not a bad deal. Since that time vodka became something akin to the water of life for me. I owe my very being to it. I also fondly remember my brother's cool-headed resourcefulness. He got us out of a deathtrap.

IN JEOPARDY [SEVERAL MONTHS LATER]

We had been on the march. Before us lay the large industrial city of Iuzovka (later Stalino). The sluggish river Kal'mius flowed here. This was a historical river, once called Kalka. On its shores in 1223 the Russians first encountered the Tatars and Mongols and were crushed by them.

Just at that time Red headquarters decided to stage a huge two-pronged assault. One prong was directed at Novocherkassk from the east and the other at Mospino, right where we were. The two prongs were to meet and envelop the Don and the Volunteer armies in a pincers.

In total ignorance of the responsibility which had fallen on our meager force we crossed the river and positioned our two field pieces some fifty strides to the left of the bridge. The rolling hills in front of us were occupied by infantry of the Markovets Regiment. The weather was wonderful, no gunfire was heard and we spread ourselves on the grass. I let my horse Dura graze, Kolzakov and Shapilovskii were on a hill in front of the battery. They were connected to us by a chain of scouts who would pass orders.

Everything seemed peaceful and quiet but suddenly artillery shells began to burst near the battery. The Reds could not see us but they suspected the battery's location. Whenever a shell burst we would throw a lump of dirt at a sleeping comrade. He'd leap up in fright, thinking that he was wounded.

But the Reds' shells came with increased frequency and we weren't laughing anymore. They had to be firing at a great distance, because we could not hear the reports.

Then suddenly four armored cars appeared. Our infantry collapsed into the tall grass and let them by. They headed for us. We began firing directly at them. They sprayed us with machine-gun fire. This lasted for the longest ten minutes, maybe longer. But despite the close distance we could not knock out an armored car nor could they inflict any losses. When you are nervous, your aim is off.

One of the armored cars chased our commanders, Kolzakov and Shapilovskii, round and round a hillock. In firing at the armored car we almost obliterated our commanders. The armored cars left, having failed to dislodge us. An intermission followed. Then dark chains of Reds appeared, one after another marching elbow to elbow. Evidently they were miners because they were in black and not in olive drab. We could see three chains but the infantry said there were nine. We were surprised at the use of such a huge force against our two artillery pieces and some fifty to sixty infantrymen. We opened up and fired fiercely in all directions because the Reds tried to turn our flanks and press the field pieces against the uncrossable, swampy river. We kept a special eye on the bridge, lest the Reds take it and cut off our only means of retreat.

Word came from our commanders that the shrapnel rounds were improperly set. I looked at the soldier setting the timing mechanism. He was wide-eyed with terror and stared at the advancing Reds while mindlessly turning the head of a round with a wrench. I pushed him aside and began setting the necessary distance myself. It was precise and attentive work, hard to do under fire because your hand shook. At that moment the artillery piece was turned ninety degrees and fired right above my head. I received a powerful, deafening shock to my ear. Blood began to flow from it. But there was no time to attend to such trifles. I worked feverishly.

Our thin chain of Markovets infantry did not flinch. Their machine gun was doing a wonderful job. Our shrapnel tore out clusters of men from the Red ranks. The first two chains faltered, but a third came up and the advance continued. They began approaching the bridge. We had to fall back. The infantry crossed on a fallen log and the battery headed for the bridge. One piece would fire point blank while the other galloped low along the river coming up within 150 strides to open fire in turn. Then the other piece would move toward the bridge, stop, and fire. Thus alternating, the battery crossed the river.

So much for the battery. My circumstances were totally different. I had let Dura loose to go graze and paid no attention to her because of the battle. When the battery took off, I ran for Dura. But she wasn't used to me yet, and ran off toward the Reds. Afraid of losing her, I ran after her in despair. Luckily, the retreating infantry turned Dura, and I caught her through dumb luck. All this took place under heavy fire from the Reds. The battery was firing back by the bridge. The infantry was crossing via the fallen tree. I was at a loss. The river was uncrossable; Dura would founder in the muck. The bridge? Was it too late? Had to try it. "Go, Dura, give it all. Go!" And she flew. First, low along the river, unseen by the Reds. And then up, streaking like an arrow along the Red infantry line which escorted her with a fusillade of rifle fire. At full gallop I turned right and Dura's hooves clattered on the bridge.

"Phew. A hell of a ride. Thank God we're out of there. Sweet girl, Dura. Well done. But you're a bitch for running away from me. I'll have to work on you, and soon."

I caught up to the battery. Examined Dura. Shrugged my shoulders in amazement. Neither she nor I had a wound. Lucky. There had been bullets all over the place.

DOLZHIK

We moved north to the village of Dolzhik. Destroyed the railroad line and went to Kazach'ia Lopan where we also did major damage to the rail lines. There were some minor engagements there. The Reds scattered. The division returned to Dolzhik.

No matter how hard we strained our ears, we could not hear any artillery to the south. Either we had gotten very far from our units or the advance of our troops, thanks to our raiding, was proceeding without the use of artillery with the Reds retreating everywhere.

We were surprised that the Reds were not harassing us, and we lived rather peacefully in Dolzhik. We were billeted in a well-kept house where I noticed a book in French in an ancient leather binding. This meant that there was an estate nearby. The woman of the house watched as I picked up the book. In answer to my question as to the existence of the estate, she feigned ignorance.

I went outside and asked the first passerby: "How do I get to the *ekonomia*?" (That is what estates are called in the south.)

"The main entrance is over that way, but there's a break in the wall over there."

The estate had been thoroughly looted, with that mindless venom which overcomes looters. Everything that could not be carried away was smashed and broken. If I can't use it, let no one else have it.

The first thing that shocked me was a grand piano hacked to splinters by an axe. Parquet, with an inlaid pattern of dark wood, had been ripped up and left scattered: they had been searching for hidden treasure. Doors, much too large for a peasant's hut, were hacked apart; some windows were carried away, others ripped out. Small furniture had vanished. Large pieces, chiffoniers and bureaus, were chopped up. Paintings were slashed. The portraits, some of them valuable, had their eyes gouged out and stomachs slashed. Porcelain was shattered . . .

This was not simple looting, but a bestial destructiveness. The ancient house was enormous, more like a palace. There is an order to looting. I have seen some fifty estates, and all were looted in the same matter.

On the top floor, apparently in the bedrooms, photographs and letters were always strewn about. The dressers had been carried off, and the letters dumped. I picked up a letter. Through it and some photographs I tried to reconstruct the past. A young woman was describing a holiday to either her friend or sister. It had been either a birthday or a name-day. "A wire was stretched between the oaks," I read, "and multicolored lanterns were hung on it." "It must be these very oaks," I said to myself. "Beyond the pond there were fireworks . . ." "And there's the pond," I thought. "I danced with Andrei and Vasilii . . ." Which one of these elegant young officers in the photographs was Andrei, and which was Vasilii? And here, probably, was the prince himself, and the princess.

I went down a broad stone staircase into an enormous hall. To my surprise, large and beautiful tapestries still hung there. They were ancient and their fabric had deteriorated in places. Apparently the looters found them useless: "The fabric is rotten, can't sew anything worthwhile out of them."

There was a library one story above. Books lay in heaps all over the floor. They had been walked on. The books in old leather bindings were of no interest to anyone. The mahogany bookcases, however, had been chopped up for firewood.

I began to dig through the books. A soft coughing caught my attention. An old servant stood before me. I was embarrassed. He probably took me for a thief as well. I greeted him and asked whose estate this was. He began to speak eagerly.

This estate, the famous Veprik, had belonged for centuries to the princes Golitsyn. It had been looted many times since the revolution but was finally devastated some three weeks ago. He showed me the stables. The horses and livestock had been taken away, the fowl slaughtered. The agricultural machinery ruined. There had been a fruit orchard—only stumps were left. This was the hothouse. The princess was fond of it and came by frequently. Rare plants grew here; peaches, orchids. Everything was smashed now, the glass panes knocked out.

With a heavy heart I started for home, that is, the house of the peasant who, of course, took part in the looting. The French book was witness to that. The housewife attentively watched my facial expression and made a very good dinner. My comrades were even surprised. I explained to them that this was reparation for the looting. I felt no love at all for the Russian people. To have destroyed such high culture and civilization was totally mindless. They probably even cut the tapestries into foot-cloths.

I suggested to Colonel Shapilovskii that we round up the estate's stolen horses for the battery. This would have been very easy to do. Find one horse, and all the thieves will inform on each other on the principle, "Well if they took mine, let them take Petr's also . . ."

"That wouldn't be bad," said the colonel. "But we're operating in the rear and must not provoke the local population. They supply us with information now, but otherwise they will inform the Reds."

Chapter Sixteen

Vera Volkonskaia, Orphaned by Revolution

Volkonskaia's story is one which was replicated in thousands of lives, that of children separated from their families and lost during the cataclysms of the Russian Revolution. She was an orphan with talents which unscrupulous people quickly recognized and tried to use. Her personal tragedy of this period was not her last. She was to endure the 900 day blockade of Leningrad in World War II as well. This is an excerpt from O. [Vera] Volkonskaia, *Tak tiazhkii mlat* [Thus the Heavy Mallet]. Paris: LEV, 1979.

The Revolution caught us in a small town in the Ukraine where father also had to come. During the October Revolution he was labeled an outlaw, since he was a prince and jurist, and mother begged him to flee abroad. My oldest sister lived with an aunt in Petrograd and being very gifted and assiduous was studying to be an architect. She knew that she would soon have to become "the father" of our family. She had to concentrate all her powers in order to obtain a good profession. But what could be accurately foreseen in this troubled time?! A huge whirlwind shook Russia, jarring individual destinies as well. Mother caught smallpox and was sent to the quarantine barracks, while we three, two younger brothers and myself, were left alone. The chances for recovery were slim. Our neighbors took us to a children's home, as orphans. There we merged with other orphans, the homeless and under-aged, young enterprising travelers, removed from the trains on which they had hitched rides.

The smell of carbolic acid, the prickly gray blankets, the thin wheat porridge, the bullying by the other children, were compensated for by the beneficent presence of the Komsomol [communist youth league] member Misha, [diminutive for Mikhail] a kind and fair leader. He organized hikes in the woods and fields during which he acquainted us with the healing herbs and described their properties. He spoke of birds, how beneficial their presence was, and how one should safeguard them.

Meanwhile, the food situation worsened and the orphanage was moved to the country. Our instructor was sent to the operational center, while the housekeeping head, without waiting for the arrival of the replacement, fled, grabbing what he could. He was a dodger. His convictions changed depending on circumstance. Taking advantage of the interregnum, those who were drawn to Tashkent, "the city of bread," walked the eight *versts* to the station in order to hop freight trains and cling to the railroad car buffers. We decided to make our way to our sister, but were taken off the train in Kiev and sent to a sorting point. This place sent underage vagrants to the families from which they had run away or to orphanages.

My younger brothers were assigned to an orphanage for boys on a dairy farm twelve kilometers from Kiev. It was said that children were well fed there and taken to a school in Kiev with the milk cans. The question of food became dominant for us. I was happy for them. It was good that they, who were inseparable, would be together. They wouldn't be miserable. Insofar as things concerned me, I was certain from my younger years that I could handle anything. Reminiscence, self-pity, sorrow—I immediately quashed these feelings within myself. I wrote the address of the orphanage on the lining of my white canvas shoes.

I was temporarily left at the site. We, the older ones, were allowed to walk around town provided we were back by six in the evening. On one of these walks I met a short fat lady who was carrying two large packets. Glancing at my uncomely clothes, she addressed me:

"Little girl, help me carry my things. I'll pay you fifty kopeks."

Strong and tall, I looked older than my years. "Where do you live? I have to get back to the orphanage shortly."

"Not far at all."

We were in the Podol area with the Dnieper flowing below. Despite late autumn, it was as warm as in spring. Having reached a tiny house standing in a small garden, the woman pushed open the wicket gate and we entered. A black shaggy dog rushed out happily in greeting. He treated me with suspicious indifference. We entered with the packages into a room whose table had a huge glass sphere and upon which playing cards with strange drawings were laid out. On an easy chair by the table sat a well-fed black cat with shiny fur. He appeared as suspicious as the dog. I did not even venture to pet it. The woman gave me the promised fifty kopeks. Puffing and panting, she sat down in the easy chair moving the cat aside. "I get tired from walking a long time. Yet, I was a dancer in my youth." She pointed to a photograph hanging on the wall of a young ballerina, thin as a blade of grass, who had nothing the least bit in common with the squat, fat lady.

"Do you want to come here tomorrow? You'll help me a bit with cleaning, and you'll get another fifty kopeks." I happily agreed. I would save some money this way!

On the following day, right after dinner, I went to the small house. I had to sweep and wash the painted floors in three rooms (the fourth was locked) and in the kitchen. "I'll take care of the fourth one myself," said Tat'iana Ivanovna, the mistress of the house. I finished my work quickly. In the orphanage I had learned how to wash floors and dishes properly, rinsing them and then wiping them dry.

"Good girl! Sit a minute and tell me about your family. Why are you in an orphanage?" I told her all that I knew. She remained quiet for awhile, then asked: "Do you know how to sing?"

"Yes, I know how to sing everything that my mother sang."

"Sing something!"

She brought out a guitar and quickly played the chords to Glinka's romances which I sang for her one after another. I always sang when cleaning or when I was in a meadow or in the woods. But it was very new and pleasant to sing with accompaniment.

"You have a good ear. Have you ever danced?"

"No."

"Well, come tomorrow. You can peel some pears for my jam, then we'll try some dancing." Squeezing the fifty kopeks in my fist, I returned to the center in an elevated mood. This way I would save money for a trip to Leningrad.

The next day, sitting on a stool in the kitchen, I commenced peeling fruit. Without breaking away from the work, I peeled a whole pan of pears. "So! Now, let's go dance. Follow what I am going to do and try to repeat it. Watch." She took off her robe and was left in black tights. She made several movements the probability of which, coming from her, was impossible to conceive. I repeated, as best I could, the steps she had executed. "Not bad. Not bad. The main thing here is to have a musical ear and a feel for rhythm. Besides that, you're pretty and it is pleasant to look at you." Everything that I heard was totally new and terribly interesting. "Tomorrow I'll teach you a simple dance." Having discovered my "choreographic talents," Tat'iana Ivanovna offered, "Would you like to stay here? I'll teach you to dance character dances. Sometimes we'll perform together and you will make a little money. In the mornings you'll go to school. I'm alone, you're alone, we'll both be happier." This offer seemed exciting to me. Everything at the center was done quickly. Tat'iana Ivanovna pledged that she would send me to school and take care of me, and I pledged that I was willing to live with her. Her address was recorded and we were told that an inspector would visit.

I was given a cheerful room in the small house, with lace curtains and pots of geraniums on the windowsill. A table and chair stood by the window. There was a small closet but I had nothing to put or hang there. A key protruded from the door to my room and Tat'iana Ivanovna ordered me to lock myself in at night.

In the morning she took me to school not far from the Podol. She spoke to the teacher for a long time, then left. There were none like me. All the girls lived nearby with their parents. They scrutinized me unceremoniously with evident contempt. My white canvas shoes in November, my worn dress and old coat did not inspire their confidence. The girl next to whom I was seated moved to the very edge of the seat as if I were a leper. No, I felt better with the street urchins. In that setting everything took place along lines of friendship and appearances had no significance. Besides, everybody looked equally bad.

With an aching heart I decided to ignore them, try to study hard and then leave immediately. But when classes ended, the teacher called me over and told me that I would be eating in school. She gave me meal tickets for a week. This was free for those without parents. She showed me how to get to the dining room. A long table covered with an oilcloth stood in a small clean room. One had to take a plate and go for food to a window which opened into the kitchen. I received a full plate of porridge with sunflower oil and a large piece of bread. Some of the girls ate here also but not even one of them sat next to me. Having finished my porridge, I put the remainder of the bread into my pocket, said thanks at the kitchen window and left. I was also given a notebook and two books for free. Returning to the small house, I saw that Tat'iana Ivanovna was not home. She left the key hanging on a nail in the little shed. Entering, I knocked on her door nevertheless. There was no answer. I took hold of the doorknob, wanting to take a look at the cat, but could not get in. The door was locked. I sat down in my room to do homework. Tat'iana Ivanovna returned at four o'clock. "We will practice the dance now. Did you eat in school?"

"Yes."

"I'll have some coffee, then I will call you." The house came to smell deliciously of coffee and something else that was good. In half an hour she called me. On the table in front of her were tights, tutus, and garlands. "Now try on all of these. I was fifteen years old when I wore these, but I was short and thin. You are so big that they might fit you now." I tried everything on in my room. The pink tights and the tutus almost fit, and I presented myself to Tat'iana Ivanovna who found this was not bad at all. "You'll grow a little more by spring and there will be no work until then anyway." I danced in front of her for about an hour, cautiously repeating the movements of the dance. "Good. We'll work this way everyday. Now go peel some potatoes and boil them. Wash my underwear that is soaking and hang it on the wire in the shed." I did all this and went to my room. I felt myself very much an orphan and in order to distract myself I began to repeat the movements of my dance.

"Come to supper!" shouted Tat'iana Ivanovna. We sat down at the kitchen table and I was given three potatoes and a piece of herring. "You have the right to get food from the ARA [American Relief Administration]. Ask your teacher tomorrow where you are to go to get it."

After lessons were over the next day, I walked up to the teacher in order to find out where I should go. She gave me an envelope with an address. Asking passersby, I finally found the street and the building. In a large room on the first floor sat a young woman who gave out food to older children from a list. When my turn came, having read the teacher's letter, she asked: "Did you bring a bag for the food?" "No, I don't have a bag!" I must have looked very upset because, smiling, she said: "Wait on the side, I will be there shortly and we'll find something." In a little while, another young woman replaced her and she went into the storeroom. Looking in the cabinets she found an old canvas bag. She gave me several cans of condensed milk, a large jar of coconut butter, a package of sugar, cocoa, and coffee. "Do you want some clothes?" asked the young woman, looking at my worn out garments. "We distribute only foodstuffs here, but there are some donated clothes as well, let's look." She quickly began to sort through items piled in the corner. Taking two dresses, she measured them up against me. Then she put a thick blue coat on me, completely new and very pretty. "There you go, we've dressed you up a bit." Thanking her, I loaded up my treasures and set off.

It was already completely dark. The unfamiliar streets had an unfriendly look. I became sad that I was alone and had no one with whom to share my feelings and the tasty things. Tat'iana Ivanovna showed no warmth toward me whatsoever. I even wondered why she took me in. At that time I was far from comprehending her desire to make some money off me and have a free servant.

Entering the yard of the little house, which I could not possibly call my home, I saw that there were no lights in the windows. Feeling for the key on the nail, I walked into the house. I was very hungry. It would be good to eat my leftover bread with some condensed milk but I didn't know what to use to open the can and went to my room. Having eaten my bread I sat down to do my lessons. Tat'iana Ivanovna still had not come. Removing the key from the keyhole of the front door so that she could enter with her key, I went to my room and lay down to sleep. I was exhausted from running around the streets, as well as from the cold and the agitation, and I fell asleep the moment my head touched the pillow.

Awakening suddenly because someone was touching my face, I opened my eyes. Light from the street lamp penetrated the room and I saw, standing next to the bed, a small person with a large head and protruding black hair. He touched my face again and I screamed wildly. A disheveled and sleepy Tat'iana Ivanovna ran in, took the person by the hand, and led him away. Returning to me, she explained: "That is my nephew. My sister died and it is a year now since he's been living here. He's a midget. He doesn't do bad things but he looks so revolting that I have to hide him. He is locked up all day and sleeps but wanders around the house at night. This time, lock your door. In the morning, you'll find cocoa ready with bread and butter." For the first time in her tone a weak shadow of sincere warmth conveyed itself, addressed to this lonely trusting creature which had so simply followed her without hesitation or doubt.

Everything was going well at school. I did my lessons carefully and was attentive. The girls changed their attitude toward me from the moment that I began coming in a pretty woolen dress, black lacquered shoes and a quality coat. But they no longer existed for me. I almost never talked to them. I hurried to the small house to clean it, prepare my lessons and learn new steps. I liked dancing very much. Sometimes when thinking of my family and nanny and feeling the onset of tears, I would begin to invent numerous new movements.

Once Tat'iana Ivanovna said: "We have a chance to make some money. There's going to be a big party with entertainment in a private home. You will come with me, sing to my accompaniment, and then dance. You are doing this quite well already." She carefully unwound the pink tights, ironed the tutu, and straightened the silk rose on the little garland. "Everything is in order. I'll put some makeup on you and you'll be a dear."

Saturday evening came and we set out for the Kreshchatik [main thoroughfare of Kiev] with two round cartons and our dresses. "This is the apartment where we're going," pointed Tat'iana Ivanovna to a series of large illuminated windows. We went up through the back entrance and the housemaid took us to a small room next to the kitchen where we changed. Tat'iana Ivanovna put on a long black evening dress, combed her hair very deftly, fastened artificial diamonds to her breast and hair, and became unrecognizable. She also combed my thick hair, binding it into a large knot at the back of my head, fastened the little charm of roses, stretched out the tights evenly, and touched up my cheeks, eyes, and lips. Glancing in the mirror, I barely recognized myself.

We entered the living room. I was carrying Tat'iana Ivanovna's guitar. The large hall was awash in light from the crystal chandelier suspended from the ceiling and a series of lamps with crystal pendants along the walls. The guests were already sitting on the sofas, easy chairs, and armchairs, Tat'iana Ivanovna fawningly greeted the lady of the house, a tall fat woman in an expensive dress. "Good evening, Iuliia Petrovna!" "Good evening, Tat'iana Ivanovna. And this is your orphan?" "Yes." I curtsied. "Hello little girl." When all the guests had gathered, Tat'iana Ivanovna gave me a signal and I walked to the center of the hall, having handed her the guitar.

I was scared and uncomfortable, but the feeling of responsibility and being yoked, having become habitual in my solitary existence, forced me to assume the ballet pose I had learned. After the introduction, I sang Glinka's "The Lark." When I finished, everyone applauded very loudly. Bowing, I sang another romance. When all was sung, I bowed again, and after an introduction danced a number arranged by Tat'iana Ivanovna. They again applauded enthusiastically. I was surrounded, people smiled, the ladies kissed me. A friendly fat girl approximately my own age brought me a basket decorated with ribbons that was full of money. I thanked everybody again and curtsied ballet-style to all sides. Everyone smiled benevolently again. They then went to eat. The girl took me by the hand and sat me next to her. Tat'iana Ivanovna came over, took the basket from my hands, and transferred the entire contents to her purse. Nina, the girl, the niece of the lady of the house, warned me, telling me that Tat'iana Ivanovna liked money very much and would always take all of it away from me. "She dresses up her midget nephew as a freak and shows him off for money at carnivals. Beware," said Nina. A young man sitting across from me offered: "If you want, I'll introduce you to the director of a terrific circus. You'll make a lot more money there."

I was not comfortable with Tat'iana Ivanovna from the very start and there were moments when I wanted to leave her and return to the center. But there—again the unknown. Where would I be sent? My goal remained to make my way to Leningrad, the St. Petersburg of my early childhood, to Varia, my older sister. What if I could really make more money in the circus and go to her? We arranged it with the young man that he would meet me in front of the school on Wednesday and take me to the circus director.

Tat'iana Ivanovna, having praised me for the concert, said nothing about the money. She said nothing about it the following day as well. On Monday, when I returned from school in the rain with wet books, I got up some courage and asked her to buy me a bag for my books and notebooks. She looked at me sideways but, nevertheless, bought me a large oilskin briefcase. On Tuesday evening I put my good dress in it, my books, and my white canvas shoes in case I would not return.

My heart, once tender in infancy, had acquired a defensive shield from the shocks and calamities. Not yet in a condition to comprehend life's fundamental dangers, I began to learn how to parry its small jolts and stings. Having finished lunch in school, I walked out into the street with my briefcase. My new acquaintance was waiting for me on the corner. He took me by the hand and we went along the streets. He told me about the circus and said that I would learn much there and make excellent money. We arrived at a small, fairly rundown hotel and knocked on the door of the room occupied by the director. This was a tall, fat man who looked unpleasant. My guide began to talk quietly in German. I could only distinguish the individual words: "Waisenkind" (orphan) and "sehr begabt" (very able). (In my early childhood, Kätchen, my governess, who was to have trained me to be a mademoiselle, had taught me to speak German.) This person instilled such fear in me that I decided immediately to return to Tat'iana Ivanovna. But, after talking for another two to three minutes, the young man, whose name I did not even know, quickly left the room. I jumped after him but the German grabbed me by the shoulder.

"You will remain here. I will teach you acrobatics and you will make good money."

"I don't want to stay here! I want to go home!"

"You don't have a home. Don't be stupid. If you protest, I'll give you a flogging."

And so, a difficult life began. It seemed that nothing worse than this had yet happened. From early morning, training in acrobatics took place. Handstands, faults, somersaults. Falling on one arm and then the other, and depicting a circle with the body and extended legs, one had to get on one's feet for one second and, again with palms on the floor, make another circle and so on around the whole arena. Each exercise was repeated countless times. My muscles hurt. All of this was done under the hostile gaze of Master Kurt. Unsuccessful movements drew a whip to my rear. Forget about school. I decided to run away at the first opportunity. But such an opportunity did not present itself. I was always under observation. I, of course, did not show that I understood his conversations with his daughter. I slept in the same room with his daughter Irma. The rest of the time was spent in the circus. There was not even a suggestion of my innocent dances. I had to become an acrobat. "She is like rubber," said Kurt to his daughter once. "She will work wonderfully."

Irma was lazy, quite dumb but not mean. She did not let me away from her even for a stride during the time that I spent with her. I was always well fed, but the words "Man does not live by bread alone" were especially applicable here. There wasn't even a hint of any warmth, friendly attitude, or joyous approach to matters at hand. All the circus people, as if specially chosen, were rude, dismal, and jealous of another's success. And everything was valued strictly in terms of money. Conditions were unpleasant, even oppressive. The animals were treated badly also. Everything was based on fear. I was full of compassion for my silent four-legged brothers.

Once I overheard Kurt say: "Two more performances—then out of this swinish country." My situation was bad. No matter what, I had to try and run away. Irma was going on her regular shopping and I implored her to take me with her. "I'll carry your packages. I never get to go outside!" She thought about it and agreed. "All right, you'll carry the goods. But be careful, father whips one very painfully!" We walked along the Kiev streets. Irma stopped in shops, bought the required produce, and loaded me with it. We proceeded. "Walk in step with me," she ordered sternly. At one spot in the street, at the very entrance to the vegetable market, a truck stood on the sidewalk. Some boxes and bags were being unloaded from it. Throwing the produce on the ground, I slid through the narrow space between the wall and the truck, leaving fat Irma on the other side, and raced up the stairs having jumped into the entrance of the very first building. Screened by the truck, my actions escaped Irma's eyes.

Reaching the third floor, I read the name V. Volkonskaia on the bronze plate. The first letter of my name, my last name, could these be close relatives of some sort? I rang. A tall woman of about forty opened the door. "Can I come in for a few minutes? I am Vera Volkonskaia." Down the street I heard Irma's shrill voice. "Come in." She let me into the room and closed the door. "Wait here a little. I will ask if Vera Andreevna can see you." Rapidly, gasping, I began to describe what had occurred, that I ran away from the Germans, that they were probably searching for me that very moment, and that I was very scared. For a long moment, attentively, the lady looked me in the eyes and then said: "All right. We will look after you."

In a quarter of an hour I was led into a room where an old lady with an elongated stern face, and all in white, was sitting on a bed. She pointed to a chair standing next to the bed, looked at me and smiled. Her smile lit up her face like the sun coming out from behind clouds. Her face immediately became warm and attractive. We were left alone. "Well, tell me everything from the beginning!" I told her everything beginning with my grandmother, my nanny and the estate, and ending with the Germans. It turned out that Vera Andereevna knew my aunt Vera Vladimirovna well. The latter had a model *gimnazium* in Moscow. We were very distant relatives of their family. "You will stay here for awhile and go to school. It is in the same building. It is our former *gimnazium*. One of my daughters is its head, another teaches there. You will receive a school lunch from the state. I will write to Vera Vladimirovna and find out about your sister from her. Go now; my daughter Anastasia Mikhailovna, will take care of you." I thanked her awkwardly and exited.

At a desk in the neighboring room sat a woman with the same elongated, stern face. I stopped, not daring to interrupt her work. She indicated the chair with her eyes and continued to write. I probably felt the way that village children did, godchildren of grandmother Vera, who were brought in by their mothers to pay their respects. Grandmother would call the child to come closer and affectionately give a pat on the cheek, as he covered his face. "Why is he hiding?" she would ask in amazement. "He don't dare" [look up], the child's mother would explain.

In this large, cold apartment with its severe imperial furniture I too "did not dare" after the less than respectable conditions to which I had become accustomed over the past period. Finally, Anastasia Mikhailovna completed her work and, knocking, entered her mother's bedroom. After a few minutes she came out smiling with the same unexpected, sunny smile as her mother. "Hi Vera, do you want to take a bath before supper? We will be eating in three quarters of an hour."

I became bewildered in the large, snow-white bathroom. Everything glistened with the surgical cleanliness of an operating room. Could I dry myself with one of the fluffy towels neatly folded in a pile on a stool? Painstakingly I rinsed the bath after using it. For the potential flight from Master Kurt, I had put on my best dress over the dirty tights, sweated through from training. I washed them in the sink, wrung them out thoroughly, and hung them on the radiator. I put the dress on over my naked body. I smoothed out my hair and, looking carefully at everything, checking to see that I had not left any dirty tracks, I walked out of the bathroom. A table was set for four in the large dining room, but nobody was in the room yet. Perhaps I'll be eating in the kitchen? I'd better get there ahead of time. Entering, I saw Vera Andreevna's other daughter, Ekaterina Mikhailovna, who had opened the door to my salvation. In a robe and a white kerchief on her head, she was preparing a supper tray for her mother. "May I help you with anything?" I asked. "No, thank you. Go to the dining room, we'll be eating right away."

We sat down at the table as soon as Ekaterina Mikhailovna finished with her mother's supper. There were two sisters, Anastasia Mikhailovna's husband, and me. The husband was cut from completely different cloth than the Volkonskii ladies. It seemed to me that he did not feel particularly at ease in this situation. Later I found out that he had been a teacher in the former *gimnazium*; that he and Anastasia had fallen in love and married after the revolution. They were totally different in terms of their background and upbringing.

Their model *gimnazium* was transferred to the state but they were left in charge to teach and, by the way, were greatly respected. Their graduates received a good and well-rounded education. Nothing had changed in the apartment or in their unfailingly strict and modest routine.

After supper I offered to wash the dishes, saying that I had learned to do this properly at the orphanage. While washing the dishes, and alone in the kitchen, I partially shook off my feelings of confusion and restraint. "A real village girl at the lords'," I thought.

I slept on a small folding bed which was kept in a closet in the living room during the day. In school, I felt that I was way behind the others. I began to be very attentive trying to get at least a reasonable hold on the subject at hand. After lessons, there was a free dinner, simple but filling. Then, we did our homework right in school. It was hard for me, but everyone around me was so busy that I could not ask anyone to explain things. I would see how things would proceed. I did not go outside even once. I was afraid of running into somebody from the circus.

Vera Andreevna found out that aunt Vera had died, but Varia was living in a students' dormitory. Soon a letter addressed to the Volkonskiis arrived from her in which she thanked them for helping me and informed me that she would come to Kiev for a few days during vacation.

Finally it came, the long awaited day of her arrival. I answered the doorbell and flung myself on her neck. "How you've grown," exclaimed Varia.

The Volkonskiis greeted her very warmly. She spent quite a long time with Vera Adreevna, and came out smiling. In the morning, she and I went to the orphanage to see our brothers. This was a row of small, new wooden houses built next to the dairy farm. On one side were meadows, on the other a pine forest. The boys looked good and, evidently, were not unhappy. The lady in charge, with whom Varia spoke, fully understood how important it was for her to graduate from college before taking the responsibility for us upon herself. "It would be good for the boys if their sister could work in our laundry. If she is sensible, she could work and go to school. And we would pay her a little." "For the trip to Leningrad," I thought. We discussed this and decided that this was not bad at all. I would see my brothers and would not be dependent on anyone except for the head of the orphanage, who appeared to be a sincere and kind person. She offered that Varia and I live there for a few days of Varia's vacation. "There is enough milk and porridge for everybody. Your sister will learn what to do in the laundry." Varia and I checked the clothes as well as the income and expense books. "When you give out clothes—get a receipt. Keep everything in order and all will be clear."

We went walking in the woods with Varia and talked of how good things would be when she graduated and began to work. She promised that as soon as she got her diploma she would take me immediately and then, later, the boys. "You understand that I now live in a dormitory and cannot pay for a room until I start working." "I understand and how!" I exclaimed, kissing her.

I was happy. There was something new to hope for. I liked the orphanage and the director was a simple and kind lady. She saw to it that the "laundry girl" was allotted a little income. She would come by to see how I was doing. Comfortable about us, Varia left for Leningrad. I wrote a letter to Vera Andreevna thanking her for everything that she had done for me.

I didn't see the boys much. They had a precise daily schedule. School in the morning, return, dinner, homework, work in the service shops, a walk, supper, and to bed at nine o'clock. It was worse with my studies. I was able to go to school three times a week. True, the teacher assigned lessons to do at home. I tried to study in the evenings but frequently fell asleep over a book.

During free time in the day I ran into the woods. In the fragrant thickets of pine, walking on dry crunchy needles, I was immersed in a kingdom of silence. The pine forest—a forest that is mysterious, dense, devoid of the singing of birds—the impenetrable forest of nanny's stories. Ivan Tsarevich [folk tale hero] galloped through it on his gray wolf. Making my way through the reddish trunks of the pines I felt a kind of indescribable joyous agitation, the expectation of "the beautiful" and vaguely foreseen. The most optimistic of hopes, the bravest of plans were born during these walks. With a living force they fed my monotonous existence divided by time spent in the laundry, the kitchen, and doing homework. The days passed slowly, marked like signposts on the road, by Varia's letters. In her last letter she related to me that a teacher from the Advancement of Arts would be in Kiev on business. He promised to take me with him on his way back to Leningrad. Varia was now living with her high school friend, Vera Naumova. I could live there with her for a while until her final exams. She would notify me about the day of departure at the last moment. I shared this happily with the director. "That is good! You made a little money and you can take it with you."

Three weeks passed after that. No other news came. Finally a letter arrived from Vera Naumova. She wrote that Varia had contracted typhoid fever, but that she was getting better and that nothing had changed regarding my trip to Leningrad. Ultimately, after another ten days of waiting, I was sitting in a second class compartment on a train heading toward the city of my youth in the company of a quiet, affable companion. The train clicked off the *versts,* bringing me closer to my longed-for dream.

A damp winter evening had fallen upon the city when, hurried along by impatience, I ran up the steps three at a time. On the fourth floor a business card on the door read: M. Naumov. I rang. They took their time behind the door which was opened by a small old lady. I entered and through the open door of the kitchen I saw the sturdy figure of Varia's friend, Vera Naumova. She stood with her back to me without moving. Her shoulders shook with sobs.

"Vera, what's the matter?"

"Variushka died. She had a recurrent wave of ulcers and could not endure it."

Stricken as by thunder, I fell upon a stool. It was all over for me. All my plans, all my joys ended in this kitchen. Everything was cut at the root. The old lady, Vera's mother-in-law, came in. She commenced to take off my damp coat, led me to the dining room, and sat me at the table. Everything occurred as if it was not me but someone else, a mannequin. Vera came in and embraced me while drowning in tears. I seemed to freeze and did not cry. I was given linden tea with something from a small bottle poured into it.

Evidently, I slept for a very long time. I awoke with the thought: Variushka is dead. I could not believe or comprehend this. I got up and walked out of the room. Some people came and talked with me, others wept. I remained quiet, my heart wrung. I could not believe it.

Only at the funeral did I realize the full extent of my misfortune. The open casket stood in the little hospital chapel. I bent over the delicate, waxen face with its closed eyes, long eyelids lowered, the thin hands crossed on the chest, the long white dress, like a bride's, and a white rose placed at the feet. I kissed her forehead which was cold as marble. And suddenly my heart was pierced by an acute sense of hopelessness and a repressed scream burst from my mouth. Unfamiliar people took hold of me from both sides.

Then, for a long time, we walked along the streets behind the funeral hearse. For a long time I walked despairingly behind the casket of my beloved sister—always so far away and now gone forever.

Chapter Seventeen

Mikhail Gol'dshtein, My First Recital

In 1937, at the age of twenty, Gol'dshtein wrote his first memoirs encompassing some 400 pages. The great composer Dmitri Shostakovich, who perused them, suggested that they be hidden well but not destroyed. Gol'dshtein burned the manuscript in fear of discovery. As he notes, in a normal country the memoirs would have readily been published. He was to emigrate to Europe in the late 1960's and continue his career as a violinist (cherishing his 1643 Amati violin). Finally, feeling at home in freedom, he turned again to his memoirs, forty years after the initial writing. The thought of that manuscript consigned to flames in 1937 never faded from his consciousness. Taken from Mikhail Gol'dshtein, *Memuary dvadtsatiletnego muzykanta* [The Memoirs of a Twenty-Year Old Musician]. New York: *The New Review*, No. 145, December, 1981.

One cannot say that people in Odessa were bloating up and dying of hunger as they were in the other cities of Russia. Tasty dishes were available in restaurants. The abundance of mackerel helped greatly. It was eaten fried, smoked or raw. Mullet, bullheads, and fluke were also served. The selection was ample. Nor was there a shortage of alcoholic beverages. Home brew came to the rescue. Drunken Bolsheviks experienced great pleasure in demonstrating their militant revolutionary spirit in restaurants. They would discharge their firearms not only at the ceiling but at living human beings as well. Babel [Isaak Babel, the famous writer] would recall that in one restaurant there was a sign next to the piano player: "Please don't shoot the piano player, he's playing the best he can." However, things were tight when it came to bread. But the Americans, out of the kindness of their heart, decided to save the Soviet regime which was being choked by hunger. Ships loaded with grain began to arrive in Odessa. Lenin outfoxed the capitalists and cleverly took advantage of their sympathy toward the starving. But there was no sympathy for the innocent victims of the terror. No one reacted to the mass executions. The murderers received bountiful food rations. They feasted. Especially during their new holidays.

I remember the time when the fifth anniversary of the October coup approached. Huge red canvases smeared with slogans were stretched over dilapidated houses. Preobrazhenskii [Transfiguration] Street was renamed Trotsky Street. The Cathedral of the Transfiguration stood on this street. The faithful managed to keep it functioning. One could regularly hear the ringing of the bells from this cathedral. But some extremely logical person decided to rename it in honor of Trotsky Street: since the street was Trotsky, the cathedral should be Trotsky as well.

Celebratory concerts were being arranged in Odessa. There was no shortage of artists. The popular couplet-rhyming singers merely moved to the workingmen's clubs. The concerts were broad in nature: mandatory revolutionary poems were read and songs were sung; magicians, acrobats, sword swallowers, comedians, and violinists playing serious classical music all performed.

Once someone came to Stoliarskii [a famous violin teacher] in order to select a violinist for a concert. I was the one chosen. I had been playing a Vivaldi concerto. After listening, the political commissar deemed Vivaldi totally compatible with the revolutionary spirit. My parents were told that I had to appear at a particular place at a particular hour or else. My parents humbly fulfilled this command and brought me to some smelly hall. I remember it even now. Someone was vomiting; someone was fighting and cursing. Apparently the audience at this concert sacredly held to the oath of Genghis Khan and did not wash. They smoked all kinds of crap. Breathing was impossible. I was choking and a vial of perfume was brought up to my nose. They stood me on a table—the better to see me. Some very tall dame accompanied me on the piano. The audience listened with great attention and rewarded me with a storm of applause.

As reward for the performance I was given a small bag of flour. This was considered a high honor, even for well-known artists. They also handed me an official paper declaring my participation in the concert and receipt of an honorarium. The document was signed by a commissar who was covered with machine-gun bandoleers from head to belly button. He spat on the seal and slammed it against the paper. Mother hurriedly removed me from the stinking hall where I could barely breathe.

Out on the street I greedily swallowed the fresh air and mother kept saying that "tomorrow we would celebrate my birthday in royal style." She kept her word. We ate *mamalyga* [a dense corn bread] with our fingers after cutting it with a string. From the flour mother baked up a tasty *pirog* of sautéed cabbage and fish. Cherry brandy appeared on the table. Intricate toasts, each carrying a subtext, were made. Jokes were told. I was made to play and performed several exercises and etudes which required no accompaniment.

Suddenly, amidst the celebration there was a pounding on the door. Shouts and gunfire were heard. One would have thought that the regime had fallen and the Bolsheviks had been cleared from Odessa. But, unfortunately, that did not occur. A gang of drunken sailors burst into our apartment. They waved pistols and fired into the ceiling, shouting "mother f—ing this" and "mother f—ing that." "What is this, the constituent assembly?" one of the enraged "guests" shouted. "The bourgeoisie is feasting during famine! We will crush all of you like bedbugs!" A sailor, who possessed a high, rooster's voice was especially furious in his invective; he kept screaming, piercingly: "What did we struggle for, what did we shed our blood for?" "You're traitors, counter-revolutionaries! Vipers! A conspiracy against the revolution! It won't happen! It won't happen!"

One of our guests discreetly disappeared during the confusion. He sensed that the situation might have a terrible outcome. These tyrants were merciless. They disregarded the screams of my sister and the weeping of women. They were ready to kill even a child. One of them ordered that all the food on the table be seized, and immediately a blanket was ripped from the bed and food thrown into it, not only the food but also plates, dishes, and flatware. Then they began pulling wedding rings off the women's fingers and ripping the crosses from their breasts. "You're all under arrest," screamed the "revolutionary" in his piercing voice. "You're all going to prison."

Mother asked me to pick up the violin and play as loud as I could. One of the monsters tried to grab the violin, but mother stood in his way, shouting: "Stab me, kill me, but don't touch the boy. Yesterday he gave a concert for the likes of you, and today, on his birthday, you want to take away his violin?! Here, read this official paper." Mother proffered the paper, but the tyrants assured her that they were illiterate and would not read any high-falutin document. The guests armed themselves with chairs. A sailor took aim at a guest, but the pistol misfired. No one was ready to go to prison for everyone knew that no one came out of there alive.

Suddenly there was insistent rapping on the door. One of the tyrants opened it. A whole squad of the Cheka [secret police] entered along with an officer. The discreetly disappearing guest had brought the squad. The appearance of an officer brought the looters into confusion. They saw that the officer was not sympathetic to them. The officer turned out to be a graduate of the private *gimnazium* which my parents had once managed. He wanted to get to the bottom of things. My mother was permitted to speak first. She presented the official paper from the concert which stated that I had received a small bag of flower. The signature on the paper was rather impressive. Mother also presented my birth certificate with the date of birth clearly indicated. How could we not celebrate it with our family? Besides, my mother added, one of the looters ate the whole *pirog* which had been baked from the concert flour. This made a great impression. The officer ordered the looters to put all their weapons on the table and to turn their pockets inside out: Gold jewelry and silver poured onto the table. The looters were tied up and led from the apartment. In parting the officer said that everything would be settled the next day and that we would be given a document safeguarding us. Then, embarrassed, he added: "These men came to rob our dear teachers; they would seize gold items and other valuables and then get on a ship and leave Russia. We know such brave types. Put a Mauser in their hands and they go off killing and robbing." The officer said a polite goodbye and promised to come the next day. It could have turned out much worse. We could have all been hauled off to prison and finished off there, having been the object of some absurd accusation.

The next morning our "savior" came with three sailors. He handed us the safeguarding document and told us that, if need be, we were to invoke the name of a particular commissar who was aware of our situation. Two small bags of American flour, expensive wines, chocolate and other edibles were placed on the table. And an invitation was proffered to perform at a concert. We had to consent.

It was a concert and a political rally. They stood me on a table and I had to play. I tuned my violin and played all three parts of a Vivaldi concerto with the accompaniment of a grand piano. When they asked me to play some more, I had nothing except for some etudes. But they wouldn't let me off the stage. So I got really brave and played a revolutionary song, "We're Blacksmiths." The audience began to sing along. The success was incredible. Finally they let me off the stage. A commissar in black leather approached my mother, gave her gifts which were precious to us, and assured her that we were "under special protection." A special directive had been issued about this. I was also asked to give professor Stoliarskii their heartfelt gratitude. But when I came for my lesson the next day, Stoliarskii had been informed of everything to the smallest detail. He was very amused that I had played an ordinary etude which was intended for the training of one's fingers.

And then in all seriousness, Stoliarskii said: "You see how beneficial it is to learn etudes, especially by heart." Stoliarskii knew that I would be invited to perform in the future and that to decline would be taken as a hostile attitude toward the Soviet regime. So, I had to consider my concert repertoire and learn some other revolutionary songs as well. But I was able to play them by ear. Stoliarskii also gave me specific instructions as to which songs I should play. God forbid that I play a song of the White Army. And so I became a child virtuoso. I performed at concerts not only in Odessa but in places a great distance away. At one such concert Isaak Babel [the famous author] came up to me. That's how our friendship began. Many years later Babel would recall our first meeting. He even meant to write a story about it. But he was not to realize his intention. His life was broken off prematurely. [He died in 1939 in a Soviet slave-labor camp.]

Chapter Eighteen

Viktor Kravchenko, Youth in the Red

Kravchenko's story as the first major defector from the Soviet Union to the West was once well known. There were others who followed his example. But our interest in selecting this passage partly reflects the subtitle of his book regarding his personal life. The various motivations which turned him to communism in his youth are absorbingly articulated: words, ideas, faith, enthusiasm. In a revolutionary setting, all of these increased sharply in meaning and resonance. Kravchenko's predisposition toward radicalism was also shaped by his father, a worker-agitator, who devoted his life to the revolutionary movement. Taken from Viktor Kravchenko, *I Chose Freedom.* Garden City, N.Y.: Garden City Publishing, 1946.

Here, for the first time, I came to know an intellectual household, where literature, music and the theater seemed as real and vastly more important than bread and work. The elder Spiridonov steered our avid reading into broader channels, not only among the Russian classics but among the works of Shakespeare, Goethe, Anatole France, Knut Hamsun, Hugo, Flaubert, Zola, Dickens.

Looking back, I am amazed by the extent and variety of my reading during that springtime of mental discovery. Somehow the beauty and the pathos of books, along with the exalted hopes of my father, became part of the revolution as it swept over an eleven-year-old boy. It seemed as if in a few weeks the distance between literature and reality, between words and deeds, was being bridged.

The storm clouds burst in the last week of February 1917 (early March in the Western calendar). Even those who had been most certain of its advent were surprised and bewildered. Revolution, which had been an intimate and half-illicit word, was suddenly in the open, a wonderful and terrifying reality.

What had seemed a simple solution of all problems had exploded into a million new problems, some of them ridiculously petty, like finding food and clothes.

The seams of accustomed life came apart. Schools, factories, public institutions lost their old meanings. The people of our city crowded into the snow-covered streets. It was as if homes and offices and workshops had been turned inside out, dumping their human contents into the squares and parks. Demonstrations, banners, cheering, flaring angers, occasional shooting—and above it all, enveloping it, almost smothering it all, there was talk, talk, talk. Words pent up for centuries broke through in passionate oratory; foolish and inspired, high-pitched and vengeful oratory.

Slogans filled the air and seemed to have a proliferating life of their own. *Down with the war! War to a victorious end! Land and freedom! The factories to the workers! On to the Constituent Assembly! All power to the Soviets!* New words and new names burst and sputtered in our minds like fireworks. Bolsheviks, Mensheviks, Kadets, Social Revolutionaries, Anarchists. . . . Kerensky, Miliukov, Lenin, Trotsky. . . . Red Guards, Whites, Partisans. . . .

Platforms grew on the main squares. Speakers followed one another in a loud procession. Men and women who had never spoken above a timid whisper now felt the urge to scream, preach, scold and declaim. Educated men with well-tended beards made way for soldiers and workmen. "Right! Right!" the crowds thundered or "*Doloi! Von!*—Down with him! Out with him!"

Once, on a day of demonstrations under a forest of homemade banners, my father spoke from a platform. Everyone seemed to know his name.

"Friends and brothers! Workers, peasants, intellectuals and soldiers!" he began.

It was the first time I had heard him speak in public and I could scarcely contain my excitement. His voice was resonant and he seemed transfigured, so that I had to reassure myself that it was, indeed, my own father. Words and ideas that had been intimately our own, almost a family secret, were miraculously public, so that everyone became part of the family. He told about prison and exile, about the heroic life of Comrade Paramonov, about the beautiful future. He pleaded for order and self-control and warned against those who would drown the revolution in blood. He spoke with marvelous simplicity and sincerity, as if these were his three sons multiplied to hundreds.

When he stepped from the platform and a band played the *Marseillaise*, I rushed toward him, elbowed a way through his admiring friends, and shouted "Hurrah, papa!" Father laughed with a full voice.

"You see, Vitenka," he said, "now people will be free. It was worth fighting for this!"

I knew then, or perhaps I only understood later, that he was justifying himself, explaining the years of penury and worry he had visited on his family.

The honeymoon of the revolution, however, soon trailed off into dissensions, accusations, suffering. Enthusiasm gave way to anger and bitterness. Stones, fists, revolver shots were increasingly mixed with the words and arguments. At the same time food became scarcer; wood, coal and kerosene seemed to disappear; some factories worked only intermittently, others closed down altogether. "There's your revolution! You asked for it!" people, especially the well-dressed people, now muttered.

My father grew more depressed, more silent, with every passing day. He became more irritable than I had ever seen him in the years of danger and sacrifice. When I pressed him for an explanation of the many parties and programs he seemed embarrassed.

"It's too complex," he would say. "You're not old enough to understand. This is a struggle for power. No matter what any party stands for, it will be bad if *one* party wins. That will only mean new masters for the old—rule by force, not by the free will of the people. It is not for this that the revolutionists gave their lives."

Another time, after we had listened to Mensheviks, Bolsheviks, Kadets [Constitutional Democrats, K D's in Russian] and others in the Mining Institute, now the headquarters of the Ekaterinoslav Soviet, he shook his head sadly and said:

"I have been fighting to overthrow Tsarism. For freedom, for plenty, not for violence and vengeance. We should have free elections and many parties. If one party dominates, it's the end."

"But what are you, papa? A Menshevik, Bolshevik, a Social Revolutionary or what?"

"None of these, Vitia. Always remember this: that no slogan, no matter how attractive, is any indication of the real policy of any political party once it comes to power."

The newspapers were shrill with the call to a better life for the country. Poor and backward Russia was at last on the highroad to progress—it only remained for everyone to dig more coal, raise more grain, acquire more culture. I read the invocations as if they were addressed personally to me. Occasionally one of the great new leaders—Petrovsky, Rakovsky or even Lunacharsky—passed through our district. Listening to them, I felt myself part of something new, big, exciting. In the Moscow Kremlin sat men whom we called simply Comrade—Lenin, Trotsky, Dzherzhinsky—but I knew them to be of the stature of gods.

Looking back to my private history as a Communist, I am inclined to date my conversion to the arrival of Comrade Lazarev, who gave a series of lectures on the problems of socialism. He was a man of about thirty, on the staff of the University of Sverdlovsk, tall, slim, neatly dressed. He talked simply in his own words, not in quotations from Marx or Lenin. What impressed me especially was that he wore a necktie, thereby bringing powerful reinforcement to those of us who argued that one could be a good Soviet citizen yet indulge in such bourgeois accessories.

One day I was in the library, engrossed in a book, when someone behind me said:

"What are you reading? I'm curious."

I turned around. It was Comrade Lazarev.

"*The Disquisitions of Father Jerome Cougniard* by Anatole France," I replied, smiling in embarrassment.

"So? Anatole France," he said. "Why not the Russian classics, or some contemporary Soviet writer?"

"I find a lot in Anatole France that I don't find in the Soviet writers," I said. "He's subtle and very honest. I do read Russian classics, but the new authors—they write only politically and seem to avoid the real life around us."

"Very interesting, let's discuss it some night. Come to my room and we'll get acquainted."

I met him again a few days later at a *subbotnik*: a work session, when hundreds of volunteers pitched in to do some urgent job without pay. On this occasion it was the removal of a mountainous heap of coal to clear a road. Comrade Lazarev was in work clothes, covered with soot and plying a shovel with great diligence. He greeted me like an old friend and I was pleased.

That evening he saw me again in the library. And what was I reading now, he wanted to know. *What to Do?* [aka *What's to Be Done?*] by Chernishevsky, I told him.

"An important work," he nodded approvingly.

"Yes, and his question, what to do, is one that bothers me now," I said.

"It's a question that has already been answered for millions by Lenin, and before him by Marx. Have you read Lenin and Marx?"

"A little of Lenin, here and there," I replied, "but not Marx. I've read the Party literature, of course, but I'm not sure that it quite answers the question what to do."

"Come over to my room, we'll have a glass of tea and some refreshments and we'll talk without disturbing anyone," Comrade Lazarev smiled.

It was a spotlessly clean, bright room. The divan was covered with a gay rug; books neatly ranged on the desk between book-ends; a few flowers in a colored pitcher. On one wall hung several family pictures, one of them of

Lazarev himself as a boy, in *gimnazium* uniform, a dog at his feet; another of a pretty sister, also in student garb. On another wall were framed photographs of Lenin and Marx and between them—this was the touch that warmed me and won me over, though I did not know exactly why—the familiar picture of Leo Tolstoy in old age, in the long peasant tunic, his thumbs stuck into the woven belt.

This isn't an obscene sailor attacking a nurse at night, I thought to myself. [Here Kravchenko is referring to an earlier incident.] *I could follow this kind of Communist.*

"Since I have to live here for several months," Lazarev explained, "I've tried to make the place homelike."

We talked for hours that night, about books, the Party, the future of Russia. My place was with the Communist minority who must show the way, Lazarev said, and I ought to join the Komsomol and later the Party. Of course, he conceded, the Party wasn't perfect and perhaps its program wasn't perfect, but men are more important than programs.

"If bright, idealistic young people like you stand aloof, what chance will there be?" he said. "Why not come closer to us and work for the common cause? You can help others by serving as an example of devotion to the country. Just look around you in the barracks—gambling, dirt, drunkenness, greed where there ought to be cleanliness, books, spiritual light. You must understand that there's a terrific task ahead of us, Augean stables to be cleaned. We must outroot the stale, filthy, unsocial past that's still everywhere, and for that we need good men. The heart of the question Vitia, is not only formal socialism but decency, education and a brighter life for the masses."

I had been "pressured" by Communists before this. But now, for the first time, I was hearing echoes of the spirit that had suffused my childhood. I argued with Comrade Lazarev; I said I would think it over, but in fact I agreed with him and had already made up my mind.

When Comrade Lazarev departed for Moscow some weeks later, I was in the large group—ordinary miners and office workers as well as the top officials of the administration—gathered at the station to see him off.

"There you are, Vitia," he singled me out. "I head by accident that you've joined the Komsomol. Good for you! Congratulations! But why didn't you tell me? I would have recommended you."

"I know, and I'm grateful, but I wanted to do it on my own . . . without patronage."

Now life had for me an urgency, a purpose, a new and thrilling dimension of dedication to a cause. I was one of the *élite*, chosen by History to lead my country and the whole world out of darkness into the socialist light. This sounds pretentious, I know, yet that is how we talked and felt. There might be cynicism and self-seeking among some of the grown-up Communists, but not in our circle of ardent novitiates.

My privileges, as one of the elect, were to work harder, to disdain money and foreswear personal ambitions. I must never forget that I am a Komsomol member first, a person second. The fact that I had joined up in a mining region, in an area of "industrial upsurge," seemed to me to add a sort of mystic significance to the event. I suppose that a young nobleman admitted to court life under the Tsar had that same feeling of "belonging."

There was no longer much margin of time for petty amusements. Life was filled with duties—lectures, theatricals for the miners, Party "theses" to be studied and discussed. We were aware always that from our midst must come the Lenins and Bukharins of tomorrow. We were perfecting ourselves for the vocation of leadership; we were the acolytes of a sort of materialist religion.

Having discovered that I could write and speak on my feet with some natural eloquence, I was soon an "activist." I served on all kinds of committees, did missionary work among the non-Party infidels, played a role in the frequent celebrations. There were endless occasions to celebrate, over and above the regular revolutionary holidays. The installation of new machinery, the opening of new pits, the completion of production schedules were marked by demonstrations, music, speeches. Elsewhere in the world coal may be just coal—with us it was "fuel for the locomotives of revolution."

Through the intercession of Comrade Lazarev I had been transferred to work in the pits. I no longer needed to envy Senia [diminutive of Arsenii] on that score. The two of us and several other young miners formed an *artel*, a cooperative group doing jobs and being paid as a unit. The *artel* system was at this time encouraged as a means of raising output. Members of efficient *artels* usually earned more than individual miners. This, however, was the least of our concerns. We bid for the most difficult and dangerous assignments, eager to prove our zeal by deeds. We even had a slogan which we solemnly communicated to the officials: "If it's necessary, it can be done."

The members of our *artel* lived together in a clean and comfortable house stocked with good books. We took turns at scrubbing the floor and other household chores. The Soviet leaders and classic Russian writers deployed on our walls looked down approvingly, I was sure, on this example of "culture" in the midst of backwardness. Among them was Sergo Ordzhonikidze, one of the men close to Lenin and later to become Commissar of Heavy Industry. I liked his rough-hewn Georgian face, with its huge eagle beak and a shaggy drooping mustache. Perhaps I had a vague premonition that this man would one day be the patron, and in a sense the inspiration, of my busiest years as a Communist.

On occasion, of course, we allowed ourselves an evening of light-hearted sociability. Friends and comrades liked to gather in our house—it was so "civilized" and the talk so "elevated." One of our crowd played the guitar superbly; we would sing and dance and dispute far into the night. A number of the more attractive girls in the community would join us on these occasions. If we had too good a time we all felt a bit guilty and did Komsomol penance by more intensive work, study and political discussion in the days that followed.

In the late fall the boastful slogan of our *artel* was put to a critical test. One of the mines had been flooded. It was propped with wooden beams for fear of collapse, but work went on without interruption. It was this mine that we offered to operate, in order to set an example to the regular miners there, mostly Tatars and Chinese.

I was in the pit, working intently though I was almost knee-deep in icy water. Suddenly the whole world seemed to shudder, creak and groan. I heard someone shriek in terror—probably it was my own voice in my ears. Part of our shaft had caved in. When I opened my eyes again I was in a large whitewashed room, in one of a row of hospital beds. A doctor in a white gown was feeling my pulse and a handsome middle-aged nurse stood by with pad and pencil in hand. She smiled in greeting when she saw I had regained consciousness.

"You'll be all right, Comrade Kravchenko, don't worry," she said, and the doctor nodded in confirmation.

They told me I had been in the water inside the caved-in mine for two or three hours. The Chinese worker next to me had been killed. Little hope had been held out for me—if I had not been finished off by the collapsing walls, I must have drowned in the ice water. But here I was, with bruised legs and a high fever, but otherwise in good shape. The fever later developed into pneumonia.

The two months in the hospital of Algoverovka, curiously, remain with me as one of the pleasantest interludes of my youth. The story of my *artel* and its climax in the cave-in was embroidered, in the telling, into a saga of socialist heroism in which I was one of the heroes. Important trade-union and Party officials came to my bedside; the boys and girls of my Komsomol unit visited me regularly and never failed to bring little gifts. I was still in the hospital on my eighteenth birthday. Members of the *artel* and its friends arrived in a body in a heart-warming show of fellowship.

The handsome nurse treated me as if I were her own son. Indeed, in the cozy languor of convalescence I had the sense of having been adopted by all of Russia—its workers, its Komsomols, its officialdom—as the favorite son of a vast and wonderful family.

The doctors forbade me to return to the mines, at least for a year, and no pleading on my part could upset their injunction, conveyed to the administration. I had no wish to go back to an office job and therefore prepared to return to the Tocsin commune and Ekaterinoslav.

In the midst of these preparations came the news that Lenin had died, on January 24, 1924. The shock and the sorrow were real and deep in this corner of the Donets valley. The reaction had little to do with politics. To the plain people in the collieries—even to the gamblers and brawlers in the barracks, the swaggerers with shoes that creaked, let alone to the Communist Youths— he had become a symbol of hope. We needed to believe that the sufferings of these bloody years were an investment in a bright future. Each of us had a feeling of personal loss.

I marched three miles, with thousands of others, to the memorial meeting outside the mine office, called "Paris Commune." It was a bitterly cold, snowy afternoon; the winds cut like sharp knives. The rostrum in the open air was draped in red and black bunting, though a pall of snow soon covered everything. One after another the orators shouted above the howling wind, declaiming formulas of official sorrow.

"Comrade miners!" a pompous delegate from Kharkov shrieked, "Lenin is dead, but the work of Lenin goes forward. The leader of proletarian revolution . . . leader of the working class of the world... best disciple of Marx and Engels. . . ."

The formal words left me depressed. Why don't they talk simply, from the heart rather than from *Pravda* and *Izvestia* editorials? Trudging home through the snowstorm I was pleased to discover that Senia and others had the same let-down feeling. The orators had failed to express how we felt about Lenin, because what we felt had less relation to the dead leader than to our own living hopes.

Several days later we read in the local newspapers Joseph Stalin's oath at Lenin's bier on Red Square in Moscow. It was a short, almost liturgical promise to follow in the path indicated by the dead leader and it moved me as the oratory at our memorial gathering had not done. Stalin was a member of the all-powerful Political Bureau, Secretary General of the Party, and had been an important figure in the new regime from the beginning. Yet this was the first time that I had become acutely aware of his existence. Strange, I thought, that his portrait was not even on our walls.

From that day forward the name Stalin grew so big, so inescapable, that it was difficult to recall a time when it had not overshadowed our lives.

Chapter Nineteen

Vasilii Ianov, The Heart of a Peasant

From the 1890's to persecutions of the mid-1930's there existed a movement in Russia which, in varying degrees, reflected the social, ethical, and religious ideas of Leo Tolstoy. Though labeled "Tolstoyism," the movement was not monolithic, nor could any of its factions claim exclusive rights to Tolstoy's legacy. There were groups of adherents, discussion circles, and publications of various kinds. Pacifism was certainly a major binding force. Vasilii Ianov (1897-1971) was a peasant and a follower of what he fervently professed to be Tolstoy's views. Memoirs of a peasant are quite rare. And certainly, even more so of one who was an ardent believer in Tolstoy's moral stance. Taken from Vasilii Ianov, "Kratkie vospominaniia o perezhitom" [Brief Memoir of my Experiences] in *Pamiat'*. Paris: YMCA Press, 1979.

MY BIRTH AND DEATH OF MY FATHER

I was born in 1897 at the end of July in Kaluga Province, district of Zhizdrensk, village of Bol'shaia Rechka. The latter is now called Malaia Pesochnia.

For some reason I do not remember all of the talk and circumstances regarding my birth, thus I will relate what I heard from others.

On this day, my father and his oldest daughter had just returned from tilling potatoes and he was unharnessing the sweaty horse. A neighbor came up to him and with a mix of bashfulness and joy said to him: "Well, Vasilii Ivanovich, I congratulate you on the birth of a son!"

"Well, thank God, thank God," answered father. And the neighbor said: "Now the family is large, your health is poor, may the Lord take the child quickly."

"It is a sin to think that way aunt Mar'ia," said father. "On the contrary, we must make all effort to raise and bring him up to be a good person and a hardworking peasant."

Father was carrying the harness to the fence when aunt Mar'ia again came up to him. "He is a real copy of you, you can't get a cry out of him. I moved him this way and that, but he stayed quiet. He's not sensitive to pain. He's forbearing like his father."

"That's good. He feels that it's silly to be irritated by trifles. Nervousness and caprice don't lead to anything good. This experience will benefit him in life." Father went into the *izba* [peasant hut] and walked up to mother who was lying on the bed. Greeting him with her large, tear-stained, but happy eyes, mother said, "Vasia, how nice he is; hurry up and look at him!"

"Thank God, thank God, and how are you doing?"

"Oh, I'm fine. I'm happy for him because he is so loveable." Father kissed mother gently. That was how my parents initially welcomed me into this world.

"We'll name our newborn Vasia, my name. I don't have long to live and I'm getting weaker all the time. I'm not a worker anymore, you can't make it too long with consumption."

"You sure gladdened me, telling me you'll die soon. And what am I to do with five of them?" said mother.

"It's good that I'll die first. What would I do with them without you? I know you'll make it with them. They won't be hungry, you'll train them, and you'll be like a bee with them. They'll have it good with a mother like you."

"Why did we make children if we feel we're not able to raise them?" asked mother.

"You're right. For momentary earthly pleasures we became blind and we did not think of the harsh consequences. We can't bring back the past. I'm to blame, forgive me."

"Don't take all the blame on yourself. I'm not a seventeen-year-old girl and have just given birth for the ninth time. It wasn't sweet each time and I bit my lips till they bled. I repented and swore not to repeat this. So, I can't blame anybody. Get up, girl, and get to work."

And my mother began to get up from the bed. But father put her back.

"Rest for a week, I'll take care of the kids."

After one year, father died from consumption. Before death, he said that he would die that day. Though mother was used to father's illness, she nevertheless burst into tears and all of us children were also crying.

The neighbors and village friends gathered more often in the house to see father one last time. He was a kind man, a superb storyteller, and probably the only person in the village who could read the Gospels.

All who came tried to move up closer, to be seen by father and hear a final word of wisdom. But at the sight of his great suffering, all became petrified and filled the *izba* in total silence. Then father called Mar'ia, our neighbor. She approached, all in tears and, looking at father, did not move. Mother was also standing next to him.

"Good people," said father with a deep sigh, "I'll soon be dying, but at the end I'd like to say my wishes. Listen, Nastia, don't give the children away, raise them yourself. Have the most pity for the little one. He'll be your breadwinner, though now he is the weakest of all. Don't marry off the girls early. They'll have enough time to experience sorrow and suffering. It would be better if they didn't marry at all in their life, as I now understand it. That would be the very best. The boys would do well if they didn't marry either, but their road is different. They'll be drafted as soldiers and they will be corrupted there in many ways."

HOME

And so I am again with my beloved family, among my fellow villagers, amidst my native fields. Around me I do not hear the sound of commands or interrogations, but calm human speech. Nor are there marches, jumping, and convulsive movements by command, but the reasonable labor so essential for all people, a labor without which no minister, poet, scholar, general, or accountant can survive—all those whose own so-called labor is frequently valued above that of the peasant. I settled into my work, but the past, again and again, inevitably rose before me. Why? Why was all this necessary? According to Tolstoy, each person is a messenger of God, of the most elevated element that one recognizes in oneself. And each of us is allotted labor in fulfillment of this supreme law of life. In carrying out this labor, one must forget and discard all that is personal, the egotistical aspirations, desires, goals. It will then be easy to accomplish God's will. There will be no doubts, disappointments, fear, sadness, or loneliness.

I only did my duty, that which the highest attributes of my essence demanded from me. I did not wish for anything personally and things went easily. I did not become infected by the spirit of malice and hostility which surrounded me everywhere in my life, neither in jail, during interrogations, in the barracks, nor on the march. I did not get angry, was not envious, was unafraid, and felt no burden. I was also happy and at peace and observed that people with whom I had contact found this catching and were kind and well disposed toward me. If I was displeased at times, it was only with myself, that much that was egotistical was still within me, that I was not fully of God's will.

MY SISTER

So I lived in my home. Suddenly I received a letter from my sister who was at the Kamenskii factory. She wrote that there was famine in their region. Her husband went for bread and died en route. Her children were swelling from hunger. What to do? How could I help my sister in such a calamity? You could not feed four people, a mother with three children by sending parcels. We had to bring her to her homeland, but where to put them?

I had to consult with family. First I spoke to my own brother. "Brother, what are we going to do? How can we help our sister and save her and her children from starvation?"

"I don't know," answered my brother. "I have my own family of four."

I then asked my sister's father-in-law. He answered in the same way: "I barely have enough for myself." Nevertheless, I decided to bring my sister, but where to get the money for the trip? We had one rich person in our village and I went to him. I explained my sister's difficult situation.

"How much money do you need for all of this?"

I told him.

"No, you won't get by with that," and gave me double the amount, wishing me success.

I told mother I had obtained the money and would now be going for my sister. Through her tears, mother said: "I am happy for you in all this, but I'm afraid that it will be hard for you with your sister. You don't know her character yet." But I went.

My sister's situation was truly difficult. The two youngest children had already died from hunger, and the other three, though they could walk, swayed from weakness. Seeing me, they roused themselves. Their pale little faces shone with happiness, and they all hung on my neck. Nudging me with their sharp elbows and knees, they climbed up on my lap hugging me and kissing me. When I told my sister why I had come, they all yelled: "Dear mother, we will all go with uncle!"

Having questioned me as to how everyone was living and what they were saying about her arrival, she told me she was not going. "I'd rather die here from hunger than live satiated under hateful looks." The children began crying.

"Why are you bawling? Here we have a roof over our heads but where will we live there? Uncle himself lives in a room of five people, my father-in-law refused us totally, and everyone in their village says his house is crowded. Who needs us?"

I expected that in saying this my sister would cry bitterly but during this period she had lived through so much that her suffering had dried up her tears and she merely looked at a single spot with sad eyes. The children kept repeating the same thing:

"We are going with uncle."

"Well, go alone, I am staying here."

The kids agreed to this as well.

"We will plant potatoes with uncle over there; we'll cook them and bake them in the ashes, and we'll send you letters that we are comfortable, that we eat our fill of baked potatoes."

My sister smiled.

"You'll eat potatoes, all right, but where will you sleep? You have no roof or clothes." Little Kuz'ka cried out delightedly: "I will take an axe, chop some wood, and bring it in. Then we'll make a big bonfire with my uncle and we'll sleep by it." Little Masha: "And I'm going to make fritters from the potatoes and eat them with uncle."

"And you're going to live next to the fire?" asked their mother. "Wherever uncle is, that's where I'll be," answered Mania [Masha].

The oldest girl, Ira [diminutive of Irina], said, "And I, uncle, will cook for all. I will do the laundry, knit socks, and darn and patch everything. I'll do spinning with grandma and we'll weave sackcloth."

"What about school?" asked the mother.

"Three grades is enough for me. When I grow up, if I have to, I'll take courses."

"Where are you going to live?" her mother asked again.

"With uncle, and grandma will live with us too," answered Ira.

In the morning, my sister said: "You came here to get us, but did you think where we will live?"

"Wherever I live, there all of you will be. That is how I thought of it, and still do, and I came for you with this in mind."

"All right. We'll see what will come of your thinking and how we'll all live in poverty."

We left on the following morning. We experienced many difficulties during the trip but my sister did not reproach me with a single word. Probably it is difficult for some people to move from dead center but then, with each step, involuntarily, they begin to get accustomed to the new. The children also, seeing my calmness, seemingly decided internally that this was the way it should be, and peacefully gave themselves up to their impressions. They were happy and absorbed themselves in everything, knowing that their loved ones, whom they fully trusted, were with them.

Similar to these children sometimes are adults who believe in their God—love, who vigilantly looks after each one of them through their conscience. Then, loving this God in themselves and in all living things, people are assuaged, knowing that God is constantly with them, preserving them with his love and blessing them.

And so we came home. Mother greeted all with her inherent motherly concern about each person and did everything possible to make things well. My older brother and his wife were, likely, not very pleased, but seeing misfortune they contained themselves and, therefore, everything was quiet and peaceful.

Things became very crowded in our house, more precisely in our room, just like in a railroad car. But extreme need did not violate the feelings of prudence and compassion and life went on its way. I occupied myself with the usual work and also with crafting wood, metal, and clay. The local youth treated me well, respectfully. I was known not only in our whole village but in the surrounding ones as well. The older peasants did not have any particular striving to understand the meaning of life. After a long and agonizing military experience and separation they had things to do and their household concerns engaged them totally.

But the young were not fully subject to life's inertia. Their inquisitiveness led in many directions and some of them were even interested in religious questions. They started coming to see me, to talk and even asked for booklets to read. I gave whatever I had read, principally Leo Tolstoy. The clear and simple language of Leo Tolstoy was accessible to all. His words addressed life's questions and they responded with concern and sympathy.

Yes, Tolstoy is a universal miracle. He emanates the light of a godly, virtuous life and raging human egoism is incapable of smearing him with mud or trampling him down. I can't say anything about the future. Perhaps Tolstoy will yet be compelled to dwell in caves, covered by misunderstanding and anger. But at some point, this godsend will be found under heaps of stone and the new humanity will sigh joyously seeing the light emanating from underneath and dissipating the gathering darkness of ages.

Yes, the future will be as it must. For now we must be grateful that in our own lives, thanks to Tolstoy, we have perceived the truth.

Dimitrii Ivanovich Grishin agreed with me more than anyone. I told him of my plans to leave the village commune in spring, leave the peasant fields, which, due to a shortage of land, were always a source of unhappiness and enmity. I decided to go build myself a "castle" on the forested lands, at the edge of the forest, like that of any bird (except the cuckoo), to clear a garden, plant some fruit trees, and live off this. Mitia [Dimitrii] happily joined me. We decided to take nothing from our homes besides saws and axes and to leave all the household goods to our brothers.

One-and-a-half kilometers from the village there was a thicket with a swampy ravine near a stream. We picked this swampy place to drain and live on so as not to incur envy, that we had taken good land.

The work went full swing. We cleared the thicket, dug a garden, and built ourselves a "skyscraper"—four meters wide and six meters long. But at the very height of our labor we were both taken to the Briansk prison which was far stronger than our castle.

The prosecutor began interrogating us as to the basis of our violation of governmental laws—building a house, cutting wood. I replied that I was ashamed to realize that there were people who imagined that the whole world belonged to them. I did not wish to affirm their sick, abnormal opinion and ask their permission to weave my own nest of marshland brushwood in a foul swamp. Having said this, I stopped. We remained standing while the prosecutor and another person consulted quietly. Then the prosecutor turned to us and said:

"Well, go! But where will you be going and what are you going to do?"

"We are going to go to our nest, try and finish it before winter, and tend to the garden so that we have something to eat this winter."

We left the office silently and were released from prison. By winter we truly did finish our "castle." We cut some shingles, covered our roof, cut up boards for the floor, made bricks, and built a Russian stove. We harvested our garden and took in my sister and her children for the winter. The kids jumped for joy and chirped happily about me. Mitia, being cheerful, also paid attention to the children and our swamp nest became a corner of paradise.

Many of the curious came to see us to find topics for their idle chatter. They were not shy about giving us all kinds of advice, how we should live so that things would be even better. We lived thus for a year when I once accidentally heard a gossipy woman telling my sister:

"Yes, all would be fine if you had milk and meat. In the village, some neighbor could spare some. Here there is no one and you can't get it from anybody."

"Yes, in the village I could earn some money for milk and meat; here there is no one even to talk to," she complained about her life isolated from any company.

In the summer, when the peasants began to reapportion land, I went to them and asked them to parcel out a farmstead for me. The commune measured one out for me with cheerful joking.

"Well, well, Vasilii Vasil'evich you've build yourself a *dacha* in the woods, now build a winter palace next to us," they joked. "Sure, sure, we're glad that you are not separating yourself from us."

So Mitia and I lugged in all kinds of junk from the ravine next to the farmstead. We mixed clay right on the spot and built a hut. We made bricks and built an oven, covered the roof, plastered the walls, put in a door and window frames, and built a table and four stools.

"Now, sister," I said, "get ready. We're going to the village into society, to your own home. You'll live freely and unconstrained."

My sister immediately broke out into tears.

"What have you planned? To get rid of me?" And the complaints started.

"I don't have a garden there. Where will I get seedlings? And what will I do there? If I had a sewing machine, I could sew and make a living, but what will I do there?"

Nevertheless, I moved her to the new home saying:

"Here you'll be a gardener yourself and you'll have enough seedlings for half the village."

She smiled through her tears: "We know these tender persuasions. Then I'll have to suffer with the children in any way I know."

Toward the winter we bought her a sewing machine and a cow. We built a spacious shed. Mother gave her some chickens. In the spring we dug a seed-plot, planted cabbage seeds, and instructed the children to water them and guard them against the hens. My sister became more cordial to Mitia and me. We often visited each other for various reasons since there are many of these among those who love each other. Mitia and I stayed alone. Then we took in two boys who had lost both parents. They spent the winter with us, got used to the place, and were happy. But for some dark reason, their grandfather then took them. Afterwards Mitia's brother and his wife died and left six children. The older brothers were already adults, about twenty years old. They remained living in their home and we helped them.

The infant girl was taken by a peasant woman, adding to her own three children. Mitia and I took the four-year-old boy. People who were curious came to us from various places expressing a desire to live with us jointly. But they soon became bored and left, finding a more attractive life style. They went where people walked about with clean hands and did not dig in the dirt, where they ate ready-baked, clean bread produced by those who lead a boring life and dig in the dirt. They became "wise leaders" thinking that peasants could not make it without their help. They engaged in all kinds of science, acting in theaters, dancing, playing football, chess, and performing somersaults beyond the clouds, etc. At the same time, however, they carefully made sure that the peasants should not eat up their own portion of bread by themselves. Otherwise, one could die from hunger with all one's cultural games and pursuits.

Only a religious-moral attitude towards life helps a person choose a requisite labor and hold to it irrespective of any difficulties. It is to be carried out urgently and only leftover time may be allotted to amusements, merriment, and carousing. Only having set upon this path of the working peasant can a person establish brotherly relationships with people, be independent, and not sell his labor, creating exploiters in so doing. Additionally, he himself can respect another such brother-toiler.

Part Three

Unrelenting Order and Terror: 1930–1953

By 1930, the first Five Year Plan was in effect. It ushered in consequences that no one could foretell, policies that no one had ever seen, and terror that no one accused could survive.

The two main thrusts were forcible industrialization and collectivization. Through centralized planning and implementation, industrialization was slated to proceed at such a rapid pace that the Soviet Union was then, theoretically, to enter the ranks of the world's leading industrial nations. Huge amounts of money were channeled into the most extensive projects—heavy industry at a massive and rapid scale. Though at an enormous cost, human and fiscal, close to a tripling of heavy industrial production was achieved by the time the plan ended in 1932.

Collectivization refers to the lumping of millions of individual farms into huge kolkhozes, or collective farms. Neither ideology nor economic theorizing could explain why this would not work. It would not have mattered anyway as the process rammed its way through the Russian countryside. Agriculture, which had shown signs of recovery in the late 1920's, was devastated with huge drops in all the standard measures, from grain production to heads of livestock. The one measure that was the most "innovative" was also the least understood by the population and the most feared. This was the brutality of forced collectivization.

Some 15,000,000 people perished by means of forced starvation, execution, or concentration camps to insure collectivization that became entrenched. At the time of the formal collapse of the Soviet Union in 1991, agriculture had yet to recover from collectivization since the system was still in place.

Violence and fear were the great handmaidens of the Stalinist era. True totalitarianism manifested itself. Though party functionaries could write off the human devastation of collectivization, it was another story with the Great Purges of 1936-1938. Here Stalin endeavored to cleanse society and the Communist Party itself of every conceivable blemish, enemy, or opponent. Most of these perceptions were a result of his paranoia. But they were manifested as mass executions of the innocent and true believer. Even the armed forces, which lost some three-quarters of its senior officers, could not avoid the purging.

Through the 1930's and right up to Stalin's death in March 1953, Soviet society is best understood in terms of unprecedented regimentation. The discussion above points clearly to order and terror. Because this was so pervasive and complete, regimentation could be attempted and effected. Socialist realism forced literature and the arts into a straitjacket. The League of Militant Atheists served as the state arm to help repress religion. Science, whether mathematics or biology, had to serve the ideological strictures of the State. History was periodically rewritten so that the "fact" fit party requirements. Informing on family or neighbors who might not be reliable citizens was strongly encouraged. And the Gulag expanded with an unparalleled rapidity since it had to absorb millions of the arrested. As the writers Ilf and Petrov pointed out, loving Soviet power was not enough. It had to love you.[1]

With the opening of numerous Soviet archives in recent years, the knowledge of the death toll under Stalin has become more precise. In referring to the Soviet State and its leaders from Lenin through Stalin, Woodford McClellan asks: "How many did they kill one way or another? The Holocaust in Russia antedated the one in the Third Reich and took as many as 40 million and perhaps as many as 60 million lives."[2] An exceedingly difficult question to answer is how a nation survives this.

Survival is, of course, the greatest theme of World War II. Bearing the brunt of Hitler's attack in June 1941, (the most powerful military operation ever), the Soviet Union was ultimately a heroic victor. The great battles of Stalingrad and Kursk proved Germany would not win. Leningrad, surviving a 900-day siege wherein over one and a half million people starved to death, proved, if one ever had doubt, a Russian tenacity and resiliency that is barely imaginable. These were also among the intangibles that allowed the Soviet Union to claim ultimate victory, even though three fourths of the German army was engaged against it, not the West. Small wonder that Stalin insisted on territorial "concessions" after the war.

The post-war years did not grant the nation any political gifts. Repression and regimentation again became the norm. The thought of any comfort social, cultural, political, religious, or economic—was only a dream foundered on a harsh reality. But death began to shift that reality, Stalin's death. The mid 1950's were to witness a collective sigh of relief, and the surge of a long dormant positive hope.

Nickolas Lupinin

NOTES

1. As pointed out by Woodford McClellan, *Russia: The Soviet Period and After*, 4th ed. (Upper Saddle River, N.J.: Prentice Hall, 1998), p. 97.
2. McClellan, 97.

Chapter Twenty

B. Brovtsyn, Dearly Beloved

The persecution of religion was a notorious feature of the Soviet State, one that began shortly after the Bolshevik seizure of power. By the late 1920's and through the 1930's, this had developed into a total attack encompassing mass destruction of churches, arrests of believers, frequently leading to dismissal from work, imprisonment and execution. In this noxious atmosphere public profession of religion was simply dangerous. Brovtsyn describes an intimate situation. He and his fiancee, both scientists, had to go to great lengths to have a secret church wedding. Taken from B. Brovtsyn, "Pervogo iunia na Lakhte" [The First of June on the Lakhta River]. New York: *The New Review,* No. 158, March, 1985.

The place, where I was born, spent the first nine years of my life, and to which I returned from the place of my parents' exile almost an adult, at age fifteen, has been best described by Pushkin:

>Along the mossy, swampy shores
>Blackened huts here and there,
>Shelter of a wretched Finn.
>And the forest, unpenetrated by light
>In the haze of the hidden sun,
>Rustled all around.

Both the mossy shore and the swampy marsh have remained. The northern shore of the Gulf of Finland from Petrograd to the west is covered with forests. In the lowlands there were marshes where in autumn bright red cranberries ripened on their thin stems. On the pine tree-covered knolls nestled stunted, dark red foxberries, with glittering, rigid little leaves. And everywhere, to the very edge of the marshes, were modest, small, sweet, Russian blueberries. One could also find mushrooms if one knew places in the seaside Finnish forest.

At the Lakhta station, as I recall, women vendors would come out to the trains with dozens of "White" mushrooms [boleti] in wooden baskets.

Lakhta is not far from Staraia Derevnia, on the outskirts of Petrograd, about several *versts* in all from it. It is separated from Staraia Derevnia by a vast and swampy marsh that is covered by stunted shrubbery, and is flooded by waters from the gulf pushed inland by the November west winds. The railroad from Staraia Derevnia to Lakhta skirts the marsh and runs along a road paved with cobblestones. Many *dachas* are located along the cobblestone road and the several streets that cross it, leading towards the seashore. In the old days these were rented to Petersburg city-dwellers. One of the cross streets, Gardnerovskaia, is connected with the history of my family.

John Gardner, master of the oakum business, came from England to Russian in the previous [19th] century. His profession was the caulking of the planks of newly built ships with oakum. Having founded his own business and conscientiously filling the orders of the Admiralty, old man Gardner became rich, as Russia became rich at the end of the previous century and the beginning of this one. At Lakhta, John Gardner built about ten *dachas*. He gave a red *dacha* to his son, Genrikh Ivanovich, the father of my cousins. Another, a big *dacha* with two annexes, he gave to his son Fedor Ivanovich, a sickly fellow for many years, who was looked after by a Russian woman, Nastas'ia Vasil'evna. After a time she became Mrs. Gardner, but the only English she ever learned was to call her pooch "doggie." On the wall of her sitting room hung a portrait of Lord Kitchener, about whom she knew very little. However, she was very proud of this portrait.

Old man Gardner left nothing to his daughter Zhanetta Ivanovna. Zhanetta Ivanovna, a slender, tall, and stately lady, who must have been beautiful in youth, married well, settled in Moscow, and had no need of a dacha in Lakhta. She married Bruno Vasil'evich Farikh, a man of prominence in pre-revolutionary Moscow, who was in the insurance business. Their two sons had good careers in Soviet times. The elder somehow received a university education and became a well-known engineer, with a specialization in the machine-tool industry. The younger, Fabio Farikh, became a prominent Soviet arctic pilot. Later, he was shot as a man of foreign origins. The very same fate befell his brother, Bruno, as well.

By the beginning of the thirties, only one Gardner dacha remained—all the rest having been burned in 1917—the dacha belonging to Nastas'ia Vasil'evna Gardner. My fate was also connected with her home.

Having been found to be a British national, she was expelled, poor thing, beyond the borders of the USSR shortly before the Soviet-German war. The English created a shelter in Estonia for such Russian-English persons, where Nastas'ia Vasil'evna, not knowing one word of English, except for the word "doggie," suffered among other half-English people. Finally, having refused British citizenship, she managed to return to the USSR. She was not permitted to go to Lakhta, since her home had already been confiscated and divided into communal apartments. She was given a room in a communal apartment in Petrograd, and on the eve of the war she was sent to Siberia.

In the beginning of the '30s, my family and I lived peacefully, but with great difficulty. Every summer my mother's brother rented one of the two-room apartments in N.V. Gardner's dacha. He lived there with his common-law wife, Elizaveta Ivanovna Shliakova, who was a resident of Petersburg. His lawful wife, having sent their daughter to her sister's abroad, went herself to France in 1929 with a Soviet visa, naively hoping that my uncle, who received the rank of midshipman of the Imperial Fleet in 1916, would join the merchant marine and on the first foreign voyage jump ship. However, he never even thought of doing this. The fate and character of my uncle reminded me of Dr. Zhivago in Pasternak's novel, although Elizaveta Ivanovna was a real Soviet worker, an accountant at *Elektrotok* [electric generation department], and not a romantic Lara, and my uncle was not a poet. However, he was indecisive and resigned to his fate, completely like Yurii Zhivago. When he was mobilized and sent to the Volga flotilla to fight against the whites, he resigned himself to this as well, instead of escaping south to join Denikin [commanding general of the White Army].

Not far from Nastas'ia Vasil'evna's dacha at the shore of the gulf stood a half-deserted church in the forest. My uncle knew the priest. Soviet life was such that to attend church, while not completely dangerous, was all the same risky. It was 1934. My aunt (once removed) on my father's side, Lidiia Petrovna Engel'ke, having provided me with the fundamentals of a religious education, had died long ago. Grandmother Brovtsyn outlived her son (my father) by two years and died in 1933, when I was away on an expedition to Sakhalin. My mother and my uncle remained Lutherans. In my rather small world there were no remaining Orthodox. The external situation, the burdens of life, and the closed churches were not conducive for contact with religion. I did not go to church. In earlier times on Easter, for many years in a row, my friends and I tried to get into the Trinity Cathedral, located on the grounds of the Izmailovskii Regiment, or into the Nikol'skii Cathedral near the Mariinskii Theater. But the crowd was always so large even outside the cathedrals, that not once did I manage to be at Easter service inside a church.

Chapter Twenty

Shortly after the New Year of 1934, I proposed to my future wife, Nina Sergeevna Miagkova. We were at that time little more than twenty years old; we were captivated by hydrology, the science of rivers, and took part in expeditions. Nina had just graduated from Petrograd [Leningrad] University.

Birth, marriage, and death are the milestones of the beginning, middle, and end of a person's journey through life. An Orthodox person's beginning coincides with the sacrament of baptism, the middle with the sacrament of marriage, and the end with extreme unction. Before me stood a task: how to secretly fulfill the sacrament of marriage so that no one would suspect anything at work and that no difficulties, with possibly lethal consequences, would arise. My fiancée's position was even more dangerous. She had been working for two years in the military section of the State Institute of Hydrology. Among the duties of my bride, a field hydrologist of the SIH, was the investigation of the western Soviet borders, for clarification of the condition of the roads, the extent of their ability to carry traffic, and the nature of vast marshes and lowlands adjacent to the western border of Belorussia. If the SIH had found out about her intentions to marry in a church, she would have been deprived of her security clearance, and she would not have been able to do field work. Not that the fact of visiting a church or attending a wedding was important for the authorities, but rather they were interested in a person's mindset, his mood. Everything connected with the church was considered disloyal by the authorities and aroused distrust in them.

My uncle talked it over with the priest of the Lakhta church. The priest agreed to marry us and suggested that we come towards evening, when almost no people would be around. We chose the first of June 1934 as the day of our wedding.

It turned out that there was no white fabric for a bridal dress, and no one to sew it, and no gold for the wedding rings. Sweet wine, for a toast to the betrothed, could not be obtained anywhere (at that time it was known not as buying but as "obtaining.") And I only knew of champagne from my mother's stories. My fiancée bought, from one of her colleagues, vouchers for Torgsin [foreign goods store], where she purchased white silk. On Fontanka at Nikol'skii Lane, in a former servants' room, lived a crippled old woman, Anna Vasil'evna. My fiancée's sister lived with her husband and daughter in the same apartment. Anna Vasil'evna was a parishioner of the Nikol'skii Cathedral and later arranged the baptismal of our daughter there. She lived without a pension, without charity, sewing clothes for acquaintants probably for money, cleaned the church, and looked after children.

Electricity was expensive for her, so she managed with a kerosene lamp (and she was not the only one in Petrograd). This Anna Vasil'evna also agreed to sew a wedding dress for my fiancée. Gold for the wedding rings was gathered: grandmother Brovtsyn's old ring, taken form her hand a year ago at her funeral; old dental crowns, and fragments of yet another grandmother's ring. We were afraid to go to a jeweler's shop, but there, fortunately, they did not ask for last names and they did not steal the gold. We received beautiful rings. My wife still wears her ring to this day, but I exchanged mine for one-and-a-half kilos of meat from a woman who lived in the forests beyond Lakhta during the siege [of Leningrad].

Finally, my mother bought a sweet wine for entertaining after the wedding, white bread (at that time we ate only gray or black bread) and a little bit of ham at the Torgsin. There, over the course of several years, we had an account. It was money remitted by a New York insurance agency in gold rubles for my father's policy, which the Soviet government, fortunately for us, won through a lawsuit in the interests of Russian pre-revolutionary investors and, largely, in its own interests. We were given half (in fact, I think even less). From this half, which was divided again in half, we received some three hundred gold rubles on account at Torgsin and three hundred in Soviet money.

The account of three hundred gold rubles at Torgsin was at that time enormous capital. Until the end of its existence in 1936, Torgsin sold groceries and materials according to the prices of 1914. Our family lived for four years on little extras of groceries from Torgsin. Otherwise, we would have been starving.

Toward the evening of June 1, everyone gathered together in the two-room apartment at Lakhta, in the home of Nastas'ia Vasil'evna Gardner: my mother, uncle, sister, who at that time was still a schoolgirl, Elizaveta Ivanovna Shliakova and Aleksei Andreevich Kruglov. Kruglov was a tenant of our Petrograd apartment, a wonderful person in many respects, senior lecturer at the department of organic chemistry of Petrograd University, a brilliantly talented man of the people. We knew him for years, but he never told us where he was from by birth. He probably had good reasons. Most likely he was of well-to-do peasants; the so-called "dekulakized" ones. I remember the enthusiasm with which he mocked Stalin, assuring us that after the title "Sun of All the Land and Workers of the World," the Caucasus mountain-man would proclaim himself emperor of the Russian proletariat and all adjoining lands. Kruglov always recounted the latest political jokes, as did Elizaveta Ivanovna.

The time came to go through the forest from Nastas'ia Vasil'evna Gardner's home to the church. We separated into two parties. One went to the seashore, then along the gulf and there turned through the forest in the direction of the church. The other went to the church straight from the Gardner home through the forest. It was a quiet, bright, northern evening. Motionless, thin clouds stood over the gulf. Water splashed barely audibly on the sandy shore. At nine in the evening we, my mother, my fiancée and I, and my sister, carefully opened the church doors and entered. The priest was already waiting for us. Kruglov, Elizaveta Ivanovna and my uncle arrived after a few minutes. The priest turned the key in the lock.

On the outside, the church had been covered by boards, painted in a dark green color, and was hardly noticeable among the greenery. The church did not have regular services, but religious rites were conducted there. The priest asked us to show our certificate from the registry office (department of registry of civic status). We did not have it. Then the priest asked us to register immediately after the ceremony. I promised, but I never fulfilled my promise.

The priest married us as in days of old: my uncle held a crown over my head, and Aleksei Andreevich Kruglov held one over my fiancée's head. Several candles burned; the evening light of the northern sun still made its way through the stained glass of the church windows. The wedding ceremony is on the whole not long, and here, under the circumstances, the priest hurried. He put the rings on our fingers, congratulated us. And we quietly set out through the woods to the Lakhta home of Nastas'ia Vasil'evna Gardner. Now it was possible for everyone to walk together, no one would ask where we were coming from, and even if someone did ask, then after all, everyone had the right to head towards their own home, even under the new regime. At the dacha a wedding feast had been prepared for seven people. On the table was sweet wine from Torgsin, ham, white bread, and pastries.

Several days later I left on an expedition to Iakutsk, for the Ministry of Water Transport, and my wife—to a frontier region of the Ukraine.

Chapter Twenty-One

Tat'iana Fesenko, Internal Dissenter

Tat'iana Fesenko (1915–1995) was born in Kiev before the Revolution into a family of that city's intelligentsia. Her father was an engineer and a professor of chemistry who had been educated in Germany before World War I. She was a young girl when the Soviet Union was established and matured with a twin sensibility. She was a student at Kiev University completing an advanced degree in Russian literature when World War II began. During the war she was a refugee and subsequently came to the United States. Taken from her memoir *Povest' krivykh let* [The Tale of Jagged Years]. New York, 1981.

Luckily, I belong to the category of "working intelligentsia" and can get into an institution of higher education in the third round. I prepare earnestly for entry in the next year, hoping to obtain permission from the People's Commissariat of Education to take the competitive examinations at age seventeen instead of eighteen. Simultaneously, taking advantage of Kolia's absence, occasioned by practical training near Odessa, I hurriedly try to look prettier for my beloved's arrival. But where should I begin? Of course, the weakest spot is my nose. It is by no means classical in form, and worst of all, covered with freckles. In my dreams I already visualize it as being of white marble, totally irresistible, but the reality is substantially worse. Because of an ignorant and overzealous application of hydrogen peroxide, my nose swelled up, became red, and the skin hung in shreds. And the freckles didn't even think of disappearing. They sat like firmly hammered copper nails. As it became clear many years later, Kolia [diminutive of Nikolai] did not even notice them.

How quickly the heart beats on this happy early autumn day when the gate will bang and our old dog will bark furiously. Then, he'll quiet down, and gently squealing, run up to the guest, humbly look at me with his blackthorn eyes and begin banging the floor in staccato fashion with his tail: "Your waiting is over."

Father will question him in detail and at length about his training. And I, catching an eager and gentle glance, will run to the kitchen—has the teapot boiled yet?—and, closing my eyes for a minute, press my hands to my chest in an attempt to hold back the exultation racing to the surface.

Mother does not let us go anywhere alone—go with others, she says—and we honestly fulfill the condition: four of us go to the yellowing Kiev parks. My bosom friend Tamara is always with us, the only one initiated into the secret of our love and its silent worshipper. But four is still two plus two. Tamara, laughing and chattering, inevitably drags her companion further away, and we wander over poorly lit paths, becoming intoxicated with the tart smell of wilting grass, of our own closeness. We approach the parapet which separates the pathway from the steep slopes of the old park. For a long, long time we stand silently looking at the lights of Podol and my hand is warmly covered by a youthful, strong hand.

The leaves have fallen, the roads have become slippery and dirty by day, but silvery from hoarfrost in the mornings. We can only meet at our house, but how am I to bear not seeing each other until the free day—Kolia is at the institute during the day and I have classes in the evening. Leaving the lectures, I impatiently look for his broad-shouldered figure. The road from school to the tramline is so disgracefully, unfairly short that our legs, on their own, carry us to the next stop. Later, trying to avoid mother's inquisitive gaze, I mumble that the tram derailed once more and I missed three cars. Luckily, the trams were always having problems—actually derailing on the steep hills of Kiev or suffering a power outage. Obviously, mother doesn't believe me—it is not just from the light autumn frost that my cheeks burn, it is not just from tiredness that I lower my guilty and shining eyes.

But winter is coming and with it the unavoidable resolution draws near. With the routine "stream" of students Kolia will graduate from the institute. I know that he must work three years on the construction of the Turksib [railway line], that he is "contracted," just as all the others in his graduating class. He cannot avoid this—instead of a diploma he would get a card indicating political unreliability.

"I will not leave you for three years, that's impossible, do you remember Chatskii's words? You must become my wife now," he repeats over and over every time we meet. And I, confused and worried, cannot fall asleep for a long time and think, think ... It's easy to say, "be my wife" when his kinfolk smilingly ask about "the bride." But father, more frequently than usual, questions me about my studies. Patting my hair with a contained kindness, he says, looking inquisitively into my face:

"I am sure, dear girl, that you will not fail us—you know that your mother and I are willing to do anything, just so you can get an education."

Oh, God, I know this, and herein lies the difficulty of my decision. But I do not hesitate solely because of them. So many times in my mind I have run up the broad steps of the red, colonnaded building [Kiev University], so many times I repeated the lovely word "student." If I go to the Turksib, I will have none of this and all the years of my parents' sacrifices will turn out to be unjustified deprivation.

"I will wait for you, I give you my word. I will occupy myself only with lectures and books, believe me, three years will pass by quickly, we are still very young. You will visit on vacation. I will write you of everything in my life. I will think of you only, I love you."

"You are still a child, you don't know how to love. I'm leaving in a week, after all, I am suffering, I must know—'yes' or 'no.' You will go to university later, I promise; answer me, answer me,"—and he earnestly looks me in the face.

"No . . . I mean, yes . . . But only not now," I murmur. He lets go of my hands, his face is tired, suddenly mature.

"You are frozen, poor thing," he realizes. "Look, we are all covered with snow, it's hard even to open the gate."

"Will you come tomorrow?" I whisper, almost crying.

"Yes, yes," he nods. "Sleep peacefully, my dear."

But I do not sleep for a long time and outside the window snowflakes fall slowly to the earth, covering the narrow path to my first, short-lived happiness.

Kolia did not come the next day, nor any other day. Maybe everything would have turned out differently if average Soviet citizens had telephones in their apartments. But there was no telephone and only the tear-stained pillow heard my sobs. Mother came, and asking nothing, stroked my hand for a long time, saying softly and wisely:

"My dear girl, the everlasting beauty of first love is often in the fact that it does not end in marriage."

After a year and a half, I received a letter bearing a postmark from Alma-Ata. One of Kolia's fellow graduates, who had often been in our home, wrote me. The end of the letter read:

"Do you still remember Kolia S.? During commencement and departure from Kiev something strange was happening to him—he was not himself. We arrived here—and it became worse: the fellow totally fell apart. Later, we suddenly found out that he married a fellow student. It was a bad and mean marriage, but then a son was born and now they both rejoice. Recently at a Komsomol meeting, a fellow classmate was being berated. It turns out that he was a priest's son. Nikolai listened and listened, then got up, put his Komsomol card on the table for the chairman and left. Of course, there was a huge outcry, and he was expelled from the Komsomol. So far, nothing else was tagged on—and he does his job very well."

Three years later still, Kolia and I walked down a familiar path in our favorite park. Ahead of us ran a little boy who could have been my son. There was lightness and sorrow, but no pain. At that time, a pair of gray eyes had already became more dear to me than the blue.

My last name is typed in the upper right hand column of the long list of those accepted to the university. Strictly speaking, only the building itself is called the university, but the educational institution goes by the name of INO [Institute of People's Education]. It is said that we too will be an independent institute—the Ukrainian Institute of Linguistics—and that we will even have a separate building.

For the present, we have gathered in a large physics auditorium and we scrutinize each other with interest.

I do not feel myself alone among my newly fledged colleagues. Besides me sits a slight, fair-haired girl in a red knit hat with a button on top. We had already become friends during the entrance examinations. During the next four years, Lena and I are always to be together, separated only in gym class when we are obligated to take the end spots according to height on the right and left flank of the women's row.

Our students are very different both in terms of height and appearance. The son of a short-haired and graying woman in glasses who looks like an owl, is already in year two of the technical college—and the lad is just slightly older than Lena and me. Animatedly he tells us:

When they came to the plant to recruit us for students, the foreman said: "Go to study, Shurka, you're a clever one anyway. I'm not sure I can exactly tell you what linguistics is, but I think you'll be a female doctor, it doesn't matter—it's useful." Well, I came, but now I'm doubtful—these bourgeois speak foreign languages well, but will I make it?

Entering the conversation, a middle-aged village teacher in a tall Astrakhan hat says: "Don't be so doubtful, boy. My nephew told me of an incident when he was entering the institute last year. A fellow was submitting papers at the same time as he, and the secretary asked him: 'Your initials, comrade?' He became confused, started to rummage through his pockets, and then said: 'Here is a reference from the factory committee, here's a recommendation from the Komsomol, but I have no initials . . .' Well what do you think, he is now number one in the studies."

But, evidently, irrespective of the effort made to attract the working masses to our institute, it was destined to remain one hopelessly comprised of intelligentsia. Languages are not in vogue now. The industrialization of the nation is taking place and youth storms the doors of the technical institutes. This is where the newly promoted party and labor administrators hope to wind up as well. By means of its allotment, the Komsomol sent us its children, but they drowned in the general mass of the "working intelligentsia."

Ivan Mikhailovich Siiak, a Galician [from western Ukraine] and old Social Democrat, was appointed director of our institute. During the winter of 1919, he was a prominent participant in a revolt against the Romanian rulers in Bessarabia. Later he commanded some sort of "steel detachment" of Galician railroad workers, and then joined the Bolsheviks. He is handsome, smart, has the habits of an experienced demagogue, and the energy of a schemer. He was able to convince the People's Ministry of Education and the students of the almost world-wide significance of the institute and, rather quickly, in an overcrowded Kiev, was able to get a building, in the center of the city, no less. Prior to the revolution, this had been a respectable bank, but was now occupied by a scientific research institute of water resources. Rather unwillingly, the latter ceded us two halls, and calmly continued to occupy the rest of the building despite the fiery tirades of Ivan Mikhailovich and stern notes from the city soviet [council].

Plywood partitions were quickly put up in the halls which converted them into a semblance of classrooms. But since materials were scarce and the partitions just slightly above human height, students in one place could easily hear neighboring lectures. Thus we very plausibly joked that even the teaching of German in our institute was permeated with dialectical materialism, which was passionately taught by the very same Ivan Mikhailovich Siiak.

Actually, he and his auditors quite rapidly became convinced that the unity of opposites is not always one of nature's basic laws, and that it is impossible to bear both linguists and hydrologists under one roof.

Having lost patience with fruitless negotiations with a venerable and grumbling academic, Ivan Mikhailovich decided to go on the attack. True, his "army," consisting principally of timid teachers, was fundamentally different from his brave "steel detachment." But Siiak was uncontrollably drawn to the romanticism of the civil war. Once after lectures, with face aglow, he led us into "the attack." The desks of the hydrologists were opened, and their tables, files, and books, were taken to the furthest room on the top floor with utmost care. Then, Ivan Mikhailovich made a speech from the stairs and ordered us not to dissolve but to spend the night "on liberated territory." The hydrologists tried complaining, wrote letters somewhere regarding arbitrariness, but the building, nevertheless, remained in the hands of the victorious students. For a long time, as a payback, the hydrologists did not remove their remaining furniture and Siiak appointed students to keep guard and maintain protection so that not even an ink well could disappear.

We were split into brigades and it was announced that studies would proceed under collectivist principles—via the laboratory-brigade method. Of course, Lena and I rushed to sign up for the same brigade but Shura Zapiller boldly cancelled the composition of the brigades as submitted and announced that the professional group and the party-Komsomol community would be vigilantly checking to see that the brigades be structured on sound production principles and not on the petty bourgeois bases of personal affinity.

"We will not permit exclusive, individualistic groups of so-called friends to form under the guise of brigades. Therefore, we will now vote on those brigades which the action committee feels it necessary to present to the general meeting."

The vote was taken, as usual, by commencing with the question "who is against?" In each brigade, the most talented and mature student was appointed brigadier, then came two or three of the middling students, and then the inevitable "blockhead for shaping and finishing." That was what the untalented and uneducated were called by students. They had obtained entry into institutions of higher learning as a result of recruitment or being pushed into it at work.

An immediate clarification: in many poorly prepared students, the lack of education was balanced by natural abilities and a sincere desire to work and learn. Such students improved rapidly and their friends willingly helped them. But there were quite a few of the lazy and the dullards. The brigade method eased their stay in the institution. The procedure was such that the brigadier and other brigade members were passed only after all members, without exception, completed their assignments. The brigadier and his deputy spent all of their free time with such a "backward pupil," endlessly reviewing the material and writing his essays and reports—which their "ward" could not even read properly in class. This system led to a situation where capable students had absolutely no time to study since the time left to them after lectures, community labor and endless meetings was taken by "working with the blockheads" from their brigades. It was especially difficult with the inept of the worst kind, those who invariably at meetings, directed harsh criticism at senior professors. Such students looked at their brigadiers, especially those from intelligentsia backgrounds, as "milk cows," demanding complete academic servicing of them.

If any of the students were depressed by the "wholesome productive atmosphere" of the brigade, built on scamming the professor and pulling the lunkheads through from year to year, and if such a student strove to work independently, searching the libraries for corresponding materials and staying late at his books and truly deepening one's knowledge, the nickname "individualist," frightening in its consequences, was hurled from the podium at meetings and cemented venomously in the columns of the wall newspaper. One then had to hurriedly repent in order to avoid trial by his comrades and even expulsion from the institute.

If a capable student, moved by good will, attempted to help a less talented friend on his own initiative, this too was considered to be reprehensible. Fearing the rise of "secret organizations" under the pretext of brigade work, party leaders paid particular attention to the splitting up of friends.

Later, seeing the nonviability of such brigades, the institute's leadership attempted to reconstitute them according to a different principle, namely the territorial wherein students living in the same district were to be united. But this too did not improve the work of the brigades. Then a final effort was made. Exemplary students were concentrated in the first brigade, good students in the second, mid-level in the third, and so on. Such an organizational principle also did not produce positive results. Those who were behind and even the average students were left without help and were unable to carry out any of the brigade assignments.

The matter kept worsening because in the time period described, the beginning of the 1930's, the institutions of higher learning in the Soviet Union, especially the newly organized ones that did not arise on the foundations of the old establishments, which were simply renamed, had problems: they did not have well equipped laboratories or studies, nor textbooks besides primitive "work books" that reminded one of self-study manuals, and which, by the way, were published in very small press runs. Unheated classrooms and students' empty stomachs did not facilitate successful learning. In such fashion, the laboratory-brigade method was destined for total failure under the conditions of Soviet higher education. However, as a result of its application over a number of years, there appeared a type of Soviet "specialist," incompetent in his field and frequently simply ignorant, who was able to graduate from an institute by hiding his squalid baggage behind the backs of brigade comrades. However, the authorities became convinced quite swiftly that such "defective production" emanating from higher education, was completely inapplicable in the nation which had an acute need for specialists. Finally, special emphasis was placed on individual student responsibility, substantially raising the requirements for those entering and graduating from higher educational institutions. Results showed themselves quickly.

One day Siiak sent for all the students who were fluent in German and announced that on the very next day we were to depart for the Pulinskii Region of Zhitomir Province in order to help in the collectivization of the German colonies.

"Bear in mind," he said significantly, "that among those being sent there are almost no party or Komsomol elements. Therefore, if you do not justify the trust being placed in you by the Soviet regime in enlisting you in such a responsible and urgent task as the collectivization of the country, I will be unable to impose any punishment of a party-Komsomol nature, but will simply posit the question of the impossibility of your presence within the walls of a Soviet institution of higher learning."

On a February morning I arrived at the institute from which we were to go to the station. I was wearing boots and a hat with earmuffs lent to me by Boria [diminutive of Boris], a childhood friend. In my soul I was uneasy: I was not quite sure whether I would fully vindicate the celebrated trust of which Siiak spoke yesterday and sorrowfully looked at the massive oak door—it may close for me forever. The faces of my friends were also gloomy and only Misha [diminutive of Mikhail], stamping his feet and clapping his hands from the cold, was daydreaming out loud:

"Boy, will I eat my fill of sour cream with bread when I get there, just like in the country when I was a kid. These non-dekulakicized devils must still have some."

The German colonies in Volynia, created under Catherine II, did not resemble Ukrainian villages with their small white huts, tightly pressed together along dusty roads. Here, one village soviet united farmsteads scattered over ten to fifteen kilometers. A wooden house, outbuildings, a small grove, fields all around—that made up each farmstead. The colonists lived prosperously even though they did not have much land. The cultivation of crops, cattle breeding, bee keeping and hops provided large incomes. But in 1932 these once attractive spots were already a desert. The notorious "dispossession of the kulaks" deprived the village of its richest, its hardest working, and most experienced peasants. They were shipped to Siberia, while many died in the torture-chambers of the NKVD.

It is not surprising that the two authorized officials sent from Kiev to "agitate," were soundly beaten by the peasants and driven out on the road to Zhitomir. The chairman of a newly formed *kolkhoz* [collective farm] had been also recently sent to the Zhitomir hospital with bullets in his hip and leg. In an area of a neighboring village soviet, where people were able to eat only frozen potatoes, the women revolted and gave much trouble to the region's party leadership.

The district party officials who sent us to work—evidently, the number of party members who knew German was insufficient—called upon the students not to eat and not to sleep, but to think of the grain that was to be deposited in the barns of future *kolkhozes*. Finding ourselves in one of the village soviets, my classmate and I immediately felt that, here, evidently, we would have to execute our directive precisely. The newly organized *kolkhoz* refused to give us provisions—"we don't have enough for ourselves"—and in the unheated classroom in the school, a handful of rotting hay had been thrown on the floor.

We began to acquaint ourselves with the situation. The belongings of the exiles were turned over to the *kolkhoz*. Hundreds of beehives which had once produced such aromatic honey, were left in a cold building where all the bees perished from cold and hunger. No one took the trouble to feed them. Horses also died from hunger and often on the snowy fields one could see a dark heap above which a flock of ravens circled. This was a horse released from the *kolkhoz* stable when its time had come or one that had simply collapsed on the road. Of course, a different fate would have befallen this horse in the city. It would have been quickly converted into sausage that was very popular in those years and which was called "Konnitsa Budennago" ["Budennyi's horse sausage," a play on Budennyi's "Red Cavalry"]. The colonists, however, though starving, resolutely refused to eat horsemeat.

All the grain had been shipped out. The small amount which each peasant saved after a poor harvest year, not even giving it to his family so that he could sow his fields anew, was mercilessly confiscated by the regime.

In the main, our responsibilities were to translate into German the pronouncements of the visiting party agitators and other officials. They either spoke at meetings or called in peasants for individual "talks." Here we observed, while shuddering with indignation, the application of "effective" measures, including putting an unyielding person's fingers into the crack of an open door and slowly closing the door. Later, such behavior was hypocritically criticized as "dizziness from success." "Guilty" lower level party workers were demonstratively removed from their posts, though they had acted on directives from the center. Sometimes they were even executed. But the deed was done. As to the German colonists, even those who were collectivized, there remained no trace of them after a few years. All of them were shipped in a direction unknown and "reliable" *kolkhozniks* were placed on their lands. As the war was to show, however, they too rapidly became unreliable.

We were without any food for almost three days. Only a delayed directive from the region forced the *kolkhoz* officials to attend to the unwelcome, though involuntary guests. We began to receive food consisting of a small bowl of watery soup and a piece of corn bread that was much akin to brick. For some reason this soup was given to us in a dark, semi-demolished house.

Once we couldn't determine what was the mass of white that had aggregated on the sides of the soup bowls. These were maggots; the soup had been made with completely rotten flour.

No, Misha was not able to treat himself to sour cream here.

We were charged with compiling a list of how much grain was still due from each farmstead and we dragged ourselves from house to house over barely walked-on, snowy paths. My city boots were soaked through and I wrapped my feet in newspaper. It froze to the soles of the boots. I was coughing violently, but I visualized the headline on the institute's wall newspaper: "Saboteurs have no place in a Soviet institution of higher education!" And I continued on, making notations with ossified fingers.

For some reason, meetings were always scheduled at night and, in hoarse voices, we translated the stereotypical speeches of the regional orators. Sometimes the *kolkhozniks* who were "adapting" spoke—those not yet acclimatized usually remained grimly quiet.

Once I was going to a women's meeting, as usual, scheduled late in the evening. My friend was occupied at the other end of our district and I struggled along on my own from the school. I tried not to lose the path and fall into knee deep snow. Clouds alternately blocked off the sky or revealed a narrow sickle of the cold moon. My path followed a sparse wood, then it led out to the public road. It was there by the woods that I saw a dark figure lying right on the trail and moving slightly to the right and to the left, the way a person does in a shooting gallery preparing for an unerring shot at the target.

I turned cold: at this instant there will be a flash from the sawn-off muzzle. I will fall into the snow and never see my mother again . . . But why would anyone shoot me? The colonists, after all, understand that we are only screws in the machine, that we are incapable of changing anything in this fearful operation. Maybe the person is lying in wait for someone else, not me? To run is hopeless—the shot would get me in the back. I tear off my hat that hides my hair and go directly at the dark figure.

But there is no shot. . . . Only having come up very close do I see that this is a dying horse moving its head in agony. Then I run across the barren, cold fields choking from the tension. Only upon reaching the road do I notice that I am still clutching my hat in my hands.

The trees are covered with bright, still sticky leaves, and baskets of lilies of the valley are being sold in the streets. I really don't want to be stuck in boring meetings at the institute. But this time I will not be able to slip away easily. My name is listed in the agenda for the day. It is proposed that I and some other friends be inducted into the professional union. This is essential in order to obtain work—but I do not worry since I feel that everything is in place. My grades are high, I have some half dozen social commitments, and my old ladies, housewives whom I am bringing out of illiteracy, are already reading in syllables. And suddenly, completely unexpectedly—rejection.

"Comrade Pavlova [the author's maiden name] must be more fully immersed in the proletarian kettle and definitively reject her bourgeois ways," drones a horse-jawed student who does not miss the occasion to flaunt his vigilance. "Even today, look at her dress!"

All stare at me and, bewildered, even I look at my humble dress, re-sewn out of something by my mother. Finding nothing reprehensible, I wait perplexed. Sustaining an effective pause, my accuser triumphantly announces:

"See how long it is? A whole quarter below the knees."

Here he is truly correct. In accordance with fashion magazines, waistlines were raised and skirts lowered—and mother's creation reflects these tendencies. In a period when engineers did not shave for weeks so as to graphically demonstrate their enthusiasm and zeal for the building of socialism—ostensibly having not even a minute for personal matters—and a student who showed up at an institute in a white shirt and tie would be immediately censured by the wall newspaper, any manifestation of femininity irritated the guardians of the purity of proletarian taste.

"I cannot consider the length of my dress to be a reason interfering with my entry into the professional union at this time," I say with a non-penitential look, "Comrade Tarasov's displeasure would be understandable if I raised my skirt a quarter above the knees."

There are giggles in the hall, but Shura Zapiller, who is running the meeting, interrupts me: "A motion has been made to postpone the entry of comrade Pavlova into the professional union until she liquidates the left-over bourgeois habits in her consciousness. In the name of the institute's professional organization, I fully support this action for re-education. Who is against?"

It is difficult to say when the necessary shifts in my behavior would have appeared. Unexpectedly, Sergo Ordzhonikidze [Minister of Heavy Industry] stopped accepting unshaven engineers and it was proposed to Komsomol secretaries that they lift the ban on white collars.

I was accepted as a union member in the fall.

Chapter Twenty-Two

Nila Magidoff, Only to Travel! Only to Live!

Nila Magidoff was born in Belarus in 1905 to a peasant family. Her family moved to Kursk in central Russia when she was still a child. There she was accepted into a school for indigent girls funded by Maria Fedorovna (Romanov), the Queen Mother. After the Revolution the active and restless Nila trained to parachute jump and joined the Soviet merchant marine. These activities were far more interesting to her than the factory work that she was doing. In 1938 she married and American in Moscow, Robert Magidoff, a noted correspondent for the Associated Press and NBC radio. She was unexpectedly able to come to America in October 1941 where she became heavily involved as a speaker and fundraiser for Russian War Relief. The book *Nila* was co-written by Willie Snow Ethridge to whom Nila narrated her story. The narration makes for the colorful and idiosyncratic English. Excerpted from N. Magidoff and W.S. Ethridge, *Nila*. New York: Keedick Press, 1956.

I worked at this factory for some time and then I want to see the world. I understand I can go to the Merchant Marines and apply to be a sailor. I had a nice, clean biography. It was absolutely pure like a white page—nothing written there. I came from poor family with no capitalists, which was all they required. So here I went. It was very strange, I suppose you think, Willie, this married life. I don't understand it myself. I loved my husband very much, and he loved me. It was just that I was young and crazy to travel and Karel at this time was so involved in his work.

I was assigned to a big freight boat, the Karl Marx. It was carrying the sunflower seeds and also butter. For weeks I hadn't seen the butter. Russia exported everything: butter, ham, caviar. There was a crew of fifty-two people, fifty man and two woman.

I don't know why, but I cut my hair then with a bang. I really looked like a gangster. Not the third-degree gangster, but the lowest gangster. I wore a brown flannel shirt and black skirt. There was no uniform; you wear what you want.

Just before we sailed some kind of political commissar came on the boat and made a long speech how you are supposed to behave highly. All the crew, new and old, was given this lecture on behavior. We must remember we represent the new Soviet Republic abroad. This, you see, was in 1926. We must not involve in any political situation, but if we are involved, we must remember we are Soviet citizens and even if we are not members of the Party we must stick to the Party line. And he gave us to understand we had members of the family left behind.

But I didn't mind the lecture. I was afraid of only one thing—that they take me off the boat. Up to the last minute I was afraid they take me off. Only to travel! Only to live! I sent a telegram to Mother, "I'm going abroad. Thinking of you."

The machinery start! I thought, that's it. Then the whistle blew which means all the crew must step ashore and be lined up. There came four NKVD man with four German wolfdogs, and everybody shout out his name. Then the NKVD man say that if anybody is hidden in the boat these dogs will tear him to pieces. The man standing next to me turned a green color and I got terribly frightened. It was something so undignifying hunting down the man with the dog. All this time, you must remember, I was an idealistic Soviet.

Well, they went on the boat and started with the top deck and suddenly you heard this barking and screaming and saw the NKVD bringing a man all bloody and his flesh torn away. My God, I don't like to think about it! Then we find out that two sailors were trying to smuggle out this priest. The boat was running on coal and in this place where the coal is they dig a hole and put a pipe so the priest can breathe, but the dogs find him and almost tear him to pieces. A very illustrating story of life in Russia. I was actually sick.

They took the priest and the two sailors away and we went back on the boat. When we came to our cabins it was just as if a cyclone came. Everything was on floor. The NKVD search everything.

Finally we sailed, but here I must explain that when you sail from Leningrad you go through the Neva River and a narrow strait until you come to this island and then on to the ocean. Up to this island is Russian water but when you go behind this island you are out of Russian water and the NKVD boat can't go. The crew was praying to get on the outside of this island and I was praying too. Why I felt so guilty and afraid I don't know. I had nothing behind me but the best work, but I was affected by this fear.

Then just when we were on the Russian side of this island the machinery went -bump, -bump,-bump. We understood the captain had got word to stop the boat. The NKVD, we knew, must have been questioning the two sailors and they had told something. And so it was. They had told about one more man and the NKVD came and got him and took him off the boat.

I was a sailor third class and I did everything—washing the floors, polishing the brass and doing everything that they call in Russia unqualified work. I organized a literary circle and was so happy for it was such a success. Man attend it 100 per cent.

We got our money in English—nine pounds a month—about $45. If a sailor has a family at home they took something for family, and pay them in rubles. Also we got a ration: sardines, cocoa, herring and all like these things. None of us eat it. We always save it and when we come to a Russian port there will be a lot of people there waiting, for they know every Russian sailor gets this ration. We weren't permitted to sell it, but it was the most profitable thing there is.

We came to Hamburg. The first officer called me to his office. "I hope you do understand," he said, "that I'm not capitalistic inclined, but we are coming to a capitalistic country and Russian citizens must look a little more presentable in capitalistic country where they notice everything."

He was right to speak to me. I was poorly dressed. The boat furnished working clothes—overalls and wooden shoes that went *clack, clack, clack,* but I had nothing for the leisure. A sailor said he would take me to a place where I could get cheap things. I bought shoes made of material—not even leather, and an advertised suit. I spent altogether $3.25. I can't tell you how I hated to spend money then on clothes.

We were the first Soviet boat that came to Germany after the war. The Russian consulate gave a dinner for the crew and for the first course we had in little glass dishes a mixture made from cherries and other fruits and we just giggled and giggled; we thought we were so capitalistic. And they gave us presents. I got a thermos, the first one I ever saw, to keep drinks hot and cold. My God, why I need it?

While we were in Hamburg the machinery of the boat broke down and we had to stay there for six weeks. Two sailors and I rented a bicycle and we went to many places in Germany. Then we came back to Hamburg and we bought together one bottle of champagne for $2.00 and saw night club entertaining. Girls were making stomach dances. They had on chiffon pants and small brassieres that just covered these little things. And their stomachs start to make this ocean movement. Believe me I never went through such an experience as these stomach dances. I saw it in its full swing—my first capitalistic entertainment. The sailor I was with got so excited with this movement, he cried, "God, isn't that something?" but in Russian even more stronger, and slapped this strange woman, almost naked, who was next to him, on the back. And immediately the man with naked woman hit him between the eyes. The sailor doubled his fist and hit him back. Then I was fighting. Then everybody threw chairs just like in movies. My God! How we were fighting! It was beautiful. People were so electrified from this stomach dance they had to discharge the excitement.

But in the middle of the fight the police came and here we were in the police station. Then somebody notified the captain and here we were back on the boat under arrest. Every day we were lectured and lectured on how to behave in capitalistic country.

Then we went to Holland, Gibraltar and Constantinople. A man in a restaurant in Constantinople told me he'd like to give me a present. Of course, I love presents and he gave me an amber stone on a chain. It was the first piece of jewelry I ever had in my life and I thought it very beautiful.

Then we went on to Odessa and from Odessa we went to many other places. Altogether my sailoring days lasted nearly a year. When they were finished, I had no money whatsoever. I had spent all of it in the countries where we stopped to see how the people lived.

I wanted to bring something for the mother, but I had nothing except some antique flowers I bought in Gibraltar. Nothing else. My sweater was in shreds and my shoes torn to pieces, but I did have enough sardines from my ration to buy a ticket to Kursk.

As I neared our house, I saw Mother talking with the woman from next door. They were outside sitting, eating the sunflower seeds. I slipped around and came in the back door and I heard Mother telling the most beautiful tale about me. How I was going about abroad, everywhere doing first-class traveling; all the places I was staying and all the beautiful clothes I was wearing.

And there I was in the old rags! Oh, how guilty I feel to break this beautiful tale she was telling! I really couldn't give her up before this woman; but after a while I say, "Sh-sh-sh," and she heard me and came inside. I gave her the sardines that were left to quiet her down. With tears in her eyes she begged me not to go out in the town, and so for two days I stayed in the house.

By now my brother Nikolai was a member of the Communist party and was assistant manager of a repair factory shop. It was a small thing, but nevertheless he was quite prominent and he gave me the coupons for some material and Mother made me a dress. She wanted me when I went out to say it came from abroad, but it could be plainly seen it was made by the mother.

THE SADDEST ROMANCE ONE CAN IMAGINE

The most important thing as can be happened to me at a big skating rink in Moscow in November of 1936. You see I loved to skate more than anything.

I was not very fancy, but fairly good that's just to be modest for once in my life, for to tell the truth, I was really very, very good.

This evening when I was striding along fast and strong I saw in front of me a quivering figure, very unsure on his feet and z-zh-ip he went down. Then quickly with a z-zh-ip I cut the ice and came to a dramatic stop, and very beautifully my full skirt went around me. Now I understand my outfit was a little strange for the skating, but it was the best I had then. I had on a quite bright blue silk dress with a circular skirt and on top of it I was wearing a quite shabby man's sweater, a beige-brown color, a black beret and heavy white socks and mits. I hadn't developed at this time the talent for matching things. But no matter, for a very big orchestra would play for the skating and everybody would look so much more beautiful with the graceful movements than he actually was.

Well, I helped the sprawled figure to his feet and immediately I saw he was a foreigner by the way he was dressed. His jacket and gloves and skates were perfect and he was also wearing a beret, which was most unusual for a Russian man in those days. He thanked me in Russian with the accent and I left him and went on my way. In Russia we consider it not polite to talk to a man you're not introduced to, and especially if he is a foreigner.

However as I went around I kept my eyes on him for my curiosity had jumped to the heaven—it was always before the Revolution and after the Revolution in Russia this great curiosity for the foreigner—and I noticed he kept his eyes on me. I pretended to pay no attention. Z-zh-ip I went by him. Z-zh-ip! Z-zh-ip! Once when I went by I heard him talking with a group of three people in English.

Then he fell down again quite close to me and as I assisted him once more to his feet I said. "It looks like I will have to help you."

"Will you?" he asked very humbly with the shining eyes.

"I can even teach you to dance," I told him and I took his hands and explained. "Now you just make this: one, two, three; one, two, three." He was a very poor dancer, but I did the complicated part going backwards. The orchestra played "The Blue Danube" waltz as if we especially asked and very soon we found we could go rhythmically together. We never spoke a word; we were so fascinated by the dancing. The evening was perfect. The music; the cold, sharp air; the lights; the gracefully moving people. We felt like we already know each other, for not even conversation can bring people so close together as dancing. Already, I suppose, it was the beginning of love.

When the music stop, we talk. He tells me he is an American, and has come one year to Russia to gather material on Russian folklore; both old and new, and I tell him I'm working on the *Journal de Moscou*.

Then the music play and we dance again. Then his friends call him. I will remember forever how the woman call, "Robert, come here!" It is the first English I ever remember, "Robert, come here," and he excused himself and went to talk to them and I just left.

For several days I didn't go back to the skating rink, but I kept very busy working in the evenings. I understood, maybe, he would come again to skate there and I was afraid of the development of this friendship because he is an American. Hundreds of people, because they were connected with foreigners, were arrested, and so I thought I had better no get involved with him.

Then I was sitting at my desk one day, writing something, and I heard two people come up and this man on the paper said very officially, "Nila, I'd like to introduce you to Mr. Robert Magidoff." Robert asked me for a walk and I forgot all my resolutions and here we go.

After that I began to see him quite regularly. We went dating out to the teeater and hiking in the country and skating on the ice rink. Then suddenly an incident happened that almost ruined the romance in the bud. We were walking and a piece of dust came to my eye and there were tears just running. Robert in any circumstance, even on an uninhabited island, will always produce a clean, nice handkerchief. So it happened this time; he produced the handkerchief and gave it to me and I put it around my eye and came home with it, saying, "I will wash it and give it back tomorrow."

The next day I washed it and put it near the window to dry and the wind blew or something and it went away. I just left the room for one second and when I came back it was gone.

I was horrified. I was sure Robert would think I wanted his friendship just for this fine handkerchief. I went to all the shops to try to find a handkerchief like this; but, my God, the few handkerchiefs I found were made of the roughest material that would tear your nose away. When I asked in one shop if they have a man's handkerchief the clerk ask, "What, madam?"

"A handkerchief," I say.

"I'm working here already for ten years," he say, "and I never heard of a handkerchief."

I even went to the second-hand stores. Americans would pay a lot with pleasure for the things they could buy in these second-hand stores: pearls, crystals, silver, rubies, diamonds, furs, grand pianos, but, of course, not one handkerchief. The old sheets and the old pillow cases when they would be torn would be used for the nose; a real handkerchief, never.

For days I would not see Robert because of this damned handkerchief. I kept telling him I had work to do and had no time to see him; but one day when I came out of my apartment house there he was waiting. I felt I ought to go through the ground I was so embarrassed. However, I never mentioned the handkerchief to him until years later and, of course, by then he had completely forgot it.

It was a long time, though, before I understood a handkerchief like this one was not so important to an American. Because of the terrible shortage of all kinds of consumer things in Russia, I felt a...a...how do you say it?...a awe, but really it was more than a awe, almost a reverence for American goods. The Russian government never considered worthwhile what the people like; it never spends the brain or the money for the bright, attractive things, just the absolute necessary things. It condemned as capitalistic tricks all the miracles of the five-and-ten.

So I admired extravagantly almost everything that Robert had; but one time I admired something that made a big joke. We were going on a picnic and he came with the dark glasses and it was the first time in my life I saw the dark glasses.

"Really, you can see through them?" I asked.

Robert got real proud of his country and said the technical technique in America is unbelievable. Take the glasses for an example. You can do anything with them. You can drop them on the floor, you can sit on them, and then be took the glasses and threw them down and they went into millions of pieces. That was the funniest thing as can be.

I wasn't an exception, though, in loving everything from America. All the Russian people loved everything from abroad. The Russians' favorite word is *zagranichnyi*—from abroad. I remember on the newspaper there was a messenger boy and he came up to me and ask me to do him the greatest favor. "Will you ask your American friend for the labels off his clothes? I want very much to have something *zagranichnyi*."

So Robert cut the labels from his pajamas, his shirts, his BVDs, his hat, from everything possible—and brought them to me in an envelope, and the next day the messenger boy showed up all in labels on the outside. There came Macy suddenly on the back of the cap and Gloomingdale [sic] on the front of the shirt, but the funniest alliance, as I understand now, was the Brooks Brothers on the Russian tie.

Every time I went out with Robert, everybody sit and wait my appearance and greet me with, "So?" which means what I learn about America? Sometimes I had no time to learn anything—we were busy loving—and then at the end I'd say to Robert, "Please tell me something quick to tell about America."

However, it was most difficult to find in Moscow a place for hugging and kissing. Robert was renting a room in one part of Moscow for a fabulous sum, but under a condition that he never bring a wife or somebody to live with him and, of course, I had no room of my own, and it was not permitted to go like to the Cherokee Park for loving, and we had no car for parking.

Then I got a wonderful idea. We would go to the big station where trains come in every few minutes, and whenever a train came in we would rush into each other's arms and kiss and kiss, and then wait for the next train. But one day the militia man came up to us and say, "You have met enough trains now. Go home!"

That was the one funny incident of our courting, for to tell you the truth it was the saddest romance one can imagine. Not because of me, but because of the circumstances. By this time I love Robert very dearly and he loves me; however, I thought his stay in Russia was almost over and if I married him I will never get permission to go out of the country. Robert will have to leave me and I know how hard that will be on him, especially if there is a child, for I understand by now how wonderfully kind and gentle he is.

So I explain him all this, but he argues he loves me so much he will fight until he gets me out. After I marry him he will register at the American embassy that I am his legal wife, not just his girl friend. I am his wife for good or for worse whom he want to take with him home.

I decided I must go out of Moscow and think it over. So I went out to a Government Home of Rest for newspaper people, musicians and artists and I ask Robert not to come there, but anyway he did. He came every day with a box of chocolates on the only train from Moscow that took three and a half hours to make the trip, spent fifty minutes with me on the station platform, and then went back on the only train returning to Moscow. I was certainly very much impressed.

Of course, I couldn't ask him to spend the night in this Home of Rest because he was a foreigner. It would be the biggest scandal ever happen at this Home of Rest to have a foreigner inside of it. This fact helped me realize that our marriage will never work. I am so proud of him. Such an educated man he is and such new horizons he opened for me, but I will always be afraid to ask him in a Russian house or to ask him to meet my Russian friends. I will always be in terror that the militia will come and arrest me and then what will he do? So I say to Robert, no, and go back to Moscow.

Then in 1937 we start to hear about new arrests in Russia. Mostly they are arresting the wives of men who were counterrevolutionists; the men who had opposed the rise of Stalin. This struck terror to my heart for of course Karel [her executed husband] was one of these counterrevolutionists. For more than a year now he had been dead; but I felt sure his fight against Stalin was not forgotten.

How right I was! One day I came home and my landlady in real Russian fashion, like I'm already dead, clasps her hands in front of her and sways from side to side and says the militia man had been there. He had come with the summons for me to appear on a certain date at the regional headquarters.

I knew, of course, what it means. This was the new technique: instead of arresting you he just left the summons for you to go to the militia where you will be given the place of your exile. What a sadness I felt! I thought I am finished as a human being. I will never come back from the militia station.

I telephoned Robert and told him I must see him at once. When we meet he knows by my face what has happened and he at once begs me to marry him. "Your only chance is to marry me immediately," he argues. "If it save you, wonderful. If not, you go to exile and I go to America." By this time Robert had got his visa extended for six months and was writing free-lance stories for United States newspapers and magazines.

The next morning Robert took his passport and I took mine and we went to the marriage office. There were no flowers, no wedding dress, no nothing. Everything was frozen in me. I still didn't know whether it was the right thing to do, but Robert kept saying, "Oh, darling, cheer up! We're going to be married."

Now they change the marriage office completely, but when Robert and I were married, there were only two windows there—one was for deaths and births and one was for marriages and divorces. The ceremony takes you ten minutes. "Passports," the man say, and *click, click,* it's finished. He fills in the names, the dates of birth, stamps the passports and gives you a certificate of marriage and that's all. No witnesses needed. Nothing. We paid him three rubles and left. A marriage certificate is the cheapest thing you can buy in Russia.

Robert says, "Let's drink champagne," and so we went to the Cafe National the most fanciest, the most expensive cafe in Russia. It's the only place you can order apple pie a la mode. And Robert say, "Now don't argue; you are my wife now and we're going to have champagne and little cakes."

I had champagne and little cakes and I was throwing out all night. Happily for the bridegroom, he was not with me then. We had no place to be together. It was five months before we lived as man and wife and then we lived in one room that Gordon Kashin, an American correspondent, let us have in his three-room apartment.

But back to the summons from the militia. When the day came, Robert walked with me to the headquarters building and wanted to go into the office, but I said, "No, better not. If they arrest us both, who will fight?" Poor Robert, he was hurt by the Communists, I feel sure, more than most other foreigners, for he came so close to the bureaucracy and cruelty of the system. You know, you sometime read in books, the hero went pale. Well, I never saw anybody so pale in my life as Robert. He was gray-pale. Even his lips were pale. My heart wrings now when I think about it. I don't know how I looked, but I was certain I'd never see Robert again. Only God knows how horribly I felt.

We held both hands and kissed. Then I opened the door and the steps went up and I thought I'd never climb there. My feet were like stones when I moved them. I came to this smelly office and I showed my summons to a man sitting there. He said, "Sit down and wait. You will be called."

Then I saw four more woman sitting there and by the expressions on their faces I knew they went through the same nightmare I did. I wanted to go down and tell Robert there is a line there and I got up, but the man say with such a roughness, "Sit down and wait your turn."

All the woman was called before I was and what impressed me most was when a woman was called, she went into the next office and never come back, and so it was completely clear for me she is arrested and taken inside to prison.

Finally the man call, "Nila Ivanovna Shevko," and I get up and go to the other office where they give me a long questionnaire. They ask your last name, your Christian name, your date of birth and your birthplace, your husband's name and his occupation and so on.

Of course, they thought they knew my husband's name and that he was already dead, so can imagine with what circumstances I wrote, "Robert Magidoff, American correspondent." Then I handed in this questionnaire and in spite of my terror, I waited with devilish pleasure for the man to get to this piece of surprising information.

Ah, it was a comedy! He took the questionnaire with the boring look, for every day hundreds of people are arrested and fill these things out. Then suddenly his hair stand on end and I enjoy myself immensely. I know that even if this marriage to Robert will not save me, the NKVD will be most unpleasantly shocked to see I have an American husband working for foreign newspapers. I understand very well that at this time they don't want an American to come so close to the real Russian life.

Then he jump from his chair and say, "Will you please sit down?"

I say nothing, but sit down very deliberately.

He disappears into the chief's office and in about three minutes he returns and say most politely, "Will you come back in a week? In the meantime you will sign this paper that you will not leave Moscow until after the second interview."

The week seemed interminable, but when I returned I was received immediately by the chief officer and he say, "The most horrible thing has happened. It's all a terrible, terrible mistake your being asked to come here." And he takes the summons with my name written on it and tears it in little pieces. "I most humbly apologize for such a stupid blunder."

"You mean I'm free?" I say, scarcely able to believe my ears.

He laugh like an amateur on the stage, 'Ho, ho, ho," and say, "Of course. Of course. You can travel where you wish—that is inside the Soviet Union. And I do hope you will try to explain to your husband it was all a mistake."

"I will do my best," I say in the meanest way. "He is downstairs now, waiting for me."

As I went out, the man in the other office, who spoke so rough to me the first time, run and open the door, but God! I didn't even notice him.

On the street just where I left him, Robert is standing, and I run to him and put my arms around him and cry, "I'm free! I'm free! I can go any place!"

After this, especially after we get the room with Gordon Kashin, is the most happiest time. It was the first time anybody take care of me. You American woman will not understand this for you are accustomed to the husband taking care of the woman, being sorry for you when you have the headache, getting a wrap for you when you are cold, asking when he comes home in the evening, "Darling, what have you being doing with yourself today?" and inviting you out for special suppers now and then; you know, showing the attention in all these little things. Well, I never experienced it before and I just bask in it with such a pleasure. It was pure and untouched happiness.

Then Robert became assistant to the chief of the AP Bureau in Moscow and went to the United States for a short visit. While he was gone I was telephoned to from the Russian Foreign Office, where we I had applied for an apartment for a long time, that they had an apartment for us. I thought, of course, it would be a room and a bathroom, but my God, it was three rooms. I sent Robert a cable, "We got apartment," and in just two weeks he came rushing back with boxes loaded with things because the apartment was completely empty except for the most necessary furniture.

Robert had bought dishes and silver and the most terrific kitchen things — the things to turn the eggs, the pot to make the coffee, the beater to beat the eggs and frying things. Oh, to unpack it! Nothing will ever compare with unpacking these boxes. Never before did Robert like to shop, but he tell me that every time he bought something, even the can opener, he saw my happy face. There was only one disappointment. Robert has very plain taste and he bought very plain dishes. I want them all colors with big flowers.

The best thing he bought was the electric toaster with the pumping bread. Wonderful is not the word! I telephoned all my Russian friends — by this time the arrests and trials had subsided — and I said to them, "Please do come for American toast!" I ask husbands too. Everybody. When they came I put the toaster on an oval table in the middle of the room. I put two pieces of bread in it and then everybody sat around and waited.

Then z-zh-ip the toast pumped up! Ah-h-h, there is no way to express my friends' faces; their childish happiness at this miracle thing. Then I buttered the two slices and passed them around and here we went again. Everybody waited, scarcely breathing. Then z-zh-ip and two more slices. I'm really afraid to say how much we ate of this amazing American toast. It sounds unbelievable; but we spent the whole evening around this toaster and everybody eat five or six slices—about ten pounds of bread in all.

I remember I wore for the toasting a housecoat with a zipper that was going from the knee up to the neck, which Robert had also brought from America. I had never seen a zipper like this before and, naturally, none of my Russian friends had. Robert said the coat was just to wear around the house when there was no company but I thought it was absolutely beautiful—it was long to the floor with a little train in back. The guests simply adored the zipper. Poor souls, they were so fascinated with the zipper zipping and the toast pumping they were in a state of complete exhaustion by the time they went home.

Robert felt I should go around with Americans more. When we went ice skating and saw Americans, he would bring me up to them and introduce me as his wife. Soon one of these couples invited us to dinner.

I'll never forget this dinner. I was in a frenzy about what to wear, and I drove Robert into a frenzy too. Do I wear a hat? I asked him. Do I wear gloves? How long should my dress be? What color? He begged me to stop worrying. They are kind people, he said, and they know you're a simple Russian peasant.

So we came to the party and they passed the martinis and I took one and that was the first cocktail I ever had in my life. In Russia it is not customary to drink before dinner. In an ordinary home everybody just sits and tries to squeeze the conversation and then everybody will be invited to the table and will drink vodka with the food.

So here I am drinking the martini and everybody talking to me in English how difficult is the Russian language and I not understanding scarcely a word. When Robert was courting me he said he would give me some English lessons and he did, but the day we were married, he dropped the lessons dead—not one more lesson. I suppose I was not a very inspiring pupil.

As we drink and talk, a man in a white coat passes a lot of little things to eat—all very nice, but never before have I seen such *little* things—one bite. and z-zh-ip they're gone. So I whisper to Robert, "Shall I eat a lot of these little things or will there be something else?"

Then the man in the white coat came and said dinner is served and we got up and went into the dining room. The hostess put me on the right of the host but I did not appreciate the gesture for I was not acquainted with this compliment.

Do you know, before we ate a thing, the man in the white coat took off the plate that was already on the table and put another plate and a bowl with soup in its place? Then he pass the crackers and celery and olives and all those things. This was all easy, but when the second course came I was just ruined.

For the first time in my life I was served a platter of meat. I was served it even before the hostess because of this damned honor of sitting on the right of the host, so I could not watch her and see what to do. I thought I would just die.

The most I was afraid of was the servants. They were all Russians and the Russians are the most class-conscious of any people. They know I don't belong at this fancy dinner and they scorn me like I can't tell you. They really snobbed me. I was all the time like sitting on pins and needles. Poor Robert, he suffered too. He knows how serious I take these things. After the meat came the vegetables. Oh, my back was a hard nut of tense!

Finally, the servants took off everything and I thought thank God! it is over; but then came this last thing, the dessert. It was some kind of ring, a quite fat ring, with a sauce in the middle. I understand now I was supposed to cut a little piece of this one and then take sauce from the inside' but I cut all the way through this ring and the sauce rushed out and ran all around the platter.

Quickly, the servant jerked it away from me and stomped out of the room, his head high in the air and his eyes looking down his nose. I was so furious I could have struck him between the eyes. Fortunately for the other guests there was a second ring in the kitchen, and in a few minutes he returned with it, but he never approached within three feet of me.

After this torture—I really can't call it another way—we went back to the living room for coffee. When some time had passed I began once more to enjoy the beautiful life.

I must tell you from that night on I learned pretty fast the American ways. I didn't know a lot of things. You just can't imagine. American children learn them like they breathe, but nobody ever told me how to do all kinds of things: how to unfold your napkin (you know, the first dinner I had at Gordon Kashin's apartment I didn't use mine at all; I thought it would be terrible to soil its white innocence and I looked at Robert for approval, but afterwards he told me it was put there to use); how to hold your knife and fork; how to serve yourself from a platter.

Robert, of course, noticed when I married him that I didn't know these things; but he was so kind and gentle he wouldn't mention them. Now, though, when I insisted on knowing, he told me many things: not to reach across the table for something you wanted, not to eat chicken with your fingers at a formal dinner and so on.

The most complicated thing for me to learn was how to serve myself, so one day I fried a whole chicken and Robert, with a napkin on his hand, just like the man in the white coat, served it on a platter to me. He did it very seriously, not cracking a smile. Then he made me eat what I took with a knife and fork. I tell you it was real work, trying to finish this chicken without doing it naturally with the fingers.

So life went on until June 22nd, 1941, when we heard on the radio that Germany had invaded Russia. Soon after that many Americans sent their wives back to the United States and Robert was most anxious to send me. However, he couldn't get permission from the Russian government. He had applied for a visa for me soon after we were married. Then every six months he wrote a letter and asked has the decision yet been made; but like the real Russian bureaucracy, they never said no and they never said yes. They just said they had taken it under consideration and that Robert would be informed when the time came. We were both terribly afraid, of course, that they would never give the permission for me to go.

The war finally broke the stalemate. The American ambassador, Lawrence Steinhardt, called Robert one day and said, "I think I have good news for you. I think we have succeeded in getting permission for Nila to go to the United States. We have arranged with the Russians to exchange her and Pauline Habicht for two loads of high octane gas." Pauline was the wife of Herman Habicht, the assistant chief of the United Press bureau.

That was all Ambassador Steinhardt told Robert and for many years Robert bragged that he was one of two men who knew exactly what his wife was worth—one load of high octane gas. Thirteen years later he and I learned that Pauline and I and several other people were exchanged not for gas but for a prominent Russian who was being detained in the United States.

Anyway, the morning after the ambassador telephoned, I got a call from the Moscow bureau that gives visas and they invited me to come there. When I arrived they say the visa is granted, but they must warn me that I must renounce my Russian citizenship. This was no more than I expected. Nevertheless, it was a terrible wrench. I was never a member of the Communist party and God knows I had suffered at the hands of the Communist regime; still I loved my country, my family and my friends, and it hurt me to turn my back upon them.

Everybody at the American embassy, though, helped me to feel better. Robert and I went there as soon as I got my visa and they all seemed so happy that I was going to Robert's country and would some day be an American citizen. Everybody in the embassy knew there are two kinds of marriages between Russian woman and American man. One is when Russian woman's aim is to get everything she can from the American man because of the hard life, and the other one is for love. Everybody knew Robert's and my marriage was a real love.

Now we had to decide whether Robert would come with me to America. This was a very serious decision, for Robert recently had become chief of the NBC bureau in Moscow and broadcast over the radio. Robert said if I am afraid he will come with me, but I said absolutely not, for I understood how important this new job was for him. I never thought until now how brave I was to come here alone.

Freddy Rhinehardt, the first secretary of the embassy, made out an affidavit for me for, of course, when I renounced my Russian citizenship I had to give up my passport. It was a long paper with my name and a photograph and a description of me, and it had a big, red stamp on it and was rolled and tied with a red ribbon; it was really a very beautiful document.

I first went from Moscow to Vladivostok, which took nineteen days as our train had to leave the main tracks frequently to let pass trains with troops going to the front. At Vladivostok I caught a small freighter for Japan, then from Japan I went to Shanghai, and from Shanghai I sailed for San Francisco, and from San Francisco, as I told you in the very beginning, to New York and the three-room apartment on Twenty-first Street.

Chapter Twenty-Three
Tat'iana Fesenko, War-Scorched Kiev

Please see note to the previous Fesenko entry.

It's Sunday morning and father is at his favorite pastime, fiddling with the radio trying to get the world news. "War," he says. "Today German airplanes bombed Post Volynskii [a major railroad center west of Kiev]. Molotov[1] will address the nation at noon."

It is evening. As usual, Shura [diminutive of Aleksandr or Aleksandra] is here in the orange glow of our cozy living-room lamp. He and father are talking.

"It's not as simple as you think, Aleksandr Aleksandrovich, and it's too early to be gleeful. Russia is a tough nut to crack, especially since we've been preparing for war all these years."

"Pavel Pavlovich, I can't believe that the moment has finally come when we'll be rid of our beloved and wise leader with all his faithful shock workers and devoted communists. The German troops which went through Europe in a flash will do the same against the red commanders into whose skulls, Tania, you can't even pound ten English phrases, despite all your enthusiasm. Then Russia without the Soviets will again become our great and beautiful motherland."

Shura's serious eyes shone with such joy that one wanted to believe him. But I did not. He was forty and he knew another Russia. He remembered and yearned for it. But we, contemporaries of the Great October Revolution, had only one motherland: the motherland of the Soviet Union, of brave aviators, gigantic construction projects, a motherland with secure borders, with the invincible Red Army, with the romance of the distant Civil War. Most of us were convinced, as the song said, that "No one in the world// Can love or laugh like us."

Even those like myself who had seen the villages of the Ukraine starving to death in '33; who had not slept nights on end expecting the common fate of the intelligentsia, a "visit" from the NKVD during Ezhov's Terror, even we wanted to believe in a happy future. We tried to view everything that was dark, difficult and often hypocritical as inevitable "growing pains" which had to be lived through. I loved my country, though I did not like many things about it. And now my heart contracted with heavy foreboding.

How sad all the days had become. Every morning brought news of losses. The familiar and beloved world was collapsing. Faith, nurtured over many years, was collapsing. The "secure borders" were violated on the very first day. The "invincible Red Army" surrendered city after city, and a horrible question beat at one's brain: was it all a lie? We denied ourselves everything, our standard of living was much lower than that of Europe, but we were a land of giants. Courageous aviators soared in our skies, shocking the world with their daring records. The defensive might of our enormous country had grown day by day. Yet, now the arches of the Dnieper hydroelectric dam had fallen, dynamited by the retreating Soviet army. The dead, black smoke stacks of the destroyed plants at Kramatorsk stood ominously. The once aggressive "little falcon" warplanes had become shapeless, burnt-out hulks on their bomb-pitted aerodromes. With a heavy and confident tread the German armies swept across the endless Ukrainian plains, squeezing the Soviet troops, cutting off the retreating forces, seizing cities. The youth of the Soviet Union went to the front but was unable to stop the enemy onslaught.

On the very next day after the declaration of war Lenia [diminutive of Leonid], my sweet and gentle friend from graduate school, left for the front. It seemed only yesterday that he sat by my hospital bed, shyly fingering a large box of my favorite rum cherries in chocolate which the doctor had strictly forbidden after my operation. He was planning his summer vacation then. Now he was far away, somewhere out there, as a military interpreter.

Gone into an armor unit was Kolia, a blue-eyed, fun-loving engineer, my first love. My girlhood, my first secrets from mother, the first dreams of my own nest were all tied to him. Since that time the lilacs had bloomed many times in the gardens of Kiev but carefully hidden in my desk was a withered branch—the first awkward gift from an infatuated boyfriend. And now, as he kissed my tear-filled eyes, I said farewell to my carefree youth, to my familiar and beloved world.

Then Zoika was gone into the army as a medic. Always laughing, always devoted to her work, she assured us that even in the eyes of her beloved man she would first look for symptoms of conjunctivitis. Gone was Viktor, lanky and fun-loving, the favorite at all our picnics and parties. He had just become the father of as lively and fair-haired a boy as himself. Iura [diminutive of Georgii], too, was gone. My friend of many years who patiently would inquire every three months whether I'd go down to city hall with him and get married. And who instead went with me to all the theaters and movie houses and who kept all my great and lesser secrets. On a summer's evening I saw off Tolia [Anatolii], the husband of a close friend. Just recently we had celebrated their first wedding anniversary, and now he was off "with a spoon, tin cup, and change of underwear," as prescribed in the draft board notice.

Our house had become unusually empty and still. Occasionally my weeping girlfriends would come by to share their doleful news. I tried to console and hearten them, not knowing that my own greatest loss was still before me.

Nevertheless, I passed my last exam. Father beamed with a restrained but proud smile. When I arrived at the Military Academy where I had been teaching, a sentry snapped to attention and said with a swagger: "Comrade instructor, all classes have been postponed till the end of the war." All of a sudden I had a lot of time, empty and useless. I tried reading, then embroidering. But books would fall from my hands and the whimsical, bright embroidery patterns brought no joy.

One morning, having returned from center-city, I found a huge bouquet of red carnations in my room and a figure all in white—it was Andrei.

"It took me eight days to get here from Moscow," he said animatedly. "You can't get on a train. It's all soldiers going to the Ukrainian front. Finally, I squeezed into one. German planes strafed us on the way. Went to the Moscow draft board, thought I'd go straight to the front. But they wouldn't take me. Had to go to my place of residence. But they won't take me here either. I'm an odd case: with a university education I belong in the officer corps, but since I haven't been in the army I can't be a commander. So they told me to wait for induction papers."

How good it was that at least one friend arrived in these days of partings. We shared our grief and apprehension, but he brought me small comfort. He said that the mood on the home front was depressed, that the virtually unopposed German invasion had made everyone despondent. We walked the streets and parks, rustling with their luxuriant greenery, and spoke of a strange dichotomy creeping into our souls. We greedily read the papers, seeking hope and assurance in them. But the meager bulletins spoke of deeper penetration into new territory, without even mentioning the names of surrendered cities. On the third of July, Stalin came out with his famous speech. He called for livestock to be driven off, for grain to be burned, for the enemy to be denied everything of value. While reading the speech I had no inkling that within some twenty-four hours our home was to lose what, indeed, was most precious.

The night from the fourth to the fifth of July I awoke with a strange, agonizing feeling. It seemed that some icy hand had gripped my heart so it barely beat. I turned on a light and glanced at the clock—it wasn't yet four. "There will probably be an air raid, it happens a lot at dawn now," I thought to myself, opened a shutter and began to listen intently to the silence. A dog barked somewhere, another responded nearby. A vehicle passed by—probably transporting the wounded. The garden gate clicked and steps were heard on the flagstone walk, closer and closer, followed by an impatient knocking on our door. I'm throwing on a dress but mother is already unhooking the door chain with trembling hands. Poor mama, she always worries—it's probably just the usual identity papers check.

The raspberry bands of NKVD service caps flamed up in the electric light. Two of them enter without greeting, and demand that we hand over any weapons and radios. We have never had weapons and the radio had been turned in long ago. A search begins. One of the unexpected guests, dark and morose, plunges into closets, flinging out books and undergarments. The more polite one approaches father's bed, produces a small, white arrest warrant and says: "Get dressed." These words freeze my innards. What I feared so much in those terrible nights of 1937–38, when black automobiles stopped at almost every door, has come. Destiny had mercy on our family then.

But an unexpected blow is all the more painful. Mother became stone still, her hands fell into her lap, her face froze. I begin to ready papa for the sorrowful journey. I pack underwear and food. Crazily, it seems awfully important to include a needle and thread. Papa is so neat; he won't stand a missing button or the smallest hole. But it turns out that prisoners are not permitted anything sharp, not even needles. Remove the penknife from your pocket, surrender the razor, even if it is a safety razor. Money is allowed: 180 rubles, all that we have. Finally, everything is ready but I must treat papa to some tea: strong, with milk, the way he likes it. I have put the teapot on long ago and now, while the NKVD finish their paperwork, pour tea into a pot-bellied blue cup. Papa smiles meekly, drinks. He is given the papers to sign. They are in a hurry. "There's a lot of work today," says the dark one. Nothing, of course, was found during the search. They take papa's passport, employment ID and those beautiful gold-lettered commendations which he had been awarded for his scientific work.

It is time to part. Mother cleaves to father and I am afraid to look at her. Papa kisses her quickly, once again, then carefully moves her aside and says to me: "My little Tania, I entrust mother to you, keep her from harm."

Rest assured, daddy, my dear, my beloved friend. I will do everything in my power. How desperately we hold ourselves in control, both he and I, not wanting to make things more painful in these dreadful moments.

"You may come on the eighth," says the lieutenant.

"Oh, I'll come. Of course, I'll come. I'll do everything. I'll get to everyone. Dear daddy, don't worry."

"It's useless," he shakes his head wearily.

And so, they take papa away. I want to walk with him, at least another several steps together. But they don't let me. It is dawning, and I see how papa, his shoulders hunched, walks down the path. He looks back, then hastens. How hard it is for him. The door slams, the engine turns over. . . . He's gone . . . The NKVD, did in fact, have little time. That night some five thousand members of the Kiev intelligentsia, engineers, doctors, agronomists shared my father's fate.

I walked back to the empty house; tried to comfort and quiet my mother; mechanically put the strewn items in their proper places. If only morning would come. I'd call Shura. He is my "valerian drops," my tranquilizer, as I jokingly referred to him. A true and devoted friend, he would think of something, give sound advice. But Shura was powerless. Nor did my visits to the waiting rooms of the NKVD amount to anything. When I came on the eighth, the assigned day, I was told what hundreds of others were told: "It is wartime. No information about particular individuals can be given out." I came again and again only to receive the same response. I fought my way to the district attorney and to the military prosecutor. The first said laconically: "He's not on our lists." The second looked through his papers, called his secretary, made a phone call and finally said: "There is no such case." Then he glanced at my white knuckles and said in a softer voice that the NKVD had simply removed my father as an "unreliable."

Oh yes, he was unreliable—my father. After all, thirty years ago he had studied in Germany and did not hide the fact. He spoke German well, never went unshaven, and despite warnings from the party secretary at work, wore a gold wedding band. The nature of his crime was clear.

The administrators at the draft board were astounded by father's arrest. They tried to convince me that it was a misunderstanding which would soon be corrected, but refused to pay for the days my father had worked. At the publisher's where he was owed more than two thousand rubles for his latest book, they also refused to pay. It was useless to argue. All institutions were feverishly preparing for evacuation. Hardly any employees came to work. The offices were empty, the desks gutted. Stoves were crackling everywhere. Mountains of papers, documents, account books, engineers' calculations were being burned. Kiev was covered by black snow: droplets of soot and flakes of charred paper spun in the air and spread over the ground.

I stopped by the university; the scene was the same there. In a heap of documents on the floor I accidentally found my own file. Luckily, I had already received documentation of having passed my Master of Arts exams. The classrooms and offices stood starkly open. Here and there newly cobbled-together crates gave off an aroma of pine. The dean's office, always crowded and noisy, was totally empty. Not quite, a stove was blazing in the corner and the young, fashion-plate associate dean was carefully feeding it neat file-folders from his desk.

"Oh, Tat'iana Pavlovna," he said. "There's nothing new I can tell you. We weren't assigned any railroad cars, unfortunately. All the students, graduate students, and some of the faculty are evacuating on foot to Poltava, and then we'll see . . ."

He pressed my hand firmly, and I left through the echoing, empty corridors and stairwells. What was I to do? Neither mother nor I could go on foot. We both had weak hearts, and I was just recovering from surgery. We both were born and had lived all our lives in Kiev, and we had no one outside the city. And most importantly, there was father. Maybe he was here somewhere, nearby. How could we leave him? For there was nothing to fear from the enemy anymore; the greatest wound had been inflicted by our own people.

It was unbearable at home, especially at night. One neighbor, a major, was somewhere at the front. Another neighbor was stranded somewhere on an official trip. Mother asked Andrei to move into one of our empty rooms. Troops were occupying the university dormitories anyway, and it felt safer with a man in the house. Everybody was queuing up around the clock, lugging home candy, cooking oil, pearl barley. We had no money and could not stock up on anything. I tried selling a thing or two, but goods were worthless now, with hardly any takers. As always, Shura came to our aid, forcing some money on us until "better times."

Everywhere in and out of town people were digging trenches and tank traps. At first, we also took part, conscientiously hauling dirt, helping to camouflage the pits. But then, like everyone else convinced of the hopelessness of the task, we tried to avoid the zealous police. At that point, they began rounding people up everywhere—in movie houses, in food queues, right on the street. Many men began to grow the notorious "trench" beards to look older and visibly prove that they were past the established age for digging trenches.

The parks and gardens of Kiev seemed turned up by giant moles. People hurriedly dug slits in the soil and hid there the moment they heard the drone of airplanes and waited for death from the implacable German bombs. But the bombs did not fall. Every day flocks of enemy birds would appear over the city. They drew incomprehensible smoke signs in the sky and occasionally dumped a rain of white leaflets. People would watch with trepidation as these white moths circled languidly earthward. Then they would send children to gather the messages from the enemy (or was it friend?) and would avidly read the meager information. "Not a single bomb will fall on your beautiful city" they read, and fear would leave them, and fewer of them would crawl into the raw earth and more and more would watch the powerful silver birds float by in the sky, occasionally engaging the Soviet fighter planes. The results were always the same: smoky balls of explosions would dance near the silvery wings, but they, rocking gently, would calmly disappear in the distance, invulnerable.

At night people would come out to stand watch. Two or three figures with gas masks tied to their waists would stand before every house. But nothing was occurring in the city, and standing watch was as useless as the sand-bag barricades thrown up on all the streets. The summer rain fell on the tough fibers, the hot Ukrainian sun withered them, the sand bags rotted, ruptured, and golden streams of sand flowed to the pavement for children to carry to their yards. At night silver stars would arc across the velvet sky and heat lightning would blaze in the distance. These were stifling and moonless nights in which the rumble of distant artillery would fuse with the dull roll of thunder. In the gardens linden blossoms, tobacco, and petunias gave off their heady aroma. These were nights for singing, loving, laughing, slipping in a boat along the wide ribbon of the Dnieper, and for dreaming till dawn on St. Vladimir's hill. But instead, quite close, there was fighting. The Germans had occupied the Goloseev forest and buses with large red crosses painted on them constantly raced along the streets of Kiev. Sometimes they drove very slowly and then people looked at them with anguish because only the mortally wounded were transported so slowly.

But, more frequently, other vehicles would race by. One-and-a-half and three-ton trucks packed with all sorts of bag and baggage. Occasionally amidst bedsprings, mirrored chiffoniers, and rolled-up carpets there would be nestled rubber tree plants and palms—the VIP's of the city were prudently sending their families out of harm's way. But not everyone was able to leave the besieged city in such comfort. People being evacuated with their institutions and offices would sit for days at junctions and railroad yards vainly expecting departure. And those who did manage to get on the treasured trains sent desperate messages to their loved ones describing chaos, disorder, congestion and filth at the evacuation centers and the panic which had engulfed the rear.

Troops retreated through the city. First from the districts of Western Ukraine—Lvov and Tarnopol—and later from familiar, near-by places where

Kievans would go on vacation, buy strawberries and drink frothy, whole milk straight from the dairy. Unshaven, hungry, and sullen Red Army soldiers would march by, brusquely answering questions and sometimes caustically cursing their officers and political commissars who had taken off in their staff cars leaving the troops behind.

In contrast to the soldiers, the "warriors" of the newly-formed defensive battalions would proudly posture in their brand-new uniforms. They were given the noble task of fighting mighty German tanks with bottles of combustible fluid. Of course, it never came to that. Having strutted in their uniforms, the youths in a timely fashion changed into civvies and dispersed to their homes. Many of them later, under German occupation, filled the ranks of the collaborationist police, which was largely made up of the more unprincipled and brutal elements, thoroughly despised by the populace. Or else they became black marketeers who would scour villages for flour and cooking oil for resale to starving city-dwellers at incredible prices.

But in the meantime these "warriors" did not foresee the pitiful end of their military careers and did their utmost to fan the flames of spy-phobia sweeping the city. Every fair-haired and blue-eyed person, every young woman who "suspiciously" asked for directions in an unfamiliar part of the city was taken for a spy. All the police precincts were overflowing with such "fascist agents" who spent anguished hours in filthy cells, finally returning home only after establishing their identity.

The Germans were coming closer and closer. Once in the evening a dented and dirty automobile pulled up to our house. It was "uncle Andy," as the young folks called him in jest, a calm and handsome forty-five-year-old major, a family friend. He had long worn the glistening medal denoting twenty years service in the Workers' and Peasants' Red Army [1921–1946], but that evening this man who had fought in all the battles of the Soviet Union hardly resembled a sober and disciplined officer. He was drunk and his eyes revealed alarm and despair. His jokes were flat, and his lips were distorted in a forced smile. He looked at the old linden tree, the growth of jasmine by the window, and our small, cozy house with a glance of farewell. Then, tightening his fancy, yellow Sam Browne belt, he said simply, "Things are bad, things are very bad with us." The motor snorted, and his car shot out of our narrow yard. One friend less . . .

And friends were what we lacked most in those increasingly troubled days. After my father's arrest I was to lose mother, as well. Formerly friendly and happy, she became unrecognizable after that grim day when papa was led from the room where just two weeks before they had celebrated their thirtieth wedding anniversary. She was now apathetic and immobile, and had lost interest in all things. My attempts to console her were rebuffed with "Leave me alone. . . . Don't bother me."

Our tightly-knit and amicable family had disintegrated. Gone were friends, gone was my beloved profession. The useless books and notes were gathering dust. Something horrific and implacable was coming. It had shattered the habitual patterns of being, had taken thousands of lives and one did not know whether it was bringing agony to the nation or an "unprecedented flowering" as Shura kept insisting.

Andrei and I stood watch in the evenings, patrolled the yard, stood by the gate and then for a long time would sit on the steps of the porch, covered in wild grapes, listening to the distant grunting of heavy artillery. Golden stars, falling, traced the sky. It was their time [the August meteorite showers]. But even more frequently crimson and emerald-green signal flares soared upward, saying something to some unseen presence in an anxious and incomprehensible tongue.

It was stifling in the garden, even at night, and breathing was becoming increasingly difficult for Andrei. He complained of being choked by cobwebs, of a weight in his chest. And then, all of a sudden, there was a frightening, inexplicable seizure. The experienced doctor at the clinic immediately diagnosed it as severe bronchial asthma. While writing the prescription he said that it might be the after-effect of a bad cold, but could have a psychosomatic basis. The symptoms should dissipate after an injection. The prescribed regimen was bed rest.

In fact, Andrei did feel better, but not for long. He lay in bed for several days, but then leapt up. It wracked his nerves to stay in bed. He became pale to the point of transparency. He would walk around very slowly, biting his lips, trying to suppress his garroted breathing. Could this be Andrei, the tennis player, swimmer, tireless dancer, mad party-goer?

There was a rumor that army headquarters, to which my dear university friend, Lenia, was attached, was retreating through Kiev. I had not heard from him, and then suddenly there he was: a skinny man in uniform, dusty and sunburned, squeezing my hand and calling me by name.

It was a piece of luck, he said hurriedly. Headquarters was on the left [eastern] bank, but he was sent into the city. He had half an hour and was determined to see us, but the trolleys were not running, and he was about to give up. We just stood there amidst the crowd, holding each other by the hands, rushing to say all we could in the time we had, interrupting each other, sharing our news.

A day later Lenia was sitting on our porch, anxiously talking about what disturbed him. Honest, shy, and idealistic, he was indignant at the deception in which he had to take part while working in the political section at headquarters. He told us that his family's apartment had been abandoned, that his parents left in a great hurry, leaving everything, and asked whether we could keep his notes and dissertation drafts. Should he live, he said, then he would resume his work where he had left off. We managed to do all that, and as a memento I received Jerome K. Jerome's *Three Men in a Boat* with a personal inscription.

Dear friend, never again shall the three of us go for a boat ride as we used to, you and Andrei at the oars, myself at the tiller. Your notes have been left lying next to mine on the lower shelf of a bookcase in a house abandoned.

Lenia came by two more times and we expected him a third. But we never saw him again. The iron horseshoe of the German advance threatened to become an iron ring, and headquarters hurriedly retreated deeper into the rear.

Sinister conflagrations increasingly filled the sky as the retreating Red Army burned everything in its wake. And finally, the inevitable came.

An anti-tank gun thudded heavily at a nearby intersection. The staccato crack of machine guns burst through the still gardens. People instinctively inhaled deeply and whispered, "Here it comes." The sky blazed all night; all night artillery thundered; all night people huddled against each other in slits in the raw earth. At dawn everything suddenly became quiet. Only below, along the river the snap of rifle fire continued and a German mortar stubbornly fired on the retreating troops. Then the whole earth shuddered from a powerful explosion—the gorgeous Dnieper bridges settled into the water. They had been dynamited while the last troops still crossed them. And again there was silence, full of anxiety and bewilderment.

We went out. Trolley cars, dispersed from the depots, were scattered everywhere along the streets. The water works and power plants had already been blown up, and the trolleys, empty and useless, seemed to have lost their way in the huge city. But there were many pedestrians—people with baby carriages filled with sacks of flour. We recalled how the day before the locals were hauling off bright blue beds with cheerful nickel-plated ornaments. Somewhere warehouses were being plundered, freight cars broken into. The "lumpen proletariat" were joyously dragging easy wartime booty to their lairs.

But the Germans were slow to appear. Rumor had it that they were already in the city. Wide-eyed, street-smart kids would announce that some guy named Joe had seen the hugest tank at the Haymarket. But in our district the Germans appeared only toward five in the evening. People poured into the street, examining the newcomers from the west with fear and curiosity. They marched handsome and huge in their strange grayish-green uniforms. Tired, covered with dust, but clean shaven, they smiled at the populace. They would pick up children, fearlessly enter yards and houses to wash themselves. They washed themselves with pleasure, pouring cold water over their taut, muscular backs.

But our own, our cherished army was marching eastward into a huge trap where it was to lose some 660,000 men.

The first evening star appeared in the sky, timid and small. The nineteenth day of the month of September of the year 1941 was nearing its end. Mother shut the gate, looked around our quiet green garden with its dahlias and nasturtiums and said with relief: "Well, the war is over for us."

Poor mother, she had no way of knowing that the war had only just begun.

NOTES

1. Viacheslav Mikhailovich Molotov (1890–1986), foreign minister of the Soviet Union 1939–1949 and 1953–1956; negotiated the Soviet-German non-aggression pact in 1939.

Chapter Twenty-Four

Elena I. Kochina, Blockade Diary

For 900 days during World War II German armies blockaded Leningrad. At least one-and-a-half million residents of the city died from starvation, the elements, and disease. Not realizing what war would bring, E.I. Kochina, a Leningrad schoolteacher, started a diary a few days before war commenced. The diary ends in 1942 when she and her family were evacuated while the siege was still in progress. She writes sparingly but with lucid insight and observation of the horror, brutality, dehumanization, and death in its many forms. Life in its very essence deteriorated around her. She wrote with no hope that her diary would ever be published. This is an intense document of human survival and of the human spirit, which also speaks for all the mute and dead who did not survive the siege. The original, *Blokadnyi dnevnik* [Blockade Diary] was published in the collection *Pamiat'*. Paris: YMCA Press, 1981.

16 June 1941. Dima [Dimitrii] is on leave. He spends all day with our daughter: bathing, dressing, and feeding her. His well-groomed, sensitive hands of a designer tenderly manage these things. His fair hair blazes red in the sun, lighting up his happy face. "You gave birth to a daughter, but can't understand what a joy this is!" says Dima with reproach. I laugh to myself. Let him amuse himself. Lena and I know each other well. We have our own world, where we allow no one, not even Dima.

22 June 1941. Morning. Together with her multi-colored rattles I brought Lena out into the garden. The sun was busy at its work. Suddenly: cries, the sound of broken dishes. The landlady ran past the dacha. "Elena Iosifovna, it's war with the Germans! They just broadcast it over the radio!" she exclaimed, crying. War! I am 34 years old. This is the fourth war in my lifetime.

22 June 1941, Midnight. How quickly everything changes! Just this morning I was admiring the sunrise, and the Germans were already bombing our airports. Belorussian airfields have been hit especially hard.

23 June 1941. The tornado of war storms over our land with frightening speed, scattering people along the way, like eggshells in all directions. In this commotion it isn't possible to understand anything. The trains, stuffed with human flesh, head for Leningrad and leave equally stuffed.

24 June 1941. Infected with a general panic, we rushed to the city. Everything seemed ominous and alarming in the countryside. It seemed that a comforting tranquility awaited us in Leningrad.

24 June 1941. The Germans have penetrated the region of Dubno and Rovno. There are desperate battles. All of this isn't sinking in.

25 June 1941. Hitler threw the "immorality" philosophy, reeking of human degeneration, at the Germans as if they were starved dogs. In addition they received weapons, handsome full-dress uniforms and boastful slogans. This was all the German "boys" needed: every cretin and mongrel thinks he's a crusader, bringing renewal to a "decayed humanity."

25 June 1941. Many employees of our institute have joined the people's militia and are leaving for the front. All day today we sewed knapsacks and got them ready for the trip leading to "nowhere."

26 June 1941. We come earlier than usual to the institute, but work isn't going too well. We can't work at our daily tasks, braiding the thin strand of rational thought which no one needs now. We all have one wish—to work for the front.

27 June 1941. The whole earth, from the Baltic Sea to the Carpathians, is gripped by this monstrous war!

29 June 1941. Each day the Germans swallow 30–40 kilometer chunks of our territory. Let them get indigestion from such portions.

—June 1941. Spy mania, like an infectious disease, has struck everyone without exception. Yesterday near the market, an old woman resembling a flounder wearing a rain slicker seized hold of me: "Did you see? Certainly a spy!" she cried, waving her short arm toward some man.

"What?"

"He has pants and a jacket of a different color."

I began to laugh, despite myself.

"And a mustache, as if pasted on." She angrily drove her eyes into mine, sitting nearby.

"Excuse me . . ." I jerked away. Before slipping off, she trailed me along the pavement for a few steps. But even to me, many people seem suspicious, who should be under surveillance.

—June 1941. An order was issued calling all Leningraders from the ages of 16 to 50 (and women up to 45) to defend the city.

—June 1941. Today our whole laboratory dug anti-tank trenches around Leningrad. I dug with pleasure (it was something so practical) and straightened up only when I felt a sharp pain in the small of my back. Only women worked on the trenches. Their scarves blazed in the sun like so many little flames. It was as if a giant colorful flowerbed surrounded the city.

And suddenly the wings of a plane, gleaming, crossed the sky. A burst of machine-gun fire rattled past and the bullets, like small lizards, crackled and darted into the grass not far from me. Startled, I stood still, having forgotten all of the civil defense rules that I learned not so long ago.

"Run!" cried someone, grabbing me by the sleeve. I looked around. All of us diggers ran somewhere. I also ran, even though I didn't know where to run or what to do. No one else knew either. Unexpectedly, I saw a small bridge. I ran for it. There was a deep puddle of water under the bridge. For a whole hour, we squatted in it. That day we didn't work anymore.

29 June 1941. The evacuation of all institutions and of the population has begun.

30 June 1941. We continue to dig trenches. The airplanes no longer appear.

2 July 1941. They're evacuating the children now! Like frightened animals they filled all the streets, moving toward the train station. This was the demarcation line of their childhood: beyond it their life without parents began.

They took the small children in trucks. Their little heads stuck out of the trucks like the heads of small mushrooms layered in baskets. Panic-stricken parents ran behind the vehicles.

Having blended in with the crowd, I howled together with the rest of the passers-by, feeling how both fear and anxiety had crept so close to our hearts.

3 July 1941. With every minute of every hour the Germans get closer to Leningrad. After waking up, we rush to the radios. Washing down the bitter pills of war news with cold tea, we were slow to realize what was happening. Nevertheless, we continued to believe that sooner or later victory would appear before us with an apology.

Leningraders are hurriedly putting up barricades made of stone, metal, waste lumber, and of their fanatical love of the city. Camouflaging structures lean over architectural monuments with care.

5 July 1941. The institute where I work is being evacuated to Saratov. Dima was given a military deferment and told to stay in Leningrad. That's why he didn't want me to leave. We fought. Hurtful and unfair words flew between us. We were helpless before them. They took on a life of their own, independent from ours. This was our first fight. Dima came home on his break.

"I can't work, knowing that you are angry," he said. "Let's make peace."

We made up, but something remained standing between us. We already were not the same as before the fight, and not the way we were before the war. We had changed with catastrophic speed.

9 July 1941. Bitter battles over Kiev! The Germans have taken Pskov! Leningrad is threatened!

10 July 1941. The Finnish army has begun an offensive toward Lake Ladoga. Apparently, together with the Germans, they want to encircle Leningrad.

10 July 1941. Lena has diarrhea and a fever. We'll have to put off the evacuation for a few days. And in general, how is it possible to travel without sterile bottles? I just don't know.

11 July 1941. The Germans have seized almost all of the Baltics and almost all of Belorussia. They have reached the West Dvina and the Dnieper.

12 July 1941. Hitler is a non-entity which imagines itself a genius. He is trying to force his "blitzkrieg" on the USSR with all of its expansive forests and absence of roads. But the USSR isn't Poland. Sooner or later it will stick in his throat.

15 July 1941. My institute has left!

16 July 1941. Without warning, Lena's nanny left for her village, appropriating some of my things.

—July 1941. The stores have re-opened. In two days all of the food was snatched up. The only thing left was millet. I bought two kilograms. (I hate millet porridge.)

8 August 1941. The enemy rushes toward Leningrad!

10 August 1941. With fantastic speed, the Germans have launched an offensive on the line of Novgorod, Chudov, and Tosno. Bitter as it is, we need to recognize that we were not prepared for Hitler's aggression.

22 August 1941. Today, while walking with Lena to the children's clinic for milk, I saw an appeal on the wall of a building: "Comrade Leningraders, dear friends!" I couldn't read any further. I only pressed Lena closer to me.

God, how I fear for her!

23 August 1941. The Germans are between Bologoe and Tosno. The evacuation route runs through Ladoga. Lena is still sick, but we need to leave; waiting is not possible anymore.

25 August 1941. The road to Mga has been cut by the Germans. Convoys of Leningraders sat in a railroad yard for several days and then returned. Evacuation has ceased. I am to remain in Leningrad!

26 August 1941. People are fleeing from the suburbs into Leningrad, as into a mousetrap.

6 September 1941. I walked to the children's clinic for milk. From afar I saw a huge hole in the façade of a four-story building. Next to the building stood a large crowd, staring at the hole. A part of a room was visible through the hole. I wanted to ask if there were any victims, but reconsidered. What was the point? War was just beginning for us. The casualties would be many, for sure. Each one of us must be ready for anything.

7 September 1941. There is still a crowd by the building, damaged by the shell.

8 September 1941. Almost all of the large-scale enterprises have been moved out of Leningrad.

—September 1941. Today Dima came by a kilogram of cookies somewhere. He was feeding them to Lena, stirring sugar into tea with a spoon. The sound of silver bells poured into the cup.

Suddenly, the silence of the city was torn by the roar of planes. I looked out the window. Low, just above the roofs, German bombers flew.

"Get down, quick!" cried Dima, leaping up from the table and tipping over a cup of tea on himself.

We ran downstairs for the building manager's office; there was no bomb shelter in our building. A bomb explosion resounded. Then another, and another quite close. There was a jangling of broken glass.

The office was packed full of people. We had to stand in the stairwell, holding Lena in our arms. Only toward morning could we go back up to the fifth floor.

9 September 1941. The extensive Badaev food stores have been bombed: blackish-red rags of fire, blowing about in the wind, can be seen from all ends of the city, burning sugar, groats, and flour.

—September, 1941. All roads to Leningrad are cut off. What will happen to us now?

11 September 1941. The bread ration has been reduced again. We now receive 850 grams.

12 September 1941. Wreaths of black smoke still rise above the Badaev stores.

13 September 1941. The Germans bomb Leningrad every night.

10 October 1941. Our supply of rusks is rapidly diminishing. Dima is probably eating them, even though we had agreed not to touch them except for the portions allocated for dinner.

20 October 1941. The Germans continue to bomb Leningrad, but almost no one hides in the bomb shelters. I sit at home. When I hear the whine of the bombers I merely cover Lena with my body in order to die together, should death come. This makes Dima angry at me: "You have no right to risk the life of the child."

"But I haven't the strength, try to understand. And if we are killed together, that's not the worst thing that could happen."

"That's an idiotic philosophy," he screams, "we have to preserve her life no matter what. Even if we ourselves perish."

"Why? How will she live?"

We fight for a long time, each one of us holding to our own opinion.

15 November 1941. Starvation has set in. Our personal supplies have ended. An idiosyncratic Leningrad cuisine has been developed. We have learned to make buns out of mustard, soup out of yeast, meat patties out of horseradish, a sweet gruel out of carpenter's glue.

10 December 1941. Almost all Leningraders have become dystrophic. They have swelled up and gleam as if covered with lacquer—this is first stage dystrophy. Others have become desiccated—second stage. Women walk about in pants. Men in women's scarves. Everyone looks the same. Leningraders have lost all signs of gender and age.

12 December 1941. Today I felt that something strange is happening to my face. I brought a shard of a mirror from the kitchen and peered into it with curiosity. My face resembled that end of a pig where its tail grows.

"What a mug," I spat into the mirror. Dima's gaze slid down my face like a dead fish. He himself had bloated up long ago.

13 December 1941. Lena is ill. Dima's on sick call. He no longer helps me. He doesn't ever look after Lena. But he goes eagerly to the bakery and probably eats the small pieces added to make the weight. We cook "soup" from

the soft center of the bread. We eat it with tiny crusts. I pour Dima four serving spoons and two for myself. But for this I have the right to lick out the pot, though the soup is so thin, there is, in fact, nothing to lick.

Dima eats his "soup" with a teaspoon to prolong the eating. But today he ate his portion quicker than I. There was a hard crust in my soup which I chewed with pleasure. I sensed the hatred with which he watched my slowly moving jaws. "You're eating slowly on purpose," he suddenly exclaimed malevolently. "You want to torment me."

"Oh, no! Why would I do that?" I blurted, startled.

"Don't justify yourself. I see everything." He glared at me, his eyes glistening white with rage. I was terrified. Had he gone crazy? I quickly swallowed the crust and cleared the table. He kept grumbling, but I was silent. He wouldn't believe me anyway. Lately, he has become very suspicious and irritable.

15 December 1941. As I was returning from the bakery, I saw a worker running toward me, his small fox-like head pushed forward. I began to move aside as he ran by, but he snatched the loaf of bread from me. I screamed and looked around, but he was gone. I looked at my empty hands with horror, slowly comprehending what had occurred. There wasn't a crumb to eat at home. That meant that today and tomorrow, until we get our next ration of bread, we'd go hungry, and worst of all, there was no food for Lena.

My legs suddenly become heavy as irons, and I barely made it home. In the hallway I bumped into Dima and immediately told him everything. He gave me a wild look from underneath his sooty eyelashes, but said nothing.

17 December 1941. Our sense of smell has become very sharp: we now know the smell of sugar, of pearl-barley, of dried peas, and other "non-odorous" groceries. Dima hardly gets out of bed. He doesn't even go for bread. This disturbs me—those who lie about die sooner.

"Don't lie in bed all the time." I sat down next to him and cautiously touched his sleeve. He threw me a cross glance.

"What would you have me do?"

"Go up into the attic. Maybe you'll catch a cat up there?"

"So that's it," he said sarcastically.

The stupidity of what I had said suddenly struck me. All the cats had been eaten long ago. I furrowed my brow trying to think of something else.

"Maybe we ought to buy a mousetrap," I said indecisively.

"What would that do?"

"We'd eat mice."

"That's an idea," he exclaimed, sitting up.

"I think the mice would taste no worse than the cats," said I, encouraged.

"Not a bit."

"Everyday we would have meat."

"That would be terrific," he murmured indistinctly.

His animation was gone. He lay down again, his back to me, and pulled his hat over his ears. I understood that he had no faith in my plan.

19 December 1941. Having gotten up before me, Dima circled the room repeatedly, bumping into furniture and cursing. Finally he left, slamming the door. He was gone the whole day.

"Where have you been?" I asked when he returned.

"Walking around," he said vaguely. Suddenly, he winked and said, rapid-fire: "Looking for a little loaf of bread."

"What are you saying?" I was frightened. He looked at me with curiosity.

"You seem to think that I've lost my mind."

"No, no. But, after all . . ."

"Cut it out. I know that bread doesn't lie in the streets. That's not the point."

"What is the point, then?"

He didn't respond. I stood staring at him. Then he began to talk. At first slowly, then faster and faster. Suddenly he was seized by an incomprehensible agitation. He had encountered a child's sled loaded with bread. A convoy of five men was escorting the sled. A crowd followed, fixedly staring at the bread. Dima fell in with the rest. The sled was unloaded at a bakery. The crowd attacked the empty cases, fighting for crumbs. He found a large crust trampled into the snow. But some urchin grabbed the crust from Dima's hands. This vile snot-nose began to chew it, drooling and chomping. An insane rage seized Dima. Grabbing the kid by the scruff of the neck, he began to shake him convulsively. The kid's head on its thin neck began to flail back and forth like that of a Petrushka doll. But he continued chewing hastily, his eyes closed.

"It's all gone, all gone, uncle! Look!" he shouted suddenly, opening his mouth wide. Dima threw the kid on the ground. He was ready to kill him. But fortunately, a clerk rolled out of the store like a breakfast bun.

"Kish! Kish!" he shouted, waving his arms.

"As if humans were sparrows," noted Dima with offense, "and the most amazing thing is that no one pasted that scoundrel in the face." He became painfully pensive and stared at one spot.

Sensing that he was holding something back, I looked at him quizzically. But Dima sat disconnected from everything, seeing nothing and hearing nothing. This would happen to him more and more.

20 December 1941. Dima was gone again, having sharpened the stick which served him as a walking cane. He was back in about an hour. His appearance was strange. "What's wrong with you?" I asked inadvertently.

"Nothing . . . I'm just very hungry," he said, his face in a weepy grimace.

I shrugged my shoulders. We simply did not talk about hunger anymore: it was our normal condition. Suddenly he broke into a convulsive laughter, pulled a loaf of bread from under his clothes, and threw it in my lap. "Here, you silly thing, eat," he said tenderly.

I stared at the bread, dumbstruck. When my stupor passed and we ate our fill, he said: "I found a bakery where the bread is easy to steal. It's very dark there."

"Steal?"

"Yes, steal, of course. You don't think that they gave me this loaf of bread as a gift."

I was silent. Little flames of anxiety began to dance in the depth of his pupils. And suddenly a malevolent vexation scorched his face. Rubbing his face with the palms of his hands, he continued. It turned out that it wasn't all that difficult. You had to get unobtrusively to the counter, wait for the right moment, and quickly spear a loaf with the stick. That was it.

When the bread was under his coat filling his senses with its hot exhalation, Dima wanted to laugh, shout, and dance with joy. But he forced himself to leisurely leave the bakery, maintaining external calm.

Now, telling me this, he laughed like a madman. I looked at him with horror. What could I say? That stealing was wrong? That would have been idiotic. So, I only said: "Be more careful."

28 December 1941. The trams are not running. Children's sleds are the only means of transport. They move along the streets in endless convoys. They carry planks, men, corpses.

There are corpses everywhere. In these times death is not just an occasional guest. People have become accustomed to death. It constantly bumps up against the living. People die easily, simply, without tears. The dead are wrapped in bed sheets, tied with rope and pulled to the cemetery where they are laid in rows. There they are buried in common pits.

6 January 1942. Dima doesn't steal bread anymore. For days on end he lies in bed, his face to the wall, saying nothing. His face is covered with a thick layer of soot; even his fine, fair eyelashes have become thick and black [from the makeshift, un-vented wood stove]. I cannot imagine that he was once clean, well-groomed, and proper. And I, of course, am not much cleaner than he is. We are both tormented by lice. We sleep together—there's only one bed in the room—but even through the cotton wadded overcoats we shun each other's touch.

9 January 1942. We live in our room as in an ark, seeing nothing, encountering no one. We don't even know the news from the front. We only get incidental bits of news while standing in the queues. Dima and I have become a

single organism. Illness, antipathy, the foul mood of one is immediately reflected in the other. At the same time we have never been as far apart as we are now. Each one silently struggles with his own suffering. In this we cannot help each other. After all, I only sense my own heart (only I hear its beating), . . . my own stomach (only I feel its gnawing emptiness), . . . am aware of my brain (only I bear all the weight of unexpressed thoughts). Only I can coerce them to endure. We have come to understand that a human being must know how to struggle with life and death alone.

10 January 1942. Lena has unlearned how to speak. She can no longer stand or even sit. Her skin hangs in folds as if she had been stuffed into a cloak much too big for her. She quietly sings to herself all the time; evidently, asking for food.

Today I bought her some toys: a *matreshka* nesting doll, a clown and a stuffed bear. They were seated on her bed waiting for her to awaken. Upon seeing them, Lena sobbed loudly and scattered them over the floor. Of course, it was a stupid idea.

I kissed her hungry wolf-cub eyes. Looking at her soot-covered face, I myself wanted to howl like a dying she-wolf. I could not lighten her suffering with anything but kisses.

24 January 1942. It is 40 degrees below zero.

The camouflage curtain is frozen to the window. The room is in semi-darkness. The walls, smeared with oil-base paint, are clammy. Slim streams of water run down to the floor.

Setting off for bread, I wrapped myself in Lena's flanelette blanket, leaving only a slit for my eyes.

Outside, I winced, so bright was the sky. Next to the entryway a tree covered with snow and frost glistened unbearably.

Under the tree lay two bodies, haphazardly wrapped in bed sheets. The bare feet of one of them protruded from under the sheet, the big toes at an odd angle.

25 January 1942. The plumbing no longer works. We have to go to the Neva River for water. Due to the lack of water, the central baking plant has stopped working. Thousands of Leningraders who could still get about crawled out of their burrows and, having formed a human chain from river to bakery, passed buckets of water to each other with their frozen hands.

The bread was baked.

26 January 1942. The sewer system is not working. Everybody gets by as they can. Excrement is thrown from windows.

27 January 1942. Some days no bread is delivered. People stand in long lines. Some lose consciousness. Some die.

28 January 1942. There is, apparently, a limit to physical suffering beyond which a person becomes insensitive to everything except one's own self. Heroism, self-sacrifice, a great feat can be accomplished only by someone who is well-fed or has suffered hunger briefly. But we know starvation which has debased, crushed, and turned us into animals. Those who will come after us and perchance read these lines: don't judge us too harshly.

4 February 1942. We haven't washed in three months. They say that there's a working public bath somewhere. Men and women wash together there. But such a journey is beyond our strength.

5 February 1942. Excrement, like ossified geologic shapes, covers every courtyard.

10 February 1942. There are rumors that a road across Lake Ladoga has been cleared and that evacuation has begun anew. It would be so good to get out of Leningrad. Now, when the most difficult time seems behind us, it would be stupid to die.

12 February 1942. Some items are being distributed per ration cards. I got 250 grams of meat. We ate it raw.

14 February 1942. Today, per ration card, I got 75 grams of sunflower-seed oil. For a long time we sniffed it, as if perfume, and relished its golden-yellow color. Finally, after lengthy vacillation, we decided to fry up some bread. Having gotten a frying pan and some kindling, we joyfully fussed about the jerry-rigged stove, anticipating a sumptuous dinner.

Suddenly, with a careless gesture, I knocked the bottle over. The oil gushed out. I screamed in horror and froze. It seemed that it wasn't oil but my blood pouring to the floor. Dima rushed to scoop up the oil from the floor. He managed to save some twenty to twenty-five grams. I stood all red, fearing even to glance at him.

"It's OK. Don't get upset," he said abruptly. It was a chivalrous and noble thing to do. I shall never forget it.

24 February 1942. Only now have I understood the deep wounds inflicted on my city by the Germans.

In many places, instead of buildings remembered in flashes from my childhood, there now towered ruins. A huge granite building on the corner of Krasnoarmeiskaia Street and Moscow Concourse was ripped apart down to its very foundation. There used to be a boutique here. I would often pop into it in the winter to warm up and buy some trifle.

25 February 1942. Today I wandered into one of the streets next to the Moscow Railway Terminal [i.e., from which trains departed for Moscow].

The destruction which I saw there shook me deeply. All the buildings had been bombed out. An occasional wall would rise here and there. A [tile] stove was suspended from one of them like a pale blue absurdity. It gently reminded me of recently known warmth and coziness. A pure, dreamy, iridescent, blue snow covered everything. It was unmarked by tracks: neither human, nor beast, nor bird.

A tomb-like silence, like the smell of strong wine, permeated the ruins. Iron beds, twisted into spirals, were strewn about, resembling strange skeletons of ancient unearthed animals. I stood there awhile, lost in thought, then crossed the Terminal Square. It lay before me—an icy, snowbound desert. Only the wind whirled about and, like a homeless dog, licked at my legs.

26 February 1942. I left the apartment and stopped on the street, not having a sense of where to go. . . . After a while I found myself before the Technological Institute. It stood alone, huge amidst the deserted streets. I was a student here once. Its enormous doors once swallowed young people like a hungry mouth. They scattered throughout its numerous corridors, filling the building with full-blooded, boiling life. Now the doors were sternly locked.

Suddenly someone's halting call reached me. "Elena, is that you?" A middle-aged woman stood before me. Her puffy face seemed familiar.

"You don't recognize me?" she asked, her unfamiliar expression vanishing with a blink of her long lashes.

"Irina, you?"

"Me, of course. Have I changed a lot?"

"You? Well . . . no. But yes, of course. Like the rest of us," I mumbled.

Before the war she and I worked together. She was a charming young woman; now you could have given her fifty.

"Ira [diminutive of Irina], are you thinking about evacuation," I asked, changing the subject.

"Yes."

"But how?"

"With the Meteorological Institute. I work there now."

"Could I possibly go with you?"

"Can't say." She pensively rubbed the whitish tip of her nose. "I'm on my way to the institute. Come with me, if you like. It's very near."

Of course, "I liked." On the way Irina told me about herself. In January she had given birth to a premature seven-month infant. The baby died after five days. The only food in the hospital was water and vitamins. She spent twenty days there tossing in bed, tormented by hunger and fever. They brought her home nearly dead. And then salvation came: her grandmother died leaving two kilograms of fish-base glue and ration cards as inheritance.

"And where's your husband?"

Irina gave a long whistle. "He fled on a plane to Moscow."

"And what about you?"

"As you see, I'm here. When he took off, I was in the maternity ward."

"He left you all alone?"

"Yes. And to hell with him. If he were here, I would have dropped dead long ago. He ate everything I had. You know what I mean by 'everything.'"

Yes, I knew very well. In the entryway I pushed my passport through the small window [to get a building pass], but a dirty hand threw it back at me.

"What about the pass?"

"There'll be no pass," came the brief answer.

"Why?"

"Give me a piece of bread, I'll give you a pass."

"You're crazy! Where would I get bread," I exploded.

"A tiny, little piece, at least," wailed the doorkeeper with the voice of a beggar.

"Give her a pass immediately, or I'll complain to the director," shouted Irina.

A shaggy head protruded from the window and peered sideways at Irina. A pass was flung out shortly after that.

Irina wasn't very long at the director's. Coming out she said, "Everything is in order. The director does not object."

I looked at her like an idiot.

"What's wrong with you?"

"Nothing... you said, the director does not object?"

"Yes."

Tears welled up in my eyes.

"Forget it," said Irina, grasping me by the arm. "Let's go." We went out into the street. "All the evacuation trains are headed south now," she said. "Most likely we'll go to the Caucuses; we'll warm ourselves in the sun and eat all kinds of fruit."

"Eat fruit?" I was amazed. It wouldn't enter my head that somewhere there's fruit which can be held in one's hands, smelled, and even eaten.

28 February 1942. Irina lived in a large, handsome apartment house on Mayakovsky Street. The courtyard was flooded with excrement. A narrow path lead to the entrance. The door to the apartment was wide open. It was quiet in the hall. The sound of my steps rolled ahead of me, like a bowling ball. Irina sat, squatting before her makeshift stove, cooking something. A large black sheep's skin was tied to her back and chest.

"I never take it off. It sort of became part of me," she said, noticing my stare.

"You need a cat to match your colorful outfit."

"I had a cat, but I ate it."

"What are you cooking?"

"Carpenter's glue broth."

When the broth was ready, she began to eat. Of course, she did not offer me any. The tradition of offering food to your guests had long since vanished in Leningrad. In order to get food off my mind I asked a question. "Why is it so quiet here?"

"Some people have left, others have died. They're lying about in every room."

"Who?" I was confused.

"The corpses."

"Why don't they remove them?"

"Who? I told the concierge, but he said that they can lie there a long time without smelling, since it's cold now."

"Are you alone in this apartment?"

"There's some guy living at the end of the hallway. Every night he tries to force my door. Probably wants to eat me . . . I sleep with a knife."

She showed me a large chef's knife which she pulled from beneath her pillow. We went to the institute, but there was almost nobody there, and nobody knew anything.

2 March 1942. Every day Irina and I go to the institute, so as not to miss the evacuation day. But so far, nothing is known.

9 March 1942. I dropped by [the old apartment on] Moscow Street to grab a few things for the trip. Wistfully, I walked through the rooms. Almost my whole life was spent here, but I'll never live here again.

My gaze slipped along the bookcase: Bagritskii, Mandelshtam, Pasternak . . .

I chose one of the small volumes and leafed through the pages. Familiar lines came to life beneath my fingers. But they aroused nothing in me now except irritation. I snuffed the lines, slamming the book shut. Photographs tumbled out from somewhere. They fell in a fan-shape on the floor before me. The faces looking up from them seemed alien to me. Was that really me? Dima? Did we really have such fat mugs and smug, feckless eyes? A shiver ran up my spine. No, we would not have understood each other now.

I left the photographs lying on the floor.

29 March 1942. Upon arriving at the institute, we discovered that the convoy was to leave at six that evening. We had four hours to ourselves.

"Let's run to a bakery and eat our rations to the end of the month," Irina shouted.

After eating my portion right there at the counter, I ran home.

We went into a frenzy, feverishly stuffing things into sacks, afraid of being late. We had to get to the Finland [railway] Station on foot.

For the trip I put on Galia's [a neighbor] knickers from a wardrobe which stood in our room. After all, I couldn't go with my knees showing. Having put them on, I recalled how indignant I had been quite recently when Dima took a pair of pants that weren't his. And now I was doing exactly the same thing. The concept of honor had become an empty sound for us.

Finally we left. Left like swine, not saying farewell to our hosts and leaving our room in chaos and filth.

The sky was covered with clouds. One could see the outline of the sun wandering behind them, searching for an opening. Having found one, it would pour onto the street in streams of bright light. The snow would turn to slush; the sled would get stuck. Sometimes it would turn over, spilling all our "junk" along the road.

We'd fuss over it, angry, accusing each other. Finally, all in a lather, we arrived at the station. Irina was already there.

"Come quick. They're going to feed us," she said in agitation.

We were given two serving spoons of millet porridge with butter and a hunk of bread. With his plate in his hands, Dima ran around the tables looking for a seat. His frighteningly agitated face was covered with blue streaks. I gave him my chair and ate standing. Having finished the porridge, we scrupulously licked the plates clean. The next feeding was to take place only on the other side of Lake Ladoga.

Chapter Twenty-Five

N. Ianevich, Literary Politics

The chapter of Ianevich's memoirs from which this selection is taken deals with the Institute of World Literature from the 1930's through the 1970's. The selection discloses the intense politicization within the institute during World War II and after as well as the many internal vagaries aggravated by the war. The author's introspection reveals her intimate knowledge of the workings of this prestigious institute. She notes that she had been employed there practically from its very founding. Originally published as "Institut Mirovoi Literatury v 1930-e–1970-e gody" [The Institute of World Literature from the 1930's to the 1970's] in *Pamiat'*. Paris: YMCA Press, 1982.

The first months of the war were horrific. The Germans were rushing toward Moscow. Every night our colleagues stood watch on the roof of our Gorky Museum tossing off incendiary flares. The capital was being evacuated. Children, old people, priceless museum items, paintings and finally whole offices and institutions were moved out. Leonid Ippolitovich Ponomarev, our director, waited in vain for specific directives from his superiors at the Academy and complained that they were more likely concerned with their own safety than with the safety of the institutes. He was confused and overwhelmed by the sudden responsibility for the destiny of the staff and the institute itself. He clearly needed the help of youthful and energetic people. Acting on our own initiative we decided to help him.

In the course of two or three weeks several of our active women organized the evacuation of women with small children as well as of the ill and aged family members of our co-workers. They launched a furious attack on the Presidium of the Academy of Sciences until they received the necessary evacuation authorizations and destination. Then the institute received a directive mobilizing everyone, as many as possible, into work brigades for the building of fortifications outside of Moscow. I readily joined this brigade along with Liza Glatman, Olga Kuznetsova, Vera Bezuglova and other co-workers who were capable of handling a shovel. We were sent off with great pomp and speechifying, but no sooner did we get to the outskirts of the city than we were sent back. It was too late, all the approaches had been seized by the Germans. There was no place nor purpose for digging or erecting fortifications.

And on the next day—this was 16 October 1941, the notorious day of wholesale Moscow panic—our institute among many others was ordered to leave the city on foot, since there was no transportation and no point in waiting for any. Thousands of people in silent concentration, having taken with them whatever they could, marched along roads away from what seemed to be a doomed Moscow.

That was a cold autumnal day. The wind whipped pieces of burnt personal and official documents along the streets. The Institute of World Literature column, or what was left of the IWL, presented a sorry sight. Most of the men had been called into the army or had gone into the people's volunteer corps. Several of them, specifically Mark Serebrianskii, head of the Soviet Literature sector, and Misha Zabludovskii, a specialist in Western Literature, had already been killed. Some of the older scholars declined to leave Moscow (A.K. Dzhivelegov among them). Others, members of the Writer's Union, managed to leave on the 14th or 15th of October with the Writer's Union convoy. There were others who could not walk at all due to poor health. Our column, therefore, was made up primarily of women with children or aged parents who had not been evacuated earlier. Anna Arkad'evna Elistratova, even then a renowned specialist on Anglo-American literature, trudged along, short of breath, painfully moving her edematous legs. Her mother and totally decrepit father trudged along with her. Old Leonid Ippolitovich walked with difficulty in the column of the institute which had been entrusted to him. Evgenii Emil'evich Leitneker, the middle-aged and ill co-worker of the Gorky sector also marched with difficulty, carrying a heavy rucksack totally filled with his unfinished manuscript: *The Chronicle of Gorky's Life and Art*. Varvara Nikolaevna Lanina, from the same sector, walked along with her thirteen-year-old daughter, Tania. Among the hastily snatched items from their home they were carrying a new, glistening electric iron. Soon it tired their arms so much that they began dragging it by the cord. Later, of course, they had to part with it entirely.

People quickly began to tire and our younger members began putting the old and infirm on military vehicles which kept passing us. Then they found places for everybody else and by the end of the day all of us were taken care of, including the director who had refused to get on a vehicle until everybody else had been provided a place. In this manner we arrived in the city of Gorky [Nizhnii Novgorod] and then by water reached Kazan where we were housed in the university. Finally, in a convoy composed of many academic institutions, we set off for Alma-Ata in Central Asia where the Academy Presidium had assigned us. When it turned out that Alma-Ata was filled beyond capacity, we found refuge in Tashkent.

We were quartered in the building of the Tamara Khanum school of ballet on one of the central streets of the city. In an enormous mirrored hall we spread out crates of manuscripts and articles from our Tolstoy and Pushkin museums which had been sent to Tashkent in our footsteps. We arranged the crates to form small, cell-like rooms which were quickly dubbed "caves;" used anything at hand for curtains, and began to live in them as families or in groups of two or three friends.

From time to time those of us who were stronger were sent by the city council to pick cotton; a group took part in the construction of the North-Tashkent canal, but most of us academic types were utilized as lecturers in hospitals and at the various enterprises and construction sites of the region. For this work Tashkent provided us with minimal room and board.

Most of all, I recall, we suffered from the absence of potatoes—the customary Russian potatoes without which a meal is not a meal with us. But at the Alai farmer's market, the "belly of Tashkent," potatoes cost eight rubles a kilo and only those who had money or had managed to bring items for barter could buy them. There were few people like that among us. Once while strolling in the market with Olga Kuznetsova and platonically admiring the colorful rows of fruits and vegetables we spotted our director, Leonid Ippolitovich, standing off in a corner holding his hat out with embarrassment. The poor man, he intended to sell or trade it for potatoes, but did it so ineptly that no one understood him. One could think that he was holding it out for alms. We slipped away quietly.

We all loved and sympathized with "Ippolitych," despite the fact that in contrast to Luppol [the previous director] he was slow in his thinking, had poor relations with his subordinates, had a quick temper, and was unjust in his arbitrary likes and dislikes. But we knew that he was scrupulously honest, unselfish and totally helpless before his bosses, especially when he encountered liars, bribe takers, careerists and other slime of which we had more than enough. We considered it our duty to aid him in all the institute matters, especially in providing for those people whom we had led out of Moscow.

"We," the morally conscious, active group of "Tamara Khanum" who had become closely knit during the wartime disasters were: Liza Glatman, assistant director in organizational matters; Lidochka Kriuchkova, executive secretary, a warm and sweet person who completed medical school while in

Tashkent and later became an outstanding doctor at Moscow's Botkin Hospital; Varvara Nikolaevna Lanina, the irreplaceable chairman of the [city] district committee who was in charge of distributing wearing apparel—footwear, shirts, pants, etc.—and who did so with unfailing fairness and attentiveness though the goods were few and the demand high. Emmochka Evin, from the Pushkin Museum, was also part of the activist group. She was a wonderful comrade who maintained unbroken contact with all our colleagues who were at the front. There was also Tamara Motyleva, who in her business-like manner with high expectations toward herself and others, was a successful administrator throughout the evacuation. But the soul of the group was Olga Kuznetsova, who occupied no titled position, but had a fervid, generous and selfless spirit which drew everyone to her. Soon other co-workers who had fled Moscow independently of the institute began arriving at the "Tamara Khanum."

The institute gradually recovered and renewed its labors. The work on the history of Soviet literature continued. One of the "English" volumes was nearing completion under the leadership of A.A. Elistratova. In evacuation we began work on the first volume of *The History of American Literature* which was to have such a controversial, even notorious destiny. And V.M. Zhirmunskii [a noted literary critic] began a definitive study of Uzbek folklore for which he, at the age of fifty plus, had to learn the far from easy Uzbek language.

Significant shifts in attitude were occurring among the inhabitants of "Tamara Khanum" as they were occurring among most Soviet people of that time. The confusion at of the beginning of the war was replaced by a wave of patriotism. We all lived with one goal and one emotion: only to win the war. At that moment our Olga announced that, since her daughters were being taken care of by the state in a children's refuge of the Academy of Science, it was her duty to volunteer for the front where she would bring more benefit to people. And even though she was almost forty, she was sent to a military cook's school, finished it with the rank of sergeant, and was sent to the front where she spent almost the duration of the war. And, along with many others, at the front she became a member of the [Communist] Party.

THE POST-WAR PERIOD: THE "COSMOPOLITE" CAMPAIGN

The second half of the 1940's was marked by ruthless ideological pogroms accompanied by robust praise-mongering about the "most wise," the "genius," and the "beloved" great leader.

The first attack was the pronouncement of the Central Committee of the Communist Party of the Soviet Union concerning the literary journals *Zvezda* [The Star] and *Leningrad*. Just a month-and-a-half earlier the newspaper *Kul'tura i zhizn'* [Culture and Life] was founded. It was the organ of the propaganda section of the Central Committee in which loud praise for the achievements of Soviet culture alternated with ruthless vilification of its particular representatives. Each time, we opened the newspaper with horror.

Any judgement, proclaimed on its pages, was beyond appeal. Even if courageous people could be found to speak against it, their writings would not have been published anywhere. Books denounced in this manner were immediately removed from sale and from all the libraries of the nation. And their authors were subjected to lengthy and humiliating "workings over" at meetings of their institutions where they had to repent and admit their errors. Otherwise they were expelled from their positions and never hired anywhere again. In provincial cities this took on a more severe and ruthless nature. I had heard that at one such bloodletting in the city of Khar'kov the victim, who had been ultimately "worked over," stood up on a dais and said, "You have convinced me, comrades. I have finally understood, that I am not one of us!" This phrase, "I am not one of us," became a sardonic aphorism. The academic and social life at the IWL went on in an atmosphere of similar pogroms.

A [malevolent] article in *Kul'tura i zhizn'* by Viktor Nikolaev accused Leonid Grossman [a noted scholar] of placing the great Russian writer Leo Tolstoy in "the same rank with the decadent French writer Marcel Proust." This was characterized as "slavish adoration of bourgeois culture." The list of the other "accursed" persons was chosen in a very deliberate manner. Thus began within the walls of the institute the pernicious "anti-cosmopolite" campaign which was already raging in the Writer's Union and other ideological institutions and in which we did not immediately comprehend an elemental anti-Semitic pogrom that had been let loose by the highest directives of the Central Committee and "comrade Stalin personally."

A complete replacement of the leadership of the institute took place as a result of Nikolaev's article. This was followed by a series of notorious cases. The first target of the pogrom turned out to be *The History of American Literature*. The trouble with this work was that it was begun back during the war when we and the USA were in a united front against Hitler. But due to the tortoise pace of publishing, the book appeared only in 1947, at a tense time in Soviet-American relations. And then the calm, well-intentioned tone of the volume's authors toward American literature seemed unacceptable to the "ruling comrades."

An unbelievable scandal began. The book was accused of containing distortions and political errors, that the "ringing of dollars" was heard in it, and so on. The workers in the foreign sector who had even a tangential association with the creation of the book were most severely castigated and, either immediately or some time later, dismissed from the institute. Abel Isaakovich Startsev was expelled as one of the senior editors, Tamara Motyleva—as the reviewer, Anikst—as a member of the editorial board, Tamara Sil'man—as the author of the article on Edgar Allen Poe, which was deemed to be "depraved."

The repressed edition—a first effort on the history of American literature in the Russian language—was conceived by the authors in two volumes and written with great love and profound knowledge. The second volume was near completion at the time of the crushing of the first volume. But after the scandal, the materials for the second volume were rejected and destroyed without any discussion. ("I lament the fact, that we were not permitted to complete the second volume," said Startsev many years later. "They could have castigated and abused us later, but the book would have remained!")

After the reprisals against the Americanists, there came charges of "cosmopolitism" and the exclusion of a number of Jews who were Communists from the party. The "working-over" proceeded as follows. A commission would be formed within the Communist Party of the institute which would divide amongst itself the principal works of the accused, read them and elicit "ideological errors" which were evidence of the author's obeisance to the West. All of this would be consolidated and presented at a Party meeting. The overall picture would be solid and convincing, and everyone would be amazed how it was that such a cosmopolite malefactor could do his foul deeds within the walls of the institute without punishment. The "malefactor" of course would try to defend himself. But this was quite difficult to accomplish. His students and admirers suddenly "having seen the light" in the best case would blink their eyes in confusion or, in the worst case, join the pack of enraged dogs in the frenzy of pursuing their game. Then everything would be presented at a general Party meeting where, as a rule, the unanimous decision would be: "Expel from the Party and remove from work."

Today, after the passing of so many years, it is worth contemplating by what means such unanimity was achieved. It cannot be denied that elements of fear and faint-heartedness played a role in this. After all, we lived in an atmosphere of all-penetrating government terror against which struggle was impossible. However, it was more complex than that. We had all been raised to respect the collective, the mass, the opinion of the majority, to reject individualism which had become a word of censure, so that in the end we had totally lost our individual face. It would never even enter our heads to defend an opinion against the opinion of the majority, the embodiment of which we believed was the Party, or more precisely, the Party leadership. Therefore, mass psychosis, even though organized and "pushed down" from the top, gripped and convinced substantial numbers of people.

I will refer to the story of one of the contemporary members of the Party executive committee, E.M. Evnina, a member of the foreign literature division. In her words one of the most shameful acts of her life for which she is ashamed even now was connected to the "case" of Tamara Motyleva. When the first "cosmopolites," Iakovlev and Kirpotin, were expelled, E.M. reacted rather indifferently because she was not especially familiar with their work, simply believing the report of the investigative commission and what was said in the executive council. Having mindlessly voted, E.M. went on vacation, but having returned to Moscow in a month learned that the case of Motyleva had come up at the last executive meeting.

Though many considered Tamara to be an unprincipled chameleon and called her a "dry old stick" and a pedant, E.M. knew that she had a great capacity for work, clarity of purpose, was very erudite and had a command of several foreign languages. She had been an exemplary university student, always on the honor roll and maintained these qualities in her scholarly work. Upon hearing that Motyleva was being expelled from the party for having made mistakes in her doctoral dissertation, E.M. was extremely surprised since she always considered her a strong scholar and a "correct" communist.

Evnina and Motyleva worked in the same department and, while never having been close friends, knew each other quite well. Naturally, Motyleva turned to Evnina for aid and advice. Their conversation took place in the home of Motyleva in the presence of her mother, an old woman, doctor by profession, who fiercely insisted that it were not Tamara's mistakes that were the cause, but her nationality. After all, Ania Elistratova, a fellow student of Tamara's, was not being "worked over" by anyone. Tamara cut her mother short several times, returning to the main theme of the conversation. "I would like to limit it to a public censure rather than expulsion," she would repeat. E.M. thought that there were no grounds even for public censure. They parted with the understanding that E.M. would defend this position.

However, the next day the party secretary of the IWL, Ivan Andreevich Martynov, called her to his office. At length and with great conviction he explained to her what great damage the scholar-cosmopolites were dealing the party by either intentionally or unintentionally praising bourgeois literature and art at the expense of our young Soviet culture. He cited examples garnered from instructional sessions at the Central Committee, shocked her with several criminal (from his point of view) positions and citations from Motyleva's work. The point was that she was "debasing" our most great Russian writer, Leo Tolstoy, turning him over to the judgement of Western "pygmies." And as Martynov spoke, E.M. sensed that her consciousness was being smothered by something alien, penetrating and mucilaginous, and that she no longer was capable or skillful enough to object. She could not recall his reasoning but remembered that he had convinced her. She came home totally demoralized and called Motyleva to say that the matter was much more complicated than she had thought, and that she could not do anything for her.

And several days later at a party meeting of the IWL an impressive performance was played out before us. The protagonist in the Motyleva case was A.F. Ivashchenko. With a theatrical gesture he would throw back a lock of hair from his, admittedly, high and handsome forehead and loudly read some "unacceptable" phrase from Motyleva's dissertation, each time with the same refrain: "And this is being said by a Soviet scholar, a communist?!" "Shame!" Martynov would respond from the other end of the table. Then another phrase of Motyleva's would be read followed by the same refrain: "And this is being said by a Communist?!" And again Martynov's bass: "Unbelievable!!" "Shame!"

The whole assembly was shaken and struck dumb. No one objected and no one asked any questions. Those who performed mumbled something supporting the points presented by the protagonist. And our friend E.M. at Martynov's invitation stood up and like a parrot mouthed some stupid and empty words about "unacceptable" mistakes. Then we all voted to expel Motyleva from the party. We did it as if bewildered, even the most upright of us, even my Olga Kuznetsova, who now mercilessly excoriates herself for that unworthy act.

Many months later, after Motyleva had been reinstated in the party thanks to the intercession of Fadeev [a well-known writer] but not re-employed at the Institute, E.M. and I were at the first-run of some play. During the intermission we bumped into Motyleva and her mother. Tamara calmly greeted both of us without a shade of resentment. After all, she was a communist just as we were and had also voted for the expulsion of those "cosmopolites" whose cases preceded hers: Iakovlev, Kirpotin, Novich and others. But when Evnina proffered her hand to Motyleva's mother, she demonstratively turned away, and I saw how the extended hand hung in the air. The old woman, not constrained by any party "norms," would not forgive betrayal. E.M. moved away, shamed and abashed, having whispered to me, "Tamara's mother is right."

Chapter Twenty-Six

K. Vadot, The Terrorist

The act of denunciation was one of striking arbitrariness. Its encouragement and utilization, which saw a vast increase in the 1930's, transcended all social and class categories. Families were destroyed by the denunciations of children who were then exalted by the state. Since the denunciations could be anonymous and vindictive (with only a hint of "crimes against the state" to trigger action by the authorities), they were yet another aspect of life in a totalitarian system over which the individual had no control. Vadot's story deals with such a denunciation. Excerpted from K. Vadot, "V zhenskom rabochem lagere" [In a Women's Labor Camp]. New York: *The New Review*, No. 116, September, 1974.

"Anna Timofeevna, now, Anna Timofeevna, please do stop crying. Now what's really the matter? Don't go killing yourself so. Calm down."

"And how am I supposed to calm down when I find myself living in hell?"

"Straight to hell, just like that. Does that make us devils then?"

"No, you're also unfortunate wretches. So then hell itself might actually be worse than this."

"Well, don't cry; better you should drink some tea. Look, the kettle's already on the boil."

"Thank you, girls, but I don't want any tea. I'm going to die soon, anyway, so what's the point of drinking tea?"

"You'll get used to it. You won't die. People aren't cattle: we can get used to anything."

"So, have you been here long?"

"It varies. I'm here eight years. That one over there, the young one, seven years; as for the others—no one has been here less than five years."

"But Aleksandra Ivanovna, sweetie, they gave me a whole twenty-five years, it scares me to even say it."

"Yes, but that twenty-five years is your whole term. And we've all got the full bobbin: twenty-five years. I'm just talking about how much time we've already done."

"Holy Jesus . . . It's terrible to think about it."

"It's nothing; we can bear it. Better you should drink tea. It's sweet."

This conversation took place in one of the barracks of the women's camp at Vorkuta. Aleksandra Ivanovna was pouring tea into half-liter jars, and Anna Timofeevna, on whom the brand-new camp uniform still fit awkwardly, sat at a table in the middle of the barracks, along with Masha—a girl with long braids wrapped around her head, Ania—a woman of about thirty with cold eyes, and Aleksandra Ivanovna.

"Go ahead, Anna Timofeevna, I'll just splash some in a little jar for you," Masha says tenderly.

Anna Timofeevna is a small, plump woman of about fifty years. Her eyes are frightened, wary.

"Thank you kindly, little daughter. You were right. Tea is good for the nerves. And it warms you up well. While they were bringing me here, I froze like a dog."

"Now, if you want to freeze, you just wait a little. The month of March—we consider that warm. We call it spring. You wait and see—you'll change your tune come December."

"What kind of spring is this, Anechka, thirty degrees below. I'm used to Rostov."

"We were all used to it. It doesn't matter—with the years and the intense cold you'll get used to anything."

"Stop it, Ania," Masha said reproachfully, "This person is broken as it is, and you're dealing the final blow."

Anna Timofeevna looked at Masha with her eyes full of tears and in an unexpectedly low voice, so as not to let her weeping be heard, said, "You know, the main thing, girls, is that I am not guilty of anything. They sentenced me for no reason."

"Here in this barrack alone there are a hundred and twenty of us, and every one, Anna Timofeevna, sits here for no reason; every one is innocent."

"Listen, Ania, I beg you to stop, but if you can't, then no one is keeping you here by force. You've finished your tea . . ." Aleksandra Ivanovna's voice did not portend anything pleasant.

"All right, there's other stuff to talk about. I'm going to the drying shed; there at least I'll find people, not just sheared little sheep."

Ania left. Anna Timofeevna sighed.

"People like that are so rude and so difficult. It's enough to make you cry."

"Don't worry about it, Anna Timofeevna, everything will pass, like the white petals off the apple trees. So, which article did you get?"

"Fifty-eight, point eight."

"Eighth point?" Masha looked through the steam from the tea at Anna Timofeevna, whose legs didn't reach the floor and who sat entirely childlike on her stool, and smiled involuntarily.

"Well, now, the eighth point, that's for terrorism, isn't it?"

"That's right," Anna Timofeevna said in a hushed voice.

"Well how about that! A nice terrorist indeed."

"Ah, girls, as I told you, this business of mine is very distressing. This is why I'm so nervous and lost. It would be a sin for me to complain about my life. I worked as head midwife at a maternity home. And the pay was good, thank God. Thirty years of service and no one stinted on the presents. And on the side, sometimes you would get to do an abortion. And I had a little apartment; any one would love to have the likes of it. I even picked up matching furniture. And my neighbor wasn't too bad. But now look at me: I have nothing. I sit here at the edge of the world and drink someone else's tea out of a half-liter jar, and thanks be to those who gave it to me."

"I sympathize with you completely, but all the same, what has this got to do with terrorism? Because, excuse me, but making a terrorist out of you is like making bullets out of sh-t."

"I see that you're both kind women. I'll tell you only but, God forbid, don't tell anyone else or people will indeed be frightened of me."

"Our kind isn't timid. What did you do, cut someone's throat?"

"Listen to you! I used to have to get my neighbor to slaughter my chickens for me. I could never cut someone's throat. Oi, girls, it's terrible to say—I am in prison on account of Stalin. . . .Well, as I said, I was managing just fine; I couldn't ask for much more. I was respected and everyone treated me with deference. But there was one fellow in our town, a driver. An attractive blond, tall, intelligent, well-read, and in general pleasant. He wanted to become a pilot, only the entrance exam was very difficult, and he didn't pass. So, he worked as a driver. Pilot or not, he still gets to hang around motors. And so this Lenia [diminutive for Leonid] suddenly went to war and only returned last year.

From the front, he immediately landed in a camp, was given a sentence, sat it out for five years, and came out when he was amnestied. They accused him of transporting some kind of [contraband?] goods around Germany in his truck. I don't know, it's easy to pin things on people. To make a long story short, he came back to our town. His father died before the war yet, and his mother had gone to her daughter in Vladivostok to help look after the grandchildren. Lenka went to work as a driver on a poultry farm. And he brought poultry to us at the maternity home, and sometimes he came for the refuse, to collect any remains. They fed us well. There was one time when he was unloading, and I was just going off duty. So he says to me, "Come on, Anna Timofeevna, I'll give you a lift home; why tramp through the mud?" He dropped me off. I wanted to pay him. He wouldn't take it. He dropped me off once, he dropped me off twice. The third time, I say to him, "Come in, Lenia, I'll make you some tea, since you don't want to take any money for driving me."

The next day he came already dressed in civilian clothes made out of a foreign fabric. He lit his cigarette with a lighter, like in the movies, and told me everything about having been abroad. My husband had vanished at the very beginning of the war, when everything was still a muddle; I didn't even get a death telegram about him. Lenka moved in with me. Everything would have been fine if it weren't for my neighbor. Like a cancer of the womb, she gnawed at me. It was one thing and another, and the fellow is twenty years younger than you. Only she lied, it wasn't twenty, it was fifteen. He's only after your money, she says, and all of your belongings. He'll take everything, and then, like in American movies, he'll strangle you. Now I'm telling you, like a cancerous growth she ate away at me. It was all from envy. I put up with it; I didn't say anything. I just tried to do the best I could by Lenka. After all, a man can always leave. True enough, he didn't bring home his pay, but when he managed to get some extra he'd give me a hundred rubles or fifty. Shortly after Christmas, I went and bought a calendar, a pretty, tear-off one. I was always trying to buy pretty things for the house. I bought a picture with swans, gave two hundred rubles for it—a hundred of mine and a hundred of Lenka's. I boasted about it and showed it to Praskov'ia. So all at once she says, "Well, at least you'll have a picture with a proper couple in it." I brought home this calendar, and on it there was such a lovely portrait of comrade Stalin wearing officers' epaulets, all covered in medals. Lenka came home from work. I showed it to him: a calendar, I say, I bought it. All right, he says. But there were quarrels between us even before that, especially when Praskov'ia wasn't home, since I didn't want her to hear us and be gleeful. Then in the evening I wanted to go to the movies.

Lenia ate heartily and then sat down to shave. I said to him, "Let's go to the movies today." But he answered, "I can't, I met one of my army buddies today and promised to go out with him this evening for a beer." I answered him, "So what are you doing shaving your mug for an army buddy? What, he's never seen you unshaven?" One word led to another, and we wound up having a major talk. Suddenly, Lenka jumped up and said that there were two people ruining his young life—Stalin and me. "How I'd like to slash you with a razor right now," he says, "but, I never again want to go to prison." He took the razor (he never shaved with a safety razor) and one, two, three, he went and sliced up the entire face of comrade Stalin in the portrait, and then even gouged out the eyes.—He put on his coat and hat, slammed the door, and left. I sat and cried, and felt sorry for the calendar, and felt sorry for myself. To be sure, if he could have he'd cut my throat, too. He served that sentence for something—they don't put you in prison for nothing. And here comes Praskov'ia, and without malice, but out of kindness to me, says, so what are you doing, she says, you're crying. So I went and told her everything. She immediately began to tremble and said to me that we had to destroy the calendar right away. You know what might happen, she said, on account of that. She took the portrait part, nailed the pages back up to the wall, and left. Well, my Lenka returned, and we made up.

Only, three days later, my Lenia comes home at an unusual time—I was sleeping after a night shift. He's pale and trembling and says to me that he was called to the MGB. There they showed him that same sliced-up portrait and said, how is it that you could bring yourself to commit such an offense against a portrait of comrade Stalin. So, Lenka says to me, "You know, Aneta, (he called me Aneta, in the foreign fashion), I've already served one sentence and got out on amnesty. The absolute least they'll give me for recidivism is ten years. But you're a leading citizen, with irreproachable service, an exemplary worker. So I ask you, I beg you, go and say that this is your doing. They'll swear at you for it, maybe give you a reprimand, but you'll save a person's life."

The lad is right, I think. The next day, we went to the MGB. We no sooner approached the watchman, than Lenka goes and says to him, "This is about the business of the portrait of comrade Stalin. " They immediately let us in and led us to the investigator's office. Lenka says, "I've brought her. She'll tell you everything herself." And he left. I told them everything, just as Lenka taught me. The investigator wrote everything down and then gave it to me to read over. "Everything's written down correctly?" he says. "It's correct." "Then sign it." He showed me where to sign. I signed. "Now, I say, may I go home?" "No, now I'll send for the man on duty and he'll take you to a cell." "What kind of cell?" "A prison cell. You'll sit there until the trial, and then we'll see."

"What do you mean, until the trial? What trial?" "Well," he says, "We're going to try you." "What are you going to try me for? What's all this about?" "We're going to try you for crimes against the state, according to the law." Here I started to cry, and for three days in the cell I kept crying. After three days, they led me to the trial. They didn't even want to hear what I had to say. "Is it you," they say, "who signed your statement?" "Yes," I answer, "but I didn't know they would be passing judgment on it." "Now," they say, "it's too late. You should have thought about that earlier." And the witnesses were Lenka and Praskov'ia. The judges retired for five minutes. Then they returned and read out my sentence: in accordance with article fifty-eight, point eight, for a terroristic act against a portrait of our leader and teacher, friend of all the nations, comrade Stalin,—twenty-five years in a corrective labor camp. And so they brought me here.

Part IV

Apogee and Fracture: 1954–1991

Whatever the Soviet Union was under Stalin, it began to assume another face after him, though this was not always apparent. Nikita Khrushchev, impetuous and brash, seemed to contain many contrasting elements in his policies and character alike. A party official of the highest ranks, he was a faithful supporter of Stalin, and there was much blood on his hands.

However, it was Khrushchev who shocked the party (and then the world) by being the architect of de-Stalinization. The secret speech to the 20th Party Congress on February 24, 1956, attacked Stalin for numerous crimes and the cult of personality. Among the beneficial results, besides those of opening a vast new forum for discussion, was the release of millions of prisoners from the GULAG. What could be more anti-Stalinist than this? Thousands of prisoners were also rehabilitated, though this honor was initially reserved for high-ranking Communist Party members. The number of those released from the camps is generally cited to be close to eight million; at least a million continued life in the camps, however.

The other major shift credited to Khrushchev was the gradual relaxation of the strictures on literature and the arts. The term "thaw" is now universally used to denote this. If the Party itself admitted Stalin's errors, it could relax the reins in the field of cultural expression. Vladimir Dudintsev's 1956 novel *Not by Bread Alone* and Vera Panova's *The Seasons* are two early markers; fortunately they were two of many. Negative elements of Soviet society could be (albeit carefully) portrayed. Sometimes this was fragile and arbitrary. Boris Pasternak was vilified for *Dr. Zhivago*, for example. Yet, four years later in 1962, Solzhenitsyn's *One Day in the Life of Ivan Denisovich* was cleared for publication.

Khrushchev's salutary gestures in these areas must be contrasted with his frequently bellicose foreign policy. The great de-Stalinizer was also the figure who fomented the Berlin Crisis of 1958 and the inordinately dangerous Cuban Missile Crisis of 1962. Simultaneously, Khrushchev sought summit meetings with western leaders and spoke of "peaceful co-existence" in quieter moments. The latter phrasing was inherited by his successor Leonid Brezhnev who replaced him in 1964. Both leaders maintained resolutely that communism would ultimately win out even if "peaceful co-existence" prevailed.

Brezhnev's rule is generally viewed as one of stagnation, especially from the 1970's on. The system seemed often to be set in stone and major shifts in agriculture and industry could not be effected. The disproportionate percentage of the national budget allotted to the military did not help. The USSR's military posture and space program were still powerful and prestigious and were useful elements in the political wars aimed at gaining adherents in the Third World. Yet, fissures began to surface. The Soviet invasion of Afghanistan in 1979 turned into stalemate, then loss, something no one predicted.

China took a strong anti-Soviet position on the Afghanistan war. This only exemplified a truism apparent from the mid-1950's – the two dominant communist powers never consolidated their political might and agendas. The fact that Brezhnev's era saw nuclear test ban treaties signed, as well as those limiting strategic arms (e.g. SALT I in 1972), though viewed positively in the West, were seen as appeasement in Mao's China. The political heritage of Brezhnev was broken by Gorbachev.

Mikhail Gorbachev is generally seen as one of the ten most influential leaders of the 20th century. Though committed to communism, he nevertheless realized that overhaul was mandated at all levels of the Soviet enterprise. He was prepared to go to lengths whose outcomes he could not begin to guess. The effort, most noticed internationally via the twin political dictums of *glasnost* and *perestroika*, unleashed a plethora of decrees, policies, and emotions, ultimately helping to dismantle the Soviet Union. By the end of 1991, it was no more. History will always remember the irony that a true believer, though not an ideologue, oversaw the demise.

Nickolas Lupinin

Chapter Twenty-Seven

Mariia Shapiro, A Soviet Capitalist

Mariia Shapiro found herself in a woman's concentration camp in Eastern Siberia in 1946 after being arrested and sentenced for anti-Soviet writings. She was arrested in northern China, in Harbin, once a thriving Russian city established during the Russian expansion eastward. Its growth was greatly stimulated by the completion of the Trans-Siberian Railway. After the Civil War many Russians found a haven in that city since it was not in Soviet territory. M. Shapiro completed law school there and turned to journalism as a profession. Her articles dealt with aspects of émigré life, but she also concentrated on Soviet legal proceedings. This did not stand her in good stead when Harbin fell to the Soviets after the defeat of the Japanese in World War II. She managed to keep a secret log of her years in prison which she later expanded into memoirs. Excerpted from Mariia Shapiro, "Zhenskii kontslager'" [A Woman's Concentration Camp]. New York: *The New Review*, No. 158, March, 1985.

DECEMBER 9th, 1957

Once two new women appeared in our cell. They arrived loudly enough, in some sort of nervous excitement. In about two days they calmed down. The older of the women, Zoia Zhigaleva, immediately attracted my attention. I often recalled her later, already living in a camp, and tried to define the nature of this 38-year-old uneducated but clever woman with dark eyes and a quite correct, pleasant face which so distinguished her from the crowd that even our anarchist, criminal element immediately felt her power.

I soon understood that Zoia was a born leader and organizer. This is as much a talent as any other. It was as if Zoia was surrounded by a taboo. She would spread out the contents of her or her friend's food parcel on a clean napkin on the table and a few times invited me. It was strange to sit and eat the tasty things so demonstratively in the public eye and in the presence of criminals who flung evil glances at us and gnashed their teeth like hungry wolves.

Zoia was the daughter of a hardy Siberian peasant, an energetic and capable landholder in spirit (and perhaps by blood)—the descendant of courageous Siberian explorers. When the children became adolescents, the father decided to move to an absolutely out of the way place, far into the *taiga*, a few dozen kilometers down the Lena River from Iakutsk. There they built their home with their own hands and developed a large farm. Zoia told me in detail how much livestock they had, the kinds of vegetable gardens, outbuildings, etc. The house gradually acquired a cultured, urban appearance. The dining room even had a large painting and store-bought furniture. And all of this was created by the hands and labor of one family.

The wild *taiga* was mastered. Gradually other people began to settle near the Zhigalev homestead. New homesteads appeared.

The steamship lines on the Lena turned their attention to the new population center and established a landing there. The children began to go to school in town. But Zoia managed to finish only three grades. After the collapse of the White regime in Siberia and the end of the Civil War, the first wave of liquidation of private farms began. Zoia's father, having created a blossoming household in the Iakutsk *taiga* with his own hands, was declared a kulak. A tax of 10,000 rubles was imposed on him. Of course, he was not able to pay such a tax. Having understood with his sharp and practical Siberian mind that this tax was only the beginning of future misfortunes and that they were not to farm the *taiga*, he declared to his family that they had to abandon the homestead, give it up, and move to the city.

Zoia's voice trembled when she spoke about parting from her beloved place. The homestead passed into the hands of the government, and when Zoia went back after a few years to see what had become of the homestead, she found a frightening desolation. Some people still seemed to work there, but there were almost no cattle and no vegetable garden either. The house had been gutted and had fallen into complete decay, and even her favorite painting in the dining room hung in tatters on the dirty wall.

Zoia formed a definite worldview, well-considered and shaped by suffering. Rarely did I meet among educated women such clarity of mind, such comprehension, as possessed by this young Siberian woman with a third-grade education.

In her first years of marriage Zoia did not work anywhere. There was no necessity and not even the desire. The war began. Zoia's husband was registered at his plant and was not subject to being dispatched to the front. But Zoia with her sharp mind realized that she, a young, healthy, childless woman, would sooner or later be mobilized for some kind of, perhaps unpleasant, work. And she decided to take the bull by the horns. Zoia proposed to the administration of the plant where her husband worked that she take charge of the supply of provisions for the workers of the plant. The proposal was accepted and Zoia began to work.

So here was this young woman, not having had the slightest trade or business experience, not having ever worked even as a simple sales clerk, not having had even a high school education, beginning an undertaking under conditions of war and great shortages. And this very person took upon herself the task of supplying hundreds of workers scattered throughout the *taiga* and along the Lena under the conditions of the severe North, of the spring mud and the impassable *taiga* roads.

And the work went well. Zoia sent shiploads of products up and down the Lena, and entire convoys into the *taiga*. Her organizational talent and ability to direct people emerged, the talent of a guide, of a leader, inherited from her father and, in a larger sense, given to her by nature.

The plant's administration, seeing how well Zoia managed the acquisition and distribution of food, put her in charge of all the vegetable gardens and the creation of new gardens. And she was successful here as well. Then they entrusted her with the organization and supervision of the renovation of workers' and employees' living quarters. And she successfully organized this as well.

"But I didn't forget about myself," Zoia openly declared to me. "My apartment was first in line for the renovations."

The war ended. After her enormous achievement and the joyous awareness of knowing her revealed abilities and strengths, a series of humdrum days set in. The former, quiet pre-war life spent in the shadow of her husband and the reading of books no longer satisfied Zoia.

I understood Zoia's nature: during my childhood before the revolution I saw, in Siberian cities, such female merchants and gold dealers. There would be an elderly widow who, after the death of her husband, had mines, flour mills, and steamships left to her. In a city such as Blagoveshchensk on the Amur River, such an entrepreneur would leave her home in the morning in her surrey and go to the bank and her enterprises: to the mill, the basin to check the repairs to the steamships, and so forth. She would usually drive the horse and buggy herself. Often she would be barely literate, even unable to sign her name. But what an organizer, what acumen in questions of trade and, in particular, of business obligations and banking laws.

"That's not a woman, but a minister," my late father, an old, experienced barrister, would say about such women. He had dealings with such women who, after the death of their husbands, expanded the enterprises and fed hundreds of people. From the second generation of such entrepreneurs came Zoia.

After the war, Zoia started down a path which, according to Soviet law, is criminal, but in capitalist countries would be called successful business operations. Zoia busied herself with dealing in "gold" coupons.

For each gram of gold turned in to the government through its "Gold Purchasing" department, gold miners received either fifty rubles in cash or a coupon worth the same amount at a special-goods store. These stores were very well supplied. In them were lots of foreign goods—for example, English woolen cloth, which was almost impossible to obtain anywhere. Naturally, there was a great demand for these coupons, in particular by people who had no connection to the mines.

Zoia found out that besides Iakutsk there was a "Gold Purchasing" office in Irkutsk and Novosibirsk where black market dealers purchased these coupons for 600 rubles—that is, twelve times their face value. So Zoia decided to start dealing in these coupons. She began to buy up gold from prospectors and take it to Irkutsk, where she turned it in to the "Gold Purchasing" office and received coupons in return. She then sold the coupons to a speculator. She took a long-term lease on a room in Irkutsk from a landlady who could be trusted. This was very important, since she, a woman, carried large amounts of gold with her and occurrences of robbery were frequent. One had to know with whom you could stay.

During one of these trips from the Iakutsk mines to Irkutsk, Zoia met her future collaborator, Ekaterina Stepanovna, who was in the same line of work. It was convenient for them to join forces: they were safer and less afraid of drawing attention to themselves. Their operations gradually expanded and it became necessary to be more careful in order not to be noticed. In general, they had an agreement: if one of them or both were arrested, under no circumstances were they to confess to the joint venture, but insist that each of them worked individually in order not to be charged with violation of the group law from 7/VIII, for which there were only two penalties, death or a ten-year term. Amnesty was never an option under this law.

When the operations grew, they began to transport gold to Novosibirsk as well. They also rented an apartment in Novosibirsk in order to have a secure place to stay. They often made the Iakutsk-Irkutsk and the Irkutsk-Novosibirsk run by airplane for the sake of speed and comfort. They dressed well. There were suitcases with clothing both at the Irkutsk landlady's and at the Novosibirsk landlady's, whom they generously paid and gave gracious gifts to.

On the last, fateful trip to Novosibirsk, Zoia and Ekaterina Stepanovna brought with them an amount of gold worth no more nor less than 600 thousand rubles. They had decided that on the day of arrival with the gold, Zoia would turn in 150 thousand worth, and then Ekaterina Stepanovna would turn in another 150 thousand rubles' worth. On the next day they would repeat the procedure with the remaining 300 thousand. Zoia already suspected that they were under surveillance. They instructed their apartment landlady that if one of them or both did not return home that day, under no circumstances was she to call the police, but rather send word to Iakutsk to Zoia's husband. He would come to pick up her things and the 300 thousand rubles of gold that was left.

On the day of the arrival, Zoia went with half the gold, which they decided to turn in to the "Gold Purchasing" office. She handed in the gold successfully. Zoia said that a speculator approached her to whom she succeeded in passing the coupons. It seemed that this was the same Irkutsk speculator. But when she went outside, she sensed that she was being followed. She encountered a woman who began speaking to her. Wishing to save the woman from any unpleasantness, Zoia asked her to go away. When the woman had barely left, Zoia heard behind her the steps of a man overtaking her and a shout:

"Citizen, stop for one minute."

Everything was finished.

Ekaterina Stepanovna was arrested the same day either on the street or at the purchasing office itself. The two of them had another agreement: in the event of arrest outside the house, under no circumstances were they to reveal the address of the apartment so that the remaining gold worth 300 thousand rubles would not be lost. However, in spite of the instructions to the landlady, when they both did not return that day for the night, the landlady fell into a panic and reported it to the police. In this way the remaining part of the gold was lost.

"Trifles," laughed both Zoia and Ekaterina Stepanovna, saying, "Money will come with time! Money is a thing that is acquired. It was, and will be, and still be even more."

I was delighted. Not every capitalist would be so cheerful about the loss of 600 thousand rubles!

For Zoia it was most important to have the investigation and trial proceed not in Novosibirsk but in Iakutsk. In Iakutsk she had a sister who was married to a public prosecutor, another prosecutor was her cousin, and a third was some sort of relative. With such a situation and the fact that the lost 600 thousand in gold did not make up all of their liquid capital, Zoia had good reason to think that if they succeeded in having the trial in Iakutsk they would manage to smother the case and obtain freedom.

And they succeeded. They were being sent to Iakutsk for trial. It was in the process of being moved to Iakutsk that they were quartered at the Irkutsk prison. Here they waited for the Iakutsk convoy, which was supposed to arrive specially for them, since there was no regular transfer of convicts to Iakutsk.

Among the female criminals Zoia was just like a tamer in a tiger's cage. For them, I think, her calm and disdainful confidence had a most powerful effect, so that they did not dare touch her. In her, they also saw a procurer of material goods such as themselves, but on an immeasurably greater scale. Sometimes she liked to tease the "tigers," when they were already gnashing their teeth, but she was far above their criminal ways.

At that time the cell captains were appointed rather than elected by the inmates as before, and one fine day Zoia was appointed captain. How quickly did order enthrone itself in our chaotic cell! There was no extortion, no getting rations out of turn, no special privileges, no fights. Even cursing occurred less frequently.

How did Zoia achieve this? She didn't scream, as some captains did. She didn't threaten to complain to the administration. This relative order seemed to come on its own.

I would end almost every one of my sketches about the Russian women whom I met in prisons and transfer points with a question of their destiny. I wanted to know whether they managed to mend the broken threads of their lives. And I would especially have liked to know about the future of Zoia Zhigaleva.

She undoubtedly was an extraordinary person. How often in the ensuing years in the camps would I remember seeing the helplessness of captains and sometimes even the brigadiers before the anarchic criminal convicts, plain hooligans and even those women who were convicted on article 58 [political prisoners]—not criminals, but more vile than the criminals. How often in the Akmolinsk camp during the wild screaming of obscenities and utter lawlessness frequently ending in injury and even murder did I think to myself: "If only Zoia were here!" With her mere presence, with her calm and derisive response to hooligan behavior, she brought order and organization where there had been rampage.

I would say to her: "Zoia, in an earlier time in Russia or in the West, you would have become one of the great agents in the nation's industry or commerce. But here they consider you a transgressor of the law, a speculator, that is, an enemy of the people." I didn't notice that Zoia had any repentance or wish to stop her interrupted activity. On the contrary, temporary failure and a clash with the Soviet laws strengthened her daring and desire for success despite all obstacles.

Chapter Twenty-Eight

Valerii Leviatov, My Path to God

The first paragraph of this selection sets the theme. How does a child of committed communists, who feels an intense hatred for religion and believes in its eradication by force, turn to God while a teenager? Cases of this type lead to broader questions peculiar to the twentieth century—what are the psychological factors which make an individual a dissident in a dictatorial state? Originally published as "Kak ia prishel k Bogu" [How I Came to God] in *Grani, Nos. 111–112, 1979.*

The saying "He was Saul and became Paul" applies to me. Raised by parents who were devoted communists, I was not, like most children my age, simply indifferent to religion—I hated it. I dreamed of the time when the last devout old woman would die and the last church would be closed. I was perturbed with the government for mollycoddling believers. Why wait for the last old woman believer to die? Just close the churches and be done with it. There certainly would be no believers from my generation, that's for sure. How could an educated person believe in the flood and in a God with a beard? And if you had told me, a ten-year old boy, that in seven years time I would be baptized of my own accord, I would have laughed out loud. But that's what happened.

With the best of intentions, my parents played a dirty trick on me, but it worked out for the best because I was led to God. With the best of intentions my parents, as did our literature, served up fantasy for reality. They believed that the truth could be harmful to a child's developing worldview. And so they taught me that the goal they worked for, "man is a friend, comrade and brother to man," was already achieved or almost achieved; that with rare exceptions, all of our people were good, conscientious, and placed the interests of society ahead of their own. But when I encountered life, I found nothing of the kind.

In my children's books I read about child volunteers who helped the sick and elderly and about teachers who devoted their lives to children, but in life I found none of this, either.

My parents and our writers had obscured my vision with rose-colored glasses and when I removed them, my eyes hurt.

Evtushenko [Evgenii Evtushenko, the poet] wrote that a "chain of inconsistencies could lead to loss of faith." But he put it very mildly. In fact, inconsistencies did make many lose faith. It's no accident that among my generation, those who were sixteen or seventeen in 1956, there are so many "superfluous" people. Fortunately, my disillusionment in one faith led me to another. But that all came later. For the time being, at nine and ten years old, I only bumped into sharp corners and sustained bruises.

It began with my ethnicity. My father is Jewish and my mother is Russian. If I don't look Jewish, than I look even less like a Russian. The first blow was when the kids in the courtyard that we moved to when I was six years old called me a short, small, three-letter word: Yid. The concept of different nationalities was a very vague one for me. Thanks to my parents, I figured approximately thus: there is the Soviet Union and then there are other countries. And those who live in the Soviet Union are all Russians, all Soviets.

When I came home and told my parents that the other children had called me some strange word and refused to play with me, my parents explained that in the dark past Jews were called that word, that my father was indeed a Jew, but now that no longer meant anything. The parents of the children who called me this name were probably just very backward. This consoled me, but then in the courtyard, at school, and the young Pioneer camp, I continued to hear that word.

For a long time I could not understand and tried to explain: "What do you mean, guys? I was born in Moscow, after all. My homeland is Russia, I don't even know the Jewish language."

"But you're still a Yid, since your father's a Yid," was the answer.

When I finally came to realize that these kids would never accept me, that I would always remain a Yid to them, even though I was no more Jewish than Russian (and even more Russian than Jewish), and despite the fact that I did not have those character traits for which Jews are despised, I recall how I crawled under the table and cried for hours.

From then on, probably to assert myself, I started to fight with my offenders. I fought often, with all of them, and was often beaten, but the kids in the courtyard came to respect and even like me. And subsequently in every new group, I always had to prove I was bold and brave from the start.

The courtyard where I grew up caused me to part rather early with the illusions which my parents had spoon-fed me. (I write this now on a positive note. At the time, however, the incongruity of life with my illusions was a tragedy.)

This is the sort of courtyard it was: all the older boys were thieves—some had been jailed for stealing once, some twice, some three times. Our courtyard's past was shrouded in legends about certain big-time criminals, known throughout the Soviet Union, and about how it used to be that passers-by crossed the street to avoid our building. The courtyard resembled a well—a dark, narrow space surrounded by buildings. Not a single shrub or blade of grass, only asphalt. In the evening the older boys played cards for money and we, the younger ones, hung around, ran after cigarettes and vodka for them, listened, enraptured, to the stories of their criminal life and learned their underground songs. The air was thick with juicy profanity, and bloody fights often broke out between the card players. It's no wonder that the seven and eight-year old boys cursed as not every adult could, and at eleven or twelve they could split a half-liter of vodka "three ways" and were somber realists. (At twelve I had a much more sober view of life than did my communist parents.)

At first I remained untainted and did not take part in any of this. After all, I had been told that none of this existed. I only looked on in horror. In the fall, I watched how boys my age stole watermelons from the produce shop, smashed them and swore. So, was it that my parents had deceived me? Or did I just have the misfortune of living in a bad courtyard full of degenerates? That was probably the case. Surely in all the other courtyards, all of them except our own, there lived good, conscientious children of good, conscientious parents. But the older I became, the more bad exceptions I encountered. As it was in our courtyard, so it was at school, the Pioneer camp and the village outside Moscow, where we rented a *dacha* in the summer. Nothing was as my parents or the books said it was.

And then I thought, it couldn't be that I always encounter only exceptions to the rule. So they must not be exceptions, but the norm? And so it was. My parents and those books had been deceiving me. My parents' faith showed fissures. But only so far as everyday matters were concerned. I simply convinced myself that the time when my ideals would be realized was still a long ways off. I remained an ardent communist and dreamed of universal brotherhood. I only lamented that I saw no principled people around me for whom an idea could take precedence over their own personal interests.

In 1954, when I turned fourteen, my mother and I visited the village of Inta in the Komi ASSR [Autonomous Republic]. We went there because in 1943 my older brother had been wrongfully convicted. My parents explained to me that there had been a mistake, and that justice would be restored. It was regrettable that comrade Stalin and his aides knew nothing about this, that it was kept from them; for if they had found out, my brother would be freed and those responsible for the mistake severely punished. Justice, however, was slow in coming. Comrade Stalin managed to die by the time my brother's sentence was reduced from ten to six years (the time he had already served) and he remained exiled in Inta. (Later, after 1956, my brother was rehabilitated.)

And so, since Mohammed wasn't coming to the mountain, that summer my mother and I went to see him in Inta. Revelations of things hidden from me began on our way there. From around Kotlas onwards there were endless guard towers with sentries. Those were the camps—and only the ones along the railroad. How many more were farther away, out of sight? It was as if the whole country north of Moscow was inhabited by criminals; that there were more criminals than non-criminals.

Inta consisted almost entirely of prisoners and former prisoners in permanent exile. The crowds of women in tattered gray clothes, surrounded by dogs and soldiers with automatic weapons, were a pitiful sight. But I still really considered them enemies. My visit to Inta enabled me to learn personally what most people found out only after 1956. Only I saw it all in a truer and more horrifying version.

I returned to Moscow a totally different person. I had lost all faith in the correctness of our ideas. In school I had been taught to believe that nothing in history happens by chance. From that time on I began to ponder many things. And my thoughts were one darker than the other. I no longer believed that man would ever learn to construct his life in accordance with the laws of goodness and justice.

"It's not society that is bad, but man himself," I decided. "No matter how you change social structure, man will always find an opportunity to be selfish and there will always be injustice."

At that time I despised people. I had an amazing ability to find the bad (the vile, as I put it) in everyone, and had a very high opinion of myself. I considered myself to be better and more intelligent than others and categorized all people as either the chosen few or the masses, placing myself in the former group, of course.

There is something else I must mention. From my earliest childhood I had experienced, not so much thoughts, as feelings, that life was meaningless. I remember, once when I was about six I crawled under a table and wouldn't come out. My father tried this and that, but I wouldn't budge.

"Well, at least explain what's with you," my father finally asked anxiously.

"What's the point of all of this, if we die?" I asked.

"What do you mean by 'all of this'?"

"Everything," I said, and made a sweeping gesture with my arms.
"You're a little young to worry about such things!" father laughed.

Then I really did stop worrying about such things. But now, at fifteen/sixteen years of age, it all came back, and with much greater force. I considered the chosen ones to be those who understood that life was meaningless and did not attempt to dissuade themselves of this. Though man always strives for happiness, he will never be happy; the same is true for individuals as for humanity as a whole. So why go on living and drag out this drudgery? Why endure sixty or eighty years of stagnant existence; is it not better to cut things short at sixteen? I could take that step myself now, before I become stricken with disease or too attached to life. We all die, after all, so what difference does it make whether it's now or in fifty years? Life is worth living when one has a goal or purpose, but if there is none—then what's the point? What's the point of living if people will never be happy; if cruelty and arbitrariness will always reign in human relations? And if humanity should someday achieve happiness—so what? "I'll still just become fertilizer for burdock." And death would be harder to bear for a happy humanity than for an unhappy one. So what should one live for—for fame? One tires of fame. For women? But they grow old and die the same as you. It remains only to live as animals: eat, drink, breed and die. That's how the majority lives, after all. Simply in order to eat and to cover their nakedness, the majority works and attempts to sweeten this bitter life with movies, books, stamps or with their labor.

So, for what purpose do we have reason? And is it worth occupying oneself with art, science, philosophy, technology, just to eat, drink, reproduce, and die? Of course not.

In school at this same time I was learning the basics of Darwinism. The basic law of the animal world, I was taught, is the struggle for survival. The strong devour the weak. Those who adapt, survive, and those who don't, perish. And man, too, is an animal, isn't he? This means that among humans the basic law is the same: the strong devour the weak; those who adapt, survive, and those who don't, perish. It then follows, that the accommodating careerists are the most normal of people, and morality is just a fabrication of the weak, made up to console them in their weakness. Yet what if I don't want to live without morality, only filling my own stomach and taking away my neighbor's portion? Why the devil would I want such a life? I thought incessantly of suicide, but kept waiting for something and putting it off.

Then I had a revelation. Once, while reading that same textbook, *Principles of Darwinism*, I came upon a certain passage on coal, about how the ancient vegetation that formed coal absorbed lots of solar energy, and that's why coal releases so much heat. A sudden spark illuminated my mind. How is it that in nature everything is so interconnected, so well thought-out? Can that really be by accident? Now, if a man doesn't look after his garden, the garden will die. So how come in nature no one looks after things, but everything is in its place, everything reasoned and wise? We need oxygen, so plants make oxygen for us. Plants need humus, so animals die and their decaying bodies provide humus.

From that moment, I concluded that nature was created by a higher intelligence, God, in other words. But this belief was still far from Christianity or any other religion.

"Of course, God is creator of all in the universe," I thought, "but that still doesn't mean that people could see Him or that He could give them some sort of commandments. Can we fathom the soul of an ant? Can an ant understand us? In religions, man has simply tried to comprehend God in human terms."

Then I began to reason somewhat differently. Of course, the difference between man and God is infinitely greater than the difference between an ant and man. And it's true that an ant can never comprehend man, just as man cannot conceive the psychology of an ant. But man did not create ants. He himself, the same as ants, was created by God. So why couldn't God understand His creations? After all, to understand something does not mean to become identical with it. So just maybe, religion is a case of God coming down to man's level to show him how he ought to live, so that humanity would be better off. The same way we tell children that they shouldn't play with matches.

In a similar fashion I came gradually to approach the notion of immortality. Well, fine, we die and our body rots, but what about our thoughts and feelings? Surely it cannot be that our thoughts and deeds, our commands to our body, our will and mind, originate in the dead gray matter in our heads—matter which we have named, the composition of which we know and can discuss. What is thought, after all? Something immaterial. You can't touch or weigh it. And how can something material create the immaterial?

Then I considered that we have something in us that does not decay, because it is not subject to decay. And that this something neither dies nor is born, because birth and death are material categories. Can that which cannot be felt, weighed or measured be born? Are molecules born and do they die?

I no longer believed the theory of evolution.

"Evolution exists, but within certain limitations," I decided. Certain muscles can be developed with protracted, regular exercise. But no matter how long you flap your arms, even for a million years, they will never become wings—that I could not believe. That would be a miracle, and what miracles can there be without God?

I was now ready for religion, but which was the true one? For truth must be singular, and there are many religions.

Together with the appearance and development of my belief in God and immortality, I was becoming more and more drawn to Christianity, largely under the influence of Fedor Mikhailovich Dostoevsky.

I was struck by *The Humiliated and Insulted*, the first novel by Dostoevsky that I read. Everything I had read prior to that seemed either a saccharine depiction of life, or hopeless despair. While here I saw a life full of suffering, people who were humiliated and insulted; yet when I turned the last page, I was filled with joy. These degraded and abused people were not alone; they loved each other and helped others like themselves, or even those more humbled than themselves. These people did not place their faith in any bright future for society, but in God; they loved not society in the abstract, but people as they were. Life was difficult for them, but they were not unhappy.

What makes man unhappy? Wanting something for himself that he is not granted. Others, who also want something for themselves, don't let him have what he wants, and they in turn also suffer. But what if you are able to forget yourself? To uproot your selfishness, and to make the happiness of others your purpose in life? If your guiding principle becomes not "take," but "give," then your happiness will depend on how much good you give others. And this depends, not on fate, but upon you yourself. And misfortunes won't be able to make you unhappy, because your own injuries won't matter to you.

With a guiding principle such as this, a person can be happy in the face of any social injustice, inequality, and so on. He won't be bothered by the fact that others live better than he does—he will be glad for them.

And then I realized that this way was the only true way to universal happiness and the kingdom of good that I had dreamed of since childhood. Since it's not society that is bad, but man himself, then however many revolutions you have, it will only be like running in place. The have-nots envy the rich, take their wealth from them and themselves become the rich ("he who was nothing has become everything"), society once again is divided along the lines of rich and poor, and so on forever. Because the very desire for equity is founded on selfishness: a person thinks that he has not received his fair share and undertakes to establish equity. Yet when every person will be glad, when he can give more to another than he takes for himself (as parents are happy, when they give the tastiest bits to their children)—that's when true justice will come into being. And this universal happiness will not be dependent on universal well-being. Material well-being has never made people happy. But they can be happy in poverty. That's why the teaching that presumes the establishment of a paradise on earth together with the attainment of universal abundance is utopian. The maxim "from each according to his abilities, to each according to his needs," is wrong. It will never be possible to satisfy man's unbridled desires (recall the fable "The Fisherman and the Fish").

There is another thing that I then understood: The only thing that can truly transform a person is to love all people, including the wicked, and to answer evil with good. While in most cases, evil begets evil.

Throughout history, humanity on the whole has lived according to the rule "an eye for and eye"—and what is the result? Endless suffering. Auschwitz and hydrogen bombs. Because an evil plus an evil equals two evils.

My final turning point occurred after *Crime and Punishment*. In Raskolnikov I recognized my former self, and in the collapse of his worldview, the collapse of mine. And our savior was the righteous sinner, Sonia Marmeladov with the Gospel in hand.

Dostoevsky brought to me fragments of the Gospel, and these fragments seemed more wonderful than anything I had known. I remember how, when I had read the final page, I went outside. There was a fine, light rain and the wind was blowing. I wandered the streets of Moscow that night and thought about how the next day, I would begin a new life, quite different from the one I had known until then.

But this new belief of mine still was not true religiosity. It was rather a reasoned belief. I simply considered that it was more proper, more reasonable to live in such a fashion (while acknowledging immortality, of course). Without that, this new life was just as senseless as everything else. Having been taught to be rational, I could not grasp the irrational. To me, the rituals of the Church seemed senseless, games old women played. Well, what would possibly occur if I were dunked in water or if I crossed myself? Then once, already as one who acknowledged the teachings of Christ and who sympathized with religion, I dropped by a church—just to take a look. The impression was incredible. Yes, it was all ornate, but the theater can also be ornate. But I was gripped by a feeling that I had never experienced in any theater. Most importantly, after that visit I became much stronger in my Christian convictions, and a simple thought occurred to me: we cannot simply think and feel, we must also express our thoughts and feelings symbolically. Our every word is in fact a symbol. Yet it doesn't seem odd to us when we, upon greeting someone, say "hello" and shake his hand. The rituals of the Church are also symbols that cannot be dispensed with. Without them the faith within one's soul will wither.

After that I had no doubts in the necessity of baptism. If the human soul in all its forms senses the difference between good and evil, and, with rare exceptions, a person who commits a vile act knows that he behaves wrongly, not humanely, and since there is nothing more humane than Christianity—it follows that in Christianity there is truth. (Later I became convinced of this in practice. And I think that if every person were to analyze his life without atheistic superstitions and prejudice, he would become convinced of the same.) A person can strive only after that which is implanted in him. After all, we don't try to make ourselves grow tails.

I then told a student acquaintance in the Theological Academy, with whom I had previously spoken only about literature (he, from a reluctance to proselytize, and I from a sense of tact, so as not offend him by mocking religion), that I wanted to be baptized.

Chapter Twenty-Nine

Valentin Kataev, A Paschal Memory

Valentin Kataev was a Russian author who had the rare privilege of going abroad during the Soviet period. On one such trip to San Francisco in the 1960's he met a woman whom he had loved in Odessa before the Bolshevik revolution. He had proposed marriage to her then, but she declined. He recalls seeing her on an Easter Sunday, *Paskha*, the central holy day of the Orthodox Church which is celebrated after seven weeks of fasting with great expectation, solemn joy, and feasting. It is customary to kiss family, friends, acquaintances, and others three times on the cheeks this day, one time each for the Father, Son, and Holy Spirit. For timid and shy people, the tradition served as a way of kissing a person one liked. The lit candles which Kataev recalls were traditionally carried home after Saturday night vespers before Palm Sunday and after the Holy Thursday "Passion Gospels," always celebrated in the evening. In many families, upon arriving home, the youngest child would get to illuminate the darkened house from her candle. Excerpted from Valentin Kataev, *Sviatoi kolodets* [The Sacred Well]. Moscow, 1979.

[Kataev begins]: "Tell me, why didn't you marry me back then?"

"I was young and foolish," she answered with an unreflecting and sorrowful lightness as if she had anticipated the question. Then, her head slightly down, she continued to look at me from beneath her brows not wiping her eyes, smiling quietly. On the wall in back of her I noticed a vaguely familiar watercolor. The only item which she managed to take with her from Russia some forty years ago. The painting was of a young woman, almost a girl, in a paisley kerchief carefully carrying before her a Holy Thursday candle in a paper cone lest the March wind blow it out. The candlelight illuminated the girl's face from below her cheeks with a bright and tender glow. The upper face was in shadow but her eyes, with a gold-leaf flame in each pupil, looked straight out at me with innocence and joy. And I immediately recalled Blok's poem.

> Little boys and little girls
> Cradling candles and pussy willows
>   Set off for home.
> The flames glimmer,
> Passersby cross themselves,
>   And it smells of spring.

"Do you remember?" I asked. And right away, reading my mind, she answered:

> Playful little wind,
> Light, little rain,
>   Don't put out my flame.
> I'll be first to rise
> On Palm Sunday morrow
>   For the sacred day.

Then it was my turn to read her mind and I saw what she saw: our first and only kiss, which never really counted as real for we did not really kiss but performed a socially accepted ritual.

Near the festively decorated table with tall Easter cakes, pink shavings of hyacinth, colored eggs in a bed of watercress, a baked ham, and a silver bottle of raspberry liqueur produced by the Brothers Shustov, stood my beloved girl. Her eyes were sleepy after the all-night Easter services, but her face was fresh and turned to me with expectation. Her arms were raised. The lace cuffs of her dress half-covered her fingers with their polished nails. She was looking at me without concealing her curiosity: what would I do? That was the first time I had seen her out of her school uniform. She was wearing a fine blouse that was a little big on her. It was honeycombed with tiny perforations through which pink silken shoulder straps showed. The outfit did not suit her at all, giving her slim figure a matronly appearance.

"Christ is Risen!" I said with more conviction than the circumstances demanded and stepped toward her with hesitation—washed clean, brushed, short on sleep, perfumed with my aunt's cologne "Brocar," with my hair larded stiff with Vaseline and my new shoes screeping.

"Truly He is risen!" she responded and asked smiling, "Do we have to kiss?"

"I guess we have to," I said, barely controlling my breaking voice.

She placed the palms of her hands on my shoulders. Her hands smelled of old-fashioned elder blossom perfume, either hers or wafting from the lace sleeves become a bit yellow with time. We kissed primly and I saw close-up her lips pressed together and stretched into a cool smile with a tiny beauty mark and her eyes revealing absolutely nothing, not even self-consciousness.

It was then that I saw her father for the first time, although I had been a frequent visitor to their home. He was never there, having just left or not yet returned from the nobleman's club.

He stepped forth in a new frock-coat and white vest, slipping starch-white cards into his billfold, ready for his upcoming round of visits. She presented myself to him saying my last name and the diminutive of my first. We kissed three times. He looked at me with too much attention and a strange curiosity, shook my icy hand, and poured two green cordial glasses of raspberry liqueur. We clinked glasses and drank. I, never before having had wine, sensed an immediate intoxication from the very aroma which filled my nostrils and throat with a wonderfully evanescent raspberry taste. Outside, beyond the windows with their dry, cracked putty, the air resounded with the constant Easter chiming of the bells of St. Michael's Monastery above the sparrows in the lilac bushes ready to burst into flower. White clouds scudded across the watery azure sky and the sun glistened in the quicksilver bubble of the outdoor Reaumur thermometer. A resurrected fly crawled along the painted windowsill and I stared at her father with pickled eyes, at his stiff snow-white cuffs and golden cufflinks, his crewcut and powerful head well set on the compact, thickset torso of a retired cavalry officer who was squandering his wife's Moldavian estate at the gaming tables of the Catherine Yacht Club.

"You remember my deceased father?" she asked, uncannily continuing to read my mind.

"I remember it all," I responded wistfully.

"So do I," she said and we both grew silent.

Chapter Thirty

Kirill Kostsinskii [K.V. Uspenskii], A Dissident's Trial

Kiril V. Uspenskii (Kostsinskii is his pseudonym) was born in Petrograd in 1915. Both his parents were active Party members after the Bolsheviks took power in 1917. The author was a military officer, though this did not forestall his first arrest in 1938. He was released and subsequently served in military intelligence. He was dropped behind German lines in the Ukraine to activate the local partisans. Captured by the German forces, he managed to escape, only to return and be excluded from the Communist Party. After World War II he devoted himself to literature. He was arrested again in 1960 and served a four-year sentence for "excessive fraternization" with foreigners. He became active in the human rights movement after his release from prison and was forced to leave the Soviet Union in 1978. Taken from K.V. Uspenskii, "Iz vospominanii" [From my Memoirs] in *Pamiat'*, Paris, 1982.

In actuality, what was I accused of by the KGB? Why were they so angry with me? To answer this question I will have to digress somewhat.

I grew up in a family of intelligentsia Bolsheviks which was fully convinced that the concepts of humanism and communism were synonymous. During the days when Lenin and Zinoviev were hiding in the famous "lean-to," N.I. Bukharin found refuge in my parents' apartment. Naturally, I don't remember this, but I do remember Bukharin's rare visits in the 20's and the beginning of the 30's. They were always important to my parents. Humanism, elevated moral principles, and friendship with Bukharin—in that order but not without a shade of deference—did not later hinder my father along with everyone else, though not so forcefully, from being indignant at the vile crimes of Bukharin as well as other heroes (or victims) of "The Great Purges." My mother, a sweet and selfless woman, admired Stalin's courage and wisdom. She had forgotten how in 1928 or 1929, after a routine visit by Bukharin, she let fall a phrase in the presence of us boys: "If that is so, then Nikolai Ivanovich is undoubtedly right: *he* is a paranoiac." It was completely clear from the context of whom she was speaking.

These contradictions were forming in the sub-conscious rather than in the conscious. "The Great Purges" elicited a morbid curiosity and a desire to understand what psychological motives induced Lenin's comrades-in-arms to take up counterrevolution and betrayal. The study of party congresses, the works of Bukharin (miraculously preserved in our home, though later destroyed), and then, after the war, Rosa Luxemburg, Kautsky and Bernstein, led to the formation of views which later, fully coincided with Dubcek's program, encompassing the total spirit of the "Prague Spring." I was not the only one to undergo a shift based on various phases of the party line. But we were living in an age of the Great Silence when open servility in science or art was labeled civic consciousness. Any pronouncement which required real civic courage and was supported by quotations from the classics of Marxism-Leninism in an adequate manner almost invariably ended with "serious unpleasantness."

Realistically, nothing of essence changed later, other than that the "unpleasantness" became less catastrophic.

At about 8:00 AM on September 30, I was taken to a building in the political prison where I was "welcomed" by the MVD [Ministry of Internal Affairs]. As at my arrest, I was taken to a neighboring windowless room. One of the guards told me to undress, squat, bend over, spread, while another, meanwhile, carefully examined the contents of my pockets.

"And what is this?"

"The accusation and notes on my case."

"That's not allowed."

"What do you mean, not allowed? You're taking me to court."

I declared that if my papers were taken away from me, I would not go to court.

"You'll go,"—and the handcuffs clinked in his hands. Luckily, the officer on duty came around and explained to the sergeant that I was right.

A prison "black mariah" stood in the yard. I must say that the soldiers of my escort unit—even though they were rotated daily—radically changed their attitude toward me after the first day. They brought me parcels, notes, cigarettes, and expressed their sympathy in many ways. When alone, and without informers around, they asked me many questions. On the way to court and back, they left a door open in the vehicle and I hungrily peered at the life of the city. I reveled in the beauty of Leningrad with an unexpected painful acuity.

The trial went on for five days. My request to subpoena the experts who labeled my unfinished works as being anti-Soviet was summarily dismissed. I asked that three well-known writers, Iu. P. German, V. F. Panova, and A. I. Panteleev, who could provide an objective analysis of my literary work, be called. This solicitation was also refused. Subsequently, everything flowed within the predetermined channel. With minor exceptions, all witnesses repeated what they had said at the preliminary inquest.

I began my testimony poorly, declaring that I recognized the objective harm of many of my pronouncements. But I could not have or did not have any "desire" or "intent" to "weaken the Soviet State." If I had been intent on an anti-Soviet line, I would have been secretive to the maximum. Furthermore, I assumed that the decrees of the Twentieth Party Congress signified a return to Leninist norms of democracy. That was why I had spoken openly regarding those deficiencies which impeded the normal development of our society, specifically in literature. I was trained as an intelligence officer and knew well the techniques of counter-espionage. I knew that my mail was being read, that the phone was tapped, and via an anonymous letter, that my apartment was bugged.

"What kind of listening devices?" examined the judge.

"What form of bugging?" roared the prosecutor.

"What are you talking about," screamed the female attorney, grabbing her head.

"I'm only speaking of the letter which I received." I continued: "The charges against me, with reference to the witness, Pavlovskii, state that 'in the Writer's Union everyone knew of Uspenskii's anti-Soviet feelings.' But even the tendentious characterization of me sent by this very same union does not contain this assertion. This fact was not confirmed by a single witness. All this speaks of the tendentiousness of the investigation which rejected testimony favorable to me. What anti-Soviet element was there in my pronouncements concerning the necessity of greater freedom in literature? Lenin and Gorky spoke of this as did even Stalin in his famous letter to Bel'-Belotserkovskii."

I also spoke of collective farms and the right to leave them, of the necessity of a free market, and of workers' councils in factories and enterprises. Why can't we introduce this type of experiment at one or two of our factories so we can verify the experiences of Yugoslavia which is, as Khrushchev recently announced, a fully socialist country. I also spoke of a two party system; such an arrangement had already existed under Soviet rule.

Then Gorbenko, the city's assistant prosecutor, with scholarly accuracy, traced my long-term anti-Soviet convictions. He evaluated my criminal activity as being worth seven years of incarceration.

Otliagova, the defense attorney, gave an excellent speech and asked that a punishment be chosen which did not entail loss of freedom. She was applauded.

I said something very brief in my last remarks. By this point nervous tension had become so overwhelming that I simply do not remember my own words.

Finally, on October 3, at about seven in the evening, the verdict was finalized. I was led via stairs, corridors, and connecting passageways to the main hall on the first floor complete with marble fireplace and columns. Through the mirror-like windows I could see the engineers' union building and the gold and red leaves of maple trees.

S.E. Solov'ev, chair of the Leningrad Municipal Court (and currently Leningrad's chief prosecutor), holding sheets of paper in hand—the verdict—looked in my direction. His calmness, his irony during the course of the proceedings seemed to be saying: "What is all the fuss about, brothers? What nonsense are you speaking? Everything has been decided long ago. And not even by me . . ."

"In the name of the Russian Soviet Federal . . ."

He suddenly stopped and looked at the door. Soundlessly, bending slightly as if somebody would suddenly shoot at them, Joseph Brodsky and Anatolii Naiman were stealing into the hall [a brave act, considering the era].

"What is it you want here?" asked Solov'ev just as calmly as he had spoken of everything prior. "Were you summoned?"

"No, but we . . ." began Brodsky.

"Leave here."

"In the name of the Russian Soviet Federal Socialist . . ."

. . . I came to my senses out of the blessed, soothing darkness. I was lying on the floor between the benches. One of the guards was sticking a vial of ammonia into my nose (what foresight!). I had lost consciousness. A weakling, egghead intellectual, in the words of the great leader.

I felt hurt and ashamed, the more so in that I had not yet heard what they had decided. Perhaps . . .

"In the name of the Russian Soviet . . ." began Solov'ev for the third time. Grabbing onto the railing and trying to look as calm as possible, I listened attentively. No, old buddy, the preamble bodes nothing good . . .

". . . to be deprived of freedom for five years." A strange buzz was heard in the hall. It was Pavlovskii fainting. This time Solov'ev did not stop and continued in the same even voice. "The sentence is to commence from . . ."

"You were nailed with a good one," said one of the soldiers sitting across from me on a bench in the black mariah as I was being driven "home."

"I've been serving here three years, seen a lot go through here, all kinds of low-life, but nothing like this!" added a second.

"After all, they don't imprison anyone for such stuff these days," the first one said, shaking his head.

Chapter Thirty-One

Iurii Krotkov, The KGB in Action

Krotkov's colorful narrative moves one to think of a film plot. KGB secrets, sex and spying, blackmail, compromising a foreign ambassador, a picturesque cast of characters. It is easy to lose sight of the pernicious intent of these activities. The KGB did have clear purpose and a defined goal. Krotkov's story is punctuated by remarkably cogent and revealing observations. He speaks of an occasional desire to forget where he was, what he was doing, to forget politics and ideology, all the reasons for the task at hand.

Taken from Iurii Krotkov, "KGB v deistvii" [The KGB in Action]. New York: *The New Review,* No.111, June, 1973.

The painstaking preparatory work began anew. For Kunavin it was the labor of Sisyphus. First he met with Georgii Mdivani, one of the leading Soviet playwrights and screenwriters (a one-hundred-percent "patriot," a pillar of the Soviet establishment). I personally knew him quite well and had included him on the list, certain that *this* one would let himself be "co-opted" easily and even eagerly. I wasn't mistaken. Kunavin had a conversation with him on the subject, and after that Zhorzh [diminutive for Georgii] came to be at my disposal. It's interesting that, while moving in the same artistic circles, having taken up the same craft of producing party plays and screenplays, he and I never touched on our other "personae" in private conversations. A strict line of demarcation separated the two realms.

Zhorzh had a wife, Taisiia Savva, formerly a famous artist of the popular stage (her act was called "artistic whistling"—that is, she whistled). In my youth, I must confess, I was in love with her. But by now she was already past her prime and had gone into retirement, though she remained an endearing conversationalist. Furthermore, she knew French reasonably well. Taichik

[Taisiia] had also been made a participant. And Kunavin had the same conversation with Nadia Cherednichenko and Larisa Kronberg-Sobolevskaia. They too agreed without objection to be "co-opted" as KGB workers, and became members of my team.

On the eve of the appointed day, Kunavin and I went to the Praga Restaurant to see the director, who had been made a direct subordinate of the KGB. In the director's office, with the doors closed, we discussed all practical concerns. He assigned two waiters to us, also KGB subordinates, and gave us the best private room in the restaurant, the "Rotonda," specially equipped for our use.

Kunavin's assistants brought in a new little Grundig tape recorder and some jazz recordings. (It's amusing to note that this tape recorder was owned by one of Kunavin's co-workers by the name of Enver, who had not long before returned from abroad, working in the KGB First Sector, and had, of course, stocked up well. He begged me to assure him that I would be the only one to turn the tape recorder on and off, to make sure it wouldn't get broken.)

Kunavin spread out his agents, blond men with tousled hair sporting identical dark blue suits, on all floors of the restaurant. He himself, in a new dark blue suit paced up and down the fourth-floor corridor, where the Rotonda was located. The table was set for a tsar. The entire operation at the Praga Restaurant most likely ran the KGB around 1000 rubles in pre-reform currency. After all, there were ten people present: Mdivani and his wife, Lida, Nadia, Lora (Larisa), myself, along with two French couples, De Jean and Gerard.

I met our guests below in the restaurant lobby by the Vorovsky Street entrance and took the elevator to the fourth floor with them.

The evening went superbly. Our rapport with the ambassador himself was firmly established. New people entered the game. Maurice, of course turned his attention to the three Russian beauties: Khovanskaia, Cherednichenko, and Kronberg-Sobolevskaia. He began to treat me with marked goodwill. As for Marcel Gerard, he emulated his boss in every respect. It was clear that Marcel was Maurice's protégé. (I later learned from Vera Ivanovna that they were somehow distantly related). In any case, the advisor of cultural affairs wrote down our home telephone numbers, invited everyone to come see him at the embassy, and in every way exhibited a favorable disposition.

At first impression (and even afterwards), Marcel Gerard appeared to me to be a person agreeable in all respects, though spiritually limited, a civil servant. I know that he even wrote a book about the USSR and furnished it with a multitude of photographs. But I'm certain that, while having spent several years in the Soviet Union, Marcel saw only the superficial, that which was put on for show, and was never able to penetrate the life of our people—and perhaps never even tried. The blinders of the embassy careerist and of the well-to-do French bourgeois prevented him.

The evening in the Rotonda, as I've said before, went splendidly and brought me closer to the ambassador. Maurice acted the part of the worldly playboy easily and naturally. He flirted with the ladies, danced with them, and was gallant and witty. I should also mention that the ambassador had a sense of humor, though that humor was sometimes a little crude and always contained sexual overtones. During his anecdotes the ladies had to modestly lower their eyes, and Marie-Claire, knowing her husband's weakness, usually tried to interrupt him or loudly and deliberately laughed in the risqué places, in order to drown out certain words with her laughter. But Maurice reached his goal by repeating them several times, his eyes narrowing and becoming two tiny slits. His cheeks became rounder, and he laughed at his own jokes soundlessly, only with his lips.

The *tamada*—that is, the master of ceremonies—was, of course, Zhorzh Mdivani, a Georgian, merry and grandiloquent. He masterfully made the toasts: political, ideological, patriotic, lyrical, and so on. We conversed in three languages: Russian, French, and English. And Maurice, Marie-Claire, and Marcel Gerard began to use their Russian. Upon parting, Maurice invited us all to the embassy for dinner. This was exactly what Gribanov had been after.

After we left, Kunavin's agents filtered into the Rotonda, as he told me afterwards. Lora Kronberg-Sobolevskaia stayed behind with them. After all, someone had to finish up the food and (more importantly) the drink. And the vodka, cognac, and wine were more than plentiful. The revelry of the "plebeians" went on until dawn, so riotously that one of the agents, either Lora, or the "waiter" had his watch lifted. In the end, Kunavin had to deal with this scandalous affair.

At the meeting at the Rotonda I had personally become convinced that the ambassador had an Achilles' heel, and that heel was the opposite sex. Nevertheless, as I mentioned in my report, that evening Maurice did not show a specific preference for any one of our three young ladies. He was, so to speak, equally disposed towards all of them. The KGB offered him a choice: take one, don't be shy, but apparently had had decided not to hurry. My job was to connect the ambassador with the lady he would "point to," and facilitate his liaison with her, taking into account all of the difficulties connected with his high position, his wife's presence, and the general Soviet conditions. Of course, Marie-Claire certainly complicated the matter: she wasn't especially jealous, but she tried to keep her husband from making all sorts of mistakes. I think that she even warned him about this—in fact, I think that this was precisely true, since both Kunavin and Vera Ivanovna were not particularly enamored of Marie-Claire at the time.

Actually, as I've already noted, Vera Ivanovna existed for the purpose of distracting Mashenka [Russ. diminutive for Marie] from Maurice. This was her number-one duty. Besides, I remember that once Marie-Claire asked me offhandedly whether I knew Vera Ivanovna Gorbunova, an interpreter from the Ministry of Culture. Having been warned by Kunavin about the possibility of such a question, I answered in the affirmative.

It was at that time that Vera Ivanovna became Marie-Claire's "close" friend. As a result, she often had to "go out and have fun" with Marie-Claire. She was a KGB major in the Lubianka by day, and the wife of a Soviet party boss by night. However, there were moments when Vera Ivanovna would tire of Marie-Claire, especially in the winter. The Frenchwoman was an unstoppable cross-country skier, and Vera Ivanovna, a full-figured woman, would wear herself out trying to keep up. And so, almost every ski outing ended badly for Vera Ivanovna: she would come down with a cold, while Marie-Claire felt wonderful.

Finally, the night of the dinner at the French Embassy arrived—the first dinner party of many to follow.

We were already embracing each other as intimate friends. We enjoyed ourselves noisily in the luxurious halls of that beautiful residence in the *Russe* style on the Iakimanka [in the 1960's, Dmitrova Street]. We ate the famed French onion soup (the very same soup eaten by Louis XIV!) and Parisian partridge, and drank martinis, champagne, and burgundy. I was enchanted by the scarlet roses on the dinner table, fresh every day. According to Marie-Claire, the Air France crews brought in roses from Paris every day for De Jean. It was splendid! Everything in the residence was elegant and attractive, but at the same time simple and cozy. And what wonderful music we listened to, sitting in the living room. Marie-Claire had an excellent record collection.

Soviet freaks of nature that we were, we all felt the same thing at different times, I think: we all felt happy there and wanted our lives to go on in the same environment, having forgotten, of course, for the time being, about politics and ideology, and, first and foremost, who we were and what we were doing there. In reality we were all General Gribanov's puppets—all of us. Well, it's possible that Taisiia Savva didn't know the whole story; maybe Zhorzh didn't disclose to her his conversation with Kunavin in the Hotel Moscow. Maybe she could only guess what was going on.

And again I could report to Kunavin that the dinner had been held in the ceremonial hall of the embassy, I could list the dishes, and the wines, but I couldn't report to my boss that Maurice had set his sights on Cherednichenko, Kronberg-Sobolevskaia, or Lidiia Khovanskaia (the preferred choice being the last). Maurice was clearly waiting for something. But what?

Here I must digress a little. I don't remember exactly whether this happened at the first dinner party or later, but we were sitting at the table, drinking to the health of the new head of the French government, the president of France,

General de Gaulle. This was a special cause for celebration for the ambassador. It was, incidentally, no less a cause for celebration for Gribanov. I found out from Kunavin and Vera Ivanovna that after General de Gaulle's rise to power, De Jean's position became stronger and he could hope to become the French Minister of Foreign Affairs, since he had already served as the Commissioner of Foreign Affairs in de Gaulle's wartime government-in-exile in London. The KGB considered the close personal relationship between De Jean and de Gaulle to be important. I don't know how closely that corresponded with the truth. In any case, the ante had been raised. Gribanov's plan grew fantastically in size, although the risk of the entire operation grew as well. However, in this case behind the KGB stood none other than Nikita Khrushchev.

I will note that according to my observations, neither De Jean nor Marie-Claire took advantage of their special relationship with the new French president. Their tact never failed them. Only once when they showed us the elegantly decorated guest rooms, located at the back of the embassy, did they say that were General de Gaulle to visit Moscow, he would stay there.

But back to the operation.

Suddenly, coincidence came into play. An exhibition of the Georgian artist Lado Gudiiashvili opened at the Kuznetskii Most. I knew the artist well, since he was a friend of my father, and used to visit us in Tbilisi. I liked his work, which was distinguished by its unique qualities: a rare blend of Western modernism with something distinctly Georgian. Lado was no follower of socialist realism; he had studied in Paris in his youth, and upon his return to the already-Soviet Georgia fell into disfavor, and was the subject of constant criticism by party officials, even though he was very popular among the larger circles of the intelligentsia. Even Mdivani liked him, despite the fact that an abyss separated their artistic principles.

The Lado Gudiiashvili exhibit was very quickly closed since, according to our ideologues, it caused an "unhealthy" interest on the part of Muscovites, its occurrence during the last stage of the "Thaw" notwithstanding.

It was Zhorzh, in fact, who gave me the idea to invite De Jean and Gerard to this exhibit. Kunavin immediately seized upon this suggestion. Gribanov liked it as well. At that time Vera Ivanovna took Marie-Claire to Leningrad, I think. The ambassador was alone. We decided that, in addition to myself and Mdivani, Lidiia Khovanskaia would accompany him as his interpreter to the exhibition of Gudiiashvili's works.

I called Maurice. He agreed immediately and arrived at the exhibit hall at the designated hour, accompanied by Marcel Gerard. The ambassador arrived in his Chevrolet with the French flag, and Gerard drove his own Citroen.

This was truly a cause for celebration for the old and distinguished master. After all, his exhibit was visited by none other than the ambassador of France,

Gudiiashvili's beloved France, the country where he spent, perhaps, the best years of his youth. Lado thanked Zhorzh and me profusely for arranging this. Oh, if he only knew that it was the KGB that had arranged this, and for what purpose it had been arranged!

Maurice and Gerard spent about an hour and a half at the exhibition. Lado himself provided commentary in French. Sometimes Lidiia Khovanskaia would put in a word or two. Lado came close to tears when the French ambassador and the cultural advisor left comments of exalted praise in the guestbook.

Seeing the Frenchmen off, I stepped onto the narrow, noisy Kuznetskii Most [actually a street in Moscow's historic district]. Lidiia came out of the exhibit hall with me, and right near Maurice's car, she smiled very sweetly and asked De Jean to give her a ride home. And this was the entire *raison d'être* for the operation of visiting Gudiiashvili's exhibit. This alone. It goes without saying that Maurice gallantly opened the door of the Chevrolet for Lida, and behind the steering wheel was "our" Boris. We said good-bye. De Jean left to take Khovanskaia home.

And what came next?

If Maurice had been the ambassador in England or Brazil, then, dear reader, what follows would hardly interest you, and this book would never have seen the light of day. If he had lived in England or Brazil, the question of his safety would never have arisen. But, alas, De Jean was the ambassador to the USSR—and this changed everything.

By Kunavin's account, and later, Khovanskaia's, this is what transpired: the ambassador took Lida home, to a house on Vnukovskii Road—or, more precisely, the corner house where the road began. They had to enter the noisy courtyard of a newly constructed Moscow building. Lida, of course, invited the ambassador to come up to her apartment for a cup of coffee. The apartment happened to be empty—the children were out. And why not visit the house of a common Soviet woman? That is very likely what Maurice thought. Or maybe he thought differently. In any case, Khovanskaia was not common. If only the common people lived the way she did!

All in all, Boris waited about two hours in the car. During that time, Lida became De Jean's lover.

It was a done deal. One could suppose that Gribanov was already gleefully rubbing his hands together. The quarry was in the bag.

Lida met Maurice several more times. He would come to visit the common Soviet woman while the children were at school. Their liaison became stronger. Both played the part of lover very well, and did not give themselves away with a single look or gesture when all of us, including Marie-Claire, would wind up spending time together, eating French onion soup. Lida didn't hide it from me, seeing me as a "superior." She even told me that the ambassador was pretty good as a lover, and that being with him was pleasant and fun.

Naturally, Cherednichenko and Kronberg-Sobolevskaia receded into the background. Everything had been planned down to the last detail. Khovanskaia had been chosen. But two or three weeks later everything suddenly changed. Why? Because the little Napoleon from the Lubianka realized that he had made a mistake. He'd planned and planned, but had missed the "elephant" right in front of him. And Khovanskaia had to be retired the same way that Valia and Rita (Zoia) had been retired previously. Removing her from the stage entirely would have been awkward, and would have been noticed by the ambassador, and might even have irritated him. Using different pretences, she simply began to meet Maurice less and less frequently as a common Soviet woman—that is, alone. And so why did Gribanov discontinue Khovanskaia? What was his oversight?

I can only say the following regarding this matter: the operation thought up by Oleg Mikhailovich was hindered by the fact that Khovanskaia's first husband, a diplomat by profession, had worked for several years in Paris and was, of course, very well-known. Khovanskaia had left him, as I wrote earlier, but she had had children with him. Now he served in the Ministry of Foreign Affairs where he held an important position. Incidentally, several years afterwards Khovanskaia's daughter married the son of Podtserob, the general secretary of the Ministry of Foreign Affairs and a former aide to Molotov. All of this complicated the game and increased the risks. What had Gribanov been thinking of when planning this operation? Why had he included Lida if she was "defective?" Or perhaps there had been a mistake, but since it had been committed by those from the higher echelons, everyone pretended that everything was just fine. Perhaps while Gribanov was consulting with Serov, Mironov, or even Khrushchev himself, it had been decided not to use Khovanskaia for the ultimate set-up. It's possible that Gribanov, considering the psychological circumstances, decided to lull De Jean into a false sense of security with a series of these love intrigues (Valia, Rita, Lida) in order to deliver the final blow unexpectedly.

Whether or not this was the case, I had to start over. Kunavin now gave the order to offer either Nadia Cherednichenko or Lora Kronberg-Sobolevskaia to De Jean.

I'd known Lora for a long time. As I've already noted, my cousin, a chemistry professor, met her by chance, and they had an affair. He certainly loved her and she, perhaps, loved him as well, though she always made him do her bidding. Lora was a perfect bohemian, flighty and willful. But she had many gifts. She was a great actress, an excellent chess player, a wonderful card player, a good mathematician, and a poet as well. After breaking up with my cousin she got together with the screenwriter Pomeshchikov, destroyed his life by breaking up his family, left Pomeshchikov, got together with some boxer, and in the interludes there were different actors, directors, cameramen, screenwriters, and so on. Lora became renowned within our circles for her temperament.

But, she was completely unsuited to everyday life. She owned nothing but the clothes on her back. Her parents and brother lived in Podolsk, and she would rent tiny closet-rooms in different areas of Moscow, and she always had difficulty with her residency permit. Moreover, Lora was careless in her appearance. When we went to receptions at the embassy, I had to check the way she was dressed beforehand.

When Lora entered the game, she was also in the process of entering into yet another affair with the old Soviet film director Feinzimmer. She would meet him in her hole-in-the-wall rooms. Often, when I came to get her, I would encounter Feinzimmer in her apartment, and I would take her away, despite his presence. In short, Lora Kronberg-Sobolevskaia was an unusual creature and I, for one, was constantly telling Kunavin that it was *her* we had to use.

There were many, very many receptions of every sort at the French Embassy and many private meetings with Maurice and Marie-Claire. I became such a close friend that they even invited me to lunches and dinners held for representatives of trade delegations, financiers, technical experts, and other guests from France. It goes without saying that I would be there when actors, directors, producers, artists, musicians, and others came to visit. The ambassador sometimes invited Georgii Mdivani as well. It was easier with Zhorzh there. After all, every visit to the embassy was a nerve-wracking affair, since each time we had to make arrangements with Kunavin, set specific goals for the meeting, and write up post-meeting reports. (I recall, for example, meetings with the screenwriter Spaak, with the film actor Jean Maret, with the film producer Mnushkin.)

But one time, on Kunavin's orders, I invited De Jean on a trip to the countryside, and to dinner afterwards at the Volna Restaurant at the Khimki Riverport. It had been decided that on that night Lora would show active interest in Maurice and set up a date with him. This had been discussed with Kunavin in my presence at the Hotel Moscow. Lora was very enthusiastic. It fell to me to create the necessary atmosphere and to assist her in every possible way.

We had arranged it so that right outside the French Embassy Marie-Claire got into our car, a large ZIM, the state luxury car, which, according to our cover story, I had borrowed from the Ministry of Culture. Lora got into De Jean's car with the little flag, and they rode together the whole way—she and

Maurice. Zhorzh Mdivani and Taichik were with us and, I think, Cherednichenko.

We set off for the Planernyi Region . . .

Somewhere at the edge of the forest we got out of our cars, walked around, and took a lot of pictures. At around eight o'clock, we arrived at the restaurant, where a table had been reserved for us in advance. Despite Kunavin's efforts, a small mishap occurred right at the beginning of the evening. It turned out that there were foreign journalists, Americans, in the dining area, and among them, if my memory serves me right, was the wife of the American journalist Stevens (as Kunavin later told me), who, of course, recognized Maurice De Jean and Marie-Claire and watched us intently throughout the entire meal.

While dancing was going on, I saw that Lora, who had drunk a fair amount, was pressing herself up against the ambassador. And he was smiling and whispering something in her ear. Marie-Claire either didn't notice, or pretended not to notice. Lora was really letting herself go that night. When I danced with her, she pressed herself up against me, too. I whispered in her ear, "I'm not the ambassador, babe."

After the evening was over and we had said good-bye to the De Jeans, I took Lora home by taxi. But all of a sudden she got stubborn and said that she wanted to come spend the night at my place, that she been attracted to me for a long time, and that she wasn't going to let this opportunity get away.

We arrived at my place, having bought champagne at the Praga Restaurant along the way. There Lora told me that Kunavin, speaking on authority for General Gribanov, had promised her, in the event of success, a room of her own in Moscow—no, not an apartment, but a *room*. But soon afterwards, she'd forgotten about Maurice and the room, and was remembering my cousin and her love for him with tears in her eyes. And then, no longer crying and having forgotten my cousin, she consoled herself with me. There was something pathological in all of this, for her as well as for me.

Soon afterwards Marie-Claire left for France. Summer came. Gribanov decided to force events.

I was given a special, top-secret note from the chairman of the KGB, General Serov, to the USSR State Planning Committee, which allowed me to purchase a new Volga automobile, using my own money, through the intercession of the Ministry of Trade. This was an unheard-of stroke of luck. I felt like a little boy on his birthday. After all, in those years only the very highly placed, the chosen ones, could buy a car this way. Mere mortals had to stay on a waiting list for several years, or spend 75,000 rubles buying a Volga on the black market, nearly risking their lives in the process. My Volga was intended for the Maurice De Jean operation. Gribanov's chief assistant, Vasily

Stepanovich, congratulated me over the phone, saying, "Well, now you're fully armed. Go for it!" Kunavin, an old automobile enthusiast, some other KGB administrator, and I went to buy a Volga at the only automobile dealership in Moscow, on Bakuninskii Street. Kunavin said that this was a big present for me, and I agreed, even though I was paying 40,000 rubles of my own money for this present.

Finally we approached the final stage of the Lora Kronberg-Sobolevskaia epic. In the end, Gribanov wasn't fully certain of Lora (or perhaps that was simply his style—having doubles and back-ups), and that's why one more girl was brought into the operation. This was Alla Golubova (code name: Petrova), a beautiful young woman who now works for Intourist. I was to introduce her to Maurice as a straw widow—that is, as the wife of a sailor always out at sea who rarely returned to Moscow. According to the cover story, Alla had a separate apartment on the Arbat in building #41, apartment #14. In actuality, it was an apartment owned by the KGB where I would often meet with lower-ranking agents. Alla really lived with her aunt's family, and didn't even have her own room.

Kunavin brought us together in advance at that same ill-starred Moscow Hotel, where we discussed our plan of action, went over the history of our acquaintance, details of Alla's biography, etc. Then I called up Maurice at the embassy and said that I'd like to invite him out for a picnic, especially since before she left for France Marie-Claire had asked me not to abandon her husband, to entertain him from time to time. Maurice agreed. I said that Larisa and another friend of mine were coming.

The night before, Kunavin and I went to the village of Kriukovo, within a forty-kilometer radius of Moscow, where the writer Georgii Briantsev and his wife Tonia had their dacha. [Foreigners were restricted to this 40km. radius.] In the past he had been a big man in the KGB and the Ministry of State Security; his wife had also worked for the KGB.

Someone at the Lubianka called Briantsev beforehand. He met us cordially and readily agreed to help. We revealed some of our cards to him and acquainted Tonia with what was going on. Kunavin's assistants brought fresh food, drinks, and fruit right away. I made sure I remembered the directions, in order not to get lost the next day.

The day after, Lora, Alla, and I drove my new Volga up to the French Embassy. Guarding the Embassy were three militiamen, employees of the KGB First Sector who sullenly looked us over, even though they had been apprised of our coming, as usual. The Chevrolet sat near the entrance, with Boris behind the wheel. De Jean came out exactly at the pre-arranged time. I offered him a ride in my new Volga, but he preferred his Chevrolet. Then we decided that Lora would go with him, and she got into his car. We set off. Later Boris said that De Jean got a little nervous when he noticed we were approaching the 40-kilometer mark, since diplomats were forbidden to cross it, but it was then that we turned off onto a side road and soon reached our destination.

We left our cars in the clearing and walked to Briantsev's dacha, which was about 300 meters away. We went in pairs. Maurice was with Lora, and I was with Alla. I was already pretending that Alla was my girl, since I saw whom Maurice clearly preferred.

At Briantsev's well-appointed, comfortable dacha, we had dinner, and drank quite a bit. Briantsev, a short, stocky man with sharply defined features, a little crude in conversation, delivered several completely obscene jokes. But Maurice wasn't embarrassed in the least.

After a short walk and a game of catch, we left for Moscow while it was still light. (Maurice, of course, invited the Briantsevs to visit him, but they never took him up on his offer.) We said good-bye at the center of town. I took Alla home, and Maurice took Lora home.

Home?

Yes, since by that time an apartment had been set up for her in building #2/4 on Ananiev Lane. Her apartment was on the first floor, and next to it on the same level, and with an entrance on the same landing, was a different KGB apartment—the same arrangement as on the Arbat. This system of paired apartments was intended for special operations.

The furnishings in the apartment prepared for Lora were okay—not luxurious, but not cheap, of course. The fact of the matter is that, according to the cover story, Lora's husband was a geologist, who spent most of the year on faraway expeditions. Could Maurice check up on this? No. And why would he want to check up on something that was so convenient, from his standpoint? Lora had no children (both in real life and according to the cover story), nor did she have any relatives. She lived all alone, poor soul.

And so, Maurice took Lora to Ananiev Lane. She, like Lida Khovanskaia before her, asked the ambassador in for a cup of coffee, and also to see how a common Soviet movie star lived. (Alas, not at all the way Brigitte Bardot lives.) Maurice agreed. In these cases he was amazingly amenable. The ambassador did not spend a long time there. The driver waited in the car for half an hour. And during that time nothing happened between Lora and De Jean.

A few days later, Maurice invited us over for breakfast. Everything was orderly and elegant. Breakfast was served in the reception hall, in the right corner near the window. For an hour-and-a-half we lived among antique tapestries and furniture worthy of a museum.

Later there came another invitation to the Briantsevs'—not to Kriukovo, but to their Moscow apartment, which was in the Writers Building, on Cherniakhovskii Street. De Jean accepted the invitation at first, but the next day I received a call at home from his interpreter, who asked to move the date of the meeting. Oh, what a fright the call from the French ambassador caused in my communal apartment! I wasn't at home. When I returned, my neighbor, Valentina Zevakina, told me with wide-open and clearly frightened eyes that I had received a call from the French Embassy, from the ambassador himself, and that they had requested that I call the embassy immediately.

The second meeting at the Briantsevs', officially a dinner, was only an intermediary step necessary to put Lora and Maurice on a more intimate footing, to bring them closer together smoothly and naturally.

When we left the Briantsevs' and said good-bye, Maurice got into his car and left alone. Alla set out on foot, since she lived quite close. Lora jumped into my Volga, and ordered me to rush at top speed to Ananiev Lane. On the way Lora told me that De Jean would be visiting her in an hour, and that they had arranged this inconspicuously at dinner (this was what these dinners were for!), and that she didn't know what to do, since this hadn't been pre-arranged with Kunavin. When we arrived at the apartment on Ananiev Lane, we called every KGB number we knew: Kunavin, Vera Ivanovna, Melkumov, and even Gribanov himself—that is, his office. Imagine, dear reader, none answered their telephones, or the secretaries didn't know where their bosses were. This happens sometimes, even in the KGB.

We were forced to make an independent decision, which, of course, is not recommended in KGB practice.

Lora said, "To be or not to be?"

I said, "Almost Hamlet."

She said, "It's funny. This is the first time in my life when *it* depends not on myself, but on the KGB."

I said, "Babe, you gotta fall."

And Carthage fell.

The affair between Lora and Maurice continued afterwards. She got ahead of General Gribanov's schedule. He had to rework everything on the fly. It was obvious that Lora had captivated the ambassador; he was taken with her. And to be snared by her . . .

Getting ready for the dénouement, Gribanov ordered her to hold off. De Jean would call Lora at home, but she wouldn't answer. And the meetings with Khovanskaia had also ceased. The poor ambassador remained without a woman's attentions. They had barely given him a taste, and all of a sudden—well, there you go. But the predatory wolf from the KGB knew his business. He had planned precisely, taking into account even such factors as physiology.

During this short interlude, the necessary organizational tasks were completed. The first thing Gribanov did was to call Kunavin back from a vacation that had started several days beforehand. From Kazan he summoned Misha, a KGB operative and a really big bruiser ready for anything. I had heard that he was used regularly in these types of cases—that is, when decisiveness and brute force were called for. Lora's room on Ananiev Lane was wired; that is, there was a very sensitive microphone hidden somewhere, whose wires led to the apartment next door, where a short-wave radio transmitter and receiver were set up.

Gribanov himself decided to meet with Lora. This meeting took place in a private room at the Metropole Restaurant. Besides Oleg Mikhailovich, Melkumov, Kunavin, and Misha—and Lora, of course—were present. All of the tiniest details were planned. Kunavin told me about it later. Gribanov stated again that if everything went well, Lora would receive a room in Moscow. A room, not an apartment. The KGB men had a champagne toast. After Gribanov and Melkumov left, Lora remained in the company of Kunavin and Misha, in order to get to know Misha better—after all, he was her husband, the very enthusiastic geologist. This was the role he had to play at the crucial moment. And to help him, he had a friend, Kunavin—also a dedicated geologist. Melkumov met with me; we went over my part in the script.

And, finally, the fateful day arrived for Maurice De Jean.

I invited him out for a picnic again. He agreed when he found out that Lora and Alla would be there. (Alla was my "love interest"—that's how I presented her, in order to make everything clear.) We decided to have this picnic out in the open, somewhere in a forest clearing. At Lora's request, we drove in the direction of the Lenin Hills. Afterwards I found out that this was all planned at the dinner at the Metropole Restaurant. De Jean rode in the car driven not by Boris this time, but by a different chauffeur, and took some folding metal furniture—a table and chairs—a huge umbrella for protection from the sun, and a lot of snacks and alcoholic beverages. And in our car we were carrying those items prepared by Kunavin's agents.

It was like this: Alla and I went ahead in my Volga, and Maurice and Lora followed in the Chevrolet. Twenty kilometers outside of Moscow, the Chevrolet unexpectedly pulled ahead of us, and soon turned off the road into a clearing, and proceeded to go deeper into the forest. I realized that Lora knew this place, and that we were going to set up things right there. (Later she told me that that was her "secret" place, where she met with my cousin and Pomeshchikov and other lovers.) And the grove really did turn out to be charming: a little ravine, a brook, and a sown field already thick with rye.

We sat down in the shade, made ourselves comfortable, and had a bit to eat and drink. The chauffeur had a bit to eat as well, and then went for a long walk. When we'd left Moscow and got into the country road, I'd noticed a GAZ-64 [a jeep] with an enclosed rear, which followed us constantly at a distance. Near the turn-off from the main road, I noticed another car, a Pobeda.

I hadn't been warned about this. I found out some of the technical details of the operation post factum, but certain professional secrets were so obvious that I had caught on to them by myself. But Lora, I think, had known about these cars—that is, she had known that we would be monitored for control and to prevent any sort of unforeseen occurrences.

Now we had one of those occurrences. I don't think that this was arranged with Gribanov in advance. What happened was that a couple of hours later, a light gray Volga appeared in the forest grove, about 100 meters away from us. The half-drunk Lora whispered to me that her Feinzimmer had arrived. (Yes, I had heard previously that he had recently bought a Volga, after having spent several years on the waiting list.) Lora was right. It was Feinzimmer. Paying us no attention, he got out of his car, got undressed down to his underwear, opened the hood of his car, and began to fiddle with the engine. Of course, he noticed Lora among us, but he pretended that he didn't see her.

De Jean realized that the arrival of this unknown person signified something to Lora, and, watching Lora, he realized that she was not wholly indifferent towards this person. Familiar with the mores of movie actors, he became jealous, naturally, even though he was showing it in a jocular manner. And Lora enflamed his jealousy. I directed her in a whisper to go down into the ravine and followed after her, while Alla flirted with De Jean.

In the ravine I gave Lora a berating directive. I told her that she was wrecking Gribanov's operation, that she was introducing the element of anarchy and self-initiative into it. I asked her who gave her permission to tell Feinzimmer that she was going to be here, and not alone but with friends? She began to defend herself and answered that this was all purely an accident, and that she hadn't told Feinzimmer anything. However, I think she was lying. She had decided, with a woman's logic, to kill two birds. On the one hand, probably having had a fight with Feinzimmer, she was demonstrating her prowess as far as men were concerned through this encounter. On the other hand, she was really getting De Jean worked up. Lora herself was overly excited, and this was making me nervous. Maurice, however, was looking at her with desire. This was Lora's improvisation—an improvisation which, in the event of failure, would have cost her dearly. But right sides with the victors. Since she triumphed, everything was forgiven, and she was even praised for much that had been unexpected. (But I don't know how Lora explained this entire episode to Feinzimmer after she married him.)

And so we were having a picnic while Kunavin and Misha sat in the KGB apartment next to Lora's apartment, wearing clothes for an expedition, in waterproof hob-nailed boots, with backpacks and plywood suitcases, like real geologists, while Gribanov and Melkumov waited for news, hovering over the radio operator. Our picnic outing was being reported in great detail. After all, both vehicles, the GAZ-64 and the Pobeda, were equipped with radio transmitters.

It had been decided that we would return to Moscow at five o'clock. Melkumov had given me strict orders not to be late. I tried to hurry Lora along, but she dallied.

Finally, we set out on our return trip. (Feinzimmer left earlier, not having approached Lora after all.) Somewhere on the road I pulled ahead of a car in a no-passing zone. (I didn't have a KGB permit to avoid a license and registration check, since my Volga wasn't an operative car.) I was stopped by a highway patrolman. The Chevrolet pulled over behind me. This was immediately reported to Gribanov via radio. As Kunavin later told me, Gribanov cursed both me and the highway patrolman. But the latter, having verified my documents and glanced at the little French flag on the ambassador's car, quickly saluted and let me go on my way. As we were nearing Moscow we came up to a small and rather dirty lake. Lora suddenly decided to go for a swim, and asked the ambassador to stop the car. I noticed this in the rearview mirror and also stopped.

We walked up to the lake. I was hissing at Lora, recalling Melkumov's order, since we were already running late. She just laughed in response and did whatever she pleased. (We made sure the ambassador didn't hear us arguing, of course.) O, great is the power of woman! How right Lora was in everything, listening to her intuition and acting in accordance with some sixth sense. I was forced to follow her into the lake. Maurice and Alla didn't swim, and Lora didn't have a bathing suit. And so right in front of the ambassador's eyes, she began undressing and climbed into the water in just her slip, which immediately conformed to her body, and when she came out of the water, she looked not just naked, but naked twice over. She came out of the water several times and walked around on the shore looking like this. Poor Maurice!

Whenever we swam out from shore, I would hurry Lora as much as I could, reminding her of Melkumov's order to return to Moscow no later than five. She just waved me off.

At this time, according to Kunavin, Gribanov was sitting near the receiver, listening to the reports from the scene of the events. They told him about Lora's swimming. Gribanov couldn't contain himself any longer and called her a prostitute.

In half an hour the prostitute—or, better yet, the mermaid—got out of the water and somehow got dressed. We got into our cars and continued on to Moscow. We split up at the fork near the Danilov Market. The ambassador took Lora home. Along the way they arranged for him to come see her in forty minutes.

Upon returning to the embassy, Maurice changed and got a new chauffeur, for some reason. He took Boris, as if realizing that he was more dependable.

As soon as De Jean walked into Lora's apartment, she showed him a telegram lying around on the table, which she had "received" the day before from her "husband." The telegram said that he was arriving the next day. At the end it said, "Love, your Misha." (As might be easily guessed, this was a KGB forgery.)

And what followed would have been unbelievable even in the movies. Only in the Soviet Union, where the KGB was all-powerful, could this take place.

Lora and Maurice, naturally, having been left alone, gave way to human temptation.

Gribanov and Melkumov, pressing up against the speaker, or maybe wearing headphones, were listening to everything going on in the neighboring apartment. Perhaps one of them may have even envied De Jean. But they were waiting for the pre-arranged signal, the code word. Lora herself had come up with this word in the private booth at the restaurant at the Metropole. She had to say the word "Kiev" in some phrase. As soon as she said the word, Gribanov would give Kunavin and Misha the go-ahead. But Lora drew it out and out and out, all but frazzling the remnants of Gribanov's nerves of steel. And Kunavin and Misha got completely soaked in sweat in their geological expedition gear.

"Kiev!" Gribanov and Melkumov distinctly heard, "Kiev." Lora had clearly said, "Kiev. . . ."

Chapter Thirty-Two

Vladimir Azbel, Siberian Adversity

In the 1970's the Western press was filled with reports about the "refuseniks." These were Russian Jews who petitioned the Soviet government for exit visas, principally to Israel. Under fierce international scrutiny, the government acceded, and previously unimaginable numbers of refugees left the country. Vladimir Azbel's story is set within this period. His very relocation to Irkutsk in Siberia was a direct consequence of his family's filing papers to leave the USSR. Taken from Vladimir Azbel', "Dva goda v Sibiri" [Two Years in Siberia]. New York: *The New Review*, No. 116, September, 1974.

In 1972 I was completing the tenth grade of a secondary school in Moscow. During this time frame, our family submitted the required documents for moving abroad. Three months prior to final examinations, I had to leave school since presenting these documents to OVIR [The Department of Visas and Registration of Foreign Citizens] would have led to immediate expulsion. Now, having become a "refusenik," I had to decide where and how to continue my education. I began by submitting documentation to the division of external studies and took the final exams for the tenth grade. The next problem was more difficult—entry into an institute. I had long planned to enroll in a medical institute, but this was impossible in Moscow. Column five of the questionnaire impeded this [nationality]. Then, on the advice of relatives and acquaintances living in Siberia, in Irkutsk, I decided to enroll in the Irkutsk Medical Institute. Judging by accounts, there was not as much anti-Semitism there as there was in central Russia. This turned out to be true. Without thinking too long, I bought a plane ticket and after a seven-hour flight, I arrived at the capital of eastern Siberia—Irkutsk.

Irkutsk was the city of my birth. When I was one-and-a-half years old, my family moved to Moscow. We came to Irkutsk twice after that to visit our relatives. During these trips we saw Siberia almost in the way that foreign tourists coming to Lake Baikal see it. The beautiful embankments of the Angara River, several new buildings in the center of town, a trip to Baikal, the new city of Angarsk—all this left a good impression. Now, having been a resident of Irkutsk for two years, I observed other, seamier sides of Siberian life.

I had very many acquaintances in Irkutsk; thus I was able to observe the life of Siberian society. From the beginning it was noticeable that the inhabitants of Siberia differed from those of Russia's western provinces. It was surprising that no one expressed dissatisfaction with their lives. They considered that everything which occurred was in the scheme of things. Thus, for example, in Angarsk (forty kilometers from Irkutsk), the air was constantly poisoned by gases coming from the chemical plants. There were filtration systems, but they only operated during the week. Saturdays and Sundays were off days. The management went to their dachas. But the factories kept operating in order to fulfill the plans more quickly. The harmful gases were released bypassing the filters. This speeded the process but the people in the city choked. No residents spoke against this openly. Protests were heard only within circles of close friends and relatives. If the air was poisoned by gases, that meant that it was the way it had to be. The majority of the population was convinced of this. Generally speaking, very few people in the Soviet Union voiced their protests openly. The majority preferred to remain quiet. This was particularly noticeable in Siberia.

To this day people in Siberia live in the Stalinist atmosphere of terror before the national security organs. Siberians will never engage a foreigner in conversation and never mention their difficult life in the presence of a stranger.

An asphalt road leads from Irkutsk to Listvianichnyi Bay on Baikal, the part of the lake closest to the city. For forty years, only one boat has traversed Baikal. Even if people do reach distant spots on the lakeshore, only the local taiga dweller or hunter can live there. Therefore, the people of Irkutsk, living only fifty kilometers from the lake, go to the Black Sea for vacation even though in terms of beauty there is nothing comparable to Baikal. The mountain ranges and the taiga of Baikal remain as wild, remote, and unexplored as hundreds of years ago. I made it to places which civilization had not yet reached. There were remote Buriat settlements where people led a nomadic life of cattle-breeding and hunting. They spent months in the saddle returning to their own terrain only in winter.

I also spent some time in Siberian kolkhozes. Students who were not assigned to construction brigades in the summer were obligated to work on a kolkhoz. Beginning with this year, students were forcibly enrolled in construction gangs. Earlier, when the initial brigades were formed, students signed up willingly, since they could earn some money. Under the compulsory system, students working on the most demanding construction projects received less money than workers. Komsomol leaders announced that students were obligated to help the nation that year in achieving the goals of the five-year plan. Thus, the mandatory "third labor semester" was introduced. Nobody protested, even though many were unhappy. In the USSR students were quiet and cowed. They little resembled western students. Every student knew that it only took a criticism of some injustice on their part to be expelled from the Komsomol. (At the Irkutsk Medical Institute, expulsion from the Komsomol signified automatic expulsion from the institute. Thus, students did not even have a say about their vacations.)

Therefore, in September 1973, having advanced to my second year of studies, I was sent to a kolkhoz for a month. We left Irkutsk in an overcrowded train and traveled for twenty-four hours, and then another 100 kilometers north by vehicle. The place where we arrived was isolated. The taiga stretched for hundreds of kilometers in all directions and a dirt track led to the village. The village stretched along the banks of a rapid and broad river. We were settled in the gym of the village school. We all slept together without undressing, in our boots and padded jackets on roughly hewn plank beds. Everybody was given a dirty mattress, a pillow, and a thin blanket. Forget about sheets. It was cold at night. Water in the pails froze. For a whole month we were promised that the heat would be turned on, but it wasn't. The boiler was broken. The bath-house, where we could go once every ten days, was heated primitively (the smoke escaped through the windows). Students were given a daily ration of food which they prepared themselves. Few people owned cows in the village. The cows from the kolkhoz were sent to the slaughterhouse in the district center. So, in order to obtain meat, the cows had to be taken to a slaughterhouse more than 100 kilometers away, and the meat brought back. But the kolkhoz could not assign a vehicle for this purpose. The chairman decided that the students themselves should slaughter the cows. In this fashion, we advanced to a state of complete self-service.

During my first day at the kolkhoz I heard an unknown language being spoken in the village. It turned out that these were Chuvash people deported from the Volga. Later I met some Russians. These were exiles. Among them were laborers from Rostov-on-the-Don. I made acquaintance with one of them. He told me that when Khrushchev instituted his monetary reform in 1961, one of the Rostov factories announced a strike. The KGB searched out the organizers of whom my acquaintance was one. He received a ten-year prison sentence. After release in 1972, he was exiled. He was not allowed to leave the village. His family remained in Rostov-on-the-Don. They could not visit him for lack of money.

It turned out that there were exiles not just in this village but also in many others. Villagers frequently hid convicts who had escaped from the camps. Only the students worked the fields. The kolkhoz dwellers preferred to work on their own vegetable plots at this time. Our village was called Burkhun, which meant "residence of God" in Buriat, but this was far from a heavenly place. The poverty was staggering. One felt he had walked into the previous century. The homes were old, crooked, and unpainted. The roofs were grown over with moss. The yards were small and dirty. The street, which went the length of the village, was totally rutted and there were heaps of manure everywhere. The people were grim and came to life only at the stall where vodka, sticky dirty candy, and soap were sold. There was a store with humble wares: bottled kerosene, hunting boots, cologne, a doll with a fierce face, bread, and the ever-present vodka which was delivered regularly. Almost the whole male population was at the store each morning. By mid-day not a sober person could be seen, from the mailman to the drivers. The drivers and vehicles were sent from town to the kolkhozes to help in harvesting. Every evening the drunken drivers came to the club, the only place of entertainment and relaxation, in order to fight with the villagers or the students. The only entertainment was films which were shown nightly in the club. But they were all old ones, some twenty years old or so. New films were rare, and there were never any foreign films.

Every morning we were taken out to the fields. The kolkhoz fields stretched for many kilometers but nobody worked them other than our group. Half of the harvest was left in the fields. Potatoes, turnips, carrots, and beets froze in the ground. There was a fair amount of mechanical equipment on the kolkhoz but it was all broken. Machinery, tractors, and combines were left under the open skies and were rusting away. The kolkhoz was served by two truck farming operations in town. Some trucks brought potatoes from the fields to the warehouse, others from the warehouse to town. One group of students in the field gathered potatoes in buckets and filled a dump truck which then went to the warehouse. The potatoes were dumped right on the ground, and another group of students, again using buckets, would load a truck which then went to town. As was later explained to us, the town and the trucking operation could not agree on trucks going directly to town.

Once, the kolkhoz chairman came and told us that if we moved all the potatoes out of storage, we could go home. We had ten days of work left. In order to return to Irkutsk earlier, we organized the work in three round-the-clock shifts.

We emptied the warehouse in three days. Satisfied with our successful effort, we went to the chairman to get our accounts squared. But he categorically refused to release us, saying that there was much work yet to be done on the kolkhoz. We students were indignant and refused to go to the fields the next day. The chairman ordered that we be denied food. Two days of unwitting hunger strike commenced. On the morning of the third day the director of agriculture, the secretary of the regional Komsomol, and a representative from the institute arrived by car. We were not allowed to say one word in self-justification. Only the director and the secretary spoke. They demanded to know who was the first person to suggest the work stoppage. The students replied that they all went out together, there was no first person. When the "commission" found out that the chairman had denied us food, they pretended to be very angry and promised to reprimand him. The regional secretary declared to the kolkhoz chairman that the Komsomol had its own methods of combating such negative phenomena. As a result, we had to work another week.

I found out accidentally that not only students were brought to work on the kolkhoz. Once I had to go to the regional center to make an emergency phone call to Moscow. To do this I needed an off day, but we had to work without them. I asked the team leader to assign me to the grain threshing operation on the night shift. In the evening, a covered truck arrived there. Fifteen prisoners, guarded by three sub-machine gunners, stepped out of the truck. I found out that they were from the nearest concentration camp. Another group of students from our class worked at the storage facility. They had been doing so for a whole month side by side with prisoners loading potatoes into freight cars.

All the students returned from the kolkhoz together. Four dilapidated, shaky cars were added to the freight train. But the students noticed nothing since this was payday. For a month of work we were allotted thirty-five rubles, but after taxes we were each given thirty.

Two cases of vodka appeared immediately in the railroad car. The medical students were celebrating something akin to a harvest festival. By morning the cases were empty and we were all dead asleep. Drunkenness in the USSR was a constant problem. Everybody drank, and drank a lot, especially the youth. On the streets of Irkutsk, one could see drunken people from morning to night. Girls and women drank; school children and students drank. In the vestibule of the Irkutsk Medical Institute there was a wall placard called the "Komsomol Spotlight." It was titled "War on Drunkenness." Every week the names of students who wound up in the city's medical drying-out ward were listed on it. Sometimes interns from sixth level classes made the list.

Young doctors working in villages were especially prone to alcoholism. Not a single student party took place without vodka. I knew students from the

Polytechnic Institute and journalism majors form the University of Irkutsk. It was the same picture—an absence of enthusiasm and interests. They got together to drink, tell the latest jokes and leave—no, crawl away. Young women drinking on an equal footing with the men was especially unsightly. Obviously, there were exceptions. There were students at the institute who had a passion for music, books, and sports. Maybe this was the case only in Siberia but it seems to me that only in Moscow, Leningrad, and some other large cities was the youth different from that of Irkutsk. Upon graduating from the institutes, people became better educated but not better mannered. This was particularly applicable to those graduating from the higher educational institutions of Irkutsk.

So passed my two years of voluntary Siberian exile. I was torn away from all the events occurring in Moscow. I learned of them through telephone conversations, occasionally over the radio. Only the radio station Voice of America was heard in Irkutsk. Many members of the local intelligentsia listened to it. They spoke of what they heard in whispers or behind closed doors. If one listens to foreign radio broadcasts, he styles himself a freethinker.

Irkutsk Jews (and there are many Jews in Siberia) viewed our decision to leave the USSR with surprise and sometimes with negativity. Even though there were people in Irkutsk who would have liked to go to Israel, they would never mention this aloud for fear of losing their job and means of livelihood. They would say: it's nice for you in Moscow; there are many of you; there are foreign correspondents around; and you organize demonstrations. What do we have? The taiga is the law, the bear is the prosecutor (Siberian proverb). Even complaints to courts of appeal in Moscow never get there. On several occasions I was asked to mail letters in Moscow in order to avoid the district censorship. People were afraid of becoming victims of the arbitrariness of local rulers.

I experienced this arbitrariness myself. During the winter, evidently, when there aren't many foreign tourists in Irkutsk, there weren't too many people whom the local KGB could spy on. I noticed that I was being tailed in October of 1973 during an exhibition in Irkutsk titled "Tourism and Relaxation in the USA."

There was a young American woman of Jewish heritage at the exhibition—A.W. While in Moscow, she met with activists of the Jewish movement and knew our family. She wore a large six-pointed star which drew the attention of local Jews, but especially the KGB. When I first arrived in Irkutsk with a Star of David around my neck, my relatives and acquaintances begged me to remove it. To wear such an item in Siberia was considered very dangerous. My mother was visiting me that October and together we went to see the

American exhibition and talked to her. She visited one of our friends several times. At each meeting, we sensed that we were being watched. Several days after attending the exhibition, a man came to our relatives' residence, where we were then living, and presented the credentials of a KGB officer. He asked if we lived there. He then asked for our last names and addresses in Moscow and where I was studying. My frightened relatives did not know what to think. The agent came several times but could not catch us at home. Once he waited for a long time, telling us he wanted to talk. Unable to wait that long, he left and returned no more. Half a year later, I found out that there was a move to accuse me of forming, allegedly at my father's instigation, a Zionist organization and of meeting with an American spy. In the city there was talk that one of the guides was a spy, but at the institute this subject was not discussed with me.

However, provocations were attempted. A young man named Tatarinov, who introduced himself as a student, came to our apartment in Moscow during vacation. He asked if he could leave some ancient icons for two days. Then in Irkutsk, he asked me to sell a watch, jeans, a record player, and other items. He offered me incredible sums of money. I immediately understood the approach used by the luckless KGB employee—the attempt was to build a case of black marketeering against me. Toward the end, three KGB agents followed me. They tailed me constantly by car and waited near my home. I thought they might provoke me into a fight. One never left the apartment building. The people "guarding me" rang the doorbell, and would burst into the apartment.

On the next to last day I went to the institute to declare that I was leaving it and going to Moscow. I could not even imagine what a surprise awaited me. At the institute, I approached the assistant dean. Seeing me, he heaved a sigh of relief and said that everyone had been looking for me since morning. I understood that, presumably, all was known. I was asked to go to the Komsomol committee. There were already about twenty-five people there. Present at the meeting were the institute's Komsomol committee, the dean, the union organizer, the rector, and several individuals who, as it later turned out, were KGB officials. I was asked to stand at the end of the table and then it was triumphantly announced that competent agencies had that day made the institute's administration aware of the fact that this student intended to depart for the state of Israel. So it began! The meeting lasted for more than four hours. Prior to obtaining the visa, similar meetings often took place in other Soviet cities. But this was the first for Irkutsk. And a first in the USSR after a visa had already been obtained. The "court" was headed by the rector, Rybalko. The first to speak were the Komsomol members. They would speak and then question me in turn. It was noticeable that it was difficult for them to speak without notes. Some forgot what they were supposed to say and became confused. I replied calmly and confidently. There was nothing special in my answers. When I spoke, there was deathly silence and there was fear and bewilderment in the faces of those assembled.

The rector sat in silence, focusing his gaze on a single spot. He was the last to find out and this drove him crazy. Finally, he took his turn to speak and, as usual, overdid it. When he discovered that my father was a professor, he began to scream that the Soviet government had given him everything and that he could never repay it. I protested, saying that my father had worked for sixteen years without pay. This surprised the rector very much and he demanded an explanation as to where it was in the USSR that people work without pay. When I replied that father spent sixteen years in Stalin's concentration camps and prisons, he was curious as to which ones. I replied that father had traveled the whole "Archipelago." Rybalko then asked me if I had read Solzhenitsyn. I answered in the affirmative and then asked him the same question. An explosion of indignation! However, the culminating point came a bit later when I said that we had exit visas in hand. The rector left for some fifteen minutes. When he returned he announced that I would not be going anywhere except to Kolyma and that he would try to have our visas classified as expired. The rector then asked me to go home with the KGB officials and get my student documents. Until they were placed on his desk, I would not be allowed to go home.

When my mother walked into the judgement room, having waited in the hallway for four hours, the rector fell upon her and demanded that she leave. If not, he would call the police and she would be taken out. When I tried to go out into the hallway, my path was blocked by two KGB agents. At that juncture the Komsomol secretary declared that I would not be held by force, but I stated that it was already being done. The rector promised that he would provide no certificate regarding my two years of study at the institute, and he kept his word! He also ordered that my school diploma not be returned to me.

Toward the end of the meeting, I was questioned as to who my friends were. I did not answer, so they provided names themselves. They tried to elicit whether I told them of my plans. A girl in my class whom I knew well was particularly besmirched. The filthiest rumors were circulated about her, the type that could only be heard at a Komsomol members meeting. She was then brought in for a demeaning confrontation and told to choose her friends more carefully. Our whole class of twenty-five came to see me on the day of departure. They had begged off from their philosophy seminar. They told their instructor that they were seeing off a friend who was leaving for Israel. He was stupefied and advised them not to go. Still, the students came and we parted in friendship.

The same two KGB agents tailed us at the airport and there was another one from the institute. Evidently, this was to confirm that my student identification was invalid. When we submitted our tickets for verification, they demanded my student identification. Determining that I did not have it, they demanded that I surrender my plane ticket. Without a passport, a new ticket could not be purchased (my passport had already been turned in by my father in exchange for the visa). We were already prepared to go by train when luck helped us. In the confusion at the ticket counter, we were able to buy a ticket for another flight. We did not present our passports. Instead, we left the change for the ticket seller. When we were walking to the plane, we were noticed, for upon our arrival in Moscow, we discovered that our suitcases were forced open, the locks wrenched out, and the belongings searched.

Two weeks later we were already in Vienna, and Siberia was only a nightmare in our memory. Thank God!

Rome 8/VI/74

Chapter Thirty-Three

Leonid Shebarshin, Three Days in August

Leonid Shebarshin had a long and successful career in the KGB. He was the station chief at the Soviet Embassy in Teheran during the collapse of the Shah's regime and endured a siege by Iranian militants. He later served as head of the First Directorate, the chief of intelligence. During the three-day coup attempt against the government of Mikhail Gorbachev (August 19–21, 1991) he was the de facto head at KGB headquarters. The selection which follows describes the days of the attempted coup. Taken from Leonid Shebarshin, "Avgust" [August] in *Druzhba narodov,* Moscow, Nos. 5–6, 1992.

In the organizational structure of the KGB [Committee for State Security] the head of the intelligence branch is one of the vice-chairmen and thus a member of the highest leadership circle of the Committee.

The First Directorate is somewhat physically as well as organizationally and psychologically removed from the Committee [KGB headquarters]. Nevertheless, intelligence gathering is an integral part of State Security and whatever took place at the highest levels of the Committee concerned us. The rank and file heard echoes of internal conflicts and was the object of the chairman's orders and of the Collegium of the KGB. As a rule all this was of little concern to us. The highest levels limited themselves to general instructions on the surveillance of foreign agents, on anti-Soviet organizations abroad, and on centers of ideological subversion. The First Chief Directorate [the intelligence service] was procedurally occupied with problems and directives from above and kept sharp surveillance over any particular situation.

It was not customary to hold meetings with all the vice-chairmen present. Kriuchkov [the KGB chairman] would meet with each separately. Meetings of the committee leadership were frequently called. These would include the heads of the major independent subdivisions. The Collegium of the Committee convened regularly and invited representatives of all the principal directorates and, on occasion, the KGB heads of the various Soviet republics, regions and districts.

Once or twice a week I would go from the First Chief Directorate to KGB headquarters on Lubianka Square in order to meet with my colleagues in an informal atmosphere and find out the latest news. At precisely 1330 hours [1:30 PM] the chairman and his vice-chairs would gather in the dining room on the fourth floor near the chairman's office and seat themselves at a huge table. The meals were ordinary; the portions modest, with no lavish dishes. The service was quick and attentive.

During the meals conversation would flow freely. Hardly a day would go by without complaints at the mass media. Its attacks on the KGB were unrelenting. The magazine *Ogonek* was a particular irritant but other publications were also criticized for their lack of objectivity. The mood of the conversation was generally pessimistic, although Kriuchkov was by nature an optimist. One of his favorite sayings was: "We can lose anytime, what we ought to do is win." It was significant, however, that upon listening to some joyless piece of news he would limit his response to a prolonged "ye-s-s" without expressing his opinion or giving orders.

The elections to the parliament of the Russian Federation went by. [Nikolai] Ryzhkov [chairman of the USSR Council of Ministers] who was supported by the KGB suffered defeat. We discussed the results. Here was a conversation among the leaders of the best informed and politically savvy agency of the nation—the KGB. What were the inferences? First inference: The mass media have duped the public. But then the logical question "Why wasn't the party with its huge propaganda apparatus not been able to dupe the public?" hung suspended in an uneasy silence. The second inference: The elections were rigged and the ballot count falsified. But then where were the election officials and the party functionaries? And precisely at which point did the rigging take place? And a final argument based on the numbers voting and the percent supporting the victors. It turned out that less than half of the population voted for the victors. How many then voted for the losers? I suspect that such "informal analysis" was all the committee was capable of. To look with a dispassionate eye at the mood of the people was frightening. The Committee tried to hide behind the particulars in order not to see the whole.

According to tradition, the relations among the vice-chairmen were once marked by a spirit of competition. This was no longer true in my time, and, at the least, I could count on the understanding of my colleagues in all practical matters.

The vice-chairmen did not make up an unofficial collective ruling body. Kriuchkov's authority was too great for that and it kept his immediate subordinates in check. In the KGB as well as in other state agencies the power of the chief and the extent of his influence were determined by his relations with the government leaders. His competence, expertise and the respect of his staff were factors of secondary importance. A huge role in professional advancement was played by personal loyalty to one's superior. The Committee imitated the laws and customs which ruled Party behavior. It could not have been otherwise. These laws were universal throughout the whole system. I think that they were instrumental in my career as well. In any case as is expected of an officer, and all cadre of the KGB, I always strove to execute all orders conscientiously, even if they did not appeal to me, and avoided conflicts with my superiors. It was uncharacteristic of me to bull my way through situations and promote my point of view at any cost in debates with those above me. In such circumstances it frequently seemed to me that I could be in the wrong. Doubts about the fullness of my knowledge, validity of my deductions and suggested solutions have always haunted me. I have long suspected that today's absolute convictions may tomorrow become grave errors; science becomes superstition and heroic acts become mistakes or crimes. But doubts were not a primary factor. Over many years we were trained in the spirit of severe discipline, submission to superiors, and faith in their professional and ruling wisdom.

We had to believe our leaders in all respects. Our doubts would be discussed in a tight circle of trusted people. Public apostasy from the general line was persecuted. In more severe times an apostate would be anathematized by the party and dismissed. For lesser sins he would be moved to some secondary position and denied the possibility of independent work and professional growth. Thus the limits of disagreement and conflict with the leadership were evident to every associate. I was not among that small number who broke the unwritten rules of the KGB.

In contemplating the vicissitudes of professional life and the necessity to dissemble (this occurred with some frequency), to scheme, to repeat the lies of others, I came to a sad formulation: A person who receives a salary cannot lay claim to intellectual freedom.

However, differences with Kriuchkov did arise. They were precipitated by constant tension, anxiety about the internal condition of the country, and simple fatigue. Brief firefights over the telephone with the chairman became increasingly frequent. He rarely visited the First Directorate and even more rarely called me in for a personal report. In early August of 1991 Kriuchkov rebuked me over a trifle, accused me of vainglory and promised to come out and give me a serious talking to. I accepted the vainglory accusation with some modification. I sensed that he had wanted to knock me down a peg for some time. But that "talking to" never did take place.

In the first half of June of 1991, the penultimate plenary session of the Central Committee of the Communist Party of the Soviet Union was held. I had previously categorically declined Kriuchkov's suggestion that I become a candidate at the 28th Party congress for Central Committee membership. However, I was still invited to the plenary sessions. At the June plenary the General Secretary of the Central Committee, Mikhail Gorbachev, was subjected to very severe criticism. He defended himself and went on the attack in what was, in my opinion, a very improper style. The plenary came to nothing; the status quo was maintained. The whole event had an inexpressibly burdensome effect on me. It was not just that the nation's and the party's grave situation had been revealed. This was not a secret anymore. One was struck by the atmosphere of hopelessness, the absence of any concept of the future, and the falsifying of thought by phrase-mongering.

According to tradition the chief of intelligence informed the secretaries of the party organs within the First Directorate of what transpired at the plenary. I did so in a neutral tone without leaving out the particulars of each speech and ended with a summary of my gloomy conclusions. I insisted that we must do everything to preserve the intelligence team, to carry out our duties honorably, and to maintain discipline. I remarked that the First Chief Directorate [FCD] should not distance itself from the KGB for our ranks should be very tightly drawn during these perilous times. My remarks were received calmly. But the questions came afterwards: "What will become of the Party? Of the nation? What should we do and what do the leaders intend to do?" I had to break with all tradition which presupposed the omniscience of the leadership and simply say: " I don't know."

I reported to Kriuchkov about my meeting with the various secretaries. But he offered no comments. Naturally the same day the KGB party secretary ("the big secretary") found out about my report, but no comments came from him as well. This was a very alarming sign. Our leadership also did not know what to do.

Events cannot be dispassionately assessed at the moment they occur. Observers, and, even more so, participants are overwhelmed by emotion. They can rarely distinguish the actual from the apparent. They are confused by the rush of contradictory information and by their hyper-excited state. In time the picture of what transpired takes on more definite contours but telling details recede from memory and the general comprehension of all that took place is molded by personal bias, fear and hope.

Exactly two weeks have gone by since the morning of 19 August 1991. Perhaps this is the most appropriate time to try and recreate the tapestry of events at the point they overcame me.

18 AUGUST

A cool clear morning and the day promises to be a good one. At 0800 (0 eight hundred) as is usual on Sundays, I am headed on foot from the government dacha, to the "object" [the grounds of the FCD]. An hour-and-a-half of tennis with my aide Iurii Ivanovich Novikov, then a five minute sauna, a quick shower and to work. As usual, I'd look through the telegrams, the news agency communications and sign off on the materials. On the 18th of August no significant information had come in and there was nothing to report. An hour later I was back on the path to the dacha through the familiar grove of trees.

Around 1500 [3:00 PM] the telephone gave an ululating call—it was the Kremlin. Such a call on a Sunday promised nothing good—either some emergency or some rush assignment from Kriuchkov who was at his desk round the clock. I cursed out loud (there was no one in the room) and picked up the receiver. Grushko was on the line.

"Kriuchkov has ordered you to get two combat-ready groups of commandos together by 2100, fifty men each with transport."

"By 2100, but it's after three now on a Sunday. What's the assignment?"

"Don't know, he called on the mobile phone, told me to transmit the order: two groups with transport."

"Who's to be in charge of the groups after that? Who do I call?"

"Zhardetskii [head of military counter-intelligence] will be there. He'll be in charge. That's all I know."

A nasty business. The special commando unit has long been a dead weight on the FCD. Attempts to transfer it to someone else's command had been unsuccessful. This combat outfit, intended for use under special circumstances abroad, is seen by Kriuchkov as a useful instrument in difficult internal situations as well. This unit had been sent to the city of Baku to guard the government buildings there. It was also to have been sent to Vilnius in January 1991, but fortunately was not for reasons unknown to me. I was very much disturbed by Kriuchkov's casual, unofficial and unwritten orders. My second in command and I frequently grumbled about this, even wrote a memo or two, but never had the boldness to demand written orders from Kriuchkov. At the end of July and in early August (was this just a coincidence?) at a session of KGB leaders the form of a presidential decree on the deployment of the KGB was discussed. I suggested that any decree specify that orders calling for the use of troops be issued in written form. On the 19th we were to celebrate the tenth anniversary of the special commandos.

I sensed that something was up. But what? I called the commando quarters and told the officer of the day to summon the unit commander B.P. Beskov and to gather the groups. Then I called Zhardetskii.

"What's going on, where will the groups be used?"

"I don't know myself. We just sent thirty-five agents to the Baltic states. Maybe there?"

We agreed to keep in touch and inform each other if we got definite information. Things are bad. Something is going on but there has been no disturbing news from the Baltics lately, and what does military counterintelligence have to do with it? Boris Petrovich Beskov calls. He's at his post and is executing the order.

"Where to?" he asks.

"Don't know yet. Get the men ready."

"What's the equipment?"

"Don't know, will inform you later."

At 1800 hours, or a little later, there is a call from the officer of the day at KGB headquarters: the chairman is calling a meeting in his office at 2230. This has got to be something worse than the Baltics. Has the military cooked up something? There is no one to consult. Vadim Alekseevich Kirpichenko [First Deputy of the KGB Foreign Intelligence Department], a dependable man, has just returned from vacation and won't be at work for three days. He is not at the dacha. An hour goes by. The phone rings again: the meeting has been cancelled. But the call-up is still on. At 2100 Beskov reports that the hundred men are ready, and I relay it by telephone to Grushko. But what should their equipment be?

"What sort of equipment have they got?" asks Grushko.

"They have civilian clothing, dark-colored jumpsuits, and camouflage fatigues of the border guards."

"The chairman is not at his desk. I'll find out and get back to you."

Around 2200 I call Zhardetskii. He knows nothing new; there have been no instructions. His voice is full of alarm. I call Beskov and ask permission to give the men a rest and be ready the next morning. I also inform Zhardetskii and go to bed.

19 AUGUST

At 0130 Zhardetskii calls.

"Grushko has denied permission to let the men disperse and asked that they be in a state of readiness by morning."

"What's up? Where is the unit to be deployed?"

"Possibly in Moscow. But don't give me away. You and I have not had this conversation."

"O.K." I fall asleep without calling Beskov and have the craziest dreams all night. I'm up at 0635 to walk the dog and turn on the radio: "The State Committee on Extraordinary Affairs . . . announces . . ." Something very ominous is happening. The list of the committee members suggests that it is not a military show. The phone rings. It's Ageev.

"Are the units ready?"

"They ought to be ready."

"Send them to the Central Club immediately. And send an additional hundred men to the same place."

"What's the equipment and weapons?"

"Have them take everything they've got."

The officer of the day calls: a meeting in the chairman's office at 0930. If the early morning begins with telephone calls, nothing good can be expected. A thought flashes by: my normal life is over.

I direct the communications people to tape everything that the State Committee on Extraordinary Affairs (SCEA) broadcasts and leave Iasenevo [a southern suburb of Moscow] for Lubianka Square [KGB headquarters]. As always on Monday mornings the streets are full of cars. People are coming back from their weekends. There are lines at the bus stops; it's rush hour. The center-city is calm. There's the usual crowd by Children's World [a department store across the square from KGB headquarters]. No signs of any "Extraordinary Affair."

Familiar faces greet me outside the chairman's office: members of the Collegium, heads of directorates. Everybody seems dejected; there is no conversation, no smiles. Kriuchkov starts the meeting without any preliminaries. No one knows what is going on. Out of habit I take brief notes. I try to summarize what Kriuchkov is saying in a single sentence and come up with: "A state of emergency has been proclaimed with the goal of helping to bring in the harvest." Kriuchkov is very excited and speaks in fits and starts. He concludes by saying approximately the following: "Keep working!" He does not take questions. Plekhanov, the chief of security, pops in. He looks completely crushed. Could it be that he is concerned about the health of the president? He is sick after all. Kriuchkov makes a rallying hand gesture in Plekhanov's direction, something as: "It's O.K., it's O.K. Don't worry, everything will be fine." We depart with our heads hanging, exchanging not opinions but mindless curses muttered under our breath.

An inner voice tells me that it is best to keep away from Lubianka, not to get trapped in some unpredictable assignment. Headquarters is always full of people who are eager to use others as a cat's paw. I am on my way back to Iasenevo. The streets are filled with armored columns. Occasionally there are stalled vehicles with soldiers fussing around them. The air is full of diesel exhaust as in the bad times in Kabul. The columns move without hurry and seem endless. To everyone's surprise they stop at red traffic lights. Clearly something's off.

Is Kriuchkov off on a risky venture? What's wrong with the president? Stroke? Heart attack? Can't figure out a damn thing. Along with the statements of the State Committee on Extraordinary Affairs they are reading Lukianov's letter concerning the agreement on union. In spirit he is with the SCEA but he is not its member. Where are the countless committees of the Supreme Soviet, where is the mountain, the great pyramid of law-giving authority?

The TV runs stupid cartoons and the radio broadcasts mindless stuff. We have the technical capacity to receive the American news network, CNN. It is an insane situation: we get news about the capital city of our native land from American sources, from various news services, from private telephone calls. No one knows anything. Kriuchkov is always at meetings. It is pointless to ask Grushko about anything, and who would want to.

According to CNN, crowds are starting to gather at Manezh Square [adjacent to the Kremlin] and at the White House [seat of the Russian Federation] on the Krasnaia Presnia Embankment. Telephone calls substantiate this.

Time ticks away but there are no instructions and no information. I ask that copies of the SCEA statements be sent to all stations abroad as well as an order to report on the local reactions to the events in Moscow. The reactions come swiftly—they are acutely negative everywhere except for Iraq. Iraq hails the events. I authorize the telegrams to be sent to Kriuchkov, but on his orders some are diverted to members of the SCEA. Let them read, it won't hearten them; perhaps it will give them pause.

But nothing heartens us. The airwaves are silent. The teletypes print out Yeltsin's addresses to the people. These are immediately reproduced and distributed throughout headquarters. The situation in the city is heating up but on the screens there are only cartoons and on the telephones only anxious voices of people who understand and know nothing. My own voice is among theirs.

The most important phone rings—ATS-1—the Kremlin. It is Sergei Vadimovich Stepashin whom I recently met for the first time. Along with the other members of the Supreme Soviet of Russia he visited the FCD in early summer. I don't remember his exact words but the sense was clear—something had to be done to avert the approaching tragedy. I am in total agreement with Stepashin; we are moving toward something dreadful.

"We have to talk to Kriuchkov immediately. All this must be stopped. How can we get in touch with him? We are all in Burbulis's office."

I try to find Kriuchkov on another line. I am told that he is in conference with Ianaev [vice-president to Gorbachev]. I call reception and demand that Kriuchkov be summoned. He takes the receiver. I tell him that negotiations are necessary, that an end must be put to everything. He asks for Burbulis's number and hangs up. To this day I don't know whether they had a conversation. The airwaves are silent. Toward evening Ianaev holds a press conference. He creates a stupefying impression. It is a huge nail in the coffin of the would-be dictatorship. Beskov and his commando group are in the recreation building. They have received no orders, but they are being fed.

20 AUGUST

The flow of contradictory news keeps swelling. It is clear that the people are defending the White House. At mid-day there is a report (was it the CNN or a phone call from the city center?) that the White House is about to be stormed. Stankevich [a leader of the democratic opposition] has ordered that all women be evacuated from the place. I manage to reach Kriuchkov by phone, report to him and ask that he cancel this venture. He laughs nervously: "What nonsense. Who made all this up? I just spoke with Silaev and told him that it's all nonsense."

But his denial gives me no peace. I have heard that laugh once before. It bodes nothing good. Kriuchkov is nervous and he is lying.

At 1730 Beskov calls. His men have done reconnaissance on the White House and concluded that a mad and bloody venture is being readied which will have totally disastrous consequences. I call Kriuchkov, inform him of Beskov's report and ask, beseech him to cancel the plot.

"Report to Ageev," he says. That's all. While keeping Beskov on the line so that he can hear everything, I relay the information to Ageev. On an internal line I switch in V.A. Kirpichenko and ask him and Beskov to listen to me carefully.

"Boris Petrovich [Beskov]," I say, "I command you not to execute any orders without informing me and getting my authorization." I repeat if for clarity and effect. Kirpichenko understands everything and acknowledges the order.

It's max alert. At 2115 I'm in my office at headquarters trying to find Kriuchkov and confront him. But he is not in the building and the duty officers say that he is in the Kremlin. I try to reach Beskov, but he is at a meeting with Ageev. I have him summoned to the telephone. He reveals that the storming is still being discussed despite the totally obvious opposition of all its would-be executioners, that is, Beskov himself and V. F. Karpukhin leader of group Alpha of the Seventh Directorate [specially trained antiterrorist squads].

I categorically reconfirm my instructions to refuse any order to storm the White House and to do everything possible that no such order be given. Kriuchkov is still away from headquarters.

Beskov reports that it has been decided to cancel the storming (but when? At night or in the morning?). I ask him to return the groups to their quarters in Balashikha, which he does with relief.

21 AUGUST

The session of Supreme Soviet of the Russian Federation is being televised live. Many of those who, like us, kept silent, now rush to announce their allegiance to the winning side. Everyone pretends that they knew all along that the State Commission on Extraordinary Affairs was nothing more than a bunch of conspirators. (If one were to believe everything that was said and written after 21 August, then millions of people were manning the White House barricades while the enemy consisted of eight helpless evildoers.) The twenty-first of August was not a peaceful day, rather it was a day of detensioning, the end of the first act. Later that evening the president of the USSR [Gorbachev] returned from the Crimea [where he had been held hostage].

22 AUGUST

The government is in place; the conspirators arrested; television is presenting news reports; the people are rejoicing. Does life go on? Maybe. At 0630 I take the dog, put on a vigorous and confident air for the benefit of the gate guards and proceed to the FCD. Normally these are the best twenty-five minutes of each day, but not today. What have we been thrust into? How could Kriuchkov have betrayed us? I am plagued by the naive question of a virgin: "Whom can I trust?"

The phone rings at 0900. It is a woman's voice: "Mikhail Sergeevich [Gorbachev] requests that you come to his office at noon."

"Where is it?" (A stupid, but sincere question.)

They give me directions. Things seem to be getting easier. I go to KGB headquarters in order to be closer to the Kremlin and bide my time. Grushko hastily gathers the Collegium. In a collective mood of "mea culpa" we accept the Collegium's condemnation of the conspiracy. In the condemnation the word "sullied" is used. An idiotic argument ensues: isn't it better to say "stained" or "besmirched?" It is an argument straight out of Kafka or the Supreme Soviet. We are all in a state of general and amicable mindlessness; the only unstated thought is that we are all up the creek. Yes, up the creek and how. Yesterday's impotent cursing of the chief gives no comfort. He has betrayed everyone.

The Collegium is breaking up. I stop by Grushko's office and tell him of the president's invitation. Grushko says that Mikhail Sergeevich had called from his car that morning and asked for everyone to remain calm. And Grushko is calm though his eyes are sunken and his face is somber. It was a brief conversation about nothing.

I drive to the Kremlin. My papers are thoroughly checked at the Borovitskii Gate. This is something new. In the past the guards would merely glance at the number on the car's plate. I cross Ivan Square past the gleaming domes of the great bell tower (a joyous gift to Moscow by the ill-fated Boris Godunov) toward the Soviet Ministries building where the Politburo used to meet and where the president's office is now located. There are two enormous black ZIL limousines at the entrance. I see that M.A. Moiseev, chief of the General Staff, has arrived. We meet in the reception room. The others present are I.S. Silaev [prime minister], chief justice of the Supreme Court Smolentsev, and V.P. Barannikov [head of the Interior Ministry]. Finally A.A. Besmertnykh comes in. We are all somewhat nervous but not gloomy. Moiseev and I have a friendly exchange in which we excoriate our previous bosses. More people arrive: S.S. Alekseev, chairman of the constitutional commission, E.M. Primakov [then director of the Institute of World Economy and International Relations and advisor to Gorbachev], V.N. Ignatenko, the president's press secretary, V.V. Bakatin, and someone else. "The black walnut room," cherished spot of the Soviet VIP's was full.

The president entered. I introduced myself and he immediately took me into an adjacent empty conference room. (I was to visit this room once again a day later.)

The conversation was very brief. "What were Kriuchkov's aims. What were the instructions to the Committee?" I answered with total frankness, giving a brief description of the meeting on the nineteenth. "What a scoundrel. I trusted him most of all, him and Iazov. You yourself know that." I nodded in agreement.

The president looked splendid: lively, energetic, with bright eyes and no signs of fatigue. This was the second time I saw him up close. The first time was 24 January 1989 when Kriuchkov presented me to the president before my appointment. At that time Gorbachev had been somewhat gloomy and distant. The president ordered me to summon all the vice-chairmen of the KGB and announce that I was to become acting chairman.

A three- to five-minute private session with the president does have special significance in this world. In passing through the "black walnut room" I saw convivial, even tender smiles and symbolic clasping of hands from all corners. Just in case. . . .

Outside, the golden domes of Great Ivan's bell tower had grown dim. We headed toward Lubianka Square where a crowd had gathered with obvious ill intent toward the KGB. We drove around the crowd with some difficulty and plunged into the KGB complex through a side street. (The usual shopping frenzy continued uninterrupted by the Children's World department store.)

I gathered the vice-chairmen and announced the president's decision. Immediately the group broke out in controlled but happy smiles. I distinctly remember G.F. Titov's open and honest face. He had been on vacation and took no part in any of the events. The sole issue on the day's agenda was the classic Russian one—what's to be done? It was absolutely clear that the old order was finished and something new had to be taken up. But the "absolutely clear" ended at this point. We decided to gather the KGB leadership on the next day, 23 August, to discuss the issues for the Collegium session. A Collegium meeting had to be held as soon as possible. There was nothing left to say and we broke up. (A line from a poem by Esenin ran through my head: "Before this throng of the departing //I can't conceal my sorrow.") It was to reappear again and again during those days.

My office is a hell of ringing telephones. The officer in charge of quarters reports that the crowd outside is about to storm the building. They are writing offensive graffiti on the walls and have surrounded the Dzerzhinskii monument [founder of the Cheka, the secret police].

"What are we to do?"

"No gunfire under any conditions! Lock all the gates and doors, check the gratings. We'll call city hall for help and ask them to send the police." (An instance of humiliation that is to last two days.) We get in touch with the police but they are in no hurry to help us. V.I. Kravtsev calls from the Attorney General's office: "We are sending a team of inspectors to search Kriuchkov's office."

"Good, send them." Next comes a call from the office of the Attorney General of the Russian Federation: "We are sending a team of inspectors to conduct a search of Kriuchkov's office. Molchanov from Central Television will come with the team."

"You are welcome to send them but people from the Soviet Attorney General's office are already on their way here."

"That's all right, we'll come to terms with them."

Within ten minutes my office is filled with some fifteen servants of the justice system among whom I recall only Stepankov, the attorney general of the

Russian Federation. To my surprise both groups come to an immediate understanding, find witnesses (young women from the secretariat) and surge into Kriuchkov's office. Another group sets off to search Kriuchkov's dacha where his wife has been weeping all morning. Yet another group sets off to search Kriuchkov's apartment.

The phone rings. It is M.S. Gorbachev: "I have signed the edict appointing you acting chairman of the KGB. Take charge."

I note the time—it is 1500 hours. To the constant reports ("they're smashing windows . . ." "we can't get in touch with the police . . ." "they're about to topple the monument") there is an added flood of congratulations on my appointment. Just in case. Life is becoming increasingly unbearable, but there is no time to think about it. My office windows look out into an inner courtyard and the noise of the crowd is heard dimly. How familiar the situation is. How horrible that it is taking place not in Tehran where some ten years ago I sat besieged, commanding the defenders, hearing the roar of the mob, the ring of shattering glass, the blows on the doors, gunshots . . . Horrible that it is happening here on Lubianka Square and that here, as in Teheran, there is no help coming.

But I am wrong. Two deputies of the Russian Federation appear in my office. It is their task to quiet the crowd should it turn violent. I write down their names with sincere gratitude—Leonid Borisovich Gurevich and Il'ia Mstislavovich Konstantinov. They have brought reason into the totally irrational world of my office.

There is a report that free vodka is being distributed from a truck in Serov Lane [near the headquarters]. But this has to be totally in the realm of fantasy—vodka is a valuable commodity and anyone would be happy to pay for it. Nevertheless, I have it checked. It turns out there is no distribution. (There is disappointment in the voice.) Things gradually clear up. There is no violent crowd on the square but rather a political rally which is discussing how to remove the monument. S.B. Stankevich [leader of a democratic faction] is in charge and the police are quietly maintaining order.

Slowly the white heat drops to a cherry red. Using the underground passageway I go to G.B. Ageev's office in the old building. The windows of his fifth-floor office look out on the square. At the request of the organizers of the rally we have turned on the building's projectors ("Don't assault us. See how conscientious we are."), but the square remains poorly illuminated. The crowd leaves a sizable empty circle around the monument. It is hard to estimate but there are several tens of thousands. People speechify, others shout slogans while two enormous self-propelled cranes take the measure of the monument. An ambulance drives onto the square but only to better illuminate the public execution of the founder of the secret police [Cheka], the first

Chekist. A public execution is not a new phenomenon for Russia. Though the scale is much grander with a monument, television will put things in the right perspective. It will be even more intriguing because the monument does not change its facial expression. Everything occurring is meaningless to it, and is simply the vanity of those who have not yet dissolved in eternal darkness. When you are executing a living person it is a different matter. In Iran they understood the difference well.

I force myself to watch. Do I feel anguish? No. Everything going on is the natural reckoning for near-sightedness, limitless power, for the self-indulgence of the leaders, for our sheep-like, mindless nature. The end of an era. But also the beginning of another era. The cranes rev up; the crowd bellows. There is the pop of hundreds of flashbulbs and "Iron Felix" firmly suspended by the neck hangs over the square while under the cast iron greatcoat the iron legs give a death shudder. You gave up your first earthly life for the wrong reasons, Mr. Felix Edmundovich, sir. Now posthumously you answer for the sins of your progeny.

The empty buildings of the KGB are silent and still. I have given an order to remove the guard details form the fourth and fifth floors of the new building. This was a maximum security zone where the offices of the secretariat, the leadership, and the chairman were located. And the long corridors look strange without the customary young lieutenants at all the entry points to the two floors.

My last order of the day is to the superintendent's unit: not to use firearms under any circumstances. That is it. There is nothing to be done here at night. We leave through an exit to Kuznetskii Most [a street]. The streets are deserted with only an occasional passer-by and a group of police at a distance, closer to the square. This is my city. I was born and have lived in it but at this night hour I sense its cold alienation. Lines from the poet Blok come to mind: "Night, a street, a lamp, a pharmacy.// A meaningless and murky light."

We hear the footfalls of history but do not know where to hide so as not to be crushed.

I am tormented not by the future (it is all in God's hands) but by the present and the not so distant past. I see myself immeasurably humiliated, deceived and robbed. The remnant of my human dignity is outraged at its treatment. After all, I did not live merely to fill my stomach with food and to sleep soundly. I considered myself a reasonably educated, rational, and reasonably decent person. It has seemed to me that I and those like myself have been perceived thus by others. The betrayal by Kriuchkov turned out to be the last in that long chain of betrayals of which my generation had been victim.

We were betrayed for the first time when we were made to believe in the semi-divine genius of Stalin. We were then too young to be cynical or to doubt the wisdom of our elders. (Was I the only idiot? I don't think so. What I say is true for a whole generation.) In March of 1953 my classmates and I wept real, bitter tears. Stalin had died. A black cloud of imminent ills was moving upon our country and ourselves, its miserable children. We were too inexperienced to see beyond the funereal bunting. Otherwise we would have seen the frenzied gleam in the eyes of the successors to the leader of all eras and all nations.

It is demeaning even to recall the mini-cult of our dear Nikita Sergeevich [Khrushchev], and after him the hero of the Great Patriotic War [WW II], the hero of virgin soil [previously uncultivated land], the hero of the Soviet renaissance, the dyed-in-the-wool apparatchik [functionary] Leonid Il'ich Brezhnev, and the pitiful figure of Chernenko. In February of 1984 when the death of Iu.V. Andropov was announced we sat in a small room of the information service trying to guess who our next leader would be. We tried not to admit to ourselves that it might be an ex-manager of a garage and Chernenko's one-time office manager.

Was it different under Andropov? He was a far-sighted, practical and clever man who spoke simply and to the issue. In conversing with him no one ever resorted to slogans or the usual hollow rhetoric. Had that happened, there would have been no subsequent conversations with that person. But Andropov lied as well and, voluntarily or involuntarily, had us believe in lies and lie to ourselves. (Incidentally Andropov once remarked in passing: "What gives you the idea, that you know what power is?" Once, in Afghanistan, the taciturn Kosygin said something similar. And Kriuchkov developed the theme further: "At that level, i.e., at the very top, there is no human friendship nor human devotedness.")

These are new times. If falsehood has not been annulled it has, at least, been reduced in its rights to the level of truth. The compulsiveness of a single, canonized, absolute truth, the bearer of which was a high priest with a mysterious conclave of wise elders, called the Politburo, was vanishing. It was becoming clear that each person may believe in whatever seems to be the truth and may speak of it openly. A timid hope appeared that even if our leaders are not very wise, they, at least, might be honest. But the right to the truth was again used for deception. We were betrayed yet again.

Fifty-six years constitutes a fairly long life. In it there has been war, starvation, poverty, the death of dear ones, artillery barrages and long sieges, disillusionment in myself and others—the usual events in the life of a Russian of my generation. There is nothing to especially grieve for or be especially joyous about.

One's own conscience should be one's master. And to be farther from people who lust for power. Farther from power and its companion—falsehood. That is all.